# CLAUDE MONET

## *Life and Art*

# CLAUDE MONET

*Life and Art*

PAUL HAYES TUCKER

*Yale University Press*
*New Haven & London*

Edited by Jane Havell
Designed by Gillian Malpass
Set in Monophoto Bembo by Servis Filmsetting Ltd, Manchester
Printed in Italy by Amilcare Pizzi S.p.A, Milan


**Library of Congress Cataloging-in-Publication Data**

Tucker, Paul Hayes. 1950–
    Claude Monet / by Paul Tucker.
    Includes bibliographical references and index.
    ISBN 0-300-06298-2
      1. Monet, Claude. 1840–1926 – Criticism and interpretation.
    I. Title.
    ND553.M7T79   1995
759.4–dc20

94-40130
CIP


A catalogue record for this book is available from The British Library

*Frontispiece*: Photograph of Claude Monet, ca. 1924, Musée Clemenceau, Paris.

*For Jonathan and Jennie*

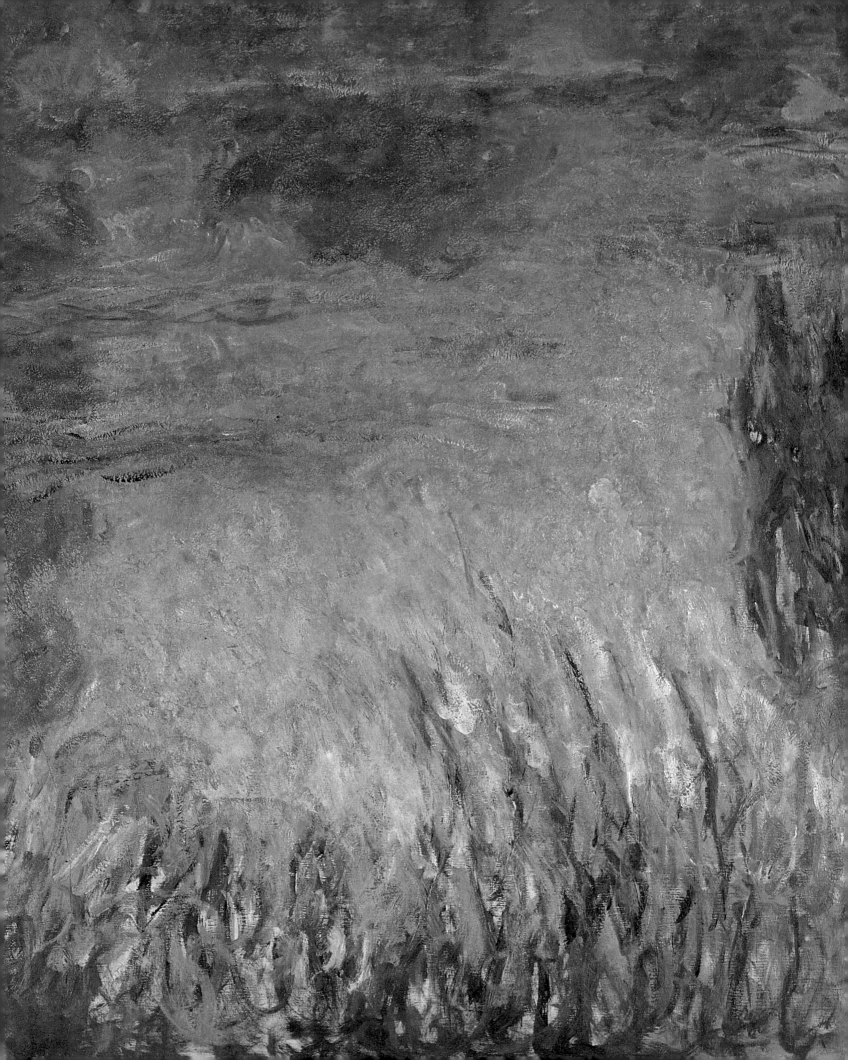

# Contents

*facing page*    Claude Monet, *Grandes Décorations. Setting Sun* (detail of Pl. 239).

# Acknowledgments

Although this book is the outgrowth of many years of work on Monet, it is the specific product of a concentrated writing campaign conducted during a sabbatical leave from my duties at the University of Massachusetts Boston in 1993–94. I would like to thank my institution of now seventeen years and my department colleagues for the precious, fitful freedom that allowed me to complete this book. I would not have been able to realize this project so quickly if it were not for the Florence Gould Arts Foundation. I am delighted, therefore, to have the opportunity to express my gratitude to John Young once again for his continued support. It also would not have been possible without the comfort of the library at Saint John's College and the beauty of Santa Fe, New Mexico.

Such a synthetic study naturally draws on the work of many people. Among the most critical for me is that of Robert L. Herbert. In addition to his seminal publications on Monet and Impressionism, Bob graciously agreed to read this manuscript and made many invaluable suggestions at its every stage. We all should be blessed to have such a mentor. I would also like to thank Daniel Wildenstein not only for his monumental biography and catalogue raisonné on which this and all modern studies of Monet unabashedly depend but also for his continued assistance over the years. I am indebted as well to Charlie Stuckey who took the time to read the final manuscript despite many other commitments and who generously alerted me to numerous errors or omissions. I would like to recognize the many other Monet scholars whose work has guided me in this enterprise, particularly Andrew Forge, Robert Gordon, Michel Hooge, John House, Joel Isaacson, Claire Joyes, Steven Levine, Charles Moffett, Grace Seiberling, William Seitz, and Virginia Spate. There are numerous art historians who have not specialized in Monet studies but who have made significant contributions to our knowledge of the artist and who have greatly influenced my thinking. They included Richard Brettell, Tim Clark, Linda Nochlin, John Rewald, Richard Shiff, and Kirk Varnedoe. I would also like to recognize Ruth Butler, the distinguished Rodin authority, for her insights and support, as well as George Heard Hamilton, Lane Faison, and Whitney Stoddard—eminent scholars who have always provided unwavering encouragement. No one could have been more helpful at different points during this project than Arnaud d'Hauterives and Marianne Delafond of the Musée Marmottan. I happily will always be in their debt. I would also like to acknowledge Norimichi Aiba, Katsunori Fukaya, and Katsumi Miyazaki for the opportunity to explore many of the ideas in this book in the catalogue for a Monet exhibition in Japan that I had the privilege of organizing in 1994, and to E. John Bullard, Harry S. Parker, and Lynn Federle Orr for the occasion to explore ideas about Monet's late work in the catalogue for an exhibition of paintings from the Musée Marmottan at the New Orleans Museum of Art and The Fine Arts Museums of San Francisco in 1995.

Many people assisted in gathering photographs for this book. I would like to thank Martha Asher, Katherine Baejter, Barbara Bernard, Philippe Brame, Phillip Charles, Gabriel Chateaubriand, Peter Findlay, Elizabeth Gombosi, Marci Gooseman, Robert Herbert, Money Hickman, Shephard Holcombe, Betra Katz, George Keyes, Jett Lamkin, Bernard Lorenceau, Anne McCauley, Katsumi Miyazaki, David Nehmad, Lynn Orr, Karen Otis, Patti Petrochuk, Lieschen Poluznik, Clive Russ, Howard Shaw, Loretta Slover, Rob Storr, Karen Stock, Karen Tates, Marie de Thézy, Lyn Voita, Sarah Watson, Kate Williams, and Ken Yeh. I owe special thanks to Malcolm Cormack, Beatrice Epstein, Neil Fiertag of Concorde Fine Arts, Robert Gordon of Marc de Montibello, Marjorie Miller of The Fashion Institute of Technology, William Acquavella, Jean Edmundson, Esperanza Sobrino, and Kim Vick of Acquavella Galleries, Inc., Ay-Wang Hsai and Joseph Baillo of Wildenstein and Company. For their cordial and efficient responses to my endless inquiries, I am deeply indebted to Mary Sluskonis and Janice Sorkow of the Museum of Fine Arts, Boston, to Sarah Ackley and David Nash at Sotheby's, New York, and to Casie Kesterson and Michael Findlay at Christie's, New York. Without them, this book would have had had far fewer color plates. My primary ally at Yale for illustrations was Sheila Lee who was a fierce and wonderful compatriot whose confidence never swerved and whose effectiveness is evident throughout this book.

I want to express special gratitude to William D. Tucker, Jr., who read the manuscript at every stage of its production and applied his editorial acumen to it with immeasurable effect. What a touchstone for sensibility. I also want to thank Jane Havell who was the final shaper of the text and the ultimate editorial red-penner who performed her task with the penultimate mixture of diplomacy and insistence. She did a marvelous job. My trusted Charlestown friend, Bruce Garr, poured over the proofs with his most welcome legal eye, as did William Tucker, both of whom saved me from many an embarrassing error. The realization of the book as a physical product, distinguished by its beauty and design, is due to the remarkable efforts of Gillian Malpass; she made the labors of Hercules seem like a light aroebic workout. No one should be prouder—or more exhausted—than she.

This is the third book that I have had the pleasure of doing with Yale. That is largely due to one person—John Nicoll—who happily insisted on publishing this one during phone calls to Santa Fe and one splendid weekend in Paris. John is a model for the profession— encouraging, discriminating, and eminently fair. I am thankful to have had him as a friend and guide for the past fifteen years.

I reserve my final thanks for my family, first for Willie and M.E. who instilled the value of education in all seven of their children and who have been unwavering in their support. Although I have said it before, I will say it again: there are not two better. When it comes to superlatives, Maggie Moss-Tucker defines the word. No one has been closer to the fire and remained as cool. No one has been as resilient or as empathetic. No one therefore could have been more desired a partner for the adventures of this book or those of the last twenty-one years, for which I will always be grateful. Best of all perhaps, it was Maggie who brought me the greatest of gifts, Jonathan, now twelve, and Jennie, eight. The two of them have reminded me of the preciousness of joy and the profundity of love. Although they have had to share their young lives with an aged and persistent M. Monet, I hope they have never doubted their father's unbounded affection for them. As a reminder of that heartfelt fact, I dedicate this book to the two of them. They deserve that and much more.

# 1  Monet Revisited

Over the course of his almost frighteningly full life—one that lasted eighty-six years and neatly bridged two centuries (1840–1926)—Claude Monet produced more than 500 drawings, 2,000 paintings, and 3,100 letters. Few artists have left such a bounteous legacy. Fewer still have received the world-wide acclaim that Monet has so long enjoyed. His views of sun-dappled waters and flowering fields, the boulevards of Paris and the cliffs of Normandy, as well as his great series paintings of the 1890s and early twentieth century of wheatstacks, poplars, Rouen cathedral, and water lilies have been a source of wonderment and inspiration for millions of people virtually from the time they appeared until today. The presence of his work in museums around the world bears eloquent testimony to his global conquest and his rightfully earned place in the history of art. In addition, the numerous reproductions of his canvases—on everything from china to swimwear—together with the mecca-like status of his house and gardens at Giverny, the second most visited site in France after Versailles, amply attest to his almost mystical appeal.[1]

Why, then, another book on this most popular of artists? The answer is simple. For all of his familiarity and appropriate fame, Monet, as an individual and as an artist, remains curiously cryptic. We think we know him well because he is consistently portrayed. We are told he was an extremely sensitive man who was keenly attuned to the natural world and who was driven by undefined inner forces to render his feelings in the presence of nature. Born into a relatively humble family who disparaged his interest in art, he struggled to make a name for himself in the competitive Parisian art world, suffering the abuse of conservative critics and resulting economic difficulties until his later years when he finally gained approval and was able to enjoy the fruits of his hard-earned success. Monet's sensitivity to nature and his ability to render it in truly remarkable ways are borne out by his letters as well as his paintings. Like the power and subtlety of his best landscape canvases, Monet's letters are filled with an endearing mixture of passion and humility about the workings of the world around him—the movements of the sea, the changing colors of autumn foliage, the varying characteristics of seasonal light, and the majesty of unassuming but fickle atmospheres in various areas of his native France as well as sites he painted beyond his nation's borders. In perusing these writings, we are treated over and over again to images of Monet's tenacity in the face of natural phenomena—wind, rain, cold, heat, blinding light, and ephemeral effects that seemed frustratingly elusive even to this man who seemed to have been able to paint them all.

Unlike his paintings, however, which appear to breathe an air of supreme confidence, Monet's letters attest to his persistent doubts about himself—his fear of failure, for example, and his struggles to realize personal goals at every stage of his long and rigorous life. Similarly, unlike the image his work often suggests, his letters show he was niggardly when it

1  Carolus Durand, *Portrait of Claude Monet*, 1867, 46 × 38, Musée Marmottan, Paris.

1

came to money, hard-nosed in his dealings with friends and business people, politically astute, and fully in touch with the cultural pulse of his moment. It becomes clear, therefore, that he was not just a talented painter who merely pursued his sensations of nature en plein air without care, forethought, or difficulty. He was a much more complicated individual with a much more multi-layered agenda.

We know, for example, that he often executed small, preparatory drawings for paintings, that he finished pictures in his studio, that he even began and ended the majority of his London series of 1900–04 in Giverny far from the English capital. We also know that despite his often expressed doubts about his enterprise and his humility in front of nature he had a large ego that needed frequent gratification. He was a terror at home, for example, when work was not going well or when he was between projects. In addition, he was always concerned about his position in the Impressionist hierarchy and how he was perceived in the Paris press. He also liked to live the good life. He constantly cried poverty, particularly in the 1870s, which has led most writers to claim he was in dire straits. But in most years he actually was making more money than doctors and lawyers in Paris. His wailings, therefore, were provoked not by his paltry earnings but by his extravagant habits and lack of fiscal restraint. They also may have been a way to drum up sympathy. Despite these cries, he generally postured as an independent male, filled with nineteenth-century machismo. Yet he was extremely dependent on his friend and confidante, Alice Hoschedé, who ultimately became his second wife. She also became a real touchstone in his life. Her influence on Monet was considerable but a relative lack of documentation limits our ability to measure accurately the dynamics of this important relationship.

Finally, it is often repeated that Monet suffered the abuse of negative critics during the early part of his career, like all of his Impressionist colleagues. While this is true in part, it is by no means the whole story, as he was not isolated to the degree that is generally implied. His very first submissions to the annual Salon in Paris in the 1860s, for example, were accepted by the Salon jury, a significant accomplishment for any emerging artist. Those same paintings were even warmly praised by reviewers in the Parisian press. And they helped find him patrons among both new and established collectors.

These kinds of contradictions—between the romantic image of Monet that his art suggests and the realities of the man himself—create a more complicated picture than normally presented. But this should not be surprising. Anyone who could have so successfully challenged the hierarchies of his day and produced as many novel paintings as Monet did over such a long period of time had to have been a more complex individual than what has often been put forth in the literature on Impressionism.

It also should not be surprising that the same is true of his art. The standard description of Monet's achievement—as being almost exclusively concerned with air, light, and particular moments in time rendered spontaneously in heightened color and broken brushwork—is fundamentally accurate but it also is overly simplistic. The intricacies of his painted surfaces alone attest to the complications of his techniques as well as to the amount of time and consideration that went into the realization of his canvases. Even his choices of color and the way he mixed his hues are tell-tale signs of his forethought and decision-making. It has been recently discovered, for example, that the nearly black tones Monet used in various parts of a painting of the Gare Saint-Lazare presently in the National Gallery, London, are not actually pure black but rather a mixture of no fewer than nine discrete colors.[2] In addition, from a conservator's point of view, the fact that Monet's paintings have stood the test of time in terms of their condition is another indication of his technical prowess and the care he took when painting his pictures. Thus, contrary to popular opinion—during his lifetime as well as now—most of his paintings (certainly all those he considered finished) were not the product of immediate inspiration or some spontaneously achieved painting process. Rather, they were carefully conceived, artfully crafted, and skillfully completed, the result of his deep involvement with his practice, his fierce desire to achieve certain specific effects, and his determination to satisfy himself, something his letters bear witness to as well.

In reconsidering what might be called the Monet myth, it seems only correct to re-examine long-held notions about Monet's choice of site and subject. Traditionally, writers have insisted that Monet's primary concern was not what he painted but how it appeared under different lighting and weather conditions. It was the sunshine that flickered across the surface of the Seine or the façade of Rouen Cathedral, for example, that was more significant than the river or the building, the atmosphere that wrapped the wheatstacks or infiltrated the sites Monet selected along the Normandy coast rather than those agrarian constructions or the specific locations on the English channel.

To support such ideas, these writers point to a variety of facts. They look first to the paintings themselves which, as a group, are clearly focused on the multiple ways in which nature reveals her many wonders. Monet obviously wanted to render the tangible presence of such evanescent matter as light, air, wind, and time. And since he did so over such a wide range of motifs, writers could insist that it did not seem to matter what motifs he chose so long as he achieved the effects he desired.

In addition to the corpus of paintings, writers emphasize the almost relentless concentration of contemporary critics who disliked Monet's innovations on the technical aspects of his work and on the ways his "degenerate" strategies compromised his ability to represent the realities he supposedly sought to render. And they refer to the fact that Monet never said anything about his subjects that would give the slightest hint of their significance to him.

But this is inverse reasoning. Few artists of Monet's generation ever spoke specifically about the meaning of their work. What good artist would? In addition, the techniques that Monet and his Impressionist colleagues developed naturally preoccupied contemporary critics; they challenged painting's basic premises while calling into question long-held notions about the very nature of art. This does not mean that critics were silent on the issue of subject matter or that Monet was indifferent to their reactions. From the 1880s onwards, Monet subscribed to two Paris clipping services to keep himself abreast of critical opinions about his work. In addition, he read widely: nineteenth-century French, Russian, and English literature; French classics by Corneille, Montaigne, Molière, and Voltaire; poems by Homer, Lucretius, and Petrarch; artists' writings by Delacroix and Michelangelo; and French history, notably the nineteen-volume history of France by Jules Michelet. He therefore was both literate and informed. He also moved in cultivated circles and counted among his friends people who cared deeply for making art about the times in which they lived, whether it be the realist painter Gustave Courbet (1819–77), the novelist Emile Zola (1840–1902), or his fellow Impressionists. Until he was almost 40 years old, he demonstrated this overtly by immersing himself in contemporary life. So passionate was he about rendering modern aspects of the world around him that Zola stated in 1868 that Monet "cannot paint a landscape without including well-dressed men and women. Nature seems to lose interest for him as soon as it does not bear the stamp of our customs. . . . Claude Monet loves with a particular affection nature that man makes modern."[3] Although this was a slight exaggeration and although Monet abandoned such subjects around 1880, he never emptied his pictures of meaning. Critics in the latter part of his career understood this and often attempted to evoke the poetic significance they sensed in his work. After seeing Monet's

*Wheatstacks* in 1891, for example, Roger Marx declared in the Parisian daily *Le Voltaire* the paintings "symbolize and sum up the labor, the sowing, and the harvesting, all of the harsh fight with the elements to fertilize the land, all the arduous and superb work of the earth."[4] Another critic saw Monet's motif for the *Poplars* of 1892 as particularly potent because the tree "summarizes all the grace, all the spirit, all the youth of our land."[5] Another critic recognized the contemporary relevance of Rouen Cathedral: "It is the historical and organic cathedral that Monet wanted to beautify because ... after centuries of embodying the mystical aspirations of the multitudes, the cathedrals have become human."[6]

The most pertinent testimony about the importance of Monet's choice of sites and subjects, however, comes from Gustave Geffroy, a leading critic of the 1880s and '90s who also became one of Monet's closest friends and staunchest supporters. Reviewing an exhibition of Monet's *Mornings on the Seine* and views of the Normandy coast in 1898, Geffroy made the following observations: "... one of the numerous fantasies born of the accidental appellation 'impressionism' is to believe in the non-choice of subjects by these thoughtful and willful artists. Choice was, on the contrary, always their lively and important concern. But it is thus that legends are made; these painters are customarily portrayed as instruments indifferently aimed at every sight, and the mistake goes along, repeating itself."[7]

These kinds of comments should make us realize that Monet's sites and subjects were critical to his art, that they were carefully considered, and that they were laden with meaning for himself and his audience. They also suggest that such observations were made more frequently than earlier writers knew or cared to acknowledge. When combined with the contrasts between Monet's private life and his public persona or when considered in relation to the gap that exists between the way he conceived, executed, and exhibited his work and the way it is generally understood today, it is apparent that we need a fuller and more complex accounting of his achievement. This book attempts to address that need by restoring the significance of contemporary history and Monet's engagement with his times to the evident subtleties of his art and life.

## 2 Between the Capital and the Coast: Monet's Early Years, 1840–1860

Monet had a penchant for controlling the facts of his own biography just as he liked to keep his ideas about his art to himself. Unfortunately, he was immensely successful at both endeavors, causing most of what has been written at least about his life to be based on what he told interviewers from approximately 1880 onwards. The facts about his early upbringing in particular are surprisingly few given his renown. They are also unrevealing, which makes them frustrating but simple to rehearse.

Monet was born on 14 November 1840 on the fifth floor of 45 rue Laffitte (Pl. 2) in the ninth arrondissement of Paris, the second son of Claude-Adolphe and Louise-Justine Aubrée Monet whose families had come to the capital in the late eighteenth century from the Dauphiné and the Essonne, respectively. Adolphe, 40, and Louise-Justine, 35, named their new son Oscar-Claude, baptizing him as such in their local parish church, Notre-Dame-de-Lorette, just steps from their house, on 20 May 1841.[1] They apparently called him "Oscar" and, like a good son, Monet obediently used that name to sign his paintings and drawings until his early twenties. He must not have found it terribly endearing, however, as he always signed his letters "Claude." Sometime in 1862, he perfunctorily dropped the "Oscar" altogether and never used it again.

There is no indication of what Adolphe Monet did for a living but it may not have been very fruitful as, several years after Oscar-Claude's arrival, Adolphe decided to leave Paris and join his brother-in-law's wholesale grocery and ship chandlers concern in the Norman port of Le Havre. The whole Monet family, therefore, moved from their fifth-floor walk-up apartment to a sizable house just north of Le Havre proper on the rue d'Épréménil in the small suburb of Ingouville (Pl. 3). For the young Oscar-Claude, it was the first of what would be hundreds of trips that he would make during the course of his life between the capital and the coast. The house, which was conveniently located near Adolphe's business, must have been a step up for the Monet family although, according to one acquaintance, Adolphe and Louise-Justine took in boarders to help make ends meet.[2]

2 Charles Marville, *La rue Laffitte*, ca. 1850, albumen print from a colodion-on-glass negative, Bibliothèque historique de la ville de Paris.

5

When Monet was 10 he entered the collège communal du Havre, a school that was within walking distance of their house and which enrolled 197 students for the year 1850–51, about a fifth of whom boarded. The school offered a typical curriculum of history, Latin, Greek, French grammar, and mathematics. It also gave drawing courses taught by a now largely forgotten artist, Jacques-François Ochard (1800–70), a student of Jacques-Louis David.[3] Ochard was a painter of some local standing. He received several commissions for public works in Le Havre and was the curator of the Le Havre Museum until his death in 1870. No records survive regarding Monet's performance in the school; we are not even certain when he left or whether he graduated. But we do know he took classes with Ochard, an earnest man whose keen interest in teaching his young students how to manipulate a pencil or piece of chalk more than compensated for his modest talent. (In addition to Monet, he counted the landscape painter Adolphe Yon [1836–97] and the genre painter Charles-Marie Lhuillier [1824–98] among his students.) We also know that Monet's mother died on 28 January 1857, some two months after Monet's sixteenth birthday and that his uncle, Jacques Lecadre, who owned the chandlers business, passed away the following year on 30 September 1858.

Beyond these modest facts, we know little about Monet's activities as a child or what kinds of experiences he had as an adolescent. Later in life he claimed he never liked school, that he favored his drawing pad over his books, and that as soon as he could he abandoned academe. He also said he drew spontaneously as a child, covering his schoolbooks with fantastic designs, but never indulging in mechanical renderings.[4] However, the evidence suggests

3 Anonymous, *View of Ingouville*, ca. 1860.

4 (below) Anonymous, *Panorama of Le Havre*, ca. 1860, lithograph, Bibliothèque Nationale, Paris.

otherwise. Although none of his school texts has ever come to light, three sketchbooks from his high school days have survived and they reveal an individual who was learning his trade in traditional fashion—by carefully copying images from drawing manuals and trying his hand at relatively standard vignettes much like those that decorated the margins of travel books of the period or circulated as independent lithographs (Pls. 5, 6, 7). The earliest of these drawings is dated 9 July 1856; the forty-six others in the first two books were done during the course of the same summer, with the last signed 12 September.[5] There are over fifty others in the third sketchbook that come from 1857 together with a few independent sheets of approximately the same date. Not surprisingly, given his later interests in landscape, most of these early drawings chronicle quaint aspects of the countryside near Monet's home—rustic cottages nestled in trees, clusters of rocks and bushes, and sailing vessels of various kinds. They also depict occupants of the area: fishermen, gardeners, and country children. Done in pencil, they are all rather tame, if not clichéd, images, but they are far too competent to have been Monet's first efforts and thus appear to reflect the training he received from Ochard. Most of them are also given quite specific dates (22 February, 29 June, 15 September) and specific locations (Graville, Epouville, Gournay) suggesting Monet's early interest in a certain kind of specificity of time and place despite the generic style of the work. What all of them suggest as well is Monet's clear preference for picturesque, non-modern subjects that affirmed the continuing charm of rural existence, despite evidence around him to the contrary.

Monet could have chosen to render quite different subjects, if he had been so inclined. The city of Le Havre, for example, was an easy walk from his house. It was rapidly expanding during his adolescent years (Pl. 4). Commerce in the continually growing port increased tremendously between 1840 and 1860, just as industries catering to the needs of that trade and

7

8 Claude Monet, *View of Saintre-Adresse*, ca. 1859, pastel on paper, 31 × 45, w.P13, Private Collection.

9 Camille Flers, *River Scene*, ca. 1850, pastel on paper, 11.5 × 28.5, Private Collection.

to the burgeoning population of northern France boomed concurrently. "It is the warehouse for the entire world," asserted Jules Janin in 1854, "the crossroads of all industrial products." The city had "few remarkable monuments," Janin admitted but it could claim a wide array of factories that produced everything from paper to porcelain as well as what Janin described as "the most beautiful . . . sugar refineries [and] construction yards in the region."[6]

Monet's interests seemed to lie elsewhere, as in these early drawings he was following the lead of his Barbizon mentors, Camille Corot (1796–1875), Constant Troyon (1810–65), Théodore Rousseau (1812–67), and Charles Daubigny (1817–78). In the 1830s and '40s, these older artists had turned their backs on the swelling cities of the nation—most notably Paris—rendering not the swarming boulevards of the metropoli or the industrial expansion of their suburbs but the tilled fields of agricultural France with its laborers and animal stock, its quiet glades and rushing streams. Like Monet's first efforts, images such as Rousseau's (Pl. 7b) were understandable antidotes to the developments of the day; intellectually at least, they were attempts to stem the march of progress and to remind everyone of what was being lost as the country experienced profound and definitive change. They also were paeans to the beauties of nature and to humans' continuous struggle to be one with that world.[7]

Monet produced several pastels at the same time as these drawings that underscore his allegiance to these very ideas (Pl. 8). They too depict picturesque subjects—grottoes, children, and unkempt stretches of the coast near Saint-Adresse, a suburb of Le Havre where his aunt and uncle lived. Monet's medium also suggests his traditional bent as pastel had been favored by many Barbizon artists—most notably Jean-François Millet (1814–75) and Camille Flers (1802–68) (Pl. 9). Their proximity in handling, color, and motif to works such as Flers's *River Scene* (Pl. 9), therefore, emphasizes the fact that Monet followed the time-honored path of learning his craft from his predecessors despite the claims he made later in his life to being an independent, self-made artist.

One of Monet's later assertions was closer to the truth, however. He often said that in addition to fantastic designs, he filled his schoolbooks with caricatures of his teachers. Although no sassy marginalia have survived, many independent drawings of this type have, including numerous portraits of Parisian notables, as well as local Le Havre residents and rival artists, such as Pls. 10, 11. In fact, there are more than sixty extant caricatures from Monet's hand and probably many more that have disappeared. The majority date from 1856 and 1857 when Monet was 16 and 17 with some coming a year or two later. Most were done as a way to earn money; some were essentially exercises (many of the latter were copied from newspapers and periodicals). According to a report by the Le Havre City Council, Monet actually made a reputation for himself on the basis of these drawings which he exhibited in a local shop that sold stationery, frames, and colors.[8] Five or six new ones appeared in the window of the shop every Sunday, much to the delight of passers-by. Witty and inventive, they suggest a person who was interested in poking fun at people and capable of realizing his ends by relying on his ability to probe beneath superficial appearances and render his sly analyses with the sure hand of an accomplished draughtsman. While such drawings were typical of his day—they appeared frequently in the press until the turn of the century— Monet's talents in this area and his humorous, mocking, even self-deprecating sides are often forgotten or downplayed. But they should be kept in mind for several reasons. They underscore Monet's artfulness as well as his ability to draw even if he did not do it often later in life. (He actually once claimed he had no talent for drawing.) They also attest to his keen eye for detail and to his interest in people. And they reaffirm his engagement with the contemporary world in many of its manifestations.

Most of these caricatures and all of the small sketchbook drawings predate the appearance of Monet's first known painting, the meticulously rendered *View of Rouelles* of 1858 (Pl. 12). Monet submitted this exquisite picture to an exhibition in Le Havre in August of 1858 where it was accepted and listed as number 380. Just as the sketchbook drawings are too sophisticated to have been Monet's first attempts at putting pencil to paper, so this painting is too refined to have been Monet's initial try at placing pigments on canvas. His touch is too sure, the color scheme too subtle, and the light and atmosphere too tangible. It is a remarkable picture, in fact, especially for someone who was barely $17\frac{1}{2}$. It proves beyond a doubt that from the very beginning Monet was an artist of talent who could compete with the leading landscape painters of his day—Daubigny, Rousseau, Troyon, and Millet, all artists whose work he saw in popular magazines and local collections prior to beginning this picture. For this modest-size canvas is a direct product of the Barbizon tradition that those older artists established. Its setting is idyllic—a small boy sitting by the side of a stream meandering through a lush landscape punctuated by poplars and illuminated by soft but brilliant light. Nothing disturbs the tranquility of the scene and nothing would lead one to believe it was painted only a short distance from the hustle and bustle of Le Havre. Like so many images by those Barbizon painters, this is not the contemporary world of change but the rewarding idyll of the untrammeled past rendered with calm, harmonious colors and carefully integrated strokes of paint that lie smoothly on the surface of the canvas.

While paintings by Troyon and Millet occasionally hung in the same stationery and art supply store as Monet's caricatures, Daubigny may have been the most important artist of this group for the budding painter; his unassuming yet carefully arranged views of various sites along the Seine and Oise rivers north of Paris and the Marne to the south, such as Pl. 13, possess the same distilled atmosphere and attention to detail as Monet's *View of Rouelles*. They

10   Claude Monet, *Caricature of Rufus Croutinelli* (a rival Le Havre artist), ca. 1858– 59, graphite on paper, 13 × 8.4, w.D495, The Art Institute of Chicago, Gift of Charter H. Harrison.

11   Claude Monet, *Caricature of Philibert Audebrand*, ca. 1858–59, graphite on paper, 32 × 24, w.D501, Private Collection, France.

9

12  Claude Monet,
*View of Rouelles*, 1858,
46 × 65, W.1, Private
Collection, Japan.

also share a rich palette of deep greens, ochers, and browns, although Monet heightens the value of his colors considerably, just as he sharpens the contrast of light and dark. The handling is common to both pictures, however, as Daubigny sets his hues down with an equal mixture of precision and fluidity. Monet's aunt actually owned a small canvas by the older artist that Monet must have studied with care and admiration. His aunt recognized his interest in the work and gave it to him sometime at the end of the decade.[9]

Monet's *View of Rouelles* strongly suggests his ability to absorb the lessons not only of his Barbizon mentors but also of a local Le Havre artist whom Monet would claim more than thirty years later to have been his primary teacher, namely Eugène Boudin (1824–98).[10] Fifteen years Monet's senior, Boudin had prowled the Normandy coast and headlands since the late 1840s painting and drawing its terrain under varying light and weather conditions. Unlike his Barbizon peers, however, Boudin did not turn his back on contemporary developments; beginning in the early 1860s, he boldly rendered such modern aspects of the once-unchanging coast as Parisian pleasure-seekers on the beach, Sunday strollers along the boardwalk, even the new hotels that began to line these watering places to accommodate the influx of tourists and day-trippers (Pl. 14). "The peasants have their painters ... but do not those middle-class people strolling on the jetty towards the sunset have the right to be fixed upon canvas, to be brought to light?" he asked his friend and dealer, Pierre-Firmin Martin in 1868. "They are often resting from hard work, those people who leave their offices, [and] consulting rooms. If there are some parasites among them, are there not also those who have fulfilled their task?"[11]

Boudin's work was often in the same shop where Monet showed his caricatures, making it likely that they would meet. According to Monet's side of the story, however, he did not want to encounter the scruffy man whose work he felt was unworthy of being called art.

13  Charles Daubigny, *The Banks of the Oise*, 1859, 90 × 182, Musée des Beaux-Arts, Bordeaux.

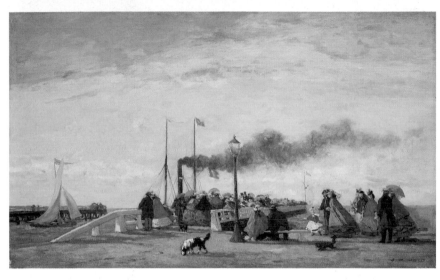

14  Eugène Boudin, *Jetty and Wharf at Trouville*, 1863, oil on wood 34.5 × 57.5, National Gallery, Washington, Collection of Mr. and Mrs. Paul Mellon.

"Often in the same show window, I beheld, hung over my own productions, marines that I, like most of my fellow citizens, thought disgusting," Monet confessed many years later. "His paintings inspired me with an intense aversion, and without knowing the man, I hated him."[12] For the more conservative, younger artist, Boudin's scenes were too exact. "To my eyes—accustomed as they were to ... arbitrary colorations, to the false notes and fantastic arrangements of the painters then in vogue—the sincere little compositions of Boudin ... drawn and painted from nature had nothing artistic and their fidelity struck me as more than suspicious."[13]

When the fateful encounter between these two artists occurred is not known, but it had to have been at least a year if not two before Monet's *View of Rouelles*. Boudin's keen sense of the moment and his feeling for the locale is clearly present in Monet's picture, elements that had to have been absorbed over a period of time. It is evident in the way Monet spreads the light across the scene and allows the landscape in all of its variety to breathe with a fullness that is not found in his drawings. It was through Boudin, Monet admitted in 1900, that "my eyes were finally opened and I really understood nature," a fact this picture eloquently bears out.[14]

Although Boudin undoubtedly encouraged Monet to follow his lead and try his own hand at different kinds of subjects, there is nothing in the older artist's oeuvre—nor anything in Monet's—that would have suggested the appearance of several paintings that Monet executed sometime shortly after the idyllic *View of Rouelles*. *Landscape with Factories* (Pl. 15) is

15   Claude Monet, *Landscape with Factories*, ca. 1858–59, 22.5 × 40, W.5, Private Collection.

16   J. Quartley after Daubigny, *Sotteville— Bifurcation of the Rouen to Le Havre Railway*, engraving from Jules Janin, *Itinéraire du chemin de fer de Paris au Havre*, Paris, Librairie de l'Hachette et Cie, ca. 1853.

one of a pair of these surprising pictures. Like the other, it probably dates from 1858 or 1859. Outnumbered by more Barbizon-like landscapes of these years, paintings such as this modest-size canvas initially seem completely anachronistic. The raw acreage in this view is littered with distant factories and anonymous structures whose desolate presence is the opposite of the reassuring hills in the background of the *View of Rouelles*. Indeed, everything about this painting is different from the bucolic image of a sun-drenched place untouched by time and change, from the troweling of the pigment and the harsher, more geometric shapes in the scene to the foreboding contrast of dark and light evident in the earth and sky. What Monet is depicting here is a landscape altered by the gritty world of industry and work, a kind of environmental assault that Emile Zola so often described in novels of the 1860s and '70s and that was occurring in and around most urban areas in France at the time.

Although these kinds of paintings are relatively limited in Monet's early oeuvre—there are only two or three of them—they nonetheless are important as they bear surprising witness to the fact that Monet did not simply focus on the seductive beauties of the rural sites surrounding his home. Instead, even at the early stage of his career, he also trained his eye on rawer, more challenging subjects, ones that may not have been as appealing as Rouelles but which were distinctly a part of his contemporary moment. Such subjects are also significant—and surprising—because they are extremely rare in French painting of the 1850s. Realist artists in Germany, such as Karl Blechen (1798–1840) and Adolph Menzel (1815–1905), depicted iron mills and forges from the 1830s to the 1870s. But outside of the paintings and drawings by François Bonhommé (1809–81) of the mines and factories at Le Creusot, Montchanin, and Fourchambault which were commissioned by the owners or the Ecole des Mines between the 1840s and 1860s, images of industry are almost non-existent in French art of the mid-nineteenth century.[15] Even among Monet's contemporaries (and soon-to-be-colleagues), Auguste Renoir (1841–1919) and Camille Pissarro (1830–1903), such views have no place. This is not unexpected as these kinds of subjects were deemed inappropriate. After all, how could the depiction of a factory raise one's aesthetic awareness, enhance one's understanding of the powers of painting, or provide even a modicum of charm or delight? Such subjects were considered too base and mundane to possess any apparent value. Thus, for Monet to have painted them at all was the more remarkable.

Given their uniqueness, it is difficult to determine what may have led Monet to choose these subjects. Perhaps it had something to do with the fact that they appeared with modest frequency in publications for mass distribution—guidebooks, for example (Pl. 16), or popular weekly magazines such as *L'Illustration*—and thus appealed to a desire that Monet would boldly manifest in the 1860s to democratize the more heralded art of painting by aligning it with such common material. Maybe Monet was attempting to follow the lead of authors he admired, such as Honoré de Balzac who had described those same subjects with graphic detail. Following his interest in caricature, perhaps it was merely his way of mocking traditional landscape painting. Whatever the reason, he vacillated between these extremes of industrial wastelands and Barbizon-like sites for his first essays and would continue to do so for the next twenty years.

Although Boudin moved to Paris in 1859 and exhibited in every Salon from that year until his death in 1899, he claimed he never really felt comfortable in the city, preferring his native Normandy. For Monet Paris was the major attraction. As the cultural capital of Europe and the center of artistic production and exchange in France, Monet knew it was where he could get serious training and be able to see significant art in abundance. Contrary to what is often said about the lack of support Monet received from his father, Adolphe Monet agreed to his son's wish to go and even wrote to the Municipal Council of Le Havre on 6 August 1858 requesting a grant to support his son's art studies in Paris. Either the request went unnoticed or was turned down because Adolphe wrote again on 21 March 1859. On the first application, Adolphe had listed Ochard and another local artist named Wissant as his son's teachers; on the second, he added Boudin's name. The second application was also accompanied by a still-life painting to demonstrate Monet's abilities. The Municipal Council rejected the request on 18 May 1859 although not without recognizing Monet's local reputation as a caricaturist—something which seems to have worked against him, however, as the council members felt he was not sufficiently serious to meet the demands of studying the high art of painting in the most prestigious place in the country.

The teenager did not wait at home for the results of the application. He headed off to Paris before the council responded, arriving sometime in early to mid-May, a few weeks after the opening of the annual Salon. With youthful enthusiasm he recorded his reactions to this immense artistic supermarket in what turned out to be the first of his surviving letters. Appropriately, it was written to Boudin.[16] Appropriately as well, the 18-year-old Monet was most enthusiastic about the landscape paintings he saw, particularly those by Troyon, Daubigny, Corot, and Diaz. Revealing an eye that was far more discriminating than his age would lead one to expect, he made surprisingly mature observations about pictures in the show in his second known letter, also to Boudin. Troyon's *View at Surenes*, for example, was "astonishing. You think you are in the middle of the country; there are herds of animals—cows in all positions; but it has movement and disorderly activity." Daubigny was "a spirited fellow who understands nature." The Corots were "unadorned marvels", the Rousseaus "very beautiful". It was his negative remarks, however, that really attest to his sophistication. Despite his admiration for Troyon, for example, he claimed the shadows in his pictures were too dark. A big dog painting by Philippe Rousseau (1816–87) was "a little confused. He is better at the details than at the whole," Monet quipped. The submissions of Emile Lambinet (1815–77) apparently had achieved considerable success but for Monet they were "all glare and glitz." Even Eugène Delacroix (1798–1863) whom Monet greatly admired had submitted pictures that, in his opinion, were only "hints or sketches." Monet reserved his strongest comments for the seascape painters. "[Eugène] Isabey [1767–1855] has produced a horrible, huge picture," while "[Jean-Louis] Hammon [1821–74] has only made terrible things ... without color or drawing. It's hypocritical and pretentious, in a word he knows nothing about nature."[17]

This is tough talk, especially from someone Monet's age, but it is also highly informed and basically accurate. In addition to revealing his sharp eye and developed taste, these observations also suggest Monet's keen desire to make his own way in that competitive art world and the confidence necessary to succeed. In fact, in both of these early letters, he constantly urged Boudin to come to Paris not only to see the Salon and take advantage of the swirl of activities in the capital, but more importantly to push his pictures as Monet rightfully recognized a void in the market for seascape painters: they "are totally absent," he told his mentor, "it's a road for you that should take you far." He raised this issue again the following year. "Come, you can only win. You know as well as I that the only good seascape painter we have, Jongkind, is dead as an artist; he is completely crazy . . . You have a perfect place waiting for you."[18] Monet even hustled sales for Boudin, working the network of artists and collectors that he was developing for his mentor and himself. Such marketeering became his modus operandi for years to come. All of this did not come without its price, however, as Monet was looking to get something for himself out of all of these efforts, another practice that also became standard. He was forthright with Boudin about this, telling him he hoped that Boudin "won't refuse me a little sketch of yours as a souvenir," a request he had the audacity to repeat two months later when Boudin apparently had not complied.[19]

It was this kind of maneuvering that Monet practiced for decades. He was not necessarily the kind of person one would want for a friend. While helpful when pushed, he generally looked out for himself, often feeling he deserved whatever he could get and whatever that was should be more than anyone else may have received. In part this feeling may have been due to the talent he knew he possessed from the beginning. In part it may have been the result of his desire to maintain the good bourgeois standards that he appeared to have enjoyed when growing up. (While running counter to the normal picture of the avant-garde artist, that desire only increased as Monet grew older and accumulated greater wealth and renown, his Giverny estate providing substantial but not complete satisfaction in this regard.) The feeling of being special may also have been due to his uncanny and unabashed ability to assess the market, size up its players, and figure out exactly where he and everyone else stood. It was as if he deserved a commission for these analytical powers which he exercised over and over again during the course of his career. Indeed, he applied them to the world of finance as well as to that of art since from the 1880s onwards he also played the stock market.

All of these activities kept him in constant contact with Paris, a city he initially found mesmerizing but later developed mixed feelings for. On his first stay in 1859 and 1860, however, he could not get enough of what it had to offer; he returned to the Salon over and over, made the round of galleries, and visited artists' studios, such as Armand Gautier's, Lhuillier's and, most importantly, Troyon's. He gathered advice from everyone he met finding that offered by Troyon to be particularly useful. Troyon urged him to draw incessantly. "One can never get enough of it. Enter a studio where you only work from the figure. Learn to draw. . . . From time to time, go to the countryside and do some studies . . . make some copies at the Louvre. . . . And then come back here to Paris definitively next winter."[20] It was this advice that Monet communicated to his father who concurred, taking to heart Troyon's apparently genuine praise for his son's work. Adolphe agreed to allow Monet to prolong his stay if he were going to enter the studio of a respectable painter, such as Thomas Couture (1815–79), whom Troyon had recommended. But Monet wanted nothing to do with an artist he claimed was prone to angry tirades and had "totally given up painting." Instead, he joined the Academie Suisse, a much less structured gathering of budding artists on the Ile de la Cité that was headed by an accommodating man from whom the school took its name.[21] Suisse ran a relatively loose shop, particularly in comparison to a traditional Paris studio. It was just what the young Monet wanted, a flexible schedule with no hierarchic course of study, no examinations or formal critiques, and no egotistical Ecole des

Beaux-Arts professor making endless demands on him. Little wonder that Monet was ecstatic about being able to stay in the capital to continue his work and to escape what he deprecatingly described to Boudin as "the dirty city of Le Havre."[22]

Monet's letters reveal several other important traits or preferences that served him well throughout his life. First, his ability to get what he needed: in this case, the right kind of studio instruction and, equally important, free studio space. He obtained the latter through the intercession of someone in Le Havre who introduced him to the still-life painter Charles Monginot (1825–1900) who in turn generously offered Monet access to his studio at any time. And, best of all, Monginot appears to have given it to Monet free of charge. Monet always managed to succeed like this whether by being at the right place at the right time or knowing how much charm or persistence he needed to apply. He also was not immune to exploiting connections his acquaintances had established, which made him careful about whom he picked as friends. Perhaps because of these talents, he often seemed to be able to influence situations or hold certain sway. While drawing from the figure, for example, as Troyon recommended, claiming it was "a fine thing" to do, he suggested that his inclination toward landscape which was shared by the other students in the academy was what ultimately would triumph. "They begin to perceive it is a good thing," he told Boudin in 1860. His prediction proved correct. For while figure painting was widely perceived in the 1860s as the most important genre, landscape assumed that position in the 1870s, undoubtedly to Monet's pleasure.

There are two final points that can be gleaned from these early letters and Paris experiences. While slightly cocky and self-centered and perhaps just going through the motions of drawing from the figure (none of these drawings has survived), Monet was immediately recognized as an artist of talent. When he brought two still lifes for Troyon to see in 1859, for example, the older artist quickly detected a facile hand. "You must do some serious work, for this is very nice but you do it too easily."[23] It was that facility that Monet treasured and developed throughout his career, relying upon it to renew his art in moments of self-doubt and to demonstrate his powers when confronting competitors or critics, particularly in the late 1880s and 1890s when he began to paint almost exclusively in series.

Finally, Monet was keenly aware of and interested in the opinions that circulated about the state of artistic affairs in France. He read newspapers and periodicals, novels and historical accounts; he moved in cultural circles, went to concerts and plays, and had many friends whose lives centered on the arts. In addition, he saw as much painting as he could. One telling instance occurred in February 1860 when he went to see what he described as a huge exhibition of modern art that centered on the School of 1830. It contained eighteen paintings by Delacroix, a dozen Rousseaus, works by Jules Dupré (1811–89) and Alexandre Decamps (1803–60), and the lesser-known Orientalist, Prosper Marihat (1811–47). In his opinion, it was a splendid show. More important, it proved to him that "we are not in as much decadence as they claim," a fact he undoubtedly found encouraging.[24] He knew how to spot mediocrity as evident from his critique of the Salon of 1859 and he certainly was not afraid to confront it. But he also was clearly sensitive to the broadly expressed cry in the contemporary press for artists who could strengthen France's artistic standing and stem the tide of its perceived decline. While taking heart in the production of his older colleagues, he also understood—no matter how naively—the role that history and his hand held for him in this most significant of challenges. And it was to its realization that he devoted his efforts during the halcyon days of the 1860s.

# 3    Meeting the Competition: Monet in the 1860s

Competition—with himself, his contemporaries, and those painters who preceded him—was innate to Monet. It surfaced in the first decade of his activity as an artist in his sardonic caricatures, his participation in the municipally sponsored exhibition in Le Havre of 1858, and his sharp judgements about the work he saw in the Paris Salons of 1859 and 1860. But it became truly apparent when he put these ritualistic beginnings behind him and decided to place his own work in front of the august Salon jury. It was a fearful moment for any artist, as the judges were notoriously harsh. And even if your work was accepted, you then had to face the often ribald and unforgiving Paris public and the ever-jealous artistic community at large. Those audiences were frequently satirized by Parisian cartoonists—rarely more wittily than by Honoré Daumier (1808–79), one of Monet's favorite artists (Pl. 18)—but they were real and their power was formidable. However, for French artists to succeed in their chosen profession, they eventually had to succumb to this time-honored, though fundamentally flawed, system—at least until the 1870s when Monet and his Impressionist colleagues established a radical alternative.

Monet bided his time, wisely perhaps, as there was no advantage to rushing into the fray. The ability of the jury to remember those who had been too eager and unprepared was legendary. In addition, Monet continued to enjoy the support of his father and his aunt and was able to live a relatively carefree life in Paris while pursuing his studies. But he held back an excessively long time—five years—until 1865 when he finally submitted two works to the infamous panel. He lost slightly more than one year from his studies (between 1861 and 1862) when he was obliged to participate in a state-run lottery to determine who among the 228 men his age living in the Le Havre area would have to serve in the army. Only those who pulled a number between one and seventy-three were drafted. Monet emerged from the drawing in that minority. (His father could have bought him out of his obligation but apparently the conditions were unacceptable to the budding artist—his father insisted he give up his studies in Paris and return to Le Havre for a traditional job.) Thinking of it as an adventure, Monet joined the Zouaves—a division of the cavalry—in July 1861 and was shipped off to North Africa (Pl. 19). The

17 (facing page) Claude Monet, *Women in the Garden* (detail from Pl. 42).

18    Honoré Daumier, *Sketch Taken at the Salon*, 1868, lithograph, published in *Le Charivari*, 16 June 1865. Courtesy of the Boston Public Library, Print Department.

period was not a complete loss to him: he had time to do some work there, and he always recalled the strong light of Algiers where he was stationed as critical to his thinking as an artist. Like his fellow inductees of the period Monet was supposed to serve a five-year term, but he came down with a strain of typhoid fever and was sent home to convalesce in August 1862. Soon after, he had the very good fortune to meet Johan Bartold Jongkind (1819–91) who was working in Sainte-Adresse and Le Havre. Although Monet had described him to Boudin two years earlier as "dead to art," Jongkind's advice to the emerging artist was apparently quite helpful. No correspondence between them has survived and there are few documented instances of their contact, but Monet greatly appreciated the guidance Jongkind gave him, admitting his immense debt to the Dutchman years later. "He was my true master from that moment onwards," he claimed in 1900, "and it is to him that I owed the definitive education of my eye."[1]

After his recovery, Monet was supposed to return to his military unit, but the 22-year-old country boy was soon back in Paris thanks to a recently enacted law that extended the buy-out option and the generosity of his aunt who put up the money to free him—over 3,000 francs, which was not an inconsequential sum: it was more than enough to support the average working-class family of four for a year.[2] Monet lived in a small fifth-floor apartment on the rue Mazarin that cost 450 francs a year and worked in a more traditional atelier—that of the well-respected though unadventurous Neo-Grec painter, Charles Gleyre (1806–74). Entering this studio was a move intended to pacify his father and aunt and thus ensure a relatively steady flow of cash from home.[3]

It proved to be astonishingly propitious, however, regardless of Monet's intentions. For while Gleyre himself painted what today are considered saccharine images of idealized figures in achingly romantic environments, he was in fact extremely tolerant and encouraged his students to pursue their own inclinations whatever they were. He was also good about dispensing advice and took the time to give critiques of his students' work. Most beneficial of all, however, was the fortuitous presence in the class of no fewer than three individuals who were to become significant figures in French art in their own right—Renoir, Alfred Sisley (1839–99), and Frédéric Bazille (1841–70). The four quickly became soulmates, particularly Bazille and Monet, and often went on painting excursions together.

Monet was the second of the four friends to try his luck at the Salon following Renoir's successful attempts in 1863 and 1864. His usual aggressiveness was perhaps tempered by the gravity of the test; if he failed, he would have to suffer not only his own disappointment but also the rebuke of his family, which was not a happy prospect given how much they had invested in him. Nonetheless, his hesitation is rather curious. He had amply demonstrated his abilities as a painter and had painted a number of pictures prior to entering the contest that were likely to have been accepted—traditional still lifes, for example, rendered with a restrained palette and highly controlled touch as well as many modest-sized landscapes that fell well within the norms established for the genre. In addition, he had already put his work in front of the public by participating in an exhibition in Rouen in October of 1864 and had received a commission for two pictures from a collector in Le Havre after having sold several canvases to other buyers. Perhaps he felt for a while that he could avoid the Salon test and make it on his own.[4]

When he did try his luck in 1865, he emerged from the review with flying colors. Both of his submissions, *The Mouth of the Seine at Honfleur* and *The Pointe de la Hève at Low Tide* were accepted (Pls. 20, 22). Both pictures were Salon-size, 90 centimeters high by 150 centimeters long, making them among the biggest he had ever painted. Both depicted scenes with which Salon-goers were familiar; such seascapes were the stock-in-trade of most landscape painters of the day. With its gusty sky and sense of immediacy the latter recalled works by Jongkind, such as Pl. 23. More important to their success, however, was the fact that the palettes in both of Monet's pictures were quite restrained as was the application of paint, formal qualities that appealed to the Salon jury and the public. Furthermore, all of the elements in his pictures were arranged in a carefully ordered fashion. The expansiveness of the view across the water in the former or down the beach in the latter is enhanced by the huge cloud-filled skies; human figures in both are concentrated in the center of the scenes and are held in check by the boats to the left and right in the port picture and by the triangular wedges of water, beach, and dunes in the coastal view. Monet artfully even has the froth of the lapping waves in the latter picture begin just at the lower left corner, and the rocky part of the beach on the right lead to the opposite corner creating a kind of traditional, Renaissance perspective system, something he underscores with the diagonal rivulets in the center of the scene.

Highly calculated, therefore, in style, subject, and composition, the paintings rightfully earned Monet important notices in the press. The tough-minded Paul Mantz, for example, writing in the conservative *Gazette des Beaux-Arts,* praised Monet's bold manner of seeing things, his "taste for harmonious colors in the play of related tones, [and] the fully thought-out quality of the whole."[5] Monet was very quickly invited to make a drawing after *The Mouth of the Seine* which was engraved and published in the popular *L'Autographe au Salon* of 1865 (Pl. 21). One could hardly have asked for a more auspicious beginning, particularly when the critic for *L'Autographe* called Monet's painting "the most original and supple, the most solid and harmonious exhibited in a long time," and fellow artists—many of whom he did not know—wrote him congratulatory letters.[6]

While such praise might have led most artists to capitalize on their success by painting similar kinds of pictures, Monet, only a few weeks after his triumph, began an entirely new group of paintings that pointed him in quite a different direction, demonstrating his desire to expand his repertoire and to step boldly to the forefront of contemporary art. Apparently responding to the widely circulated imperative for avant-garde artists to paint the world around them in order to capture, as Charles Baudelaire put it, "the eternal in the transitory" and "the heroism of modern life," Monet decided to render a scene of consummate pleasure—fashionably dressed men and women enjoying a picnic in a secluded but richly foliated corner of the Forest of Fontainebleau (Pl. 29). Numerous studies done on the site en plein air were intended to lead to a canvas of heroic proportions—4.5 meters high by more than 6 meters wide, making the dozen figures in the scene life-size and the image as a whole almost cinematic. It was a picture that clearly was to take its place in the long line of monumental canvases produced by the major figures in French art from David and Gros to Delacroix and Courbet.[7]

20    Claude Monet,
*Mouth of the Seine at
Honfleur*, 1865, 90 × 150,
W.51, The Norton
Simon Foundation,
Pasadena.

21    Claude Monet,
drawing after *Mouth of
the Seine at Honfleur*,
1865 (from *L'Autographe
au Salon et dans les
ateliers*, 24 June 1865,
76).

   As with the earlier contrast of his factory landscapes and the view of Rouelles, this painting
could not have been more different from the views of the Normandy coast of the year before.
These are not local folk as in those earlier pictures and, of course, they are not working. Their
setting is also extraordinarily lush, unlike the rougher, more threatening locales for the
Norman mariners. In addition, the colors Monet used were now deep and rich as opposed to
the tougher, more restricted hues of the former. Even the brushwork in this picture is striking
for its breadth and vigor in contrast to the restraint that is evident in the earlier canvases. It is as
if Monet allowed all of the formal aspects of this painting to be more sensuous and expressive

20

22   Claude Monet, *The Pointe de la Hève at Low Tide*, 1865, 90.2 × 150.5, W.52, The Kimbell Art Museum, Fort Worth.

23   Johan Barthold Jongkind, *The Seine at Bas Meudon*, 1865, 33 × 47, The Virginia Museum of Fine Arts, Richmond, Collection of Mr. and Mrs. Paul Mellon.

in order to heighten the attractiveness of the subject he had chosen to render, thus endowing the image—and the painting itself—with a kind of immediacy that would have a sure-fire effect on his intended Salon audience.

While the product of Monet's apparent desire to be of his time—"*il faut d'etre de son temps*"—the painting was also his reaction to recent work he had seen in the capital, particularly the paintings of two people he greatly admired, Manet (1832–83) and Courbet. The presence of the former is most apparent in Monet's choice of subject; one could not paint a picnic scene in the mid-1860s without referring, tangentially at least, to Manet's infamous

24 (top left)   Edouard
Manet, *Luncheon on the
Grass*, 1863, 208 × 264.5,
Musée d'Orsay, Paris,
Moreau–Nélaton Gift,
1906.

25 (top right)   Franz
Xavier Winterhalter,
*The Empress Eugénie
Surrounded by her Maids
of Honor*, 1855,
300 × 420, Musée
National du Palais de
Compiègne.

28 (right)   Claude
Monet, *Luncheon on the
Grass*, 248 × 217,
W.63(b), Musée
d'Orsay, Paris.

26 (above left)
Gustave Courbet, *The
Meeting ("Bonjour
Monsieur Courbet")*,
1854, 129 × 149, Musée
Fabre, Montpellier.

27 (above right)   Nicolas
Lancret, *The Picnic after the
Hunt*, ca. 1740, 61.5 × 74.8,
National Gallery of Art,
Washington, Samuel H.
Kress Collection.

*Luncheon on the Grass* which had caused such a scandal at the Salon des refusés of 1863 (Pl. 24). But instead of confounding his viewers with unexplained relationships and insulting them with the presence of such an unabashedly naked figure as Victorine Meurent who stares out from Manet's picture with extraordinary aplomb, Monet opted for a much more straightforward scene, one that was both more casual and more readable than Manet's wry concoction. By bringing his painting down to a more everyday level and making it even more accessible, Monet was attempting to outdo his colleague. Even his references are more up-to-date. Instead of basing his actors, as Manet did, on Renaissance prototypes (notably Raphael's sea gods after Marcantonio Raimondi's engraving of Raphael's tapestry cartoon), Monet plundered a wide range of prototypes from court portraiture of his very time—specifically, a painting of Empress Eugénie and her entourage by Franz Xavier Winterhalter (1805–73) (Pl. 25)—to popular fashion plates of women in the latest dresses and photographs of middle-class people enjoying themselves out of doors (Pl. 30). He also made clear reference to eighteenth-century fêtes galantes by Antoine Watteau (1684–1721) and his followers as well as to hunt and picnic scenes by rococo artists such as Nicolas Lancret (1690–1743) (Pl. 27) and Carle van Loo (1705–65). His actors, however, were identifiable contemporaries. Bazille posed for four of the six male figures—recognizable from his lanky form, mustache, and bushy muttonchops—while Monet's future wife, Camille-Léonie Doncieux (1847–79), an

29 Claude Monet, *Luncheon on the Grass*, 1865, 130 × 181, W.62, Pushkin State Museum of Fine Arts, Moscow.

30 Anonymous, fashion plate from *Les Modes parisiennes*, 30 July 1864.

23

18-year-old native of Lyons who had moved with her family to Paris when she was a child, was the model for the two women in the center and perhaps the standing figures as well.[8] Courbet is featured here, too: the poses Bazille assumes on the far left and in the center behind the woman serving plates are a variation on Alfred Bruyas and his servant in Courbet's *The Meeting* ("*Bonjour Monsieur Courbet*"), of almost ten years earlier (Pl. 26). In addition, when Bazille leans against the tree on the right, he vaguely recalls Courbet's self-portraits in several hunting scenes. The ties to Courbet are made even more apparent in the dog in the center of the composition which is stolen from Courbet's *Burial at Ornans*. The ultimate link, however, is found in one of Monet's studies for the painting in which Courbet himself appears as the seated male figure to the left of center. Ironically, Monet posed him with his hand raised on his knee in mock imitation of the figure on the right in Manet's *Luncheon*. Finally, Courbet's presence is also felt in the thick, palette knife application of paint that Monet employed in these pictures.

It is this remarkable facture which has often been cited as one of the reasons Monet ultimately abandoned this novel project in early 1866. It is said he was unable to reconcile the broad swathes of paint with the forms he was attempting to describe, that the paint asserted itself more as an independent element than as an illusionistic device by which the scene would be given form.[9] This argument is difficult to accept, however, as the two surviving sections of the final painting and the preparatory canvases are rendered with enormous confidence and skill. Given the sheer size of the picture and the fact that Monet does not appear to have begun work on the final version until some time in mid-October, it is probable that he was merely unable to complete the canvas by 20 March which was the deadline for submitting works to the 1866 Salon, a possibility made more likely by the fact that in January 1866 he had to leave the rue Furstenburg atelier that he had been sharing with Bazille and move to another, smaller space near Pigalle in the Batignolles area on the other side of Paris.

31  Anonymous, fashion plate from *Les Modes parisiennes*, 1 October 1864.

With unprecedented aplomb, Monet left his "*machine*," as such large canvases were called, in its unfinished state and quickly began another, quite different painting of Camille (Pl. 33). According to legend, Monet painted this new picture in four days, delivering it to the Salon jury at the very last moment.[10] This story is undoubtedly apocryphal since the painting is quite ambitious—Camille is life-size—and has a very complex paint surface. Drying time between working sessions alone would have required more than four days. It was also carefully planned. While painted primarily in darker tones to recall older, more traditional portraiture, it depicts a woman who is clearly dressed in the latest fashion and who assumes the disdainful but quite popular pose of models in magazines of the time (Pl. 31). It therefore is an artful combination of the past and the present, the acceptable and the aggressive, and most likely could not have been conceived and executed in short order.

To Monet's great pleasure, the canvas was accepted by the jury, together with a large landscape view of a road in the Forest of Fontainebleau that he also submitted, a notable achievement again for an emerging artist. The paintings earned Monet many favorable notices, with Ernest d'Hervilly of the widely respected magazine *L'Artiste* hailing Camille as "the Parisian queen, the triumphant woman" and Emile Zola claiming that Monet's picture held his attention more than any others: "now there is a temperament, there is a man among eunuchs."[11] A prominent Paris dealer commissioned Monet to paint a variant of the large canvas apparently for his own delectation while the two most celebrated Parisian caricaturists—Bertall and Gill—did humorous sketches of the Salon version which appeared on the front pages of their popular Parisian weeklies, *La Lune* and *Le Journal amusant* (Pl. 32).[12] As a result of all of this publicity, Monet was able to sell several other pictures that spring. And two years later Arsène Houssaye, editor of *L'Artiste*, purchased the Salon version

32  Gill, *Monet or Manet?—Monet*, caricature of *Camille*, from *La Lune*, 13 May 1866, 1.

33 Claude Monet,
*Camille (Woman in a
Green Dress)*, 1866,
231 × 151, W.65,
Kunsthalle, Bremen.

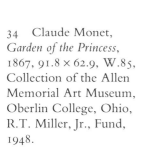

34 Claude Monet, *Garden of the Princess*, 1867, 91.8 × 62.9, W.85, Collection of the Allen Memorial Art Museum, Oberlin College, Ohio, R.T. Miller, Jr., Fund, 1948.

35 (far right) Claude Monet, *Street in Sainte-Adresse*, 1867, 79.7 × 59, W.98, Sterling and Francine Clark Art Institute, Williamstown.

of Camille from Monet for a handsome sum. Monet could not have hoped for a better outcome.[13]

As with the *Luncheon*, Camille's stylish dress and aloof, contemporary manner attest to Monet's immersion in a culture the opposite of that of his avant-garde predecessors and of his own Barbizon leanings. What the picture ultimately confirms is Monet's ability to bridge arenas otherwise considered antithetical—the city and the country, the fashionable and the ordinary, the Salon aesthetic and the popular illustration.

This dichotomy—of the old and the new, the traditional and the contemporary—became Monet's operating ground for the next dozen years following his success with this portrait of Camille. It is apparent in various pairs of paintings from the 1860s, such as his view of the Garden of the Princess from the spring of 1867 and the depiction of a street in Sainte-Adresse from the summer of the same year (Pls. 34, 35). The former is pre-eminently urban with the crisp, clean, imposed geometry of the park, the carefully tended flowers, the bustling boulevards and the cluster of apartment buildings crowned by the dome of the Pantheon, all asserting a typical Parisian air of sophistication.[14] The latter is much less assuming with its inviting dirt path leading past old stone walls and towering trees to the modest steeple of the local church. In contrast to the view of the very heart of the capital which Monet rendered from a balcony of the Louvre, everything here is literally down to earth and human scale, dignified in its own rusticity but commonly replicated throughout rural France.

A similar contrast is evident in two even more telling paintings done in the same summer of 1867 (Pls. 36, 37). Both are exactly the same size and depict the same stretch of beach in Sainte-Adresse. For all intents and purposes, therefore, they could be considered traditional pendants.[15] But what they show could not be more divergent. In one, old salts smoking pipes stand next to wooden dories while fishing vessels head out to sea under overcast skies. In the

other, the beach is reduced to a mere sliver on the left and is chock full of well-dressed men and women observing a group of sun-drenched boats engaged in a regatta. The excitement of the day in the second picture and its pleasurable activities are echoed in the strong, diagonal arrangement of the clouds and the shifting waters of the scintillating bay. The rooted serenity and conservative tone of the former picture is felt in the generous triangular wedge of beach which provides a secure foreground and a gradual entrance into the scene. It is also evident in the dories which sit weightily on the sand, in the lack of activity, in the blanketed sky, and in such artful details as the alignment of the end of the distant peninsula with the bowsprit of the departing fishing boat and the stern of the closest dory on the right. This is a moment during the week when the place has returned to its older order and reasserted its original purpose; the latter is a weekend scene when Parisian and Le Havre day-trippers invade the town and claim it temporarily for their own.[16]

Monet's advantage was that he knew both worlds from his upbringing on the Normandy coast and the years he subsequently spent in Paris. Relying on the market for his income, he was wise to use the two of them to develop a diversified portfolio of offerings. After all, he wanted to appeal to as wide an audience as possible. He was not alone in this approach as his friends from the Académie Suisse were also painting a range of pictures, particularly Renoir who produced portraits, still lifes, figure pictures, landscapes, and modern-life scenes. Like them, Monet clearly was attracted to traditional subjects just as he was swayed by the life of the city. And when he made a conscious decision to commit them all to paint he was in effect rendering opposite poles of contemporary France and his own personal biography.

Nowhere is this more apparent or more poetically expressed than in the *Garden at Sainte-Adresse* which Monet painted during that same summer of 1867 (Pl. 38). This is the consummate image of coastal life enjoyed by modern, upper middle-class people.[17] Monet's father and presumably his aunt sit peacefully on the sun-baked patio of his aunt's house looking across the mounds of flowers and foliated fence to the broad expanse of sea and sky. The brilliance of the light and the crispness of the atmosphere make the scene appear almost unreal, as if it has been painstakingly distilled from the more chaotic jumble of moments and events that comprise real life. But the palpitating presence of the encircling flowers counters the notion of this being a kind of fantasy as does the evident breeze that flutters the flags, pulling them tautly to the right, imitating the pattern of the clouds in the background and the smoke of the boats on the distant horizon. The flags themselves, one for Le Havre, the other

36 (above left) Claude Monet, *The Beach at Sainte-Adresse*, 1867, 75 × 102, W.92, The Art Institute of Chicago, Mr. and Mrs. Lewis L. Coburn Memorial Collection.

37 (above right) Claude Monet, *Regatta at Sainte-Adresse*, 1867, 75.2 × 101.6, The Metropolitan Museum of Art, New York, Bequest of William Church Osborn, 1951.

for the nation, also root the image in the real world of the 1860s as do the clothing worn by the figures, the style of the garden, and the type of boats on the sea. That sense of grounding and calculation are likewise apparent in the clean lines that divide the different parts of the picture—the concrete section of the terrace, for example, which butts up against the clearly defined grassy edge, the fence which separates the terrace from the sea, and the almost architecturally drawn horizon which divides the water and the sky.

All of these carefully mapped-out divisions attest to Monet's rational ordering of these elements and presumably to his vision of the world as a whole. The foreground terrace is clearly the world of leisure and refinement, of peace and inactivity; it is personal and domestic, meticulously ordered and evidently hierarchic. The world beyond is one of work and movement, of industry and commerce, of chance and competition. The two are inextricably linked by their forceful juxtaposition in the picture, just as they are in life. Even the flag poles which begin on the terrace tie the two by rising up though the strata beyond. The two worlds are also linked, of course, by the fact that Monet's father and aunt made their living from those steamboats and ocean-going clipper ships. They therefore have earned their leisure and place in the sun from that distant hub of mercantile activity. The final link, however, is found in the seemingly precarious placement of the dark bowsprit and jib of the local fishing boat just behind the creamy-yellow parasol of the elegantly dressed woman standing by the fence. Although it could be seen as a kind of visual joke with interchangeable punch lines, the juxtaposition actually is critical as it compresses the space between the two worlds and acts as an essential conduit between them; if the boat is removed the foreground realm of bourgeois propriety becomes hopelessly separated from the melange of traditional and modern exploits beyond, causing the picture to lose a large measure of its internal harmony and, ultimately, much of its meaning.

39  Katsushika Hokusai, *Fuji Viewed from the Sazaido in the Temple of the 500 Rakan, Edo*, from *Thirty-six Views of Mount Fuji*, 1829–33, 23.9 × 34.3, British Museum, London.

Monet once referred to this canvas as "my Chinese painting where there are some flags."[18] Although a casual reference with possibly derogatory overtones, this nonetheless suggests he associated the picture with Eastern phenomena; Japanese and Chinese products were often perceived as one and the same. Monet's enthusiasm for things Japanese in his later years is well known. He filled his house in Giverny where he moved in 1883 with his sizable collection of Japanese prints and he transformed a large portion of his property there into the magnificent water lily garden that became the focus of his attention for the last twenty-six years of his life.[19] Determining when he became enthusiastic about Japan, however, is surprisingly difficult. Near the end of his life, he claimed he came across Japanese prints in a curio shop in Le Havre when he was 16 or 17.[20] This may have been possible for, despite persistent claims to the contrary, Japanese material circulated in France long before Admiral Perry's visit to Japan which opened the country in 1854. There were histories of Japan in France in the eighteenth century, Japanese artifacts were bought and sold on the French market in the 1820s, and illustrated books containing many *ukiyo-e* images were published in Paris in the 1830s. The famous *Manga* of Katsushika Hokusai (1760–1849) was even in the collection of the Bibliothèque Nationale by the early 1840s.[21] In addition, Le Havre was a logical place for things like Japanese prints to end up given its international shipping affairs. Despite this relative proliferation, however, there is nothing in Monet's work or letters prior to his reference to the *Garden at Sainte-Adresse* that suggests he had become aware of this material at such an early age. Whenever he did encounter it, he must have been impressed with the forceful way the Japanese woodblock artists handled color, as they set it down without modulation in large areas that often created striking contrasts (vaguely reminiscent of the sunlit sections of the terrace in Monet's painting or the sea and sky beyond). He also had to have been moved by the lack of chiaroscuro in all areas of the print and thus by the clear, anti-academic way in which forms were defined. That Japanese artists concentrated on contemporary life for their subjects likewise must have been reaffirming, just as the spatial distortions they imposed—the way planes tilt up radically or forms are severely foreshortened—were equally appealing; it was precisely these kinds of violations of academic norms that the Impressionists were devising themselves (which is why people such as Pissarro claimed "the Japanese confirm my belief in our vision"[22]). The role that such material played in the development of early Impressionism, therefore, should not be overstated. Formal similarities certainly exist between Eastern and Western images, as evident when a print such as Hokusai's *Fuji Viewed from the Sazaido in the Temple of the 500 Rakan, Edo* of 1829–33 (an example of which entered Monet's collection at some point, Pl. 39) is compared with

Monet's seaside painting. But Japanese prints were only one of many sources these emerging artists absorbed—including popular prints, magazine illustrations, photography, and older as well as contemporary art. Headhunting for single references in Japanese art, therefore, is both limiting and off the point as these Impressionists were more eclectic and sophisticated than such a search implies.[23]

Despite its beauty, size, and poignant subject, Monet did not submit the *Garden at Sainte-Adresse* to the Salon jury. Like the dozens of other, albeit more modest-size views of the Normandy coast and the capital that he completed in the 1860s, Monet painted this picture for the private market of dealers and collectors that he was beginning to develop through friends and fellow artists in Paris. Sales hardly boomed but Monet must have been encouraged by the few pictures he did sell, particularly one of those Paris views, which went to the dealer Louis Latouche, and a seascape, which another dealer, Cadart, purchased that year. He also sold the *Garden at Sainte-Adresse* just a few years after he painted it.[24] Like many of his Normandy coast pictures, any of these paintings could have been candidates for the Salon; however, it appears that Monet felt Salon submissions had to be of a different magnitude—essentially two to three times as big as these canvases—which suggests the challenges he posed for himself as well as the kind of mark he wanted to leave on that most public of forums.

This is borne out by the two pictures he did submit to the Salon of 1867; one canvas depicted the Port of Honfleur and measured 2 meters wide by 1.5 meters high (Pl. 40); the other showed four women in a light-filled garden (Pl. 42) and was even bigger, 2 meters wide by 2.5 meters high. Undoubtedly emboldened by the success he had enjoyed in the previous two years, Monet was staking a claim for himself on the basis of size alone. But he went several steps further and rendered both scenes with remarkable freedom, allowing his brushstrokes to sit forcefully on the surfaces of the canvases, his colors to maintain a heightened vibrancy, and his lights and darks to meet without the calming intercession of graduated half-tones. He also devised images that were at once familiar and untraditional as he took time-honored subjects—port scenes in the one case and, in the other, pictures of women out of doors that hark back to the fêtes galantes of the eighteenth century—and rearranged their parts to produce something entirely unexpected. In the view of Honfleur, for example, Monet concentrated on a site that was well known to most Parisians. Just across the Seine estuary from Le Havre where the railroad ended linking the capital with the coast, Honfleur had become a popular getaway for city dwellers and had been painted often by landscape artists and view painters prior to Monet. Most of his predecessors, however, rendered the picturesque aspects of the port with its colorful fishing vessels and quaint, eighteenth-century timber-and-plaster houses, evoking the history-laden character of the place and the continuities of the town's seafaring traditions.

Monet includes a whole fleet of local fishing boats as well as men and women who are clearly associated with the sea by their dress and activities. But he sequesters all of this evidence on the right side of the scene while introducing quite different material on the left: a smoke-belching paddle boat that is either about to dock or to leave for open waters; two pleasure boats tacking to the right; a large, two-masted, ocean-going ship that is entering the harbor under reduced sail; and just to its right exactly where the fishing fleet begins, a second steam craft, this time a relatively new packboat used primarily to pull barges up and down the Seine and to transport cargo around the port. There is, therefore, a kind of mixture of the old and the new here that makes the scene neither delightfully nostalgic nor uncompromisingly modern, something that is evident as well in Monet's evocation of Dutch seventeenth-century precedents by painters like Aelbert Cuyp (1620–91) and Willem van de Velde (1611–

40 Claude Monet, *Port of Honfleur*, 1866, 148 × 226, W.77, Presumed destroyed during World War II. Document, Archives Durand-Ruel.

93). Instead, Monet has been able to devise a forthright, though highly calculated, image that is a commentary on the changing nature of the place—note how the top-hatted city figures on the left open the scene and the group of fishermen and their women close it on the right. It is as if he has artfully merged the two opposing Sainte-Adresse beach pictures into one, rendering this new conglomerate with strokes of paint—particularly those on the water and the sails to the right—that suggest the vitality of the moment and Monet's willingness to test the Salon jury's norms of artistic decorum.

That willingness is even more apparent in the huge *Women in the Garden* (Pl. 42). Monet always claimed he painted this picture completely out of doors by digging a trench in the backyard of a house he had rented in Sèvres in the spring and summer of 1866, raising and lowering the immense canvas with an ingenious system of pulleys. This is another apocryphal tale, however, as the trench would have to have been a veritable canal—the picture is eight feet tall! Even if he had done such excavation, we know that the unfinished painting was shipped to him after he left Sèvres for Honfleur in the late summer or early fall of 1866 and that he completed it in his studio there on the coast.[25]

Although his insistent claims can be debunked, the picture still emits the freshness of a plein air painting and possesses an extraordinary immediacy. Emile Zola thought it was one of the best pictures any artist had painted that year and designated Monet the head of a new group of artists which Zola called "Les Actualistes." In his opinion, these were "people who try to penetrate the exact sense of things and [whose] works are alive because they have taken them from life and have painted them with all the love that they have for modern subjects." According to Zola, Monet was not only the head of this group, he was also a "true Parisian; he brings Paris to the countryside. He cannot paint a landscape without including well-dressed men and women. Nature seems to lose its interest for him as soon as it does not bear the stamp of our customs. . . . Claude Monet loves with a particular affection nature that man makes modern."[26] Such recognition would have made any artist's head swell, Monet's

31

included, even if it were not entirely accurate. After all, Monet did love the quiet corners of untrammeled nature as evident from the many splendid views of the Normandy coast that he painted throughout the decade.

But the *Women in the Garden* is a remarkable painting and deserved Zola's praise. In addition to its painterly breadth and sharp junctures of light and dark, the scene appears initially at least to be clipped straight out of life, so full are the forms and so tangible the light. In addition, the women wear some of the latest Paris couture (three of the four dresses had featured in the *Luncheon on the Grass*) and they assume poses that once again imitate those in contemporary advertisements and fashion magazines (Pl. 41). Their presence is enhanced by the contrast of their gowns with the deep greens that surround them while their appeal is associated with the beauty and fragrance of the flowers that they hold, smell, and pluck.

41 Anonymous, fashion plate from *La Mode illustrée*, 27 May 1866.

While sculptural and highly readable, the scene at the same time is frustratingly cryptic. What are these exquisitely dressed women doing in this curiously ill-defined place? What are their relationships and why does one of them stare out at us so coyly? In addition, for all of their elegance, the women are haphazardly arranged just as the setting itself is inexplicably unsophisticated. The sandy path arcs oddly out of the scene after dividing the immediate foreground into three disproportionate areas. The tree is almost directly in the middle of the picture and appears to grow out of the woman's dress in front of it. Its branches stretch out to either side like the arms of a diminutive figure attempting to hold up an unruly canopy of foliage with as much grace as it can muster. It is not quite enough, however, as the branches appear too thin and ungainly, adding a note of contrast to the refined figures below. Finally, the canopy does not reach all the way across the scene, breaking on the right to allow an oval-shaped area of sky to appear. All of the parts, therefore, ultimately do not add up despite their meticulous handling and apparent veracity. It is as if Monet consciously set out to make a painting that was going to reveal the constant coexistence of slippages and sophistication that go into making grand painting, and the battle that an artist must wage between awkwardness and refinement, naiveté and polish, especially when creating an image that is so evidently decorative.

Little wonder, perhaps, that Monet's willingness in these cases to extend the norms for this kind of picture met with the jury's disapproval; both were rejected from the Salon of 1867. Zola's words were therefore even more welcome, particularly as they were part of his Salon reviews for *L'Evénement*, a major Paris newspaper that had commissioned the critic to write a series of articles on the exhibition. Obviously, Zola felt strongly enough about the painting that he devoted space to it even though it was not in the show. Monet must have felt an additional surge of satisfaction shortly after Zola's article when Bazille expressed interest in buying *Women in the Garden* and soon offered Monet the staggering sum of 2,500 francs for it. This was truly tangible retribution as factory workers at the time earned that much as an annual salary.[27]

Bazille paid Monet in installments of fifty francs a month, however, so Monet was not able to feel wealthy instantly. In fact, he cried poverty—as was his wont—constantly over the next several months, relentlessly hounding Bazille for further support and becoming more and more infuriated when Bazille did not respond. "I really don't know what to say to you," he told his friend in a typical fit of exasperation in August 1867. "You have been very stubborn in not responding to me. I have sent you letter after letter and you have done nothing . . . It is as if I were asking help from strangers. . . . Come on Bazille, there are things that one cannot leave for the next day. This is one of them and I am waiting."[28] Most of his pleading letters (which become increasingly desperate and hard-nosed) were written from his aunt's house in Sainte-Adresse where Monet had relocated for the summer and fall,

42 Claude Monet, *Women in the Garden*, 1866–67, 256 × 208, W.67, Musée d'Orsay, Paris.

ostensibly to save money. His decision to leave Paris for the coast must have been a difficult one for him because his relationship with Camille had by this time developed into something serious. Not only had she become his principal model—she posed for the three figures on the left in the *Women in the Garden*—but she was also his lover. Presumably they spent the spring and summer of 1866 together in Sèvres while Monet worked on his picture; later, that winter, she discovered she was pregnant with his child. She was due to have the baby in early August 1867 at the very time Monet was going to be nearly two hundred kilometers away.

It is difficult, if not impossible, to understand Monet's decision to leave Camille at such a critical moment in their lives. It appears, however, that it did not have as much to do with money as it did with Monet's relationship with his father. Monet had told his father how deeply involved he had become with Camille in early April 1867 which made his father furious. To the elder Monet, it was one more example of his son's negligent behavior. Monet's rejection at the Salon that spring probably did not help much, although in a letter to Bazille Adolphe Monet claimed that that setback did not make a difference, that his son had unfortunately taken "a wrong path" and that he had better get off it if he were going to enjoy the good graces of his family, particularly his aunt.[29] That meant, among other things, that Camille had to go, a threat Claude obviously took quite seriously. Not only did he give the appearance of obeying his father by moving back to his aunt's house, he also seemed to validate the underpinnings of bourgeois life which his father was propagating by painting the *Garden at Sainte-Adresse* that summer. One cannot help but feel, however, that the strain of the situation, especially the tension between himself and his father (and presumably his aunt as well) is implied in the strange serenity that hangs over this ode to middle-class conformity and the distance that separates the two couples in the picture. For while that silence and space perfectly complement the leisure moment Monet has so carefully devised, they also were distinctly a part of Monet's family experience that summer which could not have been a carefree time.

While appearing to have caved in to his father's wishes, Monet's decision to leave Camille behind in Paris also seems to have had something to do with his own struggles with the idea of becoming a father and of having a family. Not having been the most responsible of sons, he suddenly had to confront an obligation that was intimidating at best and hideous at worse. It also meant a radical change in his lifestyle, something that was equally unnerving or unwelcome. He admitted as much to Bazille that summer when he told his friend, "I beg of you my dear friend, help me from where you are because my state is visible to everyone . . . I do not want to be reproached about anything in this affair."[30]

But the main reason he became so enraged by Bazille's silence from Paris was because Monet was genuinely concerned about Camille's wellbeing, at least if one believes his letters. She apparently did not have a sou to her name and had nothing for the expected baby—no clothes, blankets, crib, or toys. Monet was relying on his friend to bail him out and provide enough money to support Camille and the child. At the same time he was torn because he wanted to please his father and aunt. It was clearly a no-win situation, something he must have realized and which undoubtedly contributed to his increased frustration.

The situation also revealed his divided feelings about Camille, something he would suggest over the next ten years in many of the paintings in which she appeared. While he was thrilled to have been able to sell two canvases before he left Paris because he "could come to the aid of that poor Camille," as he told Bazille that summer, he also could be quite condescending, describing Camille in that same letter as "a very good child" who had "become reasonable and by doing so has made me even sadder."[31] Love does not seem to have been something Monet felt in this relationship. In fact, when mentioning Camille's change of heart, he implies that she had expected something from him: a commitment, perhaps, or emotional or financial support—something he was unwilling or unable to provide.

Such divided feelings were an integral, though not always explicable or attractive, part of Monet's character and they manifested themselves in various ways over the course of his life. While they occurred most often with women and with members of his immediate family regardless of their gender, they also could quickly become part of his dealings with friends. At one moment, he could be steadfast in his devotion to them; at another, he could be ambivalent or dismissive. He told Bazille that summer, for example, that if he did not respond to the letter he was writing—the seventh in a row that had prompted no reply—he was *never* going to write him again, of that he could be sure. And yet Bazille was his best friend and his primary source of funds.[32]

This emotional tangle seems to have been partly the result of Monet's keen sense of himself with all of its attendant complexities. He always had to be in charge and be given the due he felt he deserved. Although he always accepted sympathy, indeed often demanded it, he wanted no charitable donations and no words of advice, particularly any that might smack of condescension. Again, Bazille frequently felt Monet's ire in this regard. But Monet's divided emotions also seem to derive from his own uneasiness about his emotional make-up and his capacities to become involved with someone on a deep and lasting level. He admitted this when he told Bazille that he was surprised at how he felt about the baby when he was with Camille in Paris on 8 August 1867 when she gave birth to their son, Jean. "Despite everything and I don't know how, I feel I love [him]."[33] Monet did not stay in Paris long enough to register Jean's birth at the local town hall, which occurred three days later on 11 August; at least his signature does not appear on the ledger. More than likely he had returned to Normandy because he wrote the above-quoted letter to Bazille on 12 August which he mailed from Sainte-Adresse. Not a big mark against him, perhaps, given male practice of that moment, but a curious one nonetheless. Again, not untypically of his generation, Monet did not marry Camille until three years later and then, shortly after the Franco–Prussian War broke out in July 1870, he fled to England leaving his new bride and Jean to fend for themselves. They eventually joined him in London and returned with him to set up house in Argenteuil, just outside Paris, in 1871, but from the time of their marriage until Camille's death from cancer of the uterus in 1879, there is little indication of Monet's affection for his new family (another son, Michel, was born in 1878). In fact, from September 1878 until her death a year later, Camille had to tolerate the presence of a second woman in her house Alice Hoschedé who, with her husband Ernest, Monet's principal patron of the decade, and their six children, had been taken in by Monet after Ernest went bankrupt. Unlike Monet's delayed nuptials, this *ménage à douze* was indeed unusual—if not bizarre—and represents the kind of twisted state of affairs that Monet could create for himself because of his own emotional tangle.[34]

Despite his surprised reaction to the birth of Jean, Monet spent the next seven months until March 1868 shuttling back and forth between Sainte-Adresse and Camille's tiny apartment on the impasse Saint-Louis, never remaining in the capital for any extended period, thus never raising the suspicions of his father or aunt. Work seems to have been his substitute for traditional family time, as it was so often over the course of his long career. In addition to completing approximately twenty medium-size pictures, more than he had produced during any previous seven-month period, Monet also managed to paint two huge canvases, one that depicted the wind-blown jetty of Le Havre (Pl. 43), the other showing ships leaving the Le Havre port. The latter is known only through cartoons that appeared in satirical magazines

43 Claude Monet, *The Jetty at Le Havre*, 1868, 147 × 226, W.109, Private Collection.

44 Bertall, *The Dutch Tavern Ship (Royal Palace)*, caricature of *The Boats Leaving the Port*, 1868, from *Le Journal amusant*, 6 June 1868, 2.

45 Anonymous, *Leaving the Port*, caricature of *The Boats Leaving the Port*, 1868, from *Le Tintamarre*, 6 June 1868, 4.

(Pls. 44, 45, 46), and through a description by Emile Zola, as it disappeared a year after Monet had painted it. Monet had hoped that both pictures would be accepted for the Salon of 1868 but just the now-lost canvas succeeded, and then apparently only by the intercession of the jurist Charles Daubigny who argued forcefully in its favor.[35] That Monet had at least one picture admitted to this exhibition, even if after a struggle, was still an important accomplishment and another indication of the success he continued to enjoy in this most competitive of forums. That his picture was singled out for ridicule by two of the leading satirical magazines—the *Tintamarre* and the *Journal amusant*—was also a sign of his stature, just like Zola's notice which emphasized the freshness of Monet's touch.

On Zola's advice Monet decided to leave the capital shortly after the Salon opened and take his family to Bonnières-sur-Seine, a small town more than forty kilometers north of Paris just upriver from Giverny where he would ultimately spend the last half of his life. Monet stayed there until the early summer when he left for Le Havre to finalize his submissions to an exhibition that the city was staging in July in conjunction with a huge international maritime exposition that opened there on 1 June. Ironically, the view of the port of Le Havre rejected by the Salon jury was accepted for that show and earned Monet a silver medal. Two of his other seascapes were caricatured in the local press together with his fourth submission, *Woman in a Green Dress* (Pl. 33).[36] Other developments followed. He sold his portrait of Camille to Arsène Houssaye that fall for a commendable 800 francs and learned that Houssaye was even talking about leaving it to the Musée du Luxembourg.[37] On top of that Monet received a commission from a collector in Le Havre to paint a portrait of his wife, all of which made him a happy man (although he complained about being stuck inside when working on the commission).[38] This good fortune also allowed him to bring Camille and Jean to Normandy for the first time.

After an initial stay in Fécamp, a safe distance from Le Havre and his father, they rented a house in Étretat and settled there for the winter "surrounded," as he told Bazille, "by all the things that I love. I spend my time out of doors on the beach when the weather is bad or when boats go out fishing or else I go into the countryside, which is so beautiful here that I find it perhaps more pleasant in winter than in summer... I am enjoying the most perfect tranquility ... my desire would be to remain forever in a nice corner of nature like this one."[39] Clearly, he was working in familiar territory as a native of the region, painting places that spoke to him on a personal level. The Normandy coast served as this kind of touchstone for Monet during his entire career.

Despite his enthusiasm for the natural beauties of the area, what preoccupied him most that winter were not views of the majestic chalk cliffs of this picturesque village—they would be his primary focus twenty years later. Nor did he concentrate on the old fishing boats and the rough seas which he also painted with gusto when he returned to this site in the 1880s. Instead, he worked on an interior scene simply entitled *The Luncheon* (Pl. 49). Measuring 2.3 meters high by 1.5 meters wide, it was clearly a picture destined for the Salon, perhaps as a kind of rejoinder to the jury's rejection of one of his pictures the previous year. As someone devoted to landscape and to painting contemporary life out of doors, this picture is wholly uncharacteristic; except for still lifes and portraits, Monet had never attempted such a subject. But it had been a staple for artists from the seventeenth century onwards; even Courbet had made a name for himself with it in his *After Dinner at Ornans* of 1848 (Pl. 47). That Monet took it up therefore suggests his desire once again to place himself squarely in the long line of distinguished predecessors and to challenge their collective legacy.[40]

When it came to landscape painting, Monet was a great admirer of artists from seventeenth-century Holland and those from eighteenth-century France—Watteau was one of his favorite painters. Not surprisingly, therefore, when he moved indoors for this new enterprise, he took these artists as his guides: *Luncheon* is a kind of modernized version of a Jan Vermeer or a Jan Steen or an updated François Boucher or Jean-Baptiste Chardin with echoes of Courbet's later dinner scene. All the elements are there—the rounded light that comes into the room from a window on the left, bathing the interior and warming each object it touches. There is the sense of pleasure those older works communicated engendered here by the graciousness of the setting and the physical presence of such inviting things to eat and drink and by the informality of the figures—one leaning against the window holding her hands, another gathering items from a closet in the background, a third doting on a small child who playfully raises his spoon in typical youngster fashion. There is also an apparent casualness of the moment typical of those earlier prototypes—the doll that lies discarded under the chair on the left, the newspaper and turned chair on the right that awaits its occupant, the books with their bent covers casually stacked on the edge of the buffet in the background. And there is a balanced color scheme dominated primarily by earthen tones much like older art, just as there is the evidence of careful brushwork and a highly ordered arrangement of the forms as a whole. Little wonder that Monet guarded this picture until 1874 when he included it as his most important submission to the so-called first Impressionist exhibition. He finally parted with it the following year to a discerning collector.

Little wonder as well that most writers have seen it as a heartwarming example of Monet's hard-won happiness. Monet contributed to this reading of the picture by his remarks to Bazille in the letter quoted above. "As I said to you in my little scribblings, I am very happy, very enchanted. I am like a real cock in pâté, for I am surrounded here by everything I love. I pass the time in the open air . . . and . . . then, in the evening, my dear friend, I find in my little house a good fire and a good little family. . . . it is marvelous to watch this little being [Jean] grow, and upon my word, I am really happy to have him. I am going to paint him for the Salon with other figures around him as he should be. . . . Thanks to this man from Le Havre [M. Gaudibert] who has come to my rescue, I am enjoying the most perfect tranquility since I am free of all worries, so my desire would be to to stay just like this forever, in a quiet corner of nature. . ."[41] All of this sounds wonderfully refreshing, as if Monet has been able to forget

46  Anonymous, caricatures of *Camille* (*Woman in a Green Dress*), *The Port of Honfleur*, and *The Jetty at Le Havre*, from *L'Epatoutfant*, 1868.

46a  Detail of Pl. 46 showing the caricature of *The Port of Honfleur*.

47 (above left)
Gustave Courbet, *After Dinner at Ornans*, 1865, 195 × 257, Musée des Beaux-Arts, Lille.

48 (above right)
Edouard Manet, *Luncheon in the Studio*, 1868, 118 × 153.9, Bayerische Staats-gemäldesammulungen, Munich.

the tensions of the year and a half that had just passed and truly enjoy the rewards of his hard work.

But such readings are perhaps too pat, particularly given the events of the previous eighteen months and Monet's admitted confusion about his role as father, husband, and dutiful son. They also do not conform very well to the evidence Monet presents in this picture. For there is as much awry and disturbing in this scene as there is stable and reassuring. Who is the visitor on the left, for example, and why does she assume such a curiously removed attitude even down to her odd hand gestures? Why is there no place set for her at the table and why has she made no effort either to take off her hat and gloves and stay or move around the table to leave? Why does the woman in the background, evidently a maid, seem almost trapped in the doorway as if there is not enough space for her in either the room or the closet? Why also does she appear to be intruding or listening in on something that perhaps she should not be hearing? Although the woman in the center has her arm around the child's chair, why does she look at him with such a wistful, forlorn stare? And finally, why is Monet's presence not recognized by any of the figures even though it is amply implied by the awaiting chair and newspaper and the bountiful meal? There are other curiosities as well. Why, for example, does the woman in the center already have wine in her glass and where did it come from since the bottle on the table is still corked and full? Why does the loaf of bread hang so precariously near the edge of the table on the left, and why is the woman's exit on that side blocked by the chair whose legs, while appearing out of perspective, stand on a section of the rug whose stripes are larger than those to the right?

Things become stranger when we realize that nothing is accidental here; Monet worked hard to get everything exactly the way we see it. The rather thickly painted surface attests to this as do the numerous pentimenti that are buried in the impasto. Monet altered the position of the figure's arms on the left, for example, and gave her a more formal jacket; she started off wearing a casual day dress. Even stranger, perhaps, is the difficulty of determining whether Camille posed for the woman on the left and not for the mother figure in the center which some writers have suggested was based on a neighbor. (The model for the maid is not known.) What are we supposed to make of this? Even if Camille posed for both bourgeois women, as others have claimed, the painting still does not seem to make sense.[42]

38

49    Claude Monet, *The Luncheon*, 1868–69, 230 × 150, W.132, Städelsches Kunstinstitut, Frankfurt.

It has been argued that Monet was engaged in an insider's dialogue with Edouard Manet and that the painting is a kind of clarified version of Manet's *Luncheon in the Studio* of the same year (Pl. 48).[43] But there is no indication that Monet actually saw his rival's picture which did not emerge from Manet's Paris studio until Manet submitted it to the Salon of 1869. That makes this dialogue rather unlikely.

It is more plausible to believe instead that Monet was attempting to update his heralded seventeenth- and eighteenth-century precedents, not only by making everything in his scene appear to have been taken directly from contemporary life of the 1860s but also by tinging the world of bourgeois comfort and refinement that he presents with suggestions about the complexities and contradictions of that construct. After all, this smiling child was born out of wedlock, a bastard son not a legitimate one. And his mother was not Monet's lawfully wedded wife; in the eyes of the state she was a *fille mère*. In addition, the food and setting, no less the maid, while precisely what a middle-class family would have wanted or possessed, were hardly consistent with Monet's outstanding debts and self-declared state of poverty. In fact, that very winter while he was painting this picture, four canvases that he had submitted to the maritime exhibition in Le Havre were seized by city officials and auctioned off to repay creditors. The same fate befell his Salon submission that year.[44]

Monet, of course, was not the only one engaged in this kind of posturing or caught in these kinds of lapses of economic and social responsibility. It was typical of his times. The notion of the nuclear French family, for example, long cherished as the core of the nation's strength, was under constant attack in the 1860s as critics pointed to the disturbing rate of illegitimate births, the rise in the number of prostitutes on urban streets, the increase in the amount of alcohol consumed, the decrease in the number of people attending church, the decline in literacy, and the amount of time fathers spent away from the home. To the skeptics, this was clear evidence that not only the family but the whole country was in jeopardy.

Although generally exaggerated, aspects of these claims were often the focus of avant-garde writers—Gustave Flaubert's *Madame Bovary* of 1857 is a case in point, as is Zola's *Thérèse Racquin* of 1867 in which a couple fall in love, plot the death of the woman's husband, commit the murder, and then watch their own relationship disintegrate. (Zola wrote twenty subsequent novels between 1871 and 1893—his great Rougon-Macquart anthology—in which he explored the effects of France's changing environment on one extended family.) Thus, Monet's seemingly straightforward image of a delightful bourgeois luncheon may be neither as simple nor as delightful as it initially appears. Nor is it as transparently biographical. Rooted in the complexities of Monet's contradictory life and times, it could hardly have been anything else. But it is consistent with most of his figure paintings after his initial attempt at the genre with his *Luncheon on the Grass*. And its multi-layered, sometimes opposing, readings return in different guises in the decades that followed.

Despite his preoccupation with this picture, Monet ultimately decided not to submit it to the Salon of 1869, a decision that, like the picture itself, is difficult to explain. Perhaps he was concerned about losing it to creditors. He also just might have seen Manet's studio version when he returned to Paris that spring and decided not to go head to head with the older artist. Perhaps he felt he needed to work on it more, a suggestion given strong credence by a letter that Arsène Houssaye wrote to the Salon jury (at Monet's insistence) asking them to grant Monet the opportunity to retouch his submissions before the jury made its decision. The jury turned Houssaye's request down.[45] Regardless of his reasons, it appears that it was not until the last moment that Monet decided to substitute two other pictures, a view of fishing boats sailing into the rising sun and an almost blindingly brilliant winter scene (Pls. 50, 51).[46]

It proved to be a disastrous choice, as both pictures were rejected, repeating what had occurred three years earlier in 1866 with his *Women in the Garden* and *Port of Honfleur*. This time, however, Monet was furious and after convincing the dealer Latouche to put one of his views of Sainte-Adresse in the gallery window which soon caused a stir on the sidewalk in front of the shop, he tried to convince Houssaye to buy something from him, complaining that "this fatal refusal has almost taken the bread out of my mouth and despite my prices [which are] not at all high, dealers and collectors turn their backs on me.... The worst thing is," he cried, "I cannot even work any more."[47]

Much of this was typical hyperbole undoubtedly inspired not only by his rejection but also by jealousy; his friends Renoir, Pissarro, and Bazille all had gotten pictures past the jury as had Manet and Degas (1834–1917). Monet made his anger apparent when he moved with his family in the early summer of 1869 to the small hamlet of Saint-Michel near the town of Bougival and soon found himself short of ready cash. Prompted by Bazille's suggestion that perhaps he save money by walking to Le Havre instead of taking the train or by chopping his own wood instead of purchasing it from a merchant, Monet staged a frontal assault on his friend, revealing once more the unpleasant side of his character. "The present letter is to inform you that I have not followed your (inexcusable) advice of walking to Le Havre. I have been a bit happier this month than the preceding ones, but I am still in a hopeless state.... I am brought up short because of no paints. Happy mortal, you will bring back quantities of canvases! I alone this year will have done nothing. This makes me angry at everyone; I am jealous, wicked; I'm furious; if I were able to work, everything would be all right. You tell me it is neither fifty francs nor a hundred that will get me out of this situation; that's possible but in that case there is nothing for me to do but knock my head against the wall, for I cannot look forward to any instantaneous fortune, and if all those who spoke to me as you did had sent me forty or fifty francs, etc., certainly, I would not be in this bind." Perhaps realizing how aggressive and nasty he sounded, he suddenly backed off, changing his subject as well as his tone. "I am re-reading your letter, my dear friend. It is certainly very comical and if I did not know you, I would take it as a joke. You tell me seriously, because you think it's so, that in my place you would chop wood. Only people in your position believe this, and if you were in mine, perhaps you would be more baffled than I am. It is tougher than you think, and I bet you wouldn't chop much wood. No, don't you see, advice is very hard to give and, I think, useless—no offense meant.... A propos of Renoir, that reminds me that at his brother's

50 (above left)  Claude Monet, *Fishing Boats at Sea*, ca. 1868, 96.130, W.126, Hill-Stead Museum, Farmington.

51  Claude Monet, *The Magpie*, 1868–69, 89 × 130, W.133, Musée d'Orsay, Paris.

52   Claude Monet, *La Grenouillère*, 1869, 74.6 × 99.7, W.134, The Metropolitan Museum of Art, Bequest of Mrs. H.O. Havemeyer, 1929.

house I drank wine that he had just received from Montpellier and which was awfully good. That also reminds me that it is absurd to have a friend in Montpellier and not be able to get a shipment of wine from him. Come now Bazille . . . couldn't you send us a cask the price of which you would be able to deduct from what you still owe me?"[48]

Ending up trying to coax a keg of wine out of his friend suggests Monet's priorities and places some doubt on the tales often repeated about his destitute condition at this moment. Undoubtedly it was a difficult time, perhaps one of the worst he had to endure, but it did not stop him from painting, as he claimed it had earlier. In fact, between the time he arrived in Saint-Michel in June 1869 and his departure from the Paris region just about a year later, Monet was amazingly productive, completing over twenty canvases, among them at least four views of a popular summer gathering place on the Seine known as La Grenouillère, which today are considered among the classic paintings of Impressionism (Pl. 52).[49]

These paintings were part of Monet's stated aim of doing a large canvas of this site for the Salon of 1870, a project which he was going to undertake with Renoir who was living with his parents in nearby Voisins. In his letter to Bazille quoted above, Monet claimed it would remain just a dream as by September he had "only done some bad sketches." Again, this was

42

an exaggeration as these pictures are acutely observed and boldly nuanced. Rarely had Monet ever allowed his brush to be so free. The touches of nearly pure chroma in the water in Pl. 52, for example, are remarkably deceiving in the way they alternate between describing flickering effects of light on the surface of the Seine and maintaining their complete independence as merely a collection of coordinated marks upon a canvas.

Everything about this picture is actually quite carefully planned, suggesting more than a few casual working sessions. The boat in the left foreground, for example, juts into the scene with its right gunwale coming directly out of the lower left corner of the canvas. Its left gunwale runs parallel to the wooden walkway above it on that side. The boat in the middle, while more sketchily rendered, marks the center of the canvas with its right gunwale while the upper left corner of its stern receives the rippling reflection of the bending tree beyond. The foliage on that tree flutters just above the lighter-colored leaves of the trees in the distance which Monet artfully arranges as a continuous triangle whose top edge rises gradually from the far left to the upper right, paralleling the diagonal lines of the wooden walkway on the left and the roof of the floating boat house on the right.

The passenger section of that floating structure pushes just a paint stroke higher than the creamy orange line of the shore on the opposite side of the river, while all of the figures inside are crisply silhouetted against the lighter mustard-colored foliage of the background and are neatly contained within the geometric openings of the structure's glassless windows. The whole painting therefore is a kind of theater set, made evident as well by the foliage on the upper left which hangs into the scene from a tree outside of the picture but which acts like a curtain that is being drawn back to reveal the lively activities on this painterly stage.

Just as striking as these formal subtleties was Monet's decision to paint this site in the first place primarily because it was a well-known pleasure spot that had recently received a lot of press coverage. It actually had been "discovered" about a decade earlier by artists, writers, musicians, and dancers who had been looking for picturesque escapes close to the capital. Easily reached by rail, coach, and even foot (it was only about twelve kilometers from Paris) it quickly developed into a weekenders' paradise in the 1860s and began to attract a broad cross-section of Parisian society interested in leisure activities—swimming, boating, fishing, and general carousing, the last becoming its primary orientation in the years that followed. So popular had the place become by the later 1860s that the Emperor Napoleon and his wife Eugénie paid it a visit in the very summer of 1869 that Monet and Renoir were working there. Thus, any painting of La Grenouillère appearing at the Salon the following year would have been immediately recognized as timely, if not slickly, *au courant*.

Unfortunately, Monet's did not make it that far. The canvas he appears to have submitted (Pl. 53), a work that has not been seen since the Second World War and is presumed destroyed, was rejected. The verdict probably did not come as a surprise to Monet as the painting is more broadly rendered with more independent strokes of paint than any other picture he had put before the jury. It must have been disappointing, however, as other more conservative views of similar stretches of the Seine were admitted, such as *By the Water* by Ferdinand Heilbuth (1826–89) (Pl. 54). Heilbuth had been successful because he had given his picture the guise of an eighteenth-century fête galante. The female figures in particular are more elegantly dressed and generally more fashionably posed. Even the dog on the right sits obediently erect. Most important, the paint is applied with considerable restraint, causing brushwork to be appropriately disguised. In addition, Heilbuth's palette is much more subdued with none of Monet's garish color combinations or contrasts. Monet did not want to compromise himself in this fashion. As with *The Luncheon*, he was subtly but unabashedly going to take those century-old prototypes and transform them so that they would be

53  Claude Monet, *La Grenouillère*, 1868, 75 × 100, W.136, Destroyed during World War II. Document courtesy of Robert Gordon.

unmistakably of his own moment. Thus, when he formulated this project and began to work on his suite of canvases, he too looked to eighteenth-century sources, such as Watteau's *Embarkation from the Isle of Cythera*, but he left no trace of that beloved image in the final product.

Undoubtedly more surprising to Monet was the jury's decision to reject his other submission, *The Luncheon*. This picture did not overstep the bounds of artistic decorum in any of the ways that his view of La Grenouillère did; in fact, when Monet showed it four years later in the so-called first Impressionist exhibition, it was consistently singled out as a remarkable work. The rejection in 1870 would have been all the more painful because most of Monet's colleagues—Renoir, Bazille, Pissarro, and Sisley—again were represented at the exhibition which itself was unusually large containing nearly 3,000 canvases. There was some compensation—Daubigny and Corot quit the jury in protest and several critics mentioned the setback, including Arsène Houssaye who wrote an article under a pseudonym in *L'Artiste* saying in print what had circulated by word of mouth that he was going to leave Monet's portrait of Camille to the Musée du Luxembourg.[50] But Monet must have been increasingly aware that success was more fickle than ever, particularly as this was the second year in a row that he was not represented in this all-important show. It also must have convinced him that an alternative to the Salon needed to be devised, an initiative he and his friends had discussed before and soon took up, realizing it finally in 1874.[51] This rejection was Monet's last, as it was the last time until 1880 that he placed himself before the jury. And after his relatively successful return that year—one out of two paintings was accepted—he never went back to the Salon again. The 1870 debacle, therefore, was an important turning point.

1870 also was a critical year for him personally, as three months after receiving the bad news from the Salon officials, Monet legalized his relationship with Camille by marrying her on 28 June in a civil ceremony at the *mairie* of the 8th arrondissement in Paris. It must have been a small affair as it was witnessed by only four friends: Courbet, an unknown Gustave Monet, a doctor, and a journalist who collected Monet's work. It is difficult to know why

54  Ferdinand Heilbuth, *By the Water*, 1870, 90.8 × 116, Private Collection.

Monet took this step after four years of living with Camille off and on. There is no indication he was responding one way or the other to any directives from his father. And if it was done with an eye toward obtaining a dowry from Camille's parents, he was soon to be disappointed. They promised 12,000 francs but stipulated that the sum would not be paid until after M. Doncieux's death. All the newly-weds received immediately was 1,200 francs which represented two years of interest on the dowry at 5 per cent a year.[52]

As usual, Monet was able to spend that money quickly. He bought some new canvases and supplies and left the city as the summer heat arrived, taking his family to Trouville, a delightful town on the Normandy coast, across the Seine estuary from Le Havre a few kilometers west of Honfleur. Unlike Honfleur, however, Trouville looked directly out on to the English Channel and sported a long stretch of sandy beach which attracted vacationers from England as well as northern France. And from the 1850s onwards, like so many other villages along the coast, it began to lose its homespun charm as more and more people taking advantage of the ever-growing transportation system came to bask in the sun, breathe the refreshing sea air, and enjoy the many distractions of the site. The railroad from Paris was extended to the neighboring town of Deauville in 1863 confirming the future development of this section of the coast. By 1870, huge hotels had been constructed along a new boardwalk that lined the shore in Trouville, a casino had opened as had numerous restaurants and souvenir shops making the maritime activities of the place rapidly a thing of the past.[53]

It is those vacationing pleasure-seekers together with Camille and Jean that Monet rendered that summer in nine pictures, including Pl. 55 which depicts the terrace in front of the brand new Hôtel des Roches Noires distinguished by its imposing façade topped by a golden statue of Neptune that stretches into the sky. Like this inviting view with its artful combination of refined drawing and painterly relish, all of these canvases are filled with crisp, clear light and are generally rendered with remarkable freedom, so much so that in certain areas, such as the rapidly brushed American flag on the left, the lightly primed canvas is clearly visible contributing to the freshness of the image and its windblown, seaside appeal. In

55 Claude Monet, *The Hôtel des Roches Noires*, 1870, 80 × 55, W.155, Musée d'Orsay, Paris.

fact, bits of sand are actually embedded in the surfaces of several of these paintings attesting to Monet's plein air practices as well as to the strength of the breezes that blew across the Channel.[54]

It was the winds of war, however, that began to blow that summer as, after a long period of military build-up, Prussian Chancellor Otto von Bismarck began flexing his muscles across the Rhine and threatening to place a member of the Hohenzollern family on the recently vacated Spanish throne. Since the Hohenzollerns were German and potentially beholden to King William I and to Bismarck, the French government feared that Spain and the Germans could easily form a pact of "blood and iron" and thereby isolate or at least threaten France on two sides.[55]

None of this, of course, can be sensed from Monet's paintings of that summer; everything in these scenes appears to be wonderfully carefree, a feeling that in fact pervaded the country. For most people believed that Bismarck was merely sabre-rattling and that even if he did start a war he was no match for the country that had dominated Europe so often in the past. Over-confidence mixed with condescension and disdain proved to be a deadly combination. For when France declared war on 19 July 1870, goaded on by the infamous Ems telegram that suggested Bismarck was going to fix the Spanish succession, no one could have predicted the outcome which came quickly, decisively, and disastrously for the French two months later. The well-oiled Prussian military machine rolled across the Rhine within days of the declaration of war and crushed one French stronghold after another, finally defeating Napoleon III and his 80–100,000 men at the battle of Sedan in September 1870. Not since Waterloo had France suffered such humiliation. To make matters worse, Bismarck's troops marched on to Paris which they encircled by 18 September and held under siege until January 1871, when terms of a settlement were worked out and the provisional government of France signed a peace agreement in the Palace of Versailles on the 29th of the month. It was a day of infamy for the country but it did not mark the end of terror.

Fearing the provisional government was looking out for itself and not for the nation, disenchanted Republicans and members of the national guard formed a loose federation in Paris known as the Commune.[56] Shortly after the armistice was signed, the Communards declared themselves the legitimate rulers of France thus setting the stage for a civil war, the ending of which was as vicious as it was predictable. French troops under General MacMahon were permitted by the besieging Prussians to sweep into the capital during seven days in May 1871. What followed was a bloody week of fratricide and destruction as nearly twenty thousand Communards were killed and hundreds of buildings demolished (Pl. 56). When the Versailles troops retreated on the 28th, an eery silence settled over the city as those who survived tried to understand the horror that had just been perpetrated or left to recover their sanity elsewhere.

To avoid the conflict (and possible military service, since he had been placed in the reserves at the time of his marriage) Monet received a passport on 5 September 1870 and left France for England, settling in London until May 1871 when the war and the bloody repression of the Commune insurrection entered into history.[57] He was not terribly productive while in

56 Anonymous, *Execution of Communards during Bloody Week of May 1871*, manipulated photograph, Bibliothèque Nationale, Paris.

47

57　Claude Monet,
*Hyde Park*, 1871,
41 × 74, W.164,
Museum of Art, Rhode
Island School of Design,
Providence. Gift of Mrs.
Murray S. Danforth.

58　Claude Monet, *Port
of London*, 1871, 47 × 72,
W.167, Private
Collection.

the English capital, painting only six pictures during his entire stay—a portrait of Camille, two superb views of London's most famous open spaces, Hyde Park (Pl. 57) and Green Park, and three memorable scenes of the Thames, including one of the port of London (Pl. 58) filled with boats and commercial activity that underscored his continuing interest in subjects that bore witness to the economic underpinnings of his times.

The stay proved fruitful, however, in other significant ways. He met a number of important people while he was there, including various French artists who had opted for flight like himself, such as Daubigny and Pissarro. He was able to visit the museums of the city and see at first hand the work of John Constable (1776–1837) and J.M.W. Turner (1775–1851) and their eighteenth-century predecessors, all of whom were poorly represented in France (there were no Constables or Turners in the Louvre until 1873 and 1967 respectively). While expensive, his trip provided him with an economic windfall as Daubigny introduced him to the Parisian dealer Paul Durand-Ruel and insisted that Durand-Ruel purchase works from this up-and-coming artist. It was probably the most important introduction Monet ever received as Durand-Ruel soon become Monet's main conduit for selling pictures and his primary source of funds for more than three decades. Although he did not buy any works from Monet that winter, Durand-Ruel did include at least one of Monet's Trouville canvases in an exhibition of modern French artists that he organized to inaugurate a new gallery he was opening on

New Bond Street in December 1870. Like Pissarro who also was in Durand-Ruel's show, Monet tried other outlets for his work as well—the Royal Academy, for example, where he was unsuccessful, and the South Kensington Museum where his luck was better. There he was able to have at least two figure paintings and perhaps a seascape in a major international show that the museum held in May 1871.[58] Again, this did not result in sales but it demonstrated Monet's desire to tend to his career even while he was in exile. It also established a track record on which he—and Durand-Ruel—would build over the coming years.

On the eve of his planned return to France in the latter part of May, Monet learned of the brutal repression of the Paris Commune by the Versailles troops and, incorrectly as it turned out, that Courbet had been killed during this week of bloodshed. Monet was very upset. "You have undoubtedly heard of the death of poor Courbet, shot without a trial," he told Pissarro on 27 May. "The vile conduct of Versailles. It is all too atrocious and sickening. I cannot put my heart into anything. It is all utterly distressing."[59] Although most likey provoked by the thought of his friend's death, Monet's anger and unabashed condemnation of the government's actions are important as they are the only indications, up until now at least, of his liberal leanings and anti-government stance. He expressed these sentiments more often later but they were clearly there in these formative years.

The volatile situation in France seems to have led Monet to think about going somewhere else before returning home. He decided on Holland, undoubtedly on the recommendation of numerous fellow artists, such as Jongkind and Daubigny, who had lived and worked in the lowlands before him. He also might have been influenced by Durand-Ruel who knew how much French clients liked Dutch scenes. Whatever the reasons, he left London at the end of May and was settled in Zaandam, a small suburb of Amsterdam, by 2 June, "after having crossed most of the country," he told Pissarro.[60] It was a long train ride to the capital of the country from the docks in Rotterdam where his boat left him, although the trip was worth it because what he saw was a "country [that] is much more beautiful than what they say." His initial impression lasted the entire summer; he was smitten with the place. In addition to the hospitality of the Dutch, virtually all of whom spoke French, and his comfortable quarters, he thought the town of Zaandam offered him everything he could want—"houses of all colors, windmills by the hundreds, and enchanting boats.... There is enough," he told Pissarro, "to paint here for a lifetime."[61]

Because he was a foreign national in exile from a nation that had just been torn apart by civil war, his presence in Holland was noted by local authorities and a police file on him was established in Zaandam (Pl. 59). In the end, any suspicions the authorities harbored about this potentially subversive *artiste–peintre* were not borne out by Monet's conduct. Like most visitors of his class and generation, he went to see tourist sites and picturesque areas of the region, rendering them in nearly twenty-five paintings, almost four times as many as he had produced during his much longer time in London (Pls. 60, 61). He had his photograph taken in Amsterdam and also went to Frans Hals's home in Haarlem and to the Trippenhuis in Amsterdam which housed the Rijksmuseum collection, although he left most of his museum visits until the end of his stay placing greater priority on his own work than on that of the past. As he informed Pissarro that June, "What I want first of all is to work, and I will allow myself all [the museum visiting] later."[62] His enthusiasm for this land of waterways and windmills which lured him back four years later did not cause him to forget his homeland and its plight. He sought out French newspapers almost immediately upon his arrival in Zaandam and reminded Pissarro that he "still was going to find beautiful things to paint in France; it is not lacking in that regard."[63] Given his confidence no less the pleasures he experienced during his summer in Holland, Monet must have been shocked when he

59  A. Greiner, photograph of Claude Monet, 1871, Private Collection.

60  Claude Monet, *The Port of Zaandam*, 1871, 47 × 74, W.171, Private Collection.

61  Claude Monet, *The Zaan at Zaandam*, 1871, 42 × 73, W.172, Private Collection.

returned to France some time in the fall of 1871 to find his native city of Paris ravaged by the war, the Prussian siege, and the government's assault on the Commune. No reports of the destruction could have prepared him for the sights that greeted him. The Hôtel de Ville, the Tuileries Palace, the Palais Royal, and the Palais de Justice all lay in ruins. The Rue de Rivoli from Châtelet to the Hôtel de Ville was in shambles as was the Palais de la Legion d'Honneur and the Cour des Comptes (Pl. 62).

Monet felt motivated to paint only one picture during the several months he spent among these bald reminders of his country's painful defeat (Pl. 63). It depicts the Pont Neuf, the oldest, most heralded bridge in Paris, wrapped in the gray, damp light of a typical winter's day. People hustle to and fro under the cover of umbrellas as carriages cross the structure in both directions. Life in the city has resumed its normal competitive pace and its usual anonymity. This is reiterated by the clouds of smoke that rise up from either side of the bridge. Emanating from boats working the river below, they are further signs of the city's revitalization. Above all this activity stand the solid and stately buildings of the famous *quartier* against which on the right is silhouetted Frédéric Lemot's equestrian statue of Henri IV, the first great Bourbon monarch of the late sixteenth and early seventeenth centuries whom Republicans and Royalists alike took as one of their most cherished former leaders.

62 Anonymous, photograph of La Rue de Rivoli after Bloody Week in May 1871, 1871, Bibliothèque Nationale, Paris.

63 Claude Monet, *The Pont Neuf*, 1871, 53.5 × 73.5, W.193, Dallas Museum of Art, The Wendy and Emery Reves Collection.

Although deep in the distance, he and his steed are carefully delineated, attesting to Monet's close attention to this important detail. His efforts could not have been more pointed as there could not have been a better figurehead for France at this wrenching moment in her often celebrated history. Nor perhaps could there have been a more subtle homage than this understated picture which boldly suggests that the devastated city and humiliated nation are recovering their poise and returning to responsibilities with sobriety and determination.[64]

In December, Monet moved from the hotel rooms he was renting by the Gare Saint-Lazare to the suburb of Argenteuil, fifteen kilometers north of the capital. He would stay in this "*agréable petite ville*," as Argenteuil was described in contemporary guidebooks, until 1878. Although a relatively short time, those seven years actually constituted one of the most important periods in his life and one of the most significant for French art.

# 4    Monet at Argenteuil: 1871–1878

On 2 January 1872, only a few weeks after Monet and his family had settled into their new house at Argenteuil, Monet's old friend Boudin wrote to their mutual acquaintance, Pierre-Firmin Martin, the Paris dealer. "I have been seeing Monet frequently these days. . . . He's settled in comfortably and seems to have a great desire to make a name for himself." Boudin was sure that Monet would accomplish this because he told Martin "he has brought back some extremely beautiful studies from Holland and I believe that he is destined to fill one of the most prominent positions in our school of painting."[1]

This is an intriguing piece of correspondence that reveals a great deal about Boudin's most celebrated student. Although it is uncertain whether the two were meeting mostly in Argenteuil or in Paris, it is clear that Monet is someone Boudin greatly admired and liked to spend time with. It also is evident that, like Troyon more than a decade earlier, Boudin recognized Monet's considerable talent and had faith in his ability to rise to the top of his profession. But what is perhaps even more important is the ambition that Monet clearly demonstrated to his mentor; he obviously was determined to succeed. Although this desire was only natural and undoubtedly expressed by every aspiring artist, it appears tinged with a kind of brashness when it comes from Monet's mouth; note that Boudin characterized it as a "great desire" not just a wish or a hope. Note also that Monet had also settled himself comfortably; he had rented a large house that was costing him 1,000 francs a year. It was as if he needed the proper setting from which to launch his career.[2]

Monet had manifested this edge earlier, of course, just as he had already demonstrated his facility as a painter over the previous dozen years. In addition, he had made real strides in establishing himself in conservative, as well as avant-garde, circles with his successes at the Salon and his intermittent, though encouraging, sales, at least up until the setbacks with the jury at the end of the 1860s and the seizure of his pictures in 1868 to compensate creditors. But coming so soon after his return to France and his nearly eighteen-month absence from the Paris art scene, his admission to Boudin suggests that Monet was setting his sights on securing one of those prominent positions in French art for new and pressing reasons.

He might have been motivated by the memory of his Salon failures for the two years before the war. Conversely, it might have been the confidence he had gained from his relative successes in London—two exhibitions and a promising relationship with a major international dealer were nothing to scoff at. In addition, the summer that he had enjoyed in Holland painting sites similar to those immortalized by his Dutch seventeenth-century counterparts must have been as reaffirming as it was regenerating. But Monet's sense of mission also seems to have been due to larger concerns. In July 1870, for example, barely a week after he married Camille, his aunt had died at the age of eighty. During his exile, his father also passed away leaving just Monet and his older brother, Léon. His personal world in

64   Auguste Renoir, *Portrait of Claude Monet Reading*, 1872, 60.3 × 48.3, National Gallery of Art, Washington, Collection of Mr. and Mrs. Paul Mellon

53

1872, therefore, was drastically different from what it had been prior to his departure. So too, of course, was his native land. Once the envy of Europe, France had sunk to an unprecedented low in most countries' esteem due to her failure in the war with the Prussians and her shameful (though in some nations' eyes, necessary) repression of the Commune. Evidence of these humiliating episodes in her recent history was everywhere to be found—in the hundreds upon hundreds of buildings and bridges that had been destroyed, the thousands of acres of farm land that had been ruined, and the more than 100,000 crosses that now marked the graves of the countrymen and women who had died during the war and the Commune, including one for Monet's friend Bazille who had been killed at the battle of Beaune-la-Roland on 28 November 1870.[3] Equally painful was the secession of Alsace and Lorraine to Germany as part of the treaty. Forty years later, when French troops marched off to the front to fight the Germans once again, they were inculcated with the bitter memories of that "*année terrible*" as Victor Hugo called it and inspired by the hopes of the entire nation for vindication and revenge.

By late 1871, however, despite the freshness of the memories and the evidence around them, there was a collective sense in the country that it had to move on, that a new decade had dawned, one that had to be scrubbed surgically clean by a single-minded determination to put the disasters of the recent past behind it and to begin anew. When he returned to Paris after the repression of the Commune, Emile Zola even went so far as to claim that he was "peacefully back at Batignolles, as if coming out of a bad dream. My little house is the same, my garden hasn't changed, not a stick of furniture or a plant has suffered, and I can believe that those two sieges were ugly farces, invented to frighten children."[4] Obviously, such an assertion was pure fabrication, as was evident from the rubble that filled the streets, the blown-up bridges, and the loved ones lost forever.

But the nation, miraculously it seemed, began the process of psychic and physical reconstruction with unprecedented speed. Even Zola felt this surge. "What makes these bad memories more fleeting for me is that I haven't stopped working for an instant. . . . Never have I had more hope or a greater desire to work, for Paris is born again."[5] His confidence was widely shared. Engineers, construction crews, and government and business officials worked with amazing efficiency to repair the damage to the country's infrastructure while citizens returned to their occupations with renewed commitment. They also dug into their collective pockets in order to pay off the indemnity imposed by the treaty with the Prussians. When the French government first floated bonds to initiate those financial reparations in January 1871, they were oversubscribed by two and a half times the amount requested; when they did it again in July 1872, the issue was oversubscribed by four times the offering (Pl. 65). The entire 5 billion franc debt to the enemy was paid off in less than two and a half years, a reminder not only of the nation's sense of obligation and its desire to erase this passage from its memory but also of how wealthy France actually was and how quickly its industries and financial institutions could resume their pre-1870 pace.[6]

Even the arts had a role to play in this revitalization process, as the *Gazette des Beaux-Arts* announced in its first issue after resuming publication in October 1871. "Today, called by our common duty to revive France's fortunes, we will devote more attention to the role of art in the nation's economy, politics, and education . . . and we will struggle for the triumph of those teachings that will help the arts rebuild the economic, intellectual, and moral grandeur of France."[7]

It is against this background of the nation's sense of renewal that Monet's paintings of the early 1870s and his determination to achieve a position for himself can be most fully understood. He stated as much in the first and only picture he completed while in Paris after

his return from exile, *The Pont Neuf* (Pl. 63). Having walked all the way from his quarters by the Gare Saint-Lazare to render this scene, he would have passed many sights that must have told quite a different story. In fact, he could have found them only two blocks from this time-honored bridge, as the Hôtel de Ville around the corner was still in shambles (Pl. 66).

Monet's participation in this collective spirit, however, is perhaps best seen in the dozens of pictures he produced soon after he moved to Argenteuil in December 1871. They bear witness not only to his continued interest in painting aspects of modern life in landscape but also to his frank confrontation with the ways in which the nation was going about healing its wounds. One of the most striking examples is *The Highway Bridge Under Repair* (Pl. 67), which depicts the bridge that led into the town. Paris is on the left, Argenteuil on the right. The first span of the structure with its reflections below frames the vista with a reassuring set of interlocking lines imposed upon the scene like the coordinates of a viewfinder. On top of the bridge are carriages and pedestrians crisply silhouetted against the pale blue-gray sky; below sit a boathouse, moored vessels, a puffing steamboat, and a turreted home all mirrored in the calm waters of the Seine's still surface. This is not a place of reverie or retreat; it does not even fall into the category of the obviously "beautiful." Instead, this is the work-a-day world of daily jobs and commuting and anonymous encounters in repetitive situations. Tentative but determined, loosely painted but highly calculated, the scene suggests that some of the dialectics of modern life are present even in those areas outside the city which many urban dwellers hoped were free of such strains. These tensions—between labor and leisure, familiarity and aloofness, the human and the natural—were particularly poignant for a nation emerging from the disasters of the previous year. They also were loaded with meaning for the residents of Argenteuil itself, as like many suburban towns it had suffered during France's humiliating defeat. The "enemy," as the Germans were so often referred to, had occupied Argenteuil after French troops, retreating to the capital, had blown up sections of the highway bridge, naively hoping that it might deter their foe's advance. The scaffolding on the right under the second span of the bridge that Monet includes in this scene was part of the rebuilding project that began after the armistice was signed.

Monet painted this bridge girthed in scaffolding not once but twice. Like the steamboats and traffic that he includes in both views, an appropriate symbol of the renewed life of the place and the country's ability to reassert itself. Similar rebuilding campaigns were underway throughout the suburbs and were often illustrated in the popular press to engender these same sentiments.[8] Monet went even further in this regard, however. While visiting his brother in

65 (above left) Anonymous, *1872*, 1872, Bibliothèque National, Paris.

66 (above right) Anonymous, photograph of the Hôtel de Ville after Bloody Week of May 1871, 1871, Bibliothèque Nationale, Paris.

67 Claude Monet, *The Highway Bridge Under Repair*, 1872, 54 × 73, W.195, Fondation Rau pour le Tiers-Monde, Zurich.

Rouen in early 1872, he painted several pictures of factories in the suburbs of Déville and Robec, including the astonishing Pl. 68. The site in this picture looks more like Le Creussot or Gary, Indiana, than anything traditionally associated with Impressionist France. Indeed, if it were not signed, dated, and fully documented its authenticity might be doubted by some. But it is as genuine as it is remarkable. The hillside is literally strewn with factories whose dozens of chimneys spew out clouds of smoke. This amazing industrial sprawl is artfully contained within the barely flexed crest of the hill whose blunt and slightly awkward arc continues across the length of the scene, echoing the unadorned activities of the factories below while forcing attention upon them. At the foot of the hill speeds a freight train whose engine likewise billows out a stream of smoke and whose dark, rectangular cars act like clarifying semaphores for the jumble above them. At the bottom of the scene stand three people, two women and a man, surrogates for Monet and his countrymen and women. Although seemingly out of place from our twentieth-century perspective, they are there to remind Monet's nineteenth-century viewers of the resurgence of the nation and its industrial prowess. They also suggest that what we might consider an erosion of the landscape was simply a part of the march of progress the fruits of which everyone would enjoy, at least according to utopian notions of the future and heartfelt expressions about France's recovery

56

after the war, something the seductive pinks, light blues, and array of greens which enliven the scene also seem to suggest. Equally surprising, perhaps, given the novelty of these pictures, is the fact that this and other factory scenes that Monet painted in 1872 were marketable. Durand-Ruel purchased *The Train* and another factory picture directly from Monet in late 1872, returning in February of the following year to buy a third. Obviously, Durand-Ruel felt they could sell, something that occurred several years later for *The Train* and at least one of the factory views.

These pictures were among thirty-eight paintings Monet sold in 1872, making it a very good year for the often complaining artist. From Durand-Ruel alone, Monet made no less than 9,880 francs. From direct sales to collectors and fellow artists, Monet was able to add 2,220 francs, making his income for the year 12,100 francs. This was an extraordinary sum, not matched even by doctors and lawyers in Paris. The following year, Monet made a staggering 24,800 francs, 19,000 of which came from Durand-Ruel. During the course of his seven years at Argenteuil, he averaged more than 14,000 francs a year, which dispels all myths about his constant so-called poverty. Although he would continue to claim he was penniless and beg friends for spare change, he clearly was not destitute. He simply lived the good life and too often spent more than he had.[9]

1872 was also an extraordinary year in terms of Monet's productivity, as he painted nearly sixty pictures, more than he had even attempted in the previous three years at Bougival, Trouville, London, and Holland combined. Forty-five of these pictures were set in his newly adopted home of Argenteuil, suggesting he was truly determined to settle down to hard

68   Claude Monet, *The Train*, 1872, 48 × 76, W.213, Private Collection, Japan.

work in order to achieve his desired goal and that the place agreed with him. Why Monet chose to live there is difficult to say. He had passed by it often on his train rides to Le Havre as it lay on the same line from the Gare Saint-Lazare. He also may have visited the town during his wanderings in the 1860s. He could have learned about it from general inquiries—it was that well known—and from articles about it that appeared in the Paris press. He may have been introduced to it specifically by Manet who owned property across the river in Gennevilliers and who could have put Monet in touch with Mme Aubry-Villet from whom he rented his first house on the rue Pierre Guyene.[10] In any case, by moving to Argenteuil Monet was following a general trend among avant-garde artists—including Berthe Morisot (1841–95) and Camille Pissarro—to leave the city for the pleasures of the country where housing was cheaper and modern subjects ample and diverse. Even Manet, the urban artist par excellence, began to paint serious pictures in the 1870s that were set outside the walls of the capital.

Argenteuil's offerings were particularly wide-ranging—pleasure boating and tilled fields, picturesque streets and new housing developments, factories large and small producing a variety of goods, and quiet corners of undisturbed nature where one could forget contemporary cares and be transported into idyllic reverie. It also was rich in history—it was the site of the medieval love affair of Abelard and Héloïse—and was famous for its asparagus, wine (albeit mediocre), and broad stretch of the Seine where regattas were held almost every summer weekend. In addition, it was conveniently located only fifteen minutes by rail from the heart of Paris. Regardless of why Monet decided to move there, Argenteuil was the first place he could call home since leaving his parents' house in the early 1860s. And it was there that he created some of the truly archetypical Impressionist paintings.

Undoubtedly what Monet must have found most appealing was the opportunity to paint the highway bridge and river traffic at one moment and at another, a scene such as Pl. 69 which appears to be miles away even though it was only about a ten-minute walk from the bridge. Completed in the same months as *The Highway Bridge Under Repair*, this picture is the epitome of springtime in the country with youthful, green foliage yearning for fullness, soft, pervasive light encouraging such growth, and the winding riverway providing appropriate nourishment as well as ample charm. The harsh lines of the bridge picture have been replaced by caressing, bending forms, the sense of the present with its elevated pressures has been exchanged for more humane evocations of the past with its rich, pastoral calm and sense of timeless continuity, something Monet suggests in the thinner application of paint with blended, almost ethereal, brushwork as well as the narrower range of hues which produces more lulling harmonies.

Like many other suburbs in the region, Argenteuil managed to retain these vestiges of rustic charm despite the rapid change it experienced from about mid-century onwards. In 1850, the town was essentially the same as it had been for hundreds of years; its population had increased only slightly since the seventeenth century while its preoccupation with agriculture and mining had remained relatively constant (its gypsum deposits, for example, contributed to what became known as plaster of Paris). In 1851, all of that was altered. In April of that year the railroad from Paris to Argenteuil was inaugurated, permitting quicker travel between these sites and the opportunity for urban dwellers to move to the country. Over the course of the next twenty years, thousands of people exercised that option, causing Argenteuil's population to double. Land was relatively cheap and the air much better than in the congested capital. The train also lured new businesses to the town and increased the construction industry as new factories and houses began sprouting up on the town's once-open acreage, a development Monet would deem worthy of painting (Pl. 78).

What really hastened this change was the railroad bridge which was built over the Seine in 1863 and which brought the train into the heart of Argenteuil. With this structure—hailed as evident testimony to the powers of progress—residents were able to commute to the capital in a quarter of an hour. From that moment onwards the town was destined to become a modern suburb. Town fathers knew this would happen even before the bridge opened. "Argenteuil is growing every day," proclaimed the editor of the newly founded newspaper the *Journal d'Argenteuil* in 1862. "It will receive a new boost when the railroad line presently under construction . . . puts Argenteuil in direct communication with the Montmorency Valley, Saint-Denis, Pontoise, etc. It is evident to everyone that under these conditions, the Argenteuil station will become the center of a very important movement of merchandise and travelers and that the commercial interests of the locality and the surrounding suburbs will have there a focus of development. The town, of course, will have roads to widen, new accesses to pierce, [and] improvements to make."[11]

Although there are numerous idyllic views like *Springtime at Argenteuil* that contain no evidence of these fundamental changes in the town's character and physical appearance, the vast majority of the pictures Monet produced during his years in this burgeoning suburb map

69   Claude Monet, *Springtime at Argenteuil*, 1872, 55 × 65, W.199, The Joan Whitney Payson Collection at the Portland Museum of Art, Portland, Maine. Promised gift of John Whitney Payson.

70 Claude Monet, *The Promenade at Argenteuil*, 1872, 50.5 × 65, W.223, National Gallery of Art, Washington, Ailsa Mellon Bruce Collection.

those shifts in both subtle and forthright ways. No example may be more perfectly crafted than *The Promenade at Argenteuil* (Pl. 70) . This is a picture of consummate beauty with the dusty path lined with stately trees and laced with ribbons of gloriously colored light leading gracefully to the turreted house in the distance (it is the same house that appears in the background of the view of the highway bridge, Pl. 67). Everything here is crystal clear from the outlines of the individual forms to the brilliantly illuminated, cloud-scudded sky. Even the boats on the left appear to be hovering on the surface of the water, so smooth and shimmering is the Seine. All of the pieces of the picture also fit together like the interlocking parts of an ideally constructed world: the wedges of water and land mating perfectly in the lower quadrant of the picture, the rectangle of sky above in absolute harmony with the smaller but equally consistent rectangle of the earth, the trees on the right providing appropriate counter to the two while closing off the scene with subtle authority. Even the. factory chimneys on either side of the house, while framing the structure, establish a rhythm with the turret itself and then rise in height as if in preparation for the trees on the right.

Because Monet painted this site no fewer than four times in the spring and summer of 1872, returned to it over and over again during the ensuing years, and ended his stay in Argenteuil

with four final canvases of it, it evidently held important meaning for him. Indeed, of all the places he painted in Argenteuil, this was probably one of the most significant, as it seemed to embody everything positive that the town, and other suburbs like it, were supposed to possess—the ideal integration of the new and the old, the natural and the human. As Pl. 70 suggests, this is a place where labor (in the form of the factory chimneys and small sheds on the right) happily co-exists with leisure (as represented by the sailboats on the river), where the presence of the human in the landscape in the form of the turreted house and the women nestled in the trees on the right seems not only appropriate but desirable (note in particular how the house sits at the apex of the converging orthogonals of the river's edge and the right side of the path). Evocative and inviting, this is the suburban paradise that was sought after in the 1850s and '60s but made all the more precious and desired after the disasters of 1870–71. Its order was exactly what was needed in post-war France, its calm the restorative balm for the nation as a whole.

When Monet turned around later that summer and looked down the same path towards the highway bridge with its scaffolding now removed, as in Pl. 71, he provided a veritable inventory of the pleasures Argenteuil offered and the benefits of a revitalized France. People walk up and down the sun-striped promenade while others lounge in the grass. Three figures

71  Claude Monet, *The Basin at Argenteuil*, 1872, 60 × 80.5, W.225, Musée d'Orsay, Paris.

are passing the time in a rowboat on the right while two women converse as they stand regally on the dock leading to the bathhouse at the water's edge. Sailboats tack back and forth in the distance while a steamboat lets out a blast as it approaches the bridge, the billowing gray smoke appearing to be as natural and appropriate as the cloud-filled sky above. The attractiveness of the scene is heightened by the deep rich colors, tactile pigment, and brilliant play of light that Monet employs. His low vantage point and carefully arranged elements also make everything appear easily accessible just as the rich impasto he applies throughout the scene lends the whole a sense of the tangible and immediate. One moves effortlessly through the picture; the descending line of trees and the converging promenade and riverbank invite one in, while the graciously paced series of horizontal elements lure one gently left and right. Monet heightens to the sense of seamless harmony by having the plunging line of the treetops point toward the end of the embankment in the distance, thereby forming a continuous curve on the surface of the canvas and a critical link between near and far. That same point of conjuncture is where the bridge begins its equally harmonious march across the river, allowing enough of the varied hills in the background to poke above its more regimented form while meeting the boathouse on the right exactly where the roof of the latter starts and the last arch of the bridge ends. From these kinds of perfectly negotiated relationships, it seems that Monet had found an ideal place to live and work. Several years later he told his Rumanian collector–friend, Dr. Georges de Bellio, that he did not want to leave his adopted town where he had been so productive.[12]

What attracted him most during the first few years there was the nautical activity that Argenteuil's position on the Seine encouraged. Although it was a working river on which barges were constantly being hauled from Paris to the coast and although swimming, bathing, and general frivolity occurred there all the time during the warmer months, Monet chose to depict the stretch of the river at Argenteuil almost exclusively as a site for pleasure boating. This was not without reason as Argenteuil had one of the deepest and widest basins north of Paris. Free of obstructions and encumbering curves, it was ideally suited in particular for sailing. And from mid-century onwards, the town fathers encouraged its development. They sponsored regattas and nautical fêtes, permitted the establishment of mooring areas and boathouses, and ingratiated themselves with the Parisian press as well as sports enthusiasts in the capital. By the later 1850s, their efforts were paying off. The town was becoming so well known for its near-perfect sailing conditions that the most important Paris sailing club had established its headquarters on the banks of the basin. Ten years and dozens of regattas later, Argenteuil was chosen as the site for the international sailing competition for the Universal Exposition of 1867. Thus, when Monet arrived in 1871, the terms "Argenteuil" and "boating" were virtually interchangeable.[13]

Only occasionally does Monet depict an actual sailing race, however. Instead, he preferred to show moored boats waiting for their skippers, isolated craft skimming across the water, such as those in the two views of the promenade, or a combination of the two, as in Pl. 72. The waterway in this picture is actually the same inlet from which *Springtime at Argenteuil* had been painted; Monet has simply moved further upriver closer to the main body of the Seine. This allows him to include several houses and the spire of the town church on the left as well as the trees that lined the promenade beyond the moored boats' masts and halyards to the right. The ideal conditions of the site are suggested by the amount of space that appears to exist between the craft on the right and the distant shore, the size of those moored boats, the light that flickers on the Seine's surface catching the edges of the boats on the right, the expansive sky, and the brisk breeze that fills the sails of the boat on the left as it whisks across the river. Complementing this evidence of the site's offerings is the harmonious balance that

72 Claude Monet, *Pleasure Boats at Argenteuil*, 1872, 47 × 65, W.228, Musée d'Orsay, Paris.

Monet strikes between horizontal and vertical elements—water, land, and sky, boats, masts, and steeple—and the triangular and rectangular forms they create. Proportionately, there is just about the same amount of canvas devoted to the town on the left and the bushes on the right with the trees appropriately linking the two. Even the moving boat is ingeniously placed just where those trees begin while extending to the right to touch the tip of the first moored boat as it looks out to the basin.

For all of its harmony, Monet's picture would have been strikingly novel to the eyes of a typical 1870s viewer. Its lights would have been too glaring, its darks too colorful, and their continuous juxtaposition, particularly in the water and boats, much too harsh. The independent strokes of paint Monet employs also would have appeared too bold and unsophisticated while the modern and momentary character of its subject would have seemed too temporal for an audience nurtured on Barbizon-like evocations of timeless continuities that dominated contemporary landscape production.

The same assault on traditional notions of artistic decorum is evident when Monet moves into his garden to paint pictures such as *Camille Reading* (Pl. 73). Although his beautiful wife sits angelically on a carpet of green grass absorbed in her book, virtually every stroke on the canvas refuses to be integrated into the kind of polished whole that an audience of the 1870s

73   Claude Monet,
*Camille Reading*, 1872,
50 × 65, W.205, The
Walters Art Gallery,
Baltimore.

would have expected from a finished picture. Camille's gown and bonnet, for example, are a collection of separate strokes of pink, lavender, and soft white while her face and hands are devoid of half-tones. Most surprising, perhaps, are the patches of green and yellow light that explode in the foreground sending several long, thin, wafting embers into the bower of foliage that arcs up and over Camille's head and leads to the larger areas of less modulated light beyond. Even the circles of light on Camille's gown appear to act on their own, having no apparent source and no reason for being there except to enliven the scene and add to its appeal. Like many of Monet's cotaneous garden pictures, this painting propagates Argenteuil's charm with unabashed verve. Everything here appears to be absolutely blissful. Camille is completely engrossed in her book, unaware of our presence which allows us the opportunity to inspect every detail of her radiant form and to savor the delicacy of her ethereal environment. She is the ultimate embodiment of feminine beauty and suburban leisure set in an enchanting locale far from the pressures and rapid pace of modern life. Fresh, alive, and invigorating, this was the dream world envisioned by most city-dwellers.

How different it is from Monet's garden pictures of the previous decade, most notably the *Women in the Garden* of 1866 (Pl. 42). The pretensions of that canvas—the posturing figures, their cryptic exchanges, the references to fashion plates, and the play of formal devices— have all vanished. Even the size of the picture has been reduced, contributing to the overall emphasis that Monet places here on ease and accessibility, relaxation and intimacy. Lacking the Salon aspirations of his earlier figure pictures, this canvas marks an important change in Monet's orientation, something he suggests in many other garden views of 1872 which exude a similar sense of reverie. Undoubtedly inspired by his own new surroundings and his efforts to put the memories of the previous year out of his mind, as many of his colleagues were doing, these garden pictures are the ultimate transformation of the eighteenth-century fêtes galantes that had become so popular in the 1850s and '60s. Their idyllic worlds filled with charm and seemingly innocent lovemaking were the arcadian antidotes to the fundamental changes that Second Empire society experienced on a daily basis.[14] During those decades and on through to the end of the century, the rococo made its impact felt on everything from poster-making to play-writing. It also stimulated scholarly inquiry. The Goncourts devoted more than fifteen years to writing a series of monographs on the eighteenth century which appeared between 1859 and 1875. In addition, mainstream contemporary artists, such as Alfred Stevens (1828–1906) and Adolphe Monticelli (1824–86), developed a veritable industry based on rococo prototypes. Monet's enthusiasm for the century of grace, therefore, was widely shared. It may have even been superseded by Renoir who said he "could more readily imagine [himself] in a Watteau landscape than in reality," which was one reason why he too painted picture after picture, particularly in the early 1870s, that were modernized versions of works that came from his most beloved period in art history.[15]

Unlike Stevens and other more acceptable painters who held more closely to rococo models, Monet tried to go beneath the charm of those seductive precedents by probing what appear to be quite private issues, thereby demarcating a territory that is different from both what he would explore elsewhere in Argenteuil and what his eighteenth-century forefathers had depicted. In fact, Monet's work of the 1870s can perhaps best be understood in terms of the dialectic he establishes between the public and the private, between those paintings that focus on his family and personal space and those that engage the world beyond his garden walls.

The broad parameters of this distinction are evident in the contrast that exists between a picture like *Camille Reading* and the views of the Deville factories or the pleasurable distractions of the Argenteuil boat basin that Monet was painting at the same time. But these extremes could become more subtle, particularly the former as exemplified by a painting such as *Jean on his Mechanical Horse*, also from Monet's first year in Argenteuil (Pl. 74). Initially, this picture appears to be a delightful portrait of Monet's nearly 5-year-old son. Dressed in his Sunday best down to his sporty English boater, Jean is playfully mounted on his steed which he has pedalled along the dirt path of his backyard racecourse to stop slightly to the left of center as if he were about to exit the scene. Jean holds the reins like an accomplished equestrian, his back appropriately arched, his legs in a commendably extended and locked position.

With further examination, however, things do not seem so innocent or easy. The horse, for example, appears to be enjoying the ride more than the boy; its open mouth and tussled mane are striking contrasts to Jean's tightly drawn lips and keen reserve. Jean may well have become bored posing for his father; the picture appears to have been the product of several sittings. But there is a blankness to his face that verges on melancholy and a distance that he seems to express that engenders a sense of disjuncture. The picture suddenly begins to ask more questions than it answers. Is it an accurate depiction of a boy who does not want to act older than he is? Is it a commentary on Monet's relation with his son? Does it have something to do with middle-class values and accepted codes of behavior? Or is it merely an insider's pun, since it so strongly recalls equestrian portraits of sixteenth- and seventeenth-century royalty, such as those by Titian and Velasquez? Unlike those earlier pictures, however, Jean's horse, of course, is mechanical. It is also manufactured from iron—that distinctly nineteenth-century material—not from nature, all of which implies a typical kind of appropriation as if

74   Claude Monet, *Jean on his Mechanical Horse*, 1872, 59.5 × 73.5, W.238, Private Collection.

75   Claude Monet, *The Red Cape*, 1872, 100 × 80, W.257, © Cleveland Museum of Art, Bequest of Leonard C. Hanna, Jr..

Monet is using the forms of the past to elevate the present while openly admitting to the awkwardness of the borrowing.

That this is a private picture cannot be doubted. In addition to its site and subject, Monet kept the canvas all his life, never exhibiting it. He then left it to Blanche Hoschedé who married Jean and who also kept it until late in her life. That it is difficult to read is important as it suggests the complexities that Monet was capable of creating when exploring such personal realms. It also attests to Monet's willingness to paint pictures that would operate on a number of levels and that like all good art would often resist simple explanations.

This is equally evident when he turned to paint his wife that winter in a picture called *The Red Cape* (Pl. 75). Again, Monet presents us with what initially appears to be an easily readable image. We are standing inside a stark, undecorated room with a typical parquet floor and a pair of double-pane French doors that give on to a snow-dappled garden. The doors are firmly shut, forming a cross in the middle of the scene. The not-quite floor-length sheer curtains are pulled back and tied to the casements on either side, creating a kind of Gothic arch through which we see Camille dressed in a heavy coat and bonnet, her face bathed in crisp winter light. She turns—suddenly, it seems—to look directly back at us although her expression, like Jean's, is ambiguous. So too are her actions. Is she coming or going or waiting for us? Does she want to come in? Does she sense she's not welcome? Does she want to move on? The picture offers no answers. The only thing we can say is Camille appears cut off from us and barred, at least momentarily, from entering the room. Pinned in

66

her position outside our space by the strict geometry of the door, she evokes our empathy but remains evidently removed.

As with *Jean on his Mechanical Horse*, this picture was also distinctly private; Monet kept it his entire life, never putting it before the public. Combined with the evidence of the painting itself, this knowledge forces us to ask a number of questions. Is Monet telling us something about the woman in this picture or revealing something about their relationship? Is he making some comment on the nature of marriage in the modern age? Or is he presenting Camille as a symbol as earlier artists might have done—a muse that he seeks, for example, or a contemporary stand-in for Mother Nature? Again, it is difficult to say, although the tug between the interior world of the foreground and the exterior one beyond, between the rational order of Monet's place of work and the ill-defined and seemingly compromised splendor of the out-of-doors are strong enough to suggest that something is awry here, whether it be in terms of the specific relationship of the artist and his model or the more general one between art and life that was such an overriding concern among advanced artists of Monet's generation.

These equivocations are generally less a part of Monet's public pictures, as if issues were clearer to him when painting landscapes where he did not have to confront family or friends and deal with difficult, if not unresolvable, questions. That does not mean his public works are less complex; they too operate on a number of levels and occasionally become equally cryptic. Such is the case with Monet's view of snow-covered fields that he painted in that same winter of 1872–73 *Vineyards in the Snow* (Pl. 76). Set about two kilometers from his house, the picture can be seen as a straightforward rendering of an area of town that appealed to Monet for its contrasted furrowed fields, crowning hill, and picturesque mill. In this reading, it would fit into the time-honored tradition of similar winter scenes from medieval manuscript illustrations through Poussin and Millet, all of which evoke the muffled sounds of the season, its muted colors, and chilling temperatures. On another level, however, like many of those precedents, this picture could also be seen as suggesting winter's difficulties as well as its age-old associations with the passing of things. The abandoned fields and scattered forms admit as much, as do the pervasive atmosphere and the isolated windmill, two arms of which stretch up into the sky as if uttering a wrenching cry.

How different this image is from numerous others that Monet painted of similar fields earlier that year, such as *The Path Through the Vineyards* (Pl. 77). Here, Monet walked up one of the hills that surrounded the town and looked back down the well-trodden path towards a distant horizon and cloud-filled sky. In contrast to the later winter scene, everything in this picture appears appropriately integrated. The ruts and rises of the central path, like the lines of a traditional Renaissance perspective system, lead gradually but logically past stakes and bushes to the town and the detailed vista beyond. The horizon is broken by factory chimneys and the steeple of the town church and then further back by the buildings of the capital. Although Monet appears to be alone on this hill, there is no emptiness here and no sense of melancholy, unlike in the winter view. The stakes of the vineyards and the abundant greenery suggest the continuing fertility of the soil and the enduring process of winemaking while the factory chimneys puffing smoke seem equally appropriate and just as welcome. Indeed, they complement the church spire by balancing its verticality and filling what would otherwise be a void in the middle of the scene. Their smoke is as wistful as the clouds above, their forms as permanent and monumental as the spire. They also imitate the stakes in the foreground, and not by chance, for Monet is presenting the town's evolution from the traditional cultivation of the soil to the new mechanized production of goods. And with the smooth progression from foreground to background, it appears that Monet is asserting that

76   Claude Monet, *Vineyards in the Snow*, 1873, 58.5 × 81, W.254, The Virginia Museum of Fine Arts, Richmond, The Adolph D. and Wilkins C. Williams Fund.

77   Claude Monet, *The Path through the Vineyards*, 1872, 47 × 74, W.219, Private Collection.

industry and agriculture, city and country, co-exist harmoniously in Argenteuil and still maintain their uniqueness as well as their individual appeal.

After a year of living in the town, however, and coming to understand its make-up better, Monet may be suggesting in his view of the snow-blanketed vineyards that his earlier notions were slightly idealistic—that, as with the paintings of his wife and son, things were not quite so simple. Everyone else in Argenteuil realized this, as there were continual discussions about the town's development in the pages of the *Journal d'Argenteuil* and at the meetings of the town council. Although most residents apparently supported nearly all forms of development, there was at least one group that did not and that, of course, was the vineyard owners. They were the ones most threatened by this change; it was their lifestyle and product no less their land that were disappearing in the face of Argenteuil's continued growth. "Buildings are going up on all sides of town," wrote a reporter for the Argenteuil newspaper as early as 1862, "gaining land little by little and making the owners of the vineyards, who

78 Claude Monet, *Houses by the Edge of the Fields*, 1873, 54 × 73, W.277, Staatliche Museen zu Berlin—Preussischer Kulturbesitz

formerly harvested their grapes from their front doors to the town borders, powerless to change the course of events."[16] Monet had witnessed similar change—along the Channel coast, for example, and throughout the Seine valley, as well as when visiting such formerly rustic places as Chailly and the forest of Fontainebleau. In the 1850s and '60s he had had no qualms about rendering that change. But when it occurred in the one place in which he had chosen to settle and raise a family his reactions were perhaps understandably tinged with an occasional sense of regret.

It was only occasional, however, at least for the first few years in this progressive *petite ville*. For during that time he painted picture after picture which suggest the opposite, none perhaps more striking in its apparent simplicity than *Houses by the Edge of the Field* of 1873 (Pl. 78). Standing in the fields on the western side of town not far from the turreted house at the end of the promenade, Monet turns to look at a series of modest homes that sit on the edge of his flower-strewn site. A few spindly saplings provide a thin screen in front of the structures while taller, more mature, trees rise up behind them, the whole once again crowned by the spire of the church. What is remarkable about this picture is not only its strong geometric divisions of field, houses, and sky, not only its bold palette and manipulated brushwork, particularly in the foreground and wind-whipped sky above, but also the fact that the houses were actually brand new, having just recently been built on once-tilled fields for Argenteuil's expanding population. Showered with light and filled with an abundance of fresh, clean atmosphere, the scene exudes a sense of excited fulfillment, as if this development was both just and good and thus deserved to be immortalized in paint, a belief Monet's friend, Gustave Caillebotte (1848–94), shared as he too rendered new houses that were built along the opposite banks of the Seine in Petit-Gennevilliers.

Monet's embrace of the newest developments in his adopted town is most clearly revealed in another painting that he completed in the summer of 1873, *The Railroad Bridge at Argenteuil* (Pl. 79). Few pictures from Monet's hand of these years tell a richer or more poignant tale. Like *Houses by the Edge of the Field*, Monet divides his scene into clear, simple shapes, illuminating them all with crisp, flowing light. Unlike the view of the housing development, however, the major elements here—land, water, bridge, and sky—move on intersecting diagonals which energize the scene, stretching it into the distance and pulling it left and right. This dynamism is a welcome complement to the activity Monet depicts—two trains moving in opposite directions (one toward Paris, the other toward Argenteuil) across the bridge that is elevated high above sparkling water on which sail two boats along lines that counter those of the trains above them. While one train slows down as it approaches the Argenteuil station out of the picture to the left, the other picks up speed, implied in the stream of smoke that billows out of its stack and in the streaking body of the trestle which rushes unobstructed across the width of this extended canvas, its creamy white color contrasting with the almost iridescent blue sky and the reflections on the water below. The sailboats scoot under the bridge, powered by nature not by machine. Running parallel to each other and to the near and far shore, they are artfully locked into the geometric spaces beneath the bridge's spans, their sails filled with the same wind that dissipates the engine's smoke above them. They therefore are subtly tied to the mechanical beast on high for like the railroad they represent the newest intrusion in Argenteuil's landscape, one inevitably linked to the faster form of railroad travel since it was the train that brought the boaters to the town in the first place. It also was industry, as symbolized by the trains, that permitted such recreational sports. Industry was more efficient than all previous forms of production, thus generating more leisure time. It also was more profitable, providing people with more disposable income to rent or purchase such leisure craft. The beauty of this union is implied in the glories of the day, with the bridge glistening in the afternoon light; in the neatly integrated parts of the scene, for like finely honed gears they all mesh perfectly, and in the two figures on the shore, surrogates once more for Monet and his countrymen and women, just like those in *The Train* (Pl. 68). They stand in front of this technological marvel, locked between the pylon and the sail, their heads just touching the distant shore. Like Albertian witnesses of the past and the figures who often appeared in popular illustrations of Monet's day, all of this is for them, all of it in theory within their reach. The picture, therefore, on one level at least, is a stunning celebration of the modern landscape whose horizon is literally being redrawn by the engineered lines of the bridge's iron trestle.

The novelty of the structure and Monet's commemoration of its presence is increased when we realize that no other landscape painters of Monet's day so dramatically embraced such contemporary elements in the countryside despite their proliferation. The older generation of Daubigny and Corot still concentrated on idyllic scenes of rural France as did their younger Salon protegés. If bridges appeared in their work, they were always hand-cut stone structures meant for humans not machines and set behind screens of trees or nestled into the countryside as if they had always been there. Even Pissarro, who shared Monet's utopian sentiments and occasionally turned his attention to such modern phenomena, tended to integrate the evidence into his landscape in ways that made them much less dramatic—as, for example, when he painted the railroad bridge at Pontoise in the very same year that Monet rendered the one in Argenteuil (Pl. 80).[17] Although Pissarro juxtaposes it with the older, arched bridge behind it, he hardly endows it with the domineering presence that Monet awards his own. And while Pissarro's brushwork is certainly noticeable, it is not as aggressive as Monet's. The choppy strokes of ocher and green in the left foreground of Monet's canvas,

79 Claude Monet, *The Railroad Bridge at Argenteuil*, 1873, 58.2 × 97.2, W.279, Private Collection.

the stream of multicolored marks along the path, and the fluttering though equally independent touches on the river are the antithesis of what would have been expected of a completed painting, just as the swirls of blue and violet along the edges of the steam and clouds in the sky defy the norms for accurate description no less artistic restraint. Pissarro's picture, by contrast, is closer to a Corot. What finally is remarkable about Monet's image is the bridge itself, as its poured concrete structure and extended iron trestle, while vaguely similar to the one at Pontoise, is here given full credit for its modern design, down to its faux-concrete capitals and its undersized abacuses. So novel, in fact, was the structure that when it was first unveiled in 1863 local residents were aghast. "Instead of an elegant construction of grandiose or bold forms," wrote the editor of the *Journal d'Argenteuil*, "there is only a heavy and primitive work which is not at the level of the progress of science. Instead of those gracious constructions on which wagons and machines slide onward to discovery, they made a wall of iron that is impenetrable to the eye . . . It is a tunnel without a roof."[18] In another writer's opinion, the piers "should have been surmounted by carved capitals instead of the bulging blocks that sit there now [and] the bridge itself should have been adorned with some cast-iron decorations, which would have broken up this relentless straight line."[19] Anything, in other words, to have it not be what it was: an industrial structure made from industrial materials.

Just prior to Monet's arrival in Argenteuil, the bridge had looked quite different (Pl. 81). Like the highway bridge, the old railroad bridge had been blown up by retreating French troops and lay in the river like a painful symbol of France's physical and spiritual collapse. It soon was wrapped in scaffolding as the nearly two-year rebuilding process began in the middle of 1871. That Monet bided his time, waiting more than a year to paint it fully

80  Camille Pissarro, *The Railroad Bridge at Pontoise*, 1873, 50 × 65, Private Collection.

81  Anonymous, Photograph of Argenteuil railroad bridge destroyed during Franco–Prussian War, 1871, Bibliothèque Nationale, Paris.

reconstructed, is ample testimony to his desire to elevate it, like the views of the highway bridge, as a potent symbol of France's powers of recovery.

Monet's engagement with the nation's revitalization is evident in numerous other pictures of these years but he gave it one of its most poetic expressions in the famous *Impression, Sunrise* (Pl. 82), a painting Monet completed during a visit to Le Havre in 1872.[20] Although long seen as a stellar example of Monet's uncanny ability to capture rich atmospheric effects and a particular moment in time with broken brushwork and heightened color, this rapidly executed picture attests to much more than just Monet's painterly prowess. The picture depicts the sun rising over the misty outer harbor of Monet's home town. That harbor had grown from the 1850s onwards from a modest shipping area to the second largest port in all

of France, something Monet witnessed as he grew up. Evidence of its present stature is found in the four-masted clipper ship that is entering the harbor to the left of center and in the numerous vertical elements to the left and right. Those to the left are the smoke-stacks of steamboats; those to the right are cranes and heavy machinery that were part of a huge construction project that had been initiated just before the Franco–Prussian War and had been taken up again after the armistice.[21] The expansion of the port was seen in the early 1870s as further testimony to France's post-war renewal. In the distance other vertical forms break the horizon—masts of other ships and chimneys of the many factories that lined the inner harbor, for not only did the port engage in huge shipping exchanges, it also was the site of some of the city's largest and most important industries. The smoky, bustling character of the place is amply revealed in a remarkable photograph taken in the late 1860s (Pl. 83). It makes it eminently clear that the hazy atmosphere in Monet's scene is due not only to the Channel and its frequent morning mists but also to the emissions of these factories and ships. And as they mix with the sun's early rays, they create a kind of beauty that is both surprising and seductive.

It is surprising only perhaps because it is hard for those living in the late twentieth century

83  Anonymous, photograph of the port of Le Havre, late 1860s, Collection Roger-Viollet, Paris.

to find beauty in places like this. But for Monet and his countrymen and women, it still was possible. Indeed, Renée Mauperin, the artist–heroine of Jules and Edmond de Goncourt's novel of the same name, could swim in the Seine near Saint-Denis in 1864 and proclaim the splendors of the site despite the shacks and belching factories that lined the banks of the river as it flowed north towards Argenteuil and Le Havre. In the context of this widely shared belief in progress, Monet's *Impression, Sunrise* is the up-dated version of Claude Lorrain's seventeenth-century views of imaginary ports illuminated by equally extraordinary light or of Joseph Vernet's commissioned paintings of actual ports around France, just as it is Monet's personal re-working of many similar harbor scenes by Turner. Monet's version, however, is observed on the site, and endowed with a kind of tangibility that earlier precedents lacked. It also is grounded in the contemporary aesthetic of post-war France. For as the sun rises over this melange of commercial and industrial activity sending its orange-red rays across the upper reaches of the sky, it is marking a very particular moment in time—the dawning of a new day for Le Havre and the nation. And as its dappled reflections move from the distance to the foreground, it draws attention to the small boats in the water in which various figures appear, a subtle reminder that the human has a special place in this seemingly impersonalized whole, a central one in fact exemplified by the craft in the middle of the scene which is the closest element to us.

This picture, among four other paintings and seven pastels, was included by Monet in what he and his colleagues called "The First Exhibition" of independent artists.[22] Soon to be referred to as the First Impressionist Exhibition, this show opened on 15 April 1874 in the former studios of the photographer Nadar on the third floor of 35 boulevard des Capucines in the heart of Paris (Pl. 84). Although it lasted only a month, the exhibition had historic importance. It was the first time that practicing artists had banded together to form a

84 Nadar, photograph of 35 boulevard des Capucines, ca. 1861, Bibliothèque Nationale, Paris.

business association—a *Société anonyme des peintres, sculpteurs, graveurs, etc.*—to stage a sizable show of their own work without government, commercial, or private support. It also was the first time that artists put their work in front of the public without the intermediary of a jury or the expectation of any prizes. All proceeds from admission fees and sales were to be split evenly among the partners, all of whom were allowed to exhibit works which were to be hung alphabetically by artist, one or two high, not stacked in multiples as in the official Salon.

The idea of such an enterprise had arisen often in the past, particularly in the later 1860s when younger artists were having difficulty getting into the Salon. But like many post-war undertakings, the timing of the early 1870s seemed right. There appeared to be a climate of support for individual initiatives because such undertakings were seen as further proof of the country's creativity and its ability to draw on its internal resources. There also was a sense that something had to be done about the Salon; the one in 1872 had been a serious disappointment to many observers. "Ideas are nil and thoughts mediocre," wrote Georges Puissant in *L'Avenir national* in May 1872. "In the heap, not a man, not a revelation, not even the promise of individuality . . . a lot of talent but once again not a heart that beats, not a soul that believes, not even a misled vanity."[23] This was all the more disappointing given the moment, as Jules Castagnary observed in the equally open-minded *Le Siècle*. "Coming after the war and the terrible events of the past year, the show should have had an original and gripping make-up." Instead, he claimed it was "totally devoid of character. . . . You walk around there without knowing what country you're in or what date it is."[24] The opportunity, as one centrist put it, "to show jealous Europe all that the genius of France could produce in the aftermath of its defeat" thus was squandered, just as it was the following year when so many artists were rejected by the Salon jury that the government was forced to hold a separate Salon des refusés.[25]

Even before the official show and its offshoot opened in May 1873, Monet and his friends Pissarro, Renoir, Degas, Berthe Morisot, and Sisley were hard at work planning their counter-exhibition for the following year. Their intentions were elliptically announced by a friend in the press, Paul Alexis, in an article that appeared in *L'Avenir national* just prior to the festivities for the two state-sponsored shows. In this short piece, Alexis denounced the jury system and urged artists to form their own corporations through which they could organize their own exhibitions, claiming that such initiatives were already being considered.[26] Monet responded on cue, writing him a letter immediately afterwards that Alexis was able to get published. "A group of painters assembled in my home has read with pleasure the article which you have published," his letter stated. "We are happy to see you defend ideas which are ours too, and we hope that, as you say, *L'Avenir national* will kindly give us assistance when the society which we are about to form will be completely constituted."[27] The artists were astute about their business, this little bit of public relations being just one example. Pissarro took the lead in guiding the group toward an agreeable resolution, as he had been involved with a similar association and, as a socialist, had an interest in organizational structures. But it took them until December to iron out their differences about who should be members and how the group should be governed. In the end they agreed to Pissarro's proposal to form a joint stock holding company (*Société anonyme*), and on 27 December 1873 the core group of six Impressionists signed the founding charter together with Pissarro's friends Edouard Bélaird (b. 1834) and Armand Guillaumin (1841–1927) and Degas's friends Ludovic Lepic (1839–89), Léopold Levert (b. 1828), and Henri Rouart (1833–1912) who had been invited to be a part of the enterprise.[28] With the Salon their obvious competition, the eleven decided to have their show run simultaneously with the State's, but to upstage it by opening theirs two weeks before the competition's. They also chose a well-known site: Nadar was one of the most celebrated photographers in Paris and the boulevard des Capucines one of the great art streets in the capital, boasting many photographers' studios and commercial galleries. In addition, Nadar had recently renovated the space, putting in the large floor-to-ceiling windows that were visible from the street and that permitted a wealth of natural light inside.[29] To capitalize on the location, the organizers decided to keep the show open from 10 a.m. until 6 p.m. and again from 8 p.m. until 10 p.m. They charged only a modest admission fee—one franc—and they published a catalogue that could be purchased for fifty centimes. The catalogue listed not only all of the participants and their submissions but also the collections from which many of the works came, thereby adding immediate prestige to what hung on the walls. The organizers offered a 10 per cent discount on works bought from the show and they spread news about the occasion by posters, word of mouth, and contacts in the press.

Their efforts paid off. They received more than a dozen notices in Paris newspapers even before the show opened and they attracted a commendable number of visitors during the show's run—3,500—which, while small in comparison to the numbers for the Salon, was still quite respectable for such a novel affair. They made a few sales, again nothing sizable but sales nonetheless. Most important perhaps, they received considerable press coverage. There were at least fifty notices and reviews in the leading newspapers of the capital.[30] Some of the latter were unduly harsh and have been taken as typical of the exhibition's reception. The pictures were "quite simply the negation of the most elemental rules of drawing and painting," announced Emile Cardon in the conservative daily, *La Presse*. "The scribblings of a child have a naiveté and sincerity that make you smile; the debaucheries of this school are nauseating and revolting."[31] But in actuality, more reviewers liked the show than not. Even those such as Cardon who had plenty of negative things to say often praised the organizers for their initiative. Cardon asserted that the show "represented not just an alternative to the Salon, but a new road ... for those who think art needs more freedom in order to develop than that granted by the administration." Many reviewers made quite insightful remarks. Armand Silvestre, for example, felt that "the means by which they seek their impressions will infinitely serve contemporary art [because] it is the range of painting's means that they have restored." Philippe Burty asserted that Berthe Morisot's painting *Hide and Seek* "is a perfect work in the feeling for observation, the freshness of the palette and the arrangement of planes." Ernest Chesneau thought that Monet's *Boulevard des Capucines* (Pl. 85) was "a masterpiece that went well into the future," and that Alfred Sisley's *Seine at Port Marly* "surpassed any work of the past or present in its ability to evoke the physical sensation of 'plein air' atmosphere."[32]

Monet's *Impression, Sunrise*, contrary to popular legend, did not attract much attention. It was singled out by one critic, Louis Leroy, for some satirical barbs which have been repeated ever since—it was no better than "wallpaper in an embryonic state," he cried—but only four other writers even mentioned the picture, all of them just in passing.[33] And while the title of the painting contained the term "Impression" it was not the actual source for the term "Impressionists" that was first applied to the group by Leroy. That name came up in Leroy's article between references to Monet's *Boulevard des Capucines*, two paintings by Paul Cézanne (1839–1906), and a Boudin beach scene. It therefore should be seen as deriving from the group as a whole and not from this particular picture.[34] It also should be pointed out that the group avoided using the term until their third exhibition in 1877 when they agreed to place a sign above the entrance to the space they had rented for that show that read, "Exposition des impressionnistes." They did this only that one time. In addition, the catalogue that accompanied that exhibition, like those for the seven other shows they staged, did not mention Impressionists or Impressionism. The exhibitions were called merely "Exposition de Peinture" and given a number. The group clearly did not want to be typecast or easily categorized.

And in many ways they were correct, as each Impressionist member of the core group—together with Caillebotte, Cézanne, and Boudin who joined the organization via Degas, Pissarro, and Monet respectively—all had quite different styles, as critics astutely noted even during this first gathering of their work. They also were distinct from the other artists who comprised the Société anonyme, as all writers on the show also observed. In addition to Degas's and Pissarro's friends who were among the original signatories, the Impressionists wisely invited a host of more mainstream artists to join their undertaking, most of whom have long since faded from history—the Ottin brothers, for example, Edouard Brandon, Alfred Meyer, Pierre-Isidore Bureau, and Antoine-Ferdinand Attendu, among others. They exhibited works that had little to do with the more adventurous submissions of the core group—engravings after paintings by Rubens and Holbein, for example, tourist views of Spain, even a bust of Ingres. Their presence was important, however, as it suggested the legitimacy of the Impressionists' enterprise while clarifying the novelty of the core group's inventions.

Monet's submissions, like those of his avant-garde colleagues, were designed to reveal his range as an artist and secure for himself that "prominent position" he so sought. In addition to *Impression, Sunrise*, he exhibited the monumental *Luncheon* of 1868–69 (Pl. 49), and three recent works—a view of fishing boats leaving the port of Le Havre, a view of poppy fields on the outskirts of Argenteuil, and, most remarkably perhaps, a view of the very boulevard on which the exhibition was taking place, seen from the very space in which the painting itself was hung, the *Boulevard des Capucines* (Pl. 85). Ingeniously, Monet had gained access to the exhibition site several months prior to the opening of the show and painted this picture looking out of one of Nadar's newly installed windows down the bustling street with its recently planted trees toward the avenue de l'Opéra. The immediacy of the scene is enhanced by the two top-hatted figures on the right who, like Monet, have assumed a position on an overhanging balcony to observe the swarm of people and vehicles below. No other picture in the show had such calculated ties to the time and place that viewers would experience; no other, therefore, better attests to Monet's keen marketing mind and his desire to give his work immediacy, something that is evident in his technique as well. For the intricately coordinated flecks of pigment that define the image, and the subtle but surprising range of color that suggests the spectrum of light and shade, are as palpitating as the scene itself.

That Monet showed more pastels than paintings in this historic exhibition also bears witness to his urge to be perceived as having the technical skills of a draughtsman, something conservative critics had long been questioning. Despite the contemporaneity of his other submissions, the pastels also suggested his ties to tradition, something the *Luncheon* with its

85 Claude Monet, *Boulevard des Capucines*, 1873, 61 × 80, W.292, Pushkin State Museum of Fine Arts, Moscow.

highly wrought forms and time-honored subject appears to have been intended to reveal as well. Monet may have been following the lead of his teacher, Boudin, who also was represented by more pastels than paintings. Both may have been hoping to attract collectors by offering them the opportunity to purchase works that were more modestly priced than the paintings (Monet wanted 1,000 francs for *Impression, Sunrise*).[35] Unfortunately, none of the critics discussed the pastels although nearly all spoke about the *Luncheon*, most of them finding it to be impressive.[36] On balance, despite the negative blasts of people like Leroy, Monet did quite well with the critics.

Although he did not sell any works from the show, he was not persuaded to change course; his urge to render the contemporary world continued unabated. During the ensuing summer months of 1874, he painted more pictures than he had ever completed in a similar amount of time—nearly forty canvases. They cover the gamut of Argenteuil's modern offerings—the railroad bridge, the light-filled promenade, the surrounding fields, the highway bridge, even two regattas. The vast majority of these pictures from this unprecedented flurry of activity concentrate on the boat basin, including such images as Pl 86. Like so many of the other boating pictures from this summer, everything here seems astonishingly vibrant, from the sparkling waters and bobbing boats to the rustling foliage and quickly moving clouds. Besides the high-keyed color and the independent touches of paint, especially those that so magically describe the waters of the Seine, what energizes the scene most of all is the bridge on the right which rushes in and out of the scene with the force of a locomotive. It is quite a different structure from when Monet first painted it under repair. While carving out the deep space in the picture, the bridge's dynamic thrust is absorbed by the horizontal bands on the

79

86 Claude Monet, *The Highway Bridge at Argenteuil*, 1874, 60 × 80, W.312, National Gallery of Art, Washington, Collection of Mr. and Mrs. Paul Mellon.

opposite shore and softened by the imitative triangle of foliage in the immediate foreground. It also is parried by the halyard of the black-hulled boat in the center which appears to balance the huge stone-and-wood form on its thin but taut line like an immense arrow on a bow.

This kind of artfulness is repeated throughout the scene. Besides the banter between horizontal and vertical shapes (river, shore, trees, and sky, versus foliage, bridge, and sails), there is the neatly integrated mast to the left of center which presumably rises from a boat below Monet's feet and out of the scene. It does not quite parallel the one to its right but it touches the black-hulled craft just where the white cabin on the deck begins. It then continues up to nudge the left side of the house in the distance and changes from orange to gray as it rises against the sky. It is at that point as well that it miraculously meets the halyard of the middle-ground boat. The halyard then continues down against the trees on the left where it just happens to meet the top of the mast of the boat under sail. It does not continue on to the end of the black boat's boom, however, as it is supposed to do. It simply stops. It is not that Monet forgot to finish it; it is merely a way of reminding us that he is cagily stitching together these disparate elements of an untidy world to make a kind of perfect place, a modern day utopia, for himself and his viewers.

80

That this was his aim in the majority of his pictures over the next few years cannot be doubted, as in painting after painting he transforms the mundane, messy matter of streets and boats and flowing fields into the orderly stuff of the ideal. Sunsets emblazon cloud-scudded skies, sculls skim effortlessly across colorful waters, and elegantly dressed women walk through flower-strewn meadows.

There are times when everything is not quite so orderly or placid, however, as in *Effect of Snow, Setting Sun* which Monet painted from behind his house looking westwards to the heart of town (Pl. 87). The sky here is brilliantly illuminated by a sun which, while hidden behind clouds, sends out thin rivulets of color between the waving branches of the tree on the left. The light does not warm the scene very much, however, as an icy blue cold pervades the view, almost seeming to cause the branches to shudder and the houses to huddle together for warmth. The structures are highly individualized but, as a group, they are a rather scruffy lot, a kind of jumble of forms that, unlike the elements in the view of the train, appear to be the product of happenstance rather than administrative decree or urban planning.

A similar sense of disjointedness is found in an occasional view of the Seine from around the same time, such as *Sailboats in the Boat Rental Area* of 1874 (Pl. 88). Monet undoubtedly painted this picture from a small boat that he had recently outfitted as a floating atelier following the example of Charles Daubigny. The boat afforded him the opportunity to be out on the river and to move up and down it as he pleased, dropping anchor wherever he wanted to work. As a kind of porter, the boat brought him physically closer to his motifs. As his place of work, it was also an aesthetic ally if not a stand-in for himself, something Monet implied when he included it in several other views of the Seine during his years in Argenteuil. Broadly painted, *Sailboats in the Boat Rental Area* depicts a set of jostling craft that were moored just downstream from the highway bridge. Their proximity to the viewer and to each other adds a peculiar note of tension to the scene, as if Monet is in some kind of crowded urban space instead of out of doors in a suburban pleasure site. This feeling is increased by the repeated vertical lines of the masts of the ships and their rippled reflections which come forcefully into the immediate foreground across slightly agitated water. Even the diagonals of the boats' booms and wrapped sails seem to be engaged in competition, parrying one another while imitating the drifting smoke in the background. The chimneys from which

87 (above left) Claude Monet, *Effect of Snow, Setting Sun*, 1874 75, 53 × 64, W.362, Musée Marmottan, Paris.

88 (above right) Claude Monet, *Sailboats in the Boat Rental Area*, 1874, 54 × 65, W.227, The Fine Arts Museums of San Francisco, Gift of Bruno and Sadie Adriani.

89 Claude Monet,
*Men Unloading Coal*,
1875, 55 × 66, W.364,
Musée d'Orsay, Paris.

that smoke appears repeat the lines of the masts, thus linking near and far—in this case, the forms of industry and pleasure. It is an uneasy alliance, however, a condition that is exacerbated by the emptiness of the boats and the lack of any human presence in the scene. It is as if the boats and the pleasure principle for which they stand have lost their *raison d'être* or that it has been temporarily suspended due to the demands of work. For this is not the glories of a Sunday as in *The Promenade at Argenteuil* (Pl. 70). It is a weekday scene when Parisians are at their jobs and when the energy and restlessness of labor permeate what otherwise should be a place of enjoyment.

One startling painting of 1875, *Men Unloading Coal* (Pl. 89), takes this notion one step further by extending Monet's confrontation with the new from his early views of Deville and the railroad bridge at Argenteuil (Pls. 68, 79). Never before or again did Monet render such a stark and sober scene. In the dingy light of a dank, overcast day, solitary workers unload barges of coal while figures and carriages move silently across the iron-and-stone bridge above them. The dark forms of the workers are made all the more ominous by the way Monet has separated them one from the other and then silhouetted them all against the murky greens and browns of the water and banks. The diagonal thrust of the boats is countered by the web of vertical, horizontal, and diagonal lines created by the pylons, masts, and factory chimneys, the bridges, planks, and mooring cables. Monet has very carefully described how the workers negotiate their way up and down those narrow planks. The men on the first walk down to the boats with their baskets on their heads and their left feet in front of their right. Those on the second move up to the shore in just the opposite fashion; their baskets are on their shoulders and their right feet are in front of their left. The figure on the fourth plank imitates the three on the first while the two on the fifth mirror those on the second. Together with those on the planks beyond, the figures as a group become cog-like, mechanical forms locked into repetitive motions similar to oiled but strained parts of a machine. There is no pleasure here and no sense of the promise that progress held out. For this is an image of manual labor in the industrialized age—anonymous, unfeeling, and dehumanizing. Little wonder that one critic at the end of the century felt that the silhouettes of these workers took on a demonic, fantastic aspect or that the scene had the qualities of an inferno.[37]

Little wonder as well, perhaps, that the painting actually does not depict Argenteuil. It is set in Asnières, one loop further up the Seine closer to Paris. Monet could have found numerous scenes like this in Argenteuil. It had plenty of factories in which people labored with similar drudgery. But Monet had to make his adopted home town into a different kind of place. Occasionally, it could reveal the strain of its own internal contradictions as a place in transition—as in *Sailboats in the Boat Rental Area*, *Effect of Snow*, *Setting Sun* or *Vineyards in the Snow* (Pls. 88, 87, 76)—but more often than not it had to attest to the utopian ideals that Monet and many of his liberal-minded, middle-class compatriots believed were available in their new modern age.

Monet, of course, had experienced the benefits of modernity. He had earned fabulous sums of money during the previous three years, so much so that he now ordered his wines from Narbonne and Bordeaux rather than drinking the local, mediocre Argenteuil vintage. He also hired a maid and a gardener, and then in 1874 he moved into a larger, more expensive house across from the railroad station on the rue Saint-Denis.[38] This house had been built speculatively on a subdivided lot during the course of the previous year. Monet had heard and seen the building going up, as the property was contiguous to his first house. He even included it in the background of a painting of 1873 representing Camille, Jean, and the family maid (Pl. 90), where it appears without its roof over the wall on the left. Monet and his family moved in October 1874, and were the house's first occupants. Life was good to him and he responded by painting dozens of pictures that celebrated the advantages of suburban existence, editing or tempering its unpleasant side in order to propagate its cherished appeal.

At least, that is what he did when working outside his garden walls. Within those confines, as in *Camille, Jean, and the Maid* of 1873 (Pl. 90), he often suggests that it was not as fulfilling as it might appear. Like the view of Camille in the red cape (Pl. 75), this picture is more than a little ambiguous. It clearly suggests an interruption of a family gathering as all three figures have stopped what they were doing to stare at us as if we were strangers entering their private space. Their faces are expressionless, which, like the elegance of the setting with its sculpted flower mound and carefully tended, sandy paths, makes the whole encounter curiously formal, as if Monet was in an urban park not in his own backyard. Camille greatly contributes to this effect, as she assumes the role of the lady of leisure. She sits; the maid stands. She does nothing; the maid tends to Jean while holding his hoop and stick. One hardly even sees the chair that supports Camille although one cannot fail to admire her elegant costume down to her white gloves and flower-studded bonnet. But what are viewers supposed to make of this? Is it another commentary on their relationship or a glimpse of the emptiness and boredom that could settle into even the most beautiful of suburban situations? Flaubert's Bouvard and Pécuchet found out what that meant shortly after they realized their dream and moved out of Paris to enjoy the pleasures of the countryside at Chavignolles. They devised

project after project to keep themselves from losing their minds, studying chemistry, geology, archeology, paleontology, history, literature, spiritualism, mesmerism, necromancy, and metaphysics, all to stave off boredom and ignorance.[39]

There are a number of pictures like this one that are as perplexing as they are ravishing. Take for instance a view of Camille and Jean from the same summer of 1873 (Pl. 92). What a curious scene this is! Jean lies on the ground like a discarded stuffed doll. He is either captivated by something outside the scene or lost in a daydream. Directly above him, Camille rises out of the thicket of foliage like a new Venus, her shapely form carefully delineated to enhance her appeal, something her raised arms and slightly tilted head contribute to as well. Unlike Jean, she stares directly out from her bower, although with an expression that again is impossible to read. Is she distressed or surprised, deliberately reserved or attempting to shirk her bourgeois formality and become a kind of temptress? Luckily, she is in the center of the scene; otherwise the whole construction would fall apart, so imbalanced is the rest of the composition. The foliage and shadows occupy a completely disproportionate amount of the canvas, leaving only a narrow strip on the right for the direct sunlight, potted plant, and radically cropped canvas chair. How far one is from the pretensions of the *Women in the Garden* (Pl. 42) or the secretiveness of *Camille Reading* (Pl. 73)! But how far also from any sure idea of what the painting is supposed to be conveying. Comparing it with a painting done by Renoir at the same time underscores this point. Popularly entitled *The Lovers* (Pl. 91), Renoir's canvas is equally daring in its brushwork and color just as its actors are likewise contemporaries, but the interaction of the resistant female and her more aggressive companion leaves considerably less to the imagination than Monet's cryptic scene. The only thing that is certain in Monet's image is that the picture is coming apart at its seams

compositionally, that its surface is extraordinarily rich, and that the viewer is left in the dark about its ultimate meaning.

The same holds true for *The Bench* of 1873 (Pl. 93), a canvas that is seductively painted with luscious colors applied with a fluid and generous brush. But the beauty of the pigments and the dexterity of the artist's hand cannot disguise the disturbing scenario that Monet has devised. Camille once again is the center of attention. Stylishly dressed in an elegant summer outfit, including the same flower-studded bonnet, she turns to look at us with another engaging but detached expression. Does she know what she sees or is this another anonymous encounter? Is her gaze tinged with longing or colored by distress, or is she as distant as the woman in the background? The intrigue is increased by the presence of the male figure behind her who lowers his head while allowing his left hand to curve seductively over the slats of the bench. His fingers almost appear to be drumming the wood, as if he was biding his time or itching to touch his female companion. We seem to have interrupted something again, perhaps their conversation. But it does not appear to have been an innocent exchange. Is this a tryst or a quarrel? The flowers on the bench imply the former as does the tradition of such juxtapositions, evident in the many popular illustrations of male figures leaning over chairs or walls behind seated females.[40] But what is this supposed to mean? Is this merely another image meant to reveal the difficulties and disjunctures of modern life whether in city or country, or does it testify to something about Monet's relationship with his wife? Once more we are left without secure answers.[41]

There are several paintings in which things seem clearer, as, for example, *A Corner of the Garden with Dahlias*, from the same summer of 1873 (Pl. 94). The resplendent thicket of red, yellow, and white flowers on the left energizes the scene and appears to fill it with petals and

93   Claude Monet, *The Bench*, 1873, 60.6 × 80.3, W.281, From the Collection of Walter H. and Leonore Annenberg.

fragrance. Together with the bending branches of the tree on the far left and the triangular divisions of the multicolored ground, the dahlias lead us to the couple in the background who stand together by the high picket fence. They appear to be almost Watteau-like figures in some enchanted environment, their intimacy suggested by their proximity to each other, the amount of foliage that surrounds them, and the artful way that Monet bends the trees on the right to form a kind of canopy for them. They are almost dwarfed by their surroundings, particularly by the house behind them which seems to look down at them in a curiously human way. Whether they are engaged in amorous conversation, merely an exchange of pleasantries, or a heady discussion is impossible to say, although it appears that the garden is an invigorating place for their meeting given its windswept character.

Regardless of how the interaction of the figures may be read, Monet has taken considerable liberties with his site, as a view of the same garden painted in the same year by Renoir reveals (Pl. 95). The house on the left in Renoir's picture is the one that appears in Monet's but the jumble of other structures that he faithfully includes on the right are nowhere to be found in Monet's version. Monet judiciously cropped them out of his scene and enlarged the trees and undergrowth on that side. Whether the flowers he includes on the left were borrowed from the neighbor's through artistic license is unknown, but Monet has clearly reduced the evidence of encroaching suburbia and in so doing has made his garden more charming and appealing.

In Renoir's picture, Monet appears perfectly happy to be outside, gazing intensely at his motif, and translating his sensations into paint. Unconcerned about his exposure to the neighbors, he is the epitome of the modern artist, something other portraits of him from the same moment by other friends, such as Manet, also affirm. But the editing that Monet performed on his view and the restlessness that pervades it suggest that he perhaps wanted the realities of his situation to be different—that instead of a standard suburban plot he was hoping for a richer, more discreet place further removed from the noise of the *quartier* and the surveillance of curious residents. After all, that was the prime reason for the suburbs in the first place and the desire of those city-dwellers who contemplated moving there.

Not surprisingly, Monet painted another picture during that same summer of 1873 that comes even closer to embodying that ideal, *The Luncheon* (Pl. 96). This is a grand-scale picture, measuring 1.62 × 2.03 meters, the largest that Monet had attempted since his return

94 (above left) Claude Monet, *A Corner of the Garden with Dahlias*, 1873, 61 × 82.5, W.286, National Gallery of Art, Washington, Partial Gift of Janice H. Levin, in Honor of the 50th Anniversary of the National Gallery of Art.

95 (above right) Auguste Renoir, *Monet Painting in his Argenteuil Garden*, 1873, 50.3 × 106.7, Wadsworth Atheneum, Hartford, Bequest of Anne Parrish Titzell.

from England and Holland, and the largest since the nearly similar-sized painting of the same name of 1868–69 (Pl. 49). Virtually every inch of the canvas emits an air of enviable contentment, from the brilliantly illuminated wicker cart in the immediate foreground with its rolls, fruits, and half-finished wine, to the sun-dappled table and its remnants of lunch. It also is apparent in the gleaming flowers, the inviting path beyond, and the light that fills the scene as a whole. Even young Jean appears happily engaged with his wooden toy on the left while the women stroll in the background.

Monet emphasizes the appeal of this seemingly perfect day by making everything remarkably immediate and at the same time wonderfully casual. The wooden bench on the left, for example, juts out dramatically from the foreground but its thrust is softened by the creamy touches of light on its slats and by the parasol and bag that one of the women has left. The edges of the wicker table and fruit plate in the foreground are boldly illuminated while the cart moves on a countering line from the bench. As was true in the earlier *Luncheon*, elements on the table are pushed precariously close to the edge—the coffee-cup on the right, the compote and partially eaten roll on the left. But these are countered by the way that Monet artfully integrates elements in the scene by having them touch or overlap others nearby. The parasol pokes the bag, for example, the bag bends to touch the handle of the cart, the cart rises to just below the edge of the table, the wine in the glass ends just at the cart's edge, its rim rising to just above the curve of the table. Similar pairings occur on the table itself. The abandoned napkin on the left overlaps the saucer, glass, and coffee-pot tray just as the saucer and nibbled roll on the left touch the bottom of the fruit compote whose triangular shape is echoed by the bush on the far left that it reaches out to meet. Everything is independent, yet subtly united. Even the figures in the background seem perfectly positioned: they are framed by the overhanging branches of the tree in the foreground while their arms are bent to meet the lower edge of the window-frames behind them. Monet also has the band of shadow at their feet parallel the edge of the flower-bed by the house and end on the left exactly where the bottom of the flower-box meets the planter's only exposed leg.

Monet described this picture as a "decorative panel" which suggests he differentiated it from his other efforts; it was the first time he had labelled any of his paintings in this way. Undoubtedly, it had something to do with its size. But unlike the earlier *Luncheon* or any previous large-scale canvas, this painting focused attention on what traditionally would be seen as non-narrative elements—the still life on the table, for example, or the areas of light and shade throughout the scene—which vie for precedence over the painting's story-telling features, such as the figures and the meal. The ability of the painting to tell a tale therefore is intentionally minimized: nothing seems to be occurring. As a consequence, interest is diverted to other matters—Monet's dexterity at mixing colors, for example, or his ability at rendering complex lighting effects. Visual beauty and formal values rise to the fore just as elements in the picture—the hat in the tree, for instance, or the serving cart—push their way to the surface of the canvas to assert themselves as part of a harmonious whole.

The problem is that the harmony here appears hard won, if not concocted. Note the way the bowl of the compote meets the stem just at the curve of the table, or the underside of the saucer on the right just happens to change from white to blue as it touches the edge of the linen on that side. There is a fragility here, in other words, that makes the beauty and desirability of the scene suspect. What contributes to this uneasiness is the fact that the subject of the picture—the shared meal—is obviously finished, causing the participants to go their separate ways and the foreground to be littered with the aftermath. There actually is little being shared here, just as there are questions that cannot be answered. How many people were at this meal? The pairs of wine glasses and coffee-cups imply two but does that then

eliminate Jean and his father? If the napkin on the table indicates a place setting, what has happened to the chair? And if both women in the background wear bonnets, whose is the one on the foreground branches and what is it doing there? Again, there are no logical answers to these questions. The only thing we can say is that by focusing on the aftermath of the event, Monet saps the picture of its potential for expectation, substituting a sense of emptiness and finality for the happiness and fulfillment the scene might possess. Thus, as in seventeenth-century Dutch genre scenes, he seems to be suggesting that suburbia can supply all the trappings of the ideal but that its realization is as temporal or as fleeting as the meal itself. The picture therefore is a kind of *memento mori* for modern French men and women and their existence in the suburbs.

But it was precisely that ideal that Monet and his countrymen and women wanted not only to believe in but also to possess, as the social observer, Eugène Chapus, asserted even in the 1860s: "One of the pronounced characteristics of our present Parisian society," he wrote, "is that . . . everyone in the middle class wants to have his little house with trees, roses, dahlias,

96 Claude Monet, *The Luncheon*, 1873, 162 × 203, W.285, Musée d'Orsay, Paris.

97 (above left)
Claude Monet, *The Red Boats*, 1875, 55 × 65, W.370, Musée d'Orsay, Paris.

98 (above right)
Claude Monet, *Summer Fields of Poppies*, 1875, 60 × 81, W.377, Private Collection.

99   Claude Monet, *The Studio Boat*, 1876, 72 × 60, W.390, © 1993 by The Barnes Foundation, Merion.

his big or little garden, his rural *argentea mediocritas*."[42] Although Monet seems to have recognized that Argenteuil was no longer able to sustain his belief in that ideal, he set out to paint pictures in 1875 that made the place appear to be nothing less than perfect. This is evident in pictures such as *The Red Boats* and *Summer Fields of Poppies*, both from the summer of 1875 (Pls. 97, 98). Monet eliminates anything that might compromise either the calm of the ducks who swim so peacefully on such appealing waters or the isolation of the elegantly dressed woman and two children in their field of flowers.

Clearly, something fundamental has changed in Monet's stance, a fact that he confirmed over and over again in 1876 when he painted almost nothing but idyllic garden pictures or views of the Seine, such as Pl. 99, that appear to be retreats into the untrammeled past. There are no railroads or sailboats here, no bridges or factory chimneys, just Monet's little *bateau atelier* floating along the quiet backwaters of an isolated stretch of the river nestled between

100 Claude Monet, *The Tuileries*, 1876, 50 × 74, W.403, Musée d'Orsay, Paris.

101 Claude Monet, *The Parc Monceau*, 1876, 59.7 × 82.6, The Metropolitan Museum of Art, Bequest of Loula D. Lasker, New York City, 1961.

thickly foliated banks. In such a place, Monet can be completely alone, contemplating the beauties of undisturbed nature much like his Barbizon predecessors.

This is not to say that Monet abandoned modern life altogether. He painted no such pictures in Argenteuil in 1876 but, for the first time since 1873, he returned to Paris for a brief campaign in the spring and early summer. However, instead of rendering the swarming boulevards as he had done previously, he focused this time on the Tuileries and the Parc Monceau (Pls. 100, 101), as if even in the heart of the capital he was going to minimize the contradictions of modernity and concentrate, as he had in Argenteuil, on the world of the garden. This became his complete preoccupation later that year when he moved to Montgeron at the request of his patrons, Ernest and Alice Hoschedé, who commissioned him to paint four large decorative pictures for the dining room of their sumptuous château (Pls. 102, 103). Monet worked in this lavish setting for approximately six months, from July to December 1876, producing not only these four huge canvases but also numerous views of the

102 (above left)
Claude Monet, *The Turkeys*, 1876, 172 × 175, W. 416, Musée d'Orsay, Paris.

103 (above right)
Claude Monet, *The Pond*, 1876, 172 × 193, W.420, Hermitage Museum, Saint Petersburg.

Yerres River which ran near the Hoschedé property and, on trips back to Argenteuil, equally idyllic pictures of the small arm of the Seine that had been the site for *Springtime at Argenteuil* of 1872 (Pl. 69). All of these pictures are painted with remarkable palettes and lively brushwork, but all of them also attest to Monet's new orientation, as none of them contains any evidence that would link them to a specific time or place.

After more than a year of painting nothing but these pastoral scenes of idyllic reverie, Monet suddenly returned to Paris in January 1877 and began one of his most ambitious modern life projects of the decade: multiple views of the Gare Saint-Lazare in the capital's eighth arrondissement (Pls. 104–9). Nothing could be further from the delights of Montgeron or the beauties of his own garden at Argenteuil than this busy, steaming station. Between January and April 1877 Monet worked like a demon, completing no fewer than twelve canvases that depict different areas in and around this celebrated depot. He had never concentrated so intensely on a single place and produced as many pictures in such a short amount of time (approximately one painting every ten days). The fire therefore still burned in him to be the painter of modern life in landscape, even if Argenteuil no longer seemed to be his preferred setting. The twelve vary greatly in size, palette, and touch, and thus are quite different from the later series paintings of the 1890s which would be conceived, executed, and exhibited as groups. In addition, instead of focusing on a single subject like those later pictures, the twelve actually lead the viewer around the station as if on a kind of tour.

As with all of Monet's subjects, the choice of the Gare Saint-Lazare was not made lightly. The station was one of the largest and most heavily used of the seven in the capital, moving 13 million passengers a year or 40 per cent of all such traffic in Paris.[43] It also was a station that Monet knew well because it served Argenteuil as well as Le Havre. In addition, it was only a block away from the small studio on the rue d'Isly that he had kept until 1874.[44] Furthermore, it was from this station that the first seventeen kilometers of track in France had been laid, leading to Le Pecq across from Saint Germain-en-Laye, and it was this station that had been substantially expanded in the 1860s to accommodate the enormous increases in rail travel. It therefore was a vivid symbol for the origins and explosive growth of one of the

104  Claude Monet, *The Small Arm of the Seine at Argenteuil*, 1876, 54 × 70.5, W.427, Private Collection.

nation's most important assets as well as one of the country's primary sources of change and advancement. The area around the station had also been the site of several other pictures by Monet's colleagues. Manet's *Railroad* of 1873 was set overlooking the railroad yards, while Gustave Caillebotte's *Pont de l'Europe* of 1876 depicted the huge new bridge that was the centerpiece of Baron Haussmann's massive renovation of the neighborhood and that crossed the web of tracks leading to and from the station. The area, therefore, already had a modern pedigree although no one had yet focused exclusively on the station and the trains.

Not that people had not called for someone to take up the subject. So enthused were some observers with the new railroad stations that the structures were often referred to as "the new cathedrals of humanity."[45] Gustave Courbet wanted to "turn them into churches for the benefit of painters: those great walls could be covered with all kinds of highly suitable subjects, such as previews of the main sites through which the traveler will pass, portraits of great men associated with cities in the line of route, picturesque and moral themes, industry and metallurgy—in short, all of the 'saints and miracles' of modern times."[46] Courbet never realized this idea, but it certainly stayed alive in Parisian art circles over the next couple of decades. Thomas Couture, for example, urged his students to portray "that strange and mysterious power which hides a volcano in its flanks, that monster in bronze and snout of fire which devours space," which must have been partially behind Manet's proposal to include images of the railroad in the decorative program for the reconstructed Hôtel de Ville in Paris in 1879.[47] Manet never received that commission and Couture's students largely ignored their teacher's urgings, but Monet's great suite of paintings can be considered the ultimate response to this modernist call.

It certainly was the way critics saw them when Monet exhibited eight of the twelve in the Third Impressionist Exhibition which opened in April 1877.[48] Having spent so much time on the Hoschedé commission and on so many other idyllic paintings, Monet must have realized that he needed some new modern-life pictures for this show which undoubtedly motivated him to consider the station as a subject. It is not clear exactly which eight he exhibited or how they were hung, but virtually all of the reviewers recognized their novelty

105 Claude Monet,
*Interior of the Gare Saint-Lazare*, 1877, 75 × 100,
W.437, Musée d'Orsay,
Paris.

106 Claude Monet,
*Interior of the Gare Saint-Lazare*, 1877,
53.5 × 72.5, W.441,
National Gallery,
London.

107 Claude Monet,
*Exterior of the Gare
Saint-Lazare*, 1877,
60 × 80, W.446, Private
Collection, U.S.A.

108 Claude Monet,
*The Pont de Rome* (*Gare
Saint-Lazare*), 1877,
64 × 81, W.442, Private
Collection.

whether they liked them or not. Preferences fell along predictable lines. Some writers were quite enthusiastic. Renoir's friend Georges Rivière felt that Monet's submissions as a whole had "an intense and personal life that no one before had discovered or even suspected," and that the Gare Saint-Lazare pictures displayed an "astonishing variety . . . Evident here, more than in any other of Monet's paintings, is the science of composition, of arranging the canvas, which is one of the masterful qualities of M. Monet." An anonymous writer for the liberal paper *L'Homme libre* was struck with the fact that Monet's "brush has expressed not only the movement, color, and activity [of the station] but also the clamor; it is unbelievable. Yet the station is full of din—grindings, whistles—that you make out through the colliding blue and gray clouds of dense smoke. It is a pictorial symphony," he asserted.[49] More conservative critics saw the same features negatively. To one, the impression of many trains whistling at once was "disagreeable" while to another the "pink, black, gray, and purple smoke" made "them look like an illegible scrawl."[50] The latter reactions were understandable as Monet took enormous liberties in these pictures. In most of them, the light is so intense or the steam so thick that forms tend to emerge and dissolve in dramatic, unpredictable ways. In addition, surfaces are either highly worked, as in Pl. 105, producing a dense scumbled texture, or so liquid and sketchy, as in Pl. 108, that there is little consistency and little attention paid to accepted methods of modeling. In certain pictures, such as Pl. 107, the canvas is not completely covered which allows its lightly primed weft and weave to be part of the image. In many cases, strokes of paint are applied with such independence that they easily become pure calligraphy, as evident in particular in Pl. 110.

The most penetrating remarks about these pictures, however, came from Frédéric Chevalier who was writing for the conservative magazine, *L'Artiste*. He liked many of Monet's submissions but he made the following generalization about the Impressionists' work as a whole that has special relevance to the Gare Saint-Lazare suite: "The disturbing ensemble of contradictory qualities which distinguish the Impressionists—the crude application of paint, the down-to-earth subjects, the appearance of spontaneity, the conscious incoherence, the bold colors, the contempt for form, the childish naiveté that they mix heedlessly with exquisite refinements, all of this is not without analogy to the chaos of contradictory forces that trouble our era."[51] This is a remarkable set of observations, given the fact that the Impressionists were clearly attempting to give their experience of contemporary life appropriate painterly form. But it also seems particularly germane to Monet's Gare Saint-Lazare series especially when they are considered as a group. For when arranged from what probably were the first pictures to those that most likely came last, they lead in a logical, though probably not predetermined, fashion from one kind of imagery to another and suggest distinctly different conclusions at the beginning and the end.

The first of the group were probably the most finished canvases, such as Pl. 105; they required the most work, they depict the most familiar lines in the station (those to Argenteuil), and they are the most symmetrical or at least the most traditionally balanced, with the enormous iron-and-glass roof placed exactly in the middle of the image in this instance. They also seem the most celebratory. The steam rises up through the network of iron tie rods, mixing with the light that floods the interior space from the novel skylights above. The weightiness of the shed's structure is therefore minimized, something Monet also suggests by including the thin columns on the right and the almost Gothic-like tracery on the left. But when he moves out from the sheds themselves, everything changes (Pl. 107). Forms become more evanescent and incomplete, just as the surface of the picture become less finely worked. When he moves further down the platforms in pictures such as Pl. 108, the Pont de l'Europe slices into the scene on an uncompromising diagonal while the tracks shoot out to

109   Claude Monet,
*Exterior View Back to the
Gare Saint-Lazare*, 1877,
60 × 80, W.445, Private
Collection, Japan.

110   Claude Monet,
*The Signal*, 65 × 81.5,
W.448,
Niedersächsische
Landesgalerie, Hanover.

the right to create a countering tension. Between these competing and roughly drawn orthogonals is the messy collection of railroad elements—sheds, signals, and engine—above which loom buildings and swirling smoke. No other painting from Monet's hand up until this point is as disjointed as this one. No other also appears as strained internally. When he turns around and looks back at the station, as he does in Pl. 109, he makes the whole thing seem like some kind of illusion, a mirage of steam and sheds, tracks and trains, as if it were a figment of his imagination, something unreal or incomprehensible.

This notion is reinforced by what may have been the last painting in the group, *The Signal* (Pl. 110). This is an astonishing picture, as crude as it is forceful, as definitive as it is suggestive. The black circles of the railroad's signalling system sit precariously on top of their thin vertical stanchions boldly silhouetted against the painterly bravura of the misty background. The independent strokes of paint that describe steam bolting forward from the middleground like electrified streamers are also unprecedented in Monet's work, just as the contrast between the forms in the picture as well as the way they are rendered are not found elsewhere. This is the ultimate embodiment of that "chaos of contradictory forces that trouble[d]" Chevalier. Those circular forms, in theory there to direct and control, are virtually rendered useless by the swirl of the steam; their rationale, just like their clarity, is mocked by the irrationality of their almost indecipherable environment. To some the sheds for this great invention of the railroad which we see in the distance on the right might have been the new cathedrals of humanity, something Monet seems to suggest by the forms between the signals which ironically appear to evoke the twin towers of a Gothic church. But the only human element here is the isolated, almost shadow-like, figure of a man on the right whose head imitates the rounded discs of the signals and whose body is rigidly locked between various vertical elements.

If the figures in his earlier views of factories and railroad bridges were surrogates for Monet's countrymen and women who seemed by their presence to embrace change as inherent to modernity, this figure like the other forms in the scene as a whole appears to be in a world that is no longer understandable. It is a world that has lost the clarity and meaning that Monet's earlier works had propagated so forcefully. And rightfully so perhaps—at least for Monet, the landscape painter. He had seen at first hand the changes wrought by the so-called positive force of progress—the increased population of suburban towns, particularly Argenteuil, the erosion of time-honored attachments to the land, the disappearance of once-open acreage, and the multiplication of factories. How could someone attached to nature and committed to rendering her many faces continue to trumpet such antithetical developments, ones which not only ran counter to his central beliefs but actually compromised the very subjects that made his life and art significant?

Obviously he could not, as his paintings were lived experiences, the product of his deep personal engagement with his moment. When he no longer felt in sympathy with the most basic tenets of that moment because he understood the world around him in more profound terms, he had to act. He could not continue to propagate a faith he no longer believed in, something these Gare Saint-Lazare paintings appear to confirm. Monet himself suggested as much when, at the very last moment, even after the catalogue for the Third Impressionist Exhibition was printed, he decided to include *The Signal* in the show—a revealing coda, perhaps, to a decade of myth-making.

As the reviews of the exhibition rolled in, Monet returned to Argenteuil where over the course of the next nine months he virtually stopped painting, completing only four pictures before the end of the year. Except for his stint in North Africa in 1861–62, Monet had never been so unproductive. This unprecedented lapse is difficult to explain. He may have wanted

111 Claude Monet, *Arguenteuil, the Bank in Flower*, 1877, 54 × 65, W. 453, Private Collection, Japan.

to take a break after painting the Gare Saint-Lazare pictures in such a short period of time; he may have had to take care of Camille who fell ill that summer; he also may have wanted to reduce his inventory and spend time negotiating sales; his account books show he sold quite a few pictures during these months. But it seems more than coincidental that this hiatus occurred immediately after he had experienced both extremes of modern life—the splendid isolation of the Hoschedé estate and the ordered chaos of the railroad station, something he implied as well in the Third Impressionist Exhibition when he included views of Montgeron with those of the Gare Saint-Lazare.

There was an added problem: Argenteuil was continuing to grow. In 1876, the town's third ironworks opened, right across from his house. By late 1877, it was employing over 250 workers and was operating on average eleven hours a day. The Joly factory, one of the largest ironworks in all of France, was up to 500 workers on a similar eleven-hour schedule. A third such factory, built in 1874 at the end of the promenade, employed 170 people by 1877. In total, these three industries had grown by more than 350 people since the last quarter of 1876. Other industries in the town could claim similar growth.[52]

There were changes on other fronts as well. A new railroad line that was to be laid across seven kilometers of Argenteuil's open acreage linking Epinay and Pont de Maisons was approved by the minister of public works in January 1877 with construction to begin the following year. In early 1877, the town council approved the establishment of a new distillery that was to be located in the heart of town. And they allowed a chemical concern to reopen and enlarge an older plant next to the ironworks across the railroad tracks from Monet's house. All of these were proof of the town's continuing development, one that had already seen the population rise by 600 people between 1872 and 1876 and then increase by 900 each year in 1877 and 1878.

Worse, perhaps, than the factory construction was the pollution of the Seine. Baron Haussmann had laid miles of new sewage pipes in Paris but he had linked them all to two main drains which ran out of the city to Asnières and Saint-Denis where they emptied their contents into the river. By the 1870s, 450,000 kilograms of filth was pouring into the Seine every day, creating a horrendous stench as well as serious environmental problems. At Argenteuil people constantly complained about the way the boat basin bubbled because of the sludge at the bottom of the river.[53]

Little wonder, therefore, that Monet was having difficulties getting motivated or that when he finally took up his paints and brushes again he returned to the one place that had embodied all of the idyllic qualities of the town when he had first arrived—the promenade. Little wonder as well that what probably was the last of the four views of that site, *Argenteuil, the Bank in Flower* (Pl. 111), confirms what the Gare Saint-Lazare suite had suggested—that something has gone awry and that the meaning Monet once had found in his modern, progressive world no longer appeared tenable. This breathtaking canvas is forcefully split in half, its bold, dark foreground contrasting with the golden atmosphere of its Claudian background. Unlike the *Promenade at Argenteuil* of 1872 (Pl. 70), there is no entrance to this scene, no invitation to stroll down the once-welcoming path, no ribbons of light to mark the way. Nor is there a sense of each part being integrated with the next. The flowers in the foreground twist and turn against the light in the distance, while the factory chimneys and steamboat spout out their smoke in mock imitation of the flowers' fluttering foliage. The place could still give rise to golden illusions—people still stroll along the banks to the right. But not for Monet. Just as the flowers that touch the background have lost their petals, so too had Monet lost his faith in the myth of progress. Soon after painting this picture, he left Argenteuil for good, moving first to Paris and then in 1878 to more rural Vétheuil further to the north. From that moment onwards, he would never paint the capital or its close suburbs again. He had left behind the contradictions of modern life for the beauties of undisturbed nature.

## 5   Monet in the 1880s and the Challenges to Impressionism

Located on the right bank of the Seine, some sixty kilometers north of Paris, Vétheuil was a sleepy, picturesque village when Monet moved there in September of 1878 after having scoured the suburbs for months in search of a new place to live (Pl. 112). It was precisely the kind of spot he had been seeking. Only twelve kilometers from Mantes which had been linked to the capital by the railroad in the 1840s, it afforded Monet easy access to Paris and her markets. But, unlike Argenteuil, Vétheuil had experienced precious little change. The town was too far from the capital for most people to commute and offered little in the way of pleasurable distractions that would have caused Parisians to go there on weekends or summer holidays. Its population in 1878, therefore, was not much more than it had been for centuries—622—which was less than a tenth of what Argenteuil claimed at the time. Most of those residents were engaged in agrarian activities, something else that had not changed in hundreds of years.[1]

Monet found a house to rent on the southern edge of town. Although its front door opened on to the road that ran from Vétheuil to La Roche-Guyon, it was pleasant and inexpensive—600 francs a year—and the road was hardly a thoroughfare. In addition, the house had a large garden on the other side of the street that led down to the river several hundred yards away. It was here that Monet was to live and work for slightly more than three years.

The place appeared to agree with him. Over the time he was there, he produced nearly three hundred paintings—one every four days. This was a remarkable output, surpassing the number of pictures he completed during his seven years at Argenteuil by a large margin. Most of these new canvases, however, were vastly different from those earlier works, as Monet now sought out spaces in and around this rural village that revealed its quiet secrets— the backwaters of the Seine, for example, as in *Seine at Vétheuil* (Pl. 113), the orchards that dotted the surrounding hills, and the well-trodden dirt paths of the little town of Lavancourt just across the river.

The differences between these many pictures and works like *Argenteuil, the Bank in Flower* (Pl. 111) are noticeable immediately. In *Seine at Vétheuil*, for example, the river stretches into the distance without any obstructions. No houses line the banks and no factories or pleasure-seekers break the silence that seems to hang so reassuringly over the scene. Monet appears alone in a place where earth and sky, land and water, the artist and the environment are in perfect accord. Satisfying deep yearnings within himself, Monet makes no pretensions in these scenes. He also welcomes no intrusions; everything has its place; everything belongs. There is a new kind of order here; it is nature's, not man's. Thus the picture possesses a new sense of resolve.

Although this view contains no houses, the town itself, like the village of Lavancourt,

112 Anonymous, nineteenth-century photograph of Vétheuil, Bibliothèque Nationale, Paris.

113 (above left) Claude Monet, *The Seine at Vétheuil*, 46 × 71.5, 1879, W.484, Private Collection.

114 (above right) Claude Monet, *The Church at Vétheuil*, 1878, 65 × 55, W.474, National Gallery of Scotland, Edinburgh.

often features in paintings that Monet did during that fall of 1878. In fact, views of Vétheuil, such as Pl. 114, are among the first he may have executed. Its collection of jostling buildings always appears quaint; the differently shaped structures nudge each other as if in a pleasant country dance. And, in most instances, the scene is crowned by the spire of the old town church. A charming thirteenth-century building that had received a new façade in the sixteenth century, it was the largest structure in the town and gained in stature by occupying a slightly raised site in the center of the village. It appears in no fewer than forty-five pictures, reaffirming traditional values and a certain sense of stability.

The ease and delight of these views, no less the sheer number of pictures Monet painted in the first year he was there, suggest he had finally found true contentment, at least when he was engaged with what he knew best—painting out of doors. When he was at home writing letters to friends and collectors, the story was quite different. He was flat broke, without a sou, and surely someone could advance him some money or purchase a picture that he knew they would like. Month after month, it is the same story of poverty and despair. "It is sad to be in this position at my age," he declared to Dr. de Bellio on 30 December 1878, "always obliged to ask [for money and] to solicit business. I am feeling the weight of my misfortune doubly at this time of year and '79 is going to begin just as this year ended, very sad above all for my family, to whom I cannot give even the most modest present."[2] He wrote like this despite having received 1,000 francs from Manet in March and selling more than 11,500 francs worth of paintings by the end of December. In 1879, he did about as well—12,285 francs—but if his letters are the only guide, he was barely one step in front of his creditors.

His family life was equally trying and even more complex. His wife Camille had developed a uterine problem after the birth of their second child, Michel, in 1878. The condition became quite serious in the first months at Vétheuil and caused Monet concern. Experiencing continued loss of strength, Camille soon had to be confined to bed. The illness—probably cancer—began to affect her entire system in 1879, causing her to vomit constantly and her limbs to swell from fluids. According to Monet's letters, she suffered terribly during that summer.[3] Mercifully, death came on 5 September. She was 32 years old. Monet was shaken by the event. This time he did not opt for metaphor or suggestion, as he had when painting her before. Instead, he portrayed her on her deathbed as her life literally ebbed (Pl. 115). More than forty years later, according to his friend Georges Clemenceau, he admitted he had been surprised when, at Camille's bedside with his "eyes fixed on her tragic forehead," he all of a sudden found himself "in the act of mechanically observing the succession . . . of fading colors which death was imposing on [her] immobile face," as if his powers of visual analysis were overwhelming any emotion he may have felt for his companion of more than fourteen years.[4]

This statement has often been seen as an example of how formal factors could take precedence over Monet's choice of subjects, but that is profoundly misleading. First, the statement was apparently made in 1920, many years after the event, and was put into words by Clemenceau not by Monet who was dead when Clemenceau's book containing this passage appeared. But even if it were true, even if Monet did find himself watching the color from his wife's face fade as she passed away, it does not mean that he cared any less about her. His letters of August and September amply attest to his affection for her as they are filled with apprehension about her condition. In addition, the painting itself, while firmly a part of the nineteenth-century tradition of deathbed portraiture, is extraordinary for the way Monet has been able to set the ethereal against the plastic and to evoke Camille's passing as much as her physical presence. This is most noticeable in the contrast between her clearly defined, mandala-shaped head and the windswept surface of the rest of the canvas; the former is sweet, angelic, and passive; the latter forceful, energized, and brimming with impasto. In this light, the picture speaks not merely about Monet's being struck by changing colors but also about his uncanny ability to evoke peace and pain, sorrow and celebration—essential conditions of those trying to deal with the reality of death, particularly of someone who, Monet admitted to Clemenceau in that same conversation of 1920, "had been and still was very dear to me."

A similar blend of contrasting emotions is found in the views of the wintry Seine, such as Pl. 116, that he completed a few months later. With its surface cluttered with huge slabs of ice from the once-frozen river, the views of the Seine in these paintings, indeed the scenes as a whole, are both sonorous and silent, energized and elegiac. The canvases appear to be filled with cries of pain and moments of wonderment, sighs of resignation and odes of hope. They suggest notions of the past cracking and splintering and concerns about whether the present

115  Claude Monet,
*Camille on Her Deathbed*,
1879, 90 × 68, W.543,
Musée d'Orsay, Paris.

116  Claude Monet, *Ice
Floes on the Seine*, 1880,
97 × 50.5, W.567,
Shelburne Museum,
Shelburne, Vermont.

was liberating or unnerving—sensations which the site, of course, could have inspired but which surely were also the result of this important passage in Monet's life.

The haunting beauty of these images is particularly apparent in *Sunset at Lavancourt* (Pl. 117), which Monet painted in the winter of 1880 in preparation for the Salon of that year. The orange orb of the sun in this picture tries to push its way through the almost opaque atmosphere that blankets the scene, obscuring the definition of the houses on the distant banks. The bushes on the left surge to the right as if struggling to make it to the haven of the shore upon which stand denuded trees shivering in the winter cold. The river bends around that point of land carrying on its curiously undisturbed surface chunks of ice of various dimensions. They float eerily into the distance in marked contrast to the struggles around them.

Once again, these kinds of oppositions could easily have been provoked by the scene itself: the Seine froze that winter and broke up with such fury that the noise rumbled through Vétheuil like the roar of locomotives. In addition, winter tends to reduce things to the elemental. But these contrasts also must have been the product of Monet's conflicting emotions about his wife's passing. For besides having to deal with her loss and with becoming a single parent for his two young children (aged 12 and 1), Monet had to deal with the fact that Camille had not died simply in the bosom of her own family; the house in Vétheuil had also been home to Alice and Ernest Hoschedé, their five daughters and newly born son. Monet had invited his patrons to live with him after Ernest Hoschedé had been forced to

117   Claude Monet, *Sunset at Lavancourt*, 1880, 100 × 152, W.576, Musée du Petit Palais, Paris.

declare bankruptcy, losing the Montgeron estate as well as his Paris apartment, art collection, and business.

Monet may have been motivated purely by humanitarian concerns, as the Hoschedés were in dire straits. But there is also the possibility that he had established a relationship with Alice in the summer of 1876 when he spent those many months at Montgeron. Alice was a very religious woman, so how close that relationship may have been will perhaps always remain a mystery.[5] In any case, it made for a strange *ménage à douze* (Monet, Camille, and their two children, Alice, Ernest, and their six children, plus the cook, the maid, and the gardener!) When Ernest finally left his family in late 1879, Monet lived with Alice for over a decade, ultimately marrying her after Ernest's death in 1891. One way or the other, it must have been curious for Monet to have had both women under the same roof, especially when one was dying and the other stepping in to take her place.

That these paintings were quite personal is evident not only from their moody subjects but also from their broad handling and unusual color contrasts. Monet himself admitted this when he told Théodore Duret, a contemporary critic and defender of the Impressionists, that Pl. 117 was painted "much more according to my own taste" while another painting he was working on at the same time (Pl. 118) was "more bourgeois."[6] The contrast between the two is striking. The latter is tamer in all respects; forms are more clearly rendered than in Pl. 117, greater attention is paid to detail, light is more consistent, and colors more harmonious, all of which make the scene more placid and accessible. In subject and handling, therefore, the two could hardly be more dissimilar. That Monet articulated this is significant, as it underscores once again his forethought and planning and his sensitivity to the differences between avant-garde and middle-class tastes. In this case, it is particularly revealing, as Monet intended to submit these two paintings to the Salon of 1880, his first attempt to re-enter that official arena in ten years. However, he told Duret he knew the former would be rejected, which in fact it was, just as the other was accepted, which he had anticipated as well.

Monet's return to the Salon was his last but it marked a decided break with his prior practice of trying to show and sell his work through the independent exhibitions that he and his Impressionist colleagues had staged since 1874. It also caused a lot of grumbling among the core Impressionists. Pissarro was particularly irate, so much so that he resisted the idea of allowing Monet to rejoin the Impressionists' group show the following year. "One should suffer just punishment for mistakes committed," he told Caillebotte who was advocating for Monet.[7] Monet's decision to go his separate way was announced in the press in an ironic but rather nasty article accompanied by a mock funeral notice that appeared in *Le Gaulois* in late January 1880. The notice read, "The impressionist school has the honor of informing you of the grievous loss it has suffered in the person of M. Claude MONET, one of its revered masters. The funeral for M. Claude MONET will take place on 1 May next, at ten o'clock in the morning—the day after the opening at the church of the Palais de l'Industrie—in M. Cabanel's gallery. You are requested not to attend." It was signed "De Profundis!" and was followed by a footnote saying the invitation had been sent "on behalf of M. Degas, head of the school; M. Raffaëlli, successor to the deceased; Miss Cassatt, M. Caillebotte, M. Pissarro, M. Louis Forain, M. Bracquemond, M. Rouard [*sic*], etc. . ., his ex-friends, ex-students, and ex-supporters."[8] Since the anonymous author was clearly well informed and since the paper traditionally supported the Impressionists' efforts, Monet suspected someone in the core group had planted the story. And with his typical mixture of sweetness and rage, he wrote a protest letter to the editor of the paper as well as terse notes to his patron, Dr. de Bellio, and his old friend, Pissarro, claiming he was determined to get to the bottom of it all and find out who leaked the information.[9] He also informed Pissarro that he was furious that he had been

118 Claude Monet, *The Seine at Lavancourt*, 1880, 100 × 150, W.578, Dallas Museum of Art, Munger Fund.

so maligned, particularly after the amount of work he had done on behalf of the group. *Le Gaulois* did not run Monet's letter and de Bellio and Pissarro, while empathetic, claimed they had no light to shed on the case. To make matters worse, the notice was reprinted the following month in *L'Artiste*.[10]

In addition to stirring up controversy, Monet's return to the Salon marked the end of his exclusive reliance upon the good offices of Paul Durand-Ruel who had supported him since the dealer's first purchases in early 1872. From 1880 onwards, Monet explored a variety of marketing strategies. He held exhibitions in elite settings, such as the offices of the newspaper *La Vie Moderne*, and the galleries of Durand-Ruel's primary rival Georges Petit, often playing one dealer off against another. He cultivated private collectors, setting his own prices for canvases, and controlling the flow of pictures out of his studio. He also began to participate in provincial exhibitions, something he had long avoided, doubting their usefulness to his reputation or bank account. But he willingly joined ones in Grenoble, Limoges, and Nancy in 1886 and 1888.[11] He also developed a much broader repertoire of subjects in order to appeal to a wider range of collectors. The latter strategy was linked to extensive trips he began taking, initially to the north to the English Channel and then later in the decade to the south which he had never before visited.

Without doubt his favorite site during the 1880s was the Normandy coast; it obviously was in his blood from his childhood in Le Havre and Saint-Adresse and was easily accessible from Vétheuil and later from Giverny where he moved in 1883.[12] Of all the places he visited on the coast, several became his most frequented—Pourville, Varengeville, Étretat, and Dieppe. The numbers speak for themselves; of the more than 400 landscapes he completed during the first half of the decade, over one third depict these spots. Their appeal lay primarily in their dramatic cliffs and stretches of beach, their simplicity, starkness, and past history. Varengeville was particularly attractive because of a gorge that time and nature's

119 (above left)
Anonymous,
photograph of the
gorge at the Petit Ailly
at Varengeville, ca.
1900, Collection Roger-
Viollet, Paris.

120 (above right)
Anonymous, postcard
of the Customs House
at Varengeville, ca.
1910.

121 (below left)
Claude Monet, *Customs
House at Varengeville*,
1882, 100 × 150, W.740,
The Brooklyn Museum,
Gift of Mrs Horace
Havemeyer.

forces had carved out of the cliffs (Pl. 119). It was also the site of a small stone house, a customs house, built during the Napoleonic blockade of Europe as a lookout post for ships attempting to skirt the siege and deliver cargo without being taxed (Pl. 120). After Napoleon's demise, the house was appropriated by local fishermen and used for storage and refuge. Monet painted it no fewer than twenty times in 1882 and returned to render it almost as frequently again in 1896 and '97. It therefore was of considerable significance to him and rightfully so. Perched high above the water and rocky beach, the house commanded a spectacular view of the channel (Pl. 123). The site also afforded him the opportunity to look to the north and follow the coast as it wound its way up to Dieppe and the Belgian border. And when he crossed the gorge and looked back to the house from the east, it suddenly became a humble element nestled in the crook of the undulating cliff as the hill abruptly but comfortingly rose above the structure.

In almost all of these views, Monet depicts the house as isolated and alone, vulnerable yet steadfast, as if it were a human being—a ship's captain perhaps, guiding his vessel from the poop deck or prow—or a member of a seafaring family awaiting a loved one's return. Whether blown by the winds or bathed in brilliant light, the house also takes on the attributes of a landscape painter alone with his motifs, enduring the elements in order to be one with

them, much like Monet himself. Little wonder, therefore, that he was so excited when he returned to the same site in 1896 and again in 1897, telling Alice Hoschedé it was "just as I had left it" and that he had obtained keys to the house so that he could use it just like local residents.[13]

When Monet painted these views of the house in February 1882, he was staying not in Varengeville, which had no facilities for tourists, but in Pourville, just a few kilometers down the coast to the east (Pl. 123). In the 1880s, Pourville was an unpretentious little village; it claimed an attractive boardwalk, a broad beach, and a few modest hotels but little else in the way of holiday distractions. Monet had never been there before this visit. He only "discovered" it when he ventured out from Dieppe four kilometers further to the east where he had initially installed himself at the beginning of the month. It was "a little nothing of a village," he told Alice, but it was "three times cheaper than Dieppe" and set in "a very beautiful region." What he found particularly appealing was the fact that he "couldn't be closer to the sea.... I only regret not coming here sooner."[14]

Monet's enthusiasm for the town is suggested by the numerous views he completed of the coast from Pourville's boardwalk, such as Pl. 125. Since he was there purposefully in the off season, the beach is almost always shown deserted, except for the occasional rowboat that lies silently on the shore. While adding a distinctly human note to the scene, the boats also reinforce the natural splendor of the area as it is the light and atmosphere that Monet relies on to fill the void created by the empty site and craft, just as it is the drama of the way he organizes the stripped-down forms at his disposal—beach, cliffs, water, and sky—that compensates for the relative inactivity of the scene.

The elemental qualities of these pictures bespeak Monet's keen interest in stripping away the superfluous and non-essential, just as they reveal his firm avoidance of any evidence of modern life. This return to fundamentals is also apparent in the simplicity of the shapes he employs and the way they carve out space or create surface patterns on the canvas. The upper edge of the cliff in Pl. 122, for example, rises and falls like a wave—appropriate for its setting—with its highest point coming exactly where the chimney of the house pushes out from the roof. As the crest of the cliff approaches the water, it begins to tumble like a wave breaking on the shore. And as it drops to meet the bottom of the picture it actually falls along a vertical line that creates a square with the left side of the canvas. Pl. 121 is based on similar subtleties. The top left edge of the cliff here rises on a line that runs parallel to the left edge of

123 (above left) Anonymous, photograph of Pourville, ca. 1890, Collection Roger Viollet, Paris.

124 (above right) Claude Monet, *Boats on the Beach at Pourville*, 1882, 60.5 × 79.5, W.709, Kreeger Museum, Washington.

122 (facing page bottom right) Claude Monet, *Customs House at Varengeville*, 1882, 81.3 × 60.3, Philadelphia Museum of Art, William L. Elkins Collection.

the roof of the house. Its highest point coincides with the dip of the cliffs in the distance while its right edge cuts back and down to meet the corner of the roof. Even the pattern of white caps on the water is echoed in the waving grass on the left side of the cliff. The care that Monet took to devise these compositional strategies is also apparent in the way that he created patterns and contrasts in his brushwork and in the calculated choices he made in terms of color relations in the scenes.

Monet took this turn to the elemental one step further in the summer of 1882 when he returned to Pourville with Alice Hoschedé and their children and painted a suite of four pictures that contain nothing but sea and sky (Pl. 125). The water stretches out to either side of the canvas unencumbered by any demarcating forms. There is nothing to indicate how vast or narrow the view actually is, although the horizontality of the strokes that describe the water and the strictness of the horizon in the distance suggest the scene is in fact endlessly expanding—indeed, that it is wider than can be taken in at a single glance. This same sensation of extraordinary spaciousness is generated by the way the water moves deep into the distance without a trace of nautical activity or anything else that might tell us what is near and far. The amount of canvas the water occupies varies in each work but the sky is present in all of them and is always rendered with brushstrokes that are quite different from those that describe the water. They also contain colors that often contrast with those below them.

By permitting nothing to be in the scene except stripped-down nature, Monet was testing his powers as a painter to make the image interesting through the limited means of color and touch; he also was literally wiping the slate clean and starting anew. He demonstrated this in one other, equally startling picture from that summer of 1882 (Pl. 126). In this remarkable, de Chirico-like view, Monet looks eastwards down the Varengeville beach towards Pourville in the distance. Although he provides plenty of clearly defined forms and enough spatial clues to make the picture understandable, he injects a strangeness into the scene and a sense of isolation that are as engaging as they are unnerving. This is primarily the result of his willingness to make the image strikingly spare. He empties the foreground of everything, for example, except the shimmering sands which stretch uninterrupted into the middleground where a solitary figure casting a distinct shadow to the left stands looking at us like some ominous yet inviting specter. Behind him, the beach recedes, again without any interruption, until it dips to meet the water. It is precisely at that juncture that three more figures emerge. Although mere specks, they add an important human note to the otherwise vacant scene. Monet locks them in position by placing them at the apex of the wedge of water. He is equally careful about locating the single figure in the middleground; he places him where the orthogonals of the ridge of sand and the cliff on the right converge, while allowing his head just to nudge the horizon. All around the figures is an almost blinding light which bleaches the ground and casts the cliffs into contrasting darkness. The light appears both tangible and elusive, as if Monet has managed to capture one of those brilliant days where everything is so crystal clear that it seems almost unreal.

These paintings forthrightly reveal what his many other canvases of the decade attest to more indirectly—namely, that he had set himself to a new task. From here on, he was going to allow nature to speak on her own about her awesome powers and boundless splendor. Her chiaroscuro, therefore, would be hailed as both concrete and other worldly, as in Pl. 126; her immensity and grandeur celebrated in the ever-expanding breadth of views like Pl. 125; her intricate wholeness subtly suggested by the interrelationship of individual parts of pictures, as in Pl. 124. The human would always have a place in this new enterprise, whether explicitly in the figures Monet often includes or by implication, as in the houses, boats, or other man-made artifacts that appear in his scenes. Even the immediacy of his forms and the physicality of his touch allow one to sense Monet's presence in the picture and thus that of an individual standing on the site as a surrogate for the viewer. These references, however, are generally subservient to the splendor of the setting that Monet chose to paint, making it clear that the relation of the human to the natural had changed dramatically in his mind from the first two decades of his career. For the energy he once found in the contradictions of contemporaneity were now to be discovered in the magisterial way in which rocks meet water and land reaches to sky. That meant that Monet's choices of what to paint became even more critical. If anecdote and visual incident were to be reduced, the site had to bear the primary burden of the value of the picture. Otherwise, the whole enterprise would collapse into cliché, something Monet consistently attempted to avoid.

The amount that Monet invested in his sites is evident in the formal decisions he made when he rendered them, in the stories that they told and, most importantly perhaps, in the enthusiasm he expressed for them. When on painting campaigns during the decade, his letters to Alice Hoschedé are filled with anguish about the difficulties of painting the places he had chosen and his unabashed delight for those same, carefully selected, sites. While in Pourville in 1882, for example, he told Alice, "What happiness it will be for me to show you all the delicious nooks and crannies here" even though he admitted that he had "worked so long on certain canvases that I no longer know what to think of them and have become decidedly more difficult [on myself]; nothing satisfies me."[15] A year later, he could extol the marvels of Étretat while suffering the same affliction. "You are right to envy me," he admitted to Alice. "You cannot have any idea of how beautiful the sea has been for two days, but what talent it will take to render it, it's crazy. As for the cliffs, they are like nowhere else. Yesterday, I climbed down to a spot where I had never ventured to go before and saw wonderful things there so I very quickly went back to get my canvases. In the end, I am very happy."[16] His only fear was "that these new [paintings] would not be that much different from my other things." But, he confessed, "I can't help but be seduced by these admirable cliffs."[17] A week later, however, he was beside himself. "I am furious, sad, grieving." Not only had fishermen moved the boats he had been painting but the weather had been terribly volatile. "I am tired of working incessantly and of fighting like this against the weather changes."[18] When he visited Bordighera on the Mediterranean the following year, he made the challenges of his practice clear. "It's necessary to have worked [in an area] with pain in order to render it accurately," he claimed, "but can one ever feel happy in front of nature and here in

127 Claude Monet, *The Church at Varengeville*, 1882, 60 × 73, W.794, Private Collection.

particular?" he asked.[19] He had already answered the question: "A true painter can never be happy with himself," he had asserted in a letter of a few days earlier, a condition the south seemed to exacerbate.[20] "Surrounded by this dazzling light [in Bordighera], one finds one's palette woefully lacking," he wrote. What he wanted was "the tones of gold and diamonds. In the end," he concluded, "I do what I can."[21]

That generally proved at least partially satisfying despite his cries to the contrary, primarily because of the emotive qualities of the sites he chose to render. When in Varengeville, for example, he turned around from where he stood in Pl. 126, walked a short distance down the beach, and painted the cliffs twisting and turning as they rose with a kind of volcanic force to lift the church on its crest high above the water (Pl. 127). The irregularity of the sheer rock wall is fully evident from the chiaroscuro which Monet now employs with great subtlety. The almost frightening way in which the cliff attains its staggering height from its absolutely flat footings in the sand is suggested by the multiple, sometimes quite bizarre, colors that Monet applies with considerable gusto. In contrast to this shrill palette and tangle of brushstrokes, Monet makes the church appear steadfast and firm. He illuminates it with crisp, even light and sets it against soft cumulus clouds, the latter cushioning the structure while countering the vertical thrust of the cliffs below. Like the customs house, the church takes on several personae. It too is like a ship navigating its way through perilous waters, or a stand-in for the seafaring family anxiously awaiting the return of a loved one. With its strong geometric forms contrasting with the tumultuous ones on which it stands, the structure also speaks about the ways in which the human has rationalized the world using its mental powers to fashion moral and intellectual shelters from the chaos of nature while attempting to be one with it.

Monet was not a religious man, but he painted this church more than half a dozen times in 1882, often evoking these very associations. They would have been especially appropriate for this particular church, as it sat on the bluff like a lighthouse or sailors' refuge. In addition, it was one of the oldest structures in the region, dating back to the thirteenth century. Its interior design was perhaps its more unusual attraction, as the nave was covered not by traditional stone vaults but by a rounded wooden roof and truss system which strongly recalled not the mysterious heavens of most Gothic churches but the hulls of ocean-going ships. Even the cemetery, which lay at the front of the church and was filled with the deceased of local fishing families, had tombstones that contained nautical references and symbols for the sea. Little wonder, therefore, that Monet painted it so frequently; it clearly spoke on numerous levels about the human and the natural.

Monet often professed his love of the sea. "You know my passion for the sea," he told Alice Hoschedé in 1886, "I'm mad about it."[22] Hardly a year went by in the 1880s, therefore, that did not find him at the coast. Even as an old man in the twentieth century he longed to see the water and actually was driven to the Channel during the First World War in order to gain strength from its sight and smell. He claimed he wanted to be buried in a buoy, a wish that went unfulfilled, but the hundreds of pictures he painted of the waters on which he would have bobbed are more than permanent testimony to his favorite and perhaps most important subject.[23]

Although he only occasionally ventured out onto the ocean and then just to get from one place to the next, he clearly had special feelings for those who did so to earn a living.[24] One of his most moving portraits of the decade, for example, depicts the fisherman Poly (Pl. 128) whom he met when painting on Belle-Isle in 1886 and who became both his porter and his soulmate. Monet kept the picture all his life, hanging it in his Giverny studio above his desk,

128 (far left)  Claude Monet, *Portrait of Poly*, 1886, 74 × 53, W.1122, Musée Marmottan, Paris.

129  Claude Monet, *Portrait of Père Graff*, 1882, 64 × 81, W.744, Österreichische Galerie Belvedere, Vienna.

like an alter ego. Another was of Paul Graff, affectionately known as Père Paul, who ran the hotel in Pourville where Monet stayed in 1882 (Pl. 129). Although born in Alsace, this humble, accommodating man spent much of his life in this Norman town, something Monet suggests in his ruddy features and hoary beard. Monet's affection for his host was also due to Père Paul's abilities as a chef, which is why Monet portrayed him in his traditional white jacket and hat. A hearty meal—particularly by the coast—was something Monet always treasured.

The one place where his interest in the sea and maritime life gained its most poetic and often repeated expression was Étretat (Pl. 130). Monet worked in this ravishing spot twenty-eight kilometers north-east of Le Havre at least once prior to the 1880s; there is a single painting of its cliffs from the late 1860s when he was living in the town while working on his huge *Luncheon* (Pl. 49). But it did not attract his attention in a serious way until he went there for three weeks in the winter of 1883. He worked in the town every year thereafter until 1886. These extended painting trips resulted in more than sixty canvases, which was more than Monet executed of any other single site during the decade. As soon as he arrived on 31 January 1883, he knew he was in his element. "I should tell you I am very happy to have come here," he informed Alice, "it's truly wonderful and I believe that I am going to do some very good things."[25]

Étretat's appeal lay primarily in the fact that it sat right on the water, just like Pourville, and was relatively inexpensive. But even more than Pourville, Étretat claimed truly breathtaking cliffs. They curved out from the town in a crescent-like form before rising to tremendous heights, their multicolored, striated surfaces capped by contrasting lush green grass. Their most dramatic features, however, came at their northern extremities, as it was there that the winds and waters after centuries of wear had sculpted three spectacular arches and an immense free-standing pinnacle (Pls. 130, 131). All three arches were truly monumental. One emerged from the sea like a whale coming up for air, while the other two plunged into the waters like the arms or legs of some gigantic, prehistoric beast.

Two of these huge arches could be seen from the town itself. The one to the east was known as the Porte d'Amont, the one to the west was the Porte d'Aval. The Porte d'Aval had a wider opening than its eastern counterpart and a thinner arm or leg. It also was right next to the towering pyramid of independent rock known as the Aiguille (the Needle). It too could be seen from the town but only if one walked eastwards around the cove, as it was tucked

132    Claude Monet, *The Manneporte*, 1883, 65 × 81, W.832, The Metropolitan Museum of Art, New York, Bequest of William Church Osborn.

behind the Porte d'Aval. When the tide was low, visitors, like Monet, could venture out on the rocks and come right up to the Porte d'Aval, something Monet did during that first February campaign. One could also cut through the arch and come into another cove that was dominated by the third stone arch. Known as the Manneporte (for Magna Porta), it was the largest of the three arches and perhaps the most impressive. By its isolation and sheer size, it was both frightening and awe-inspiring, incomprehensible and yet incredibly physical. Its drama complemented the danger that lurked in reaching the cove. For when the tide rose access through the arch became impossible. Thus a visit to the Manneporte had to be carefully timed, as one could easily became trapped. Monet experienced something of this danger. While painting a view from this cove on 27 November 1885, a huge wave came in and swept him and all of his painting equipment into the sea. "I immediately felt myself lost," he told Alice Hoschedé, "for the water held me, but finally I was able to get out on all fours, but in what a state, good God! My boots, thick socks, and coat soaked . . . and my beard covered with blue [and] yellow [paint]."[26]

The drama of this site with its towering limestone arch is evident from many of the nearly twenty paintings Monet completed during that first extended visit to the town in February 1883. None, however, is more striking than Pl. 132. Monet positions the arch in this picture so that its massive left side is perfectly aligned with the left side of the canvas. He has it rise up that side to the very top of the canvas where he then stretches it across more than half of the scene. The cool blues and low-keyed beiges and pinks that Monet uses to describe the striations on the rock contrast with both the lighter sky beyond and the curved section of the

133 Claude Monet,
*Étretat, Rough Seas*,
1883, 81 × 100, W.821,
Musée des Beaux-Arts,
Lyon.

arch which is warmed by the sun streaming into the scene from the left. All of this contributes
to evoking the arch's massiveness. So too do the rough, painterly strokes Monet employs and
the fact that he has the arch plunge into the frothing, white-capped waters of the sea with such
apparent force. But what really provides the necessary sense of scale for this great, natural
form are the two sketchily rendered figures which stand on the darkened stone under the arch
to the left. Held just beneath the horizon and carefully positioned between the sloping foot of
the arch and the blue and white spray of a crashing wave, they are mere specks in the scene,
but they are critical as they suggest the size of this monumental element and the grandeur of
the site as a whole.

Whether working in this cove or elsewhere in the town, Étretat constantly inspired Monet
to contemplate the raw power of nature and the role the human was supposed to play in the
face of its splendor. Not surprisingly, therefore, he painted numerous pictures, such as Pl.
133, that depict the cliffs battered by waves that roll in under stormy skies while figures or
human surrogates look on. In most cases, he also tries to integrate the forms as if to suggest
some larger order or whole. The arm of the arch, for example, often appears like a flying
buttress lending the cliff tentative support. It also seems like the prow of a ship riding out the
storm. Similarly, the successive crests of the waves imitate the strata of the cliff and the
undulations of its ridge, while the straw-covered roofs of the three boats on the beach seem to
be a combination of these active and passive forces. The latter association is particularly
appropriate because these craft once were fishing vessels but had been retired and converted
into storage units which is why they have thatched roofs. While speaking about time and

134 Gustave Courbet, *Cliff at Étretat after a Storm*, 1870, 133 × 162, Musée d'Orsay, Paris.

change, the boats also suggest continuities and the rightful presence of the human in this drama. They sit steadfast and immobile on the beach, their triangular peaks, like the weightiness of their forms, providing a reassuring contrast to the windwhipped waters and the sea's continuous motion. They are not like the boats to the right, however, by which stand two old salts. Those boats are the active ones, the craft these sailors might have been using if the seas were not so rough. Monet implies this by placing the boats farther to the right and therefore closer to the open sea and by having their masts and booms jut out toward the water in contrast to the huddled storage facilities on the left.

That such associations between sea and shore, the human and the natural, were a conscious part of Monet's efforts can be affirmed when his picture is compared to numerous others by artists such as Delacroix, Jongkind, and Courbet, who had been attracted to Étretat prior to Monet and who had painted this very same site (Pl. 134). Monet even admitted to Alice that he had Courbet in mind before he began this picture. "I am planning to do a big picture of the cliffs of Étretat," he told her the day after he arrived in the town, "although it will be terribly audacious on my part to do this after Courbet who had done it admirably. But," he added with his typical competitiveness, "I will try to do it differently."[27] Thus, where Courbet's scene is placid and staid, Monet's is virtually seething. This is due principally to the different weather conditions each artist had decided to render but it also is the product of the way both treat various elements in the scene, such as the water. In Courbet's, the Channel stretches calmly into the distance; in Monet's, it occupies almost half of the picture plane. It also rises with a kind of fury much higher up the surface of his canvas. Although both artists depict the cliff with relative accuracy, Monet has it emerge from the waters above the midpoint of the scene and has it rise nearly to the top of the canvas. He also extends the arm of the arch slightly and, most important perhaps, boldly emphasizes the stratification of the stone, with the effect of extending the form laterally and making it appear more alive, like the water and sky above and below.

Most of the paintings Monet completed during his two campaigns in Étretat—nearly thirty-five out of sixty—include references to the town's traditional preoccupation with the sea, and often to the ruggedness of mariners' lives and the powerful forces they had to confront. Most Parisians would not have seen Étretat under these conditions as they generally came to the town in the spring and summer, not in the middle of February when Monet painted this picture. But it would have appealed to their romantic sensibilities and reaffirmed the lulling, though no longer accurate, notion that the residents of Étretat were all still fishermen. In actuality, most of the townspeople had abandoned that life to cater to the tourists and weekenders who invaded the port in the warmer seasons. The fact that Monet ventured there in the middle of winter and opted to render so many pictures that proclaim the continuity of a vanishing tradition is extremely important, as it suggests his desire to distance himself from the vacationing crowds and to draw closer to the original spirit and occupation of the place, much as he did at Varengeville.

This is not to say Monet was blind to Étretat's charms. There are plenty of paintings that reveal the beauties of the cliffs and the lure of the beach, none more seductively perhaps than *The Needle Rock and the Porte d'Aval* of 1885 (Pl. 135). This is the quintessential view for the Étretat tourist agency. Brilliant afternoon light fills the scene, warming the crest of the cliffs while turning them creamy white. They become the perfect complement to the pale blue and rose of their more shadowed lower sections. Below, water gently laps the beach which is conveniently deserted so that we can enjoy the view by ourselves. Beyond the protected cove and the almost perfectly positioned cliffs, the channel stretches into the distance where it greets the sun anew, changing from soft greens, blues, and hazy purples to a shimmering yellow-beige. Local fishing boats under sail enliven this area while a thin veil of clouds above provides an appropriately subtle contrast to the consistent azure tone of the sky. It was days like this that tempted visitors, such as Flaubert's Mme Dambreuse from *Sentimental Education*, to pick up a few stones from Étretat's rocky shore and bring them back to Paris to keep in their bedroom as mementoes of their stay.[28] And it was the ability of the place to offer such beauty while reaffirming fundamental values that brought Monet back year after year.

Between his major campaigns in Étretat in 1883 and 1885, Monet made two important decisions which had profound repercussions on his life and work. The first and most significant came in 1883 when he decided to move his family and the Hoschedés out of Poissy where they had relocated two years earlier. Poissy had offered better schools for the children than Vétheuil and initially had seemed attractive to Monet. However, Monet quickly came to abhor the town; after only two months there, he announced it was "horrible."[29] He suffered with his mistake until April 1883 when he finally moved everyone to Giverny, a small farming village some forty kilometers further down the Seine in the direction of Rouen and Le Havre. They settled into one of the largest houses in the village that was owned by a wealthy tradesman who had originally come from Guadaloupe and had recently retired to nearby Vernon. Known as Le Pressoir or the Cider Press, this pink stucco house and two-and-a-half-acre property would be his home until his death in 1926. At first, he rented it. Then, in 1890, when the estate came up for sale, he purchased it for 22,000 francs. It was only after he bought the property that he initiated its ambitious and expensive transformation into the floral and aquatic wonderland that preoccupied him for nearly forty years and that was so admired during his lifetime.[30]

The second important decision he made also came in 1883, at the end of the year. In mid-December, he decided to accompany his friend Renoir on a trip to the south. It was the first time since his military service in Algiers that he had been so far from home and the first time he had ever experienced the Riviera. He undoubtedly had been convinced by Renoir, who had recently come back from Italy by way of Provence, that there were wonderful things awaiting them there. He was not to be disappointed. The two artists spent almost two weeks

135 Claude Monet, *The Needle Rock and the Porte d'Aval*, 1885, 65 × 81, W. 1034, Sterling and Francine Clark Art Institute, Williamstown.

traveling from Marseille to Genoa and Monet was thrilled by what he saw. Upon his return to Giverny at the end of December, he soon decided to gather up his painting supplies and go back there to work. He informed Durand-Ruel of his plans, asking him "to say nothing about [it] to anyone, not because I want to make a mystery about it but because I want to go alone. I've always worked better in solitude . . . following my own impressions."[31] His first stop was Bordighera, a charming town just over the French–Italian border that he had visited with Renoir and had found to be "one of the most beautiful spots [they] had seen."

He arrived there around 20 January 1884, intending to stay a month. Much to his dismay, however, the town was more crowded than it had been during his previous visit. Even more disturbing was the fact that when he came down from his room for his first dinner in the hotel restaurant, he discovered he was the only French person in the place. That might not have been so bad, he told Durand-Ruel, but everyone else was "German." Revealing his nationalistic bent and his disdain for his neighbors across the Rhine, he "was not going to stay there at any price."[32] Without hesitation, he moved out immediately and "after great difficulty was able to find something more accommodating," a hotel that was dominated this time by English people whom he at least could tolerate.

As would so often be the case in the 1880s when he went to work in a new locale, Monet initially was both smitten with the beauty of the area and frustrated by his inability to find appropriate motifs. Then, once he had decided on what he was going to paint, he constantly complained about how difficult it was to render things as he saw them.[33] He also missed Giverny. "If I am happy to work in this beautiful area, my heart is always at Giverny," he told Alice.[34] After about ten days he had spent six or seven sessions on at least one canvas but claimed he could not bring it to a conclusion because he still "had not come to grasp the tone of the country." It was an "enchanted land" for which he needed a "palette of diamonds and jewels" but, as he announced to Alice a few days later, it was "delicious."[35] Monet soon got over his difficulties and became completely immersed in work, so much so that his initial intention of staying one month became seriously compromised; much to Alice's displeasure, thirty days grew to be almost ninety, an extension that became the norm for his travels during the decade. But when Monet returned to Giverny in the middle of April, he brought back approximately forty-five canvases. Although he would finish most of them in the quiet of his Normandy studio, he essentially had averaged about one painting every two days, making it an extraordinarily productive time. All of them are infused with the magical light of the Riviera and all of them contain some of the colors—pinks, oranges, and brilliant blues—that Monet claimed people would not believe existed there. In addition, they cover a broad range of subjects from more conventional, almost Corot-like, views of Bordighera crowned by the tower of the town church (Pl. 136), to astonishingly exotic paintings of olive groves (Pl. 137), in which the trees perform a provocative dance, their trunks and branches twisting and turning as if moved by seductive music or imbued with some kind of sensuous potion. There are also numerous views of palm trees and mountains, subjects that Monet had never tackled before, and more than a dozen pictures that depict the Mediterranean as seen from several sites along the coast—Ventimiglia, west of Bordighera, Monte Carlo, and Menton across the border in France.

Despite Monet's initial fears, these paintings became reaffirming proof of his ability to capture effects that were radically different from what existed in Normandy and the Ile de France. While attesting to his dexterity and the sensitivity of his eye, these pictures also underscored his ability to reinvent himself and demonstrated the flexibility of his Impressionist style. As such, they suggested that Impressionism, long associated with Paris and the north, could actually be responsive to a wider, more diverse geographical base, that it might even be adaptable to the nation as a whole, a notion that became increasingly important to Monet as the decade progressed. Finally, they proved that daring continued to be rewarded as they sold extremely well. Durand-Ruel, for example, bought twenty-one of them for a total of 18,200 francs. When combined with other sales that he was able to negotiate during the year, his income for 1884 approached more than 45,000 francs, as it had done in each of the two previous years. These were staggering sums that prove he was doing well, despite his letters to dealers and collectors in which he continued to claim the opposite.[36]

It may have been this financial security as well as the amount of time he had spent away from Alice and his family that caused him to concentrate on the Giverny area for new subjects to paint upon his return from the south. Although he went back to work in Étretat for several months in the fall and winter of 1885 and took a brief, two-week excursion to Holland during the tulip season in 1886, he focused his attention on the region around his new home for the next two years. This concentration resulted in nearly eighty paintings that, like his views of the south, are remarkably diverse. There are pictures of the Seine and its tributary, the Epte, in virtually every season; there are charming scenes of winding country roads and houses nestled into the rolling hills of the area, of orchards and poppy fields, prairies and newly harvested mounds of hay. Although most of these are set in and around Giverny, many were painted in neighboring towns—Bennecourt, Port-Villez, Limetz, and Vernon— suggesting, again like his views of the south, a new-found freedom to expand his repertoire as well as his base of operations.

136 Claude Monet, *Olive Grove in the Moreno Garden*, 1884, 65 × 81, W.869, Private Collection.

137 Claude Monet, *Bordighera*, 1884, 65 × 81, W.852, The Art Institute of Chicago, Chicago, Mr. and Mrs. Potter Palmer Collection.

While ranging widely in site and subject, this large group of pictures also spans the gamut in terms of quality from those works that are superbly painted with a keen sense of touch and novel compositional strategies, such as Pl. 138, to those that are surprisingly bland, if not ill-conceived, such as Pl. 139. The latter, to be sure, are in the distinct minority—they barely number more than eight or ten—but there are enough of them to suggest that Monet was not consistently at the height of his powers when working in this region. In part, this may have stemmed from the challenges of making pictures from subjects that often contained little drama. It also may have come from the fact that one of his major preoccupations between 1882 and 1885 was a commission from Durand-Ruel for no fewer than thirty-six modest-size paintings of fruits and flowers that were to decorate the doors of the dealer's Paris apartment (Pls. 140, 141). Charming, lusciously painted, and often quite novel in terms of their organization as decorative groups, these pictures were the kind that came easily to Monet. The commission therefore may have lulled him into a certain stasis, resulting in dips in his normal level of quality. His occasional lapses also might have had something to do with his being at home. When he was alone in a hotel far from his loved ones, work was his primary concern—indeed, the only reason for being there. When in Giverny, everything was comfortable and familiar. There also were many more distractions, all of which might have combined to reduce his drive.

In any case, Monet seems to have sensed this slackening off. In the summer of 1886, following a brief visit to Holland in late April and early May, he suddenly returned to a subject he had not tried in nearly a decade, almost life-size figures in contemporary dress painted out of doors in the brilliant light of day (Pl. 143). Recalling similar views he had done in the 1870s—specifically, one of Camille and Jean of 1875 (Pl. 142)—this picture depicts Suzanne Hoschedé seen from an extremely low vantage point, her light blue scarf blowing in the wind, her green-lined parasol shielding her from the strong rays of the sun. The light filtering through that parasol turns the upper half of her white gown pastel blue and lime green while the grass at her feet and the sky beyond tint her lower half with warm pinks, strong beiges, and light indigos. Like these seductive colors, everything in the picture breathes an air of extraordinary vitality, from the bold brushwork of the undergrowth in the foreground to the colorful chiaroscuro of Suzanne's radiant form. Even the sky seems particularly charged with its dazzling mixture of deep blues and whites and its remarkable, calligraphic brushwork. The picture, therefore, is clearly more than just a view of Alice's

138 (below left)
Claude Monet,
*Hoarfrost*, 1885, 60 × 80,
W.964, Private
Collection, United
States.

139 (below right)
Claude Monet, *View of Vernon*, 1886, 60 × 81,
W.1061, Private
Collection.

140 (above)
Anonymous,
photograph of the
Grand Salon of Durand-
Ruel's apartment at 35,
rue de Rome, n.d.,
Archives Durand-Ruel,
Paris.

141 Claude Monet,
*Basket of Grapes,
Quinces, and Pears*, 1883,
51.2 × 38.1, W.954,
Columbus Museum of
Art, Columbus, Gift of
Howard D. and Babette
L. Sirak.

142 Claude Monet, *Camille and Jean on a Hill*, 1875, 100 × 81, W.381, National Gallery of Art, Washington, Collection of Mr. and Mrs. Paul Mellon.

143 (far right) Claude Monet, *Woman with a Parasol*, 1886, 131 × 88, W.1077, Musée d'Orsay, Paris.

daughter, whose facial features are deliberately obscured by her veil. It also is more than just a picture of a contemporary woman en plein air. It is a kind of demonstration piece in which Monet reveals how many ways he can apply paint, render physical forms, and evoke the presence of intangible elements, such as light, atmosphere, and the passage of time.

These concerns, of course, had long been his preoccupation, but in pure landscape, not sites occupied by contemporary figures. In addition, the urgency that these pictures emit and the varying brushwork that they reveal are not to be found in his previous canvases. Although prompted perhaps by internal concerns about the direction his work was taking, this picture and its pendant (a complementary view of Suzanne turned the other way) undoubtedly were also the product of market pressures, something the facts of the moment seem to support. It is worth recalling, for example, that in the summer of 1886 Monet was 45 years old. He had been working and exhibiting in Paris for nearly half of his life. He had established a strong base of support among dealers and collectors which had earned him a reputation as an artist of considerable talent, as well as a great deal of money. But that year also saw forces come to a head that had been brewing for some time.

First was the disintegration of the Impressionists' group. The group had always been a loose conglomeration of highly individualistic artists. Durand-Ruel had exhibited some of their works together in group shows at his London gallery in the early 1870s prior to 1874 when they banded together to stage their own exhibitions in Paris and promote their art. Between 1874 and 1886, they had mounted eight such shows (in '74, '76, '77, '79, '80, '81, '82, and '86). Each exhibition, however, was the result of a supreme effort on the part of two or three members of the group who took it upon themselves to convince other members to drop their differences and act in concert. Those same few also shouldered the responsibility of securing a reasonable space, gathering, hanging, and guarding the work, and then trying to ensure positive reaction in the press. Not surprisingly, all of the shows were marred by bickering and backbiting. Each show also had been quite different, primarily because the participants were never the same (Pissarro was the only member of the core group that exhibited in all eight). In addition, the location changed from year to year, as did the number of works each artist included.[37]

As one show followed the next, the reaction of the press became relatively predictable; conservative critics lambasted the group, centrist and liberal reviewers found much to praise. The biggest problem, therefore, was convincing participants it was worth their while. By the end of the decade, that had become increasingly difficult, if not impossible, as artists began to go their own way. Sisley dropped out of the '77 show; Renoir followed him in 1879. The following year the two of them were joined by Monet. In 1881, none of the three participated. In '82 the three returned, but Degas refused to participate. A lot of nasty things were said during these years. Caillebotte became furious with Degas in 1881 when he threatened to abstain, claiming he was "a bad character" who had "gone sour." "He spends his time orating at the Nouvelle-Athènes, when he would be much better occupied in turning out a few more pictures."[38] Gauguin labelled participants in the 1881 exhibition such as Raffaëlli "cipher[s]" and "schemers," while Renoir lambasted Pissarro the following year calling him a "Jew" and a "revolutionary." He also declared that to exhibit with "Gauguin and Guillaumin [and Pissarro] would be like exhibiting with any Socialists."[39] Monet felt the entire group had lost its integrity. "Our little temple has become a dull schoolroom," he told a journalist in 1880, "whose doors are open to any dauber."[40]

In this struggle, the merits of Impressionism as a style were seriously questioned. Renoir felt he had wrung it dry and returned to Italy to study Raphael and the antique in 1881.[41] Pissarro started to doubt its efficacy at the same time and began to develop a more highly conscious criss-cross stroke that had the texture and appearance of thatched straw. This made his pictures look more brazen but also less faithful to nature and thus more distant from the Impressionists' original principles. One of the biggest blows to the style, at least in the eyes of artists like Monet who were attempting to promote it, appeared to have been delivered by Emile Zola. The novelist had been one of the group's strongest supporters, hailing them with unabashed enthusiasm when they emerged in the 1860s. By the later 1870s, he had grown lukewarm, feeling they "were merely the forerunners of a modern school" and that their leader, Monet, "does not study nature with the passion of true creators."[42] In the mid-'80s, he struck what many of them felt was the death knell with the publication of *The Masterpiece*. The hero of this story was Claude Lantier, a mad genius of a painter whose character was largely based on Manet and Cézanne. Like the Impressionists as a whole, he fights the art establishment, insisting on the primacy of painting from nature and his ability to realize his dream of artistic perfection in a single work of art. The story turns tragic halfway through, however, as Lantier comes to doubt himself and his craft, ruins the monumental canvas which was to embody his dream, and ultimately ends up committing suicide.[43] As soon as the story began to appear in serial form in *Gil Blas* in December 1885, the Impressionists had reason to worry, as Lantier's tale of frustration and failure had too many parallels with their own struggles. When it came out in book form, Zola sent copies to many in the group, Monet included. Monet could not refrain from telling his former ally what he thought of the work. "I have always had great pleasure in reading your books," he admitted to the novelist, who had gained a national reputation by the time this new novel appeared. "This one interested me doubly because it raises questions of art for which we have been fighting for such a long time. I have read it, and I remain troubled, disturbed, I must admit. You took care, intentionally, that not one of your characters should resemble any of us, but in spite of that, I am afraid that the press and the public, our enemies, may use the name of Manet, or at least our names, to prove us to be failures, something which is not in your mind—I refuse to

144 Georges Seurat, *Sunday on the Island of the Grande Jatte, 1884*, 1884–84, 207.6 × 308, The Art Institute of Chicago, Helen Birch Bartlett Memorial Collection, Chicago.

believe it.... I have been struggling fairly long and I am afraid that in the moment of succeeding, our enemies may make use of your book to deal us a knockout blow.''[44] Monet's fears were not borne out; the book received mixed reviews among the critics and was soon pushed aside by Pierre Loti's romantic *The Iceland Fisherman*, which appeared in June 1889 and soon became one of the most popular novels of the century.

While spared potential fallout on that front, Monet and his colleagues undoubtedly were feeling vulnerable because at the very same time they were facing one of the most serious challenges they had experienced to date. It began in 1884 when the young Georges Seurat (1859–91) burst upon the Paris scene with his monumental *Bathers at Asnières* and then two years later stunned his avant-garde elders with his astonishing *Sunday on the Island of the Grande Jatte*, a picture which measured 2.05 × 3.05 meters (nearly 7 × 10 feet) and was nothing less than a direct assault on the style and subjects of his Impressionist forebears (Pl. 144). It appropriated the very matter that had been central to Impressionism but which most of the Impressionists had abandoned by then, namely contemporary figures seen out of doors engaged in leisure activities. More importantly, he had rendered this scene of modern urban life in a completely novel way—with thousands of tiny touches of paint that maintained their independence across the surface of the canvas. And, perhaps most important, he had been given the opportunity to demonstrate his prowess in the very center of the Impressionist circle. Pissarro had invited him to participate in the Eighth Impressionist Exhibition which took place in Paris between 15 May and 15 June 1886. Pissarro had been convinced that Seurat's new divisionist style was the answer to his own search for a way out of Impressionism. Not only did he invite the 27-year-old artist to join the exhibition, he also adopted his more mechanical style, claiming he was "personally convinced of [its] progressive character ... and certain that in time it will yield extraordinary results."[45] His opinion was shared by a number of critics who reviewed the show and who noted that Seurat's divisionism was destined to replace Impressionism as the avant-garde idiom.[46]

Monet clearly felt the pressure. He left for his brief visit to Holland just as final plans for the opening were being made. More importantly, he refused to join the show. And then, as soon as he returned from the lowlands, he began his studies of figures en plein air. This certainly was no coincidence; clearly these paintings were his response to the challenges posed by

Seurat and Pissarro as well as to the classical figure paintings that Renoir was producing at the same time, together with the figural work by Morisot. Their painterly surfaces, therefore, are forceful affirmations of Impressionism's vitality, their balmy winds and brilliant light attestations to the style's ability to evoke nature truthfully and energetically. Even the integration of the figure with her environment bespeaks Impressionism's inherent belief in the importance of direct contact with nature. How radically different the scene is from Seurat's crowded island whose hierarchic occupants remain distant from one another, like Egyptian sculpture in a seemingly mechanically distilled world.

Monet had declared his willingness to be Impressionism's figurehead and leading practitioner much earlier in the decade. In 1880, for example, when queried about his defection from the group, he categorically declared, "I am still an Impressionist and always will remain one."[47] Unlike Renoir or Pissarro, he stuck with the style despite abandoning its roots in depictions of modern life. Indeed, he even tested its limits during his painting campaigns in the north and south and had not found it wanting. But in 1886, he must have realized he was truly on his own and that if Impressionism was going to continue to be a viable style equal to the likes of Seurat's pseudo-scientific method, it was up to him to prove it. Thus his return to figure painting. Thus also a rare self-portrait—the first of only two in his career—which Monet painted during that same summer of 1886 (Pl. 146).

This introspective, deeply personal picture which Monet never sold or exhibited in his lifetime is ample testimony to the weightiness of his position and the mixture of worry and determination that it provoked. Dressed in his blue working-man's smock, his head crowned by a typical French beret, Monet looks at himself with eyes that are full of inquiry. His wrinkled forehead and protruding brow suggest concern, something that also is implied in the bold contrast of light and dark that divides his face in half. Worry is implied elsewhere— in the intensity of his stare, his turned head, and unkempt beard. It is felt as well in the smock—in the way it shifts to the left as if pulled by unseen forces, in the tension between its more carefully rendered left side and its summarily realized right, and in the way it creates a strain between the shapes of the blue sweater and those of the white color on either side of Monet's neck. Even the background is a study in contrast as the left side is rendered with forceful, independent strokes that rise rapidly up the canvas before leveling out to caress the soft edge of the beret and then dissipate on the right. Like the figure studies from the same summer, Monet is applying paint here in as many ways as possible, just as he is pitting his abilities to manipulate his liquid medium against his talents as a draughtsman. He certainly seems up to the challenge, for while everything initially appears open to question, it is apparent that every stroke has been set down with such astonishing confidence that the outcome is virtually foregone. Although critics and colleagues continued to throw him barbs, this was not to be a war of words for Monet; his lips are tightly sealed. Instead, it was a battle about how painters see the world and how they render visual form with tubes of colors and tools of the trade.

Soon after the exhibition closed and Monet's novel self-portrait and figure paintings were completed, he left for Belle-Isle, a windswept, ocean-pounded island in the Atlantic south of Brittany (Pl. 145).[48] This

145  Anonymous, photograph of Belle-Isle, Musée Marmottan, Paris.

147 Claude Monet, *The Rocks at Belle-Isle*, 1886, 63 × 79, W.1107, Musée des Beaux-Arts de Reims.

was perhaps the most dramatic site he had painted to date, as its fierce *côte sauvage* was a sheered-off mass of volcanic black rock that dropped precipitously to the swirling waters of the ocean. As in Étretat, time and weather had left their marks here although, unlike the former's refined white arches and pyramid of limestone, the Atlantic had clawed and gouged the black walls of this rock in a much more violent way. The stone therefore was deeply scarred in irregular patterns while multiple coves had been punctured all along the coast when huge sections of the island finally giving way to the relentless forces of nature collapsed into the water, occasionally leaving isolated needle rocks as mementoes of their former selves. Nothing could have been further from the gentility of Giverny or the task of painting his sun-drenched female figures en plein air. Nothing also could have been further from the Riviera. But like all of those previous pictures as well as his self-portrait, Monet was here to push himself to one more extreme and thus to demonstrate the versatility of his maligned, but still vibrant, style.

As with his trip to the south, Monet intended to stay on Belle-Isle for just a few weeks. Nearly three months later, he finally returned to Giverny. Although he had to brook Alice Hoschedé's ire constantly during the latter part of his stay, it proved to be a productive trip. He brought home nearly forty pictures including the portrait of his porter, Poly (Pl. 128). Once more, his productivity was a direct result of his enthusiasm for the place which he communicated to Alice in ecstatic terms on almost a daily basis. "I am going to set myself up in the little hamlet of eight or ten houses, near the place called *la Mer Terrible*," he told her after only two days on the island. "It's well named; not a tree for ten kilometers, some rocks and wonderful grottoes; it's sinister, diabolical, but superb."[49] Four days later, he informed her that everything was "so different from the Channel."[50] "The sea is incomparably beautiful," the rock formations "fantastic."[51] Almost a month later, his sense of the place was the same. "The further I go, the more I find the area pleasing; the landscape is superb."[52] The pictures confirm the excitement Monet felt: they are filled with dramatic rock formations, theatrically set against stretches of water that extend to deep horizons (Pl. 147). Many of them depict violent storms that lashed the area that fall (Pl. 148). Some suggest the remote, almost

146 Claude Monet, *Self-Portrait*, 1886, 56 × 46, W.1078, Private Collection.

148   Claude Monet,
*Storm off the Coast of
Belle-Isle*, 1886, 60 × 73,
W.1117, Private
Collection.

149   Claude Monet,
*Needle Rocks at Belle-Isle*,
1886, 60 × 73, W.1086,
Ny Carlsberg
Glyptotek,
Copenhagen.

exotic, character of the place as Monet renders oddly shaped, volcanic forms wrapped with
strange flora and illuminated by fanciful light. Perhaps the most impressive pictures,
however, are those that concentrate on the huge needle rocks that were located in the cove
known as the Port-Coton, for example (Pl. 149). Like shards from some ancient land, the
rocks rise up to various heights, few daring to overlap another. The tallest two in the center
arc their sculpted forms as if straining to see something in the distance. Monet does not allow
them to break the horizon, however, holding them eternally in their locked combat with the
sea.

What is also striking about these views is their similarity. Monet painted six of this very same site, some of which could almost be mistaken for replicas of others. This is also true for pictures he painted in the five or six other sites that he visited on the island. Monet, therefore, clearly set out to limit the number of motifs he would render and on top of that to restrict the compositional options he would exercise. He even used relatively consistent-size canvases for each group. While binding, these decisions also appear to have forced him to be even more exacting in his description of natural phenomena and thus were a conscious part of his strategy to trumpet his abilities as a painter and underscore the subtlety of his Impressionist style.

Critics recognized this when Monet exhibited eight of these pictures in the Sixth International Exhibition at Georges Petit's in the spring of 1887. Joris-Karl Huysmans, for example, was deeply moved by them and called Monet "the most significant landscape painter of modern times."[53] Alfred de Lostalot felt they possessed "the power to silence the critics."[54] Both writers were struck by the forcefulness of Monet's efforts. "You have to admire these feverish canvases," de Lostalot asserted, "for despite their intense color and rough touch, they are so perfectly disciplined that they easily emit a feeling for nature in an impression filled with grandeur." Many writers also noted their interrelationships, seeing them as forming a distinct group or series.[55] Gustave Geffroy, who from this moment onwards became one of Monet's staunchest supporters, went even further. "All of these forms and these glimmers of light speak to one another, collide with each other, influence one another, saturate each other with color and reflections." In his opinion, these paintings were the product of "a rustic alchemist, always living out of doors . . . [who is] active enough to be able to begin several studies of the same motif under different lighting conditions in the same afternoon [and who] had acquired a singular ability to see the disposition and influence of tones immediately." Geffroy was speaking from first-hand knowledge; he had gone to Belle-Isle in the fall of 1886 to write a book on the anarchist Blanqui, had met Monet, and watched him work. In his review of the Petit show, he also included a description of Monet's methods. "Quickly, he covers his canvas with the dominant values, studying their gradations, contrasting [and] harmonizing them. This procedure gives the paintings their unity. The color of the rock and the sea, the tint of the evening, and the disposition of the clouds suggest the shape of the coast, the movement of the sea, and simultaneously, the time of day. Look at these thin bands of clouds, these limpid, gloomy effects, these fading suns, these copper horizons, the violet, green, and blue seas, all these states so far from a singularly defined nature, and you will see mornings dawn before you, middays brighten, and nights fall."[56] This was the kind of description of Monet's work that was repeated over and over again, particularly in reference to his series paintings of the following decade. Although embellished by Geffroy's enthusiasm for "the prince of the Impressionists" (as the Australian painter and Belle-Isle resident, John Russell, called Monet in 1886), it nonetheless underscores the importance of the Belle-Isle campaign and points to the subtle shift towards greater focus and refinement that was taking place in Monet's art.

Monet did not want to be typecast, however, as specializing in a single theme. "One has to do everything," he told Alice while on Belle-Isle, "and it's precisely because of that that I congratulate myself for doing what I'm doing."[57] The desire to do it all had never been so strong but, of course, neither had the contemporary scene been so competitive. It was undoubtedly because of that pressure that Monet decided shortly after his return from Belle-Isle to tackle the antithesis of the "somber and terrible" island and go back to the south, this time to Antibes and neighboring Juan-les-Pins. For an avowed painter of sunlight, these Mediterranean resorts were ideal. Well known for their wonderful weather, they allowed

150   Claude Monet,
*Antibes Viewed from La
Salis*, 1888, 65 × 92,
W.1167, Private
Collection.,

151   Claude Monet,
*The Beach at Juan-les-
Pins*, 1888, 73 × 92,
W.1187, Private
Collection.

152 Claude Monet, *A Bend in the Epte*, 1888, 73 × 92, W.1209, Philadelphia Museum of Art, The William L. Elkins Collection.

him another opportunity to demonstrate his range as an artist while revealing how responsive his style could be to the geographical offerings of the nation as a whole.[58]

As in Brittany, Monet produced an astonishing number of paintings—again almost forty—in a relatively short period of time, from mid-January to the end of April. He also limited his motifs to a mere half-dozen and tried once more to extract subtle variations among the pictures in each suite. He was perfectly aware of the dangers inherent in this strategy. "I should guard against repeating myself," he admitted to Alice, a caution that was worth voicing as the weather was remarkably consistent (unlike at Belle-Isle) and the area, as he noted, "not very diverse."[59] A combination of these factors, perhaps together with his often expressed concern about being out of his element, resulted in certain paintings that are not as varied as those from Belle-Isle. In others, however, such as Pls. 150 and 151, he captured all the brilliance of the sites while providing a keen sense of their seductive appeal. Undoubtedly that is why Theo van Gogh purchased ten of them for the gallery Boussod and Valadon, another rival to Durand-Ruel, and staged an exhibition just of these works in June 1888, barely a month after Monet had returned from the south. For the second year in a row, therefore, Monet's claim to the leadership of French painting was going to be based on closely related canvases of a single locale, something once again that did not go unnoticed in the press. Geffroy made it a central part of his review, claiming Monet had been able to capture in these works "all that was characteristic about the area and all the deliciousness of the season."[60]

In contrast to most of the critics, however, Monet's former colleagues had few kind words for these pictures. Pissarro thought they were "beautiful" but that "they do not represent a highly developed art."[61] Renoir found them "retrograde," Degas, strictly commercial. They were "paintings ... made to sell," Degas told Pissarro, an opinion Felix Fénéon, Seurat's chief defender, voiced in his review as well.[62] Monet's reaction was swift. Revealing the divisions that existed between himself and the once single-minded avant-garde, he told Theo van Gogh that Fénéon's review "could have been anticipated."[63] He then proceeded to

153 (above left)
Claude Monet,
*Wheatstacks.* (*Morning Effect*), 1888–89, 65 × 92, W.1214, Private Collection.

154 (above right)
Claude Monet,
*Wheatstacks.* (*Sunset*), 1889, 65 × 92, W.1213, Museum of Modern Art, Saitama, Japan.

paint his most direct assault on Seurat and his Neo-Impressionist followers, a picture which depicts a bend in the Epte River near his Giverny estate (Pl. 152). Three-quarters of the surface of this canvas is covered with discrete touches of paint that are supposed to represent the fluttering, light-filled foliage of the curving line of poplars. But the touches are so individualized and so rich with pigment that they assert their abstract presence as paint as much as they describe any natural phenomena. Although deftly handled and virtually unique in Monet's work, they are inconceivable without Seurat's or Pissarro's divisionist dots. Monet takes almost every opportunity, however, to distinguish his touch from theirs. He limits his imitation of their style to the foliated areas, particularly that on the left. He then sets those areas off against the more typically Impressionist brushed water and sky. Most importantly, however, he makes his imitative touch much livelier than any Neo-Impressionist would dare by using dashes and curling strokes often laid one on top of the other instead of the stricter, more uniform divisionists' dots. He also has these seemingly more spontaneous touches appear to be moving into the illusionary space of the picture as if they literally were being blown by the breeze which passes through the scene. What Monet is doing here, therefore, is ironically and defiantly appropriating Seurat's idea and then bending it to fit a quite different goal, one more in line with the freedom and empiricism of his own Impressionism. He was, in short, outdoing the divisionists and asserting his superiority in the face of their ridicule.

The culmination of this counter-offensive came shortly after he completed this picture when the farmers of Giverny cut their fields and began their age-old ritual of constructing stacks made from hundreds of sheaves of bound stalks of wheat (Pls. 153, 154). When those stacks rose to their traditional height of fifteen to twenty feet and were capped with their thatched, conical roofs, Monet began a suite of five paintings that depicted these massive, sentinel-like forms under different lighting and weather conditions. These pictures, which he completed over the next few months, were the first of what eventually became thirty paintings of these same huge stacks and which constituted Monet's famous *Wheatstack* series. Even more than at Belle-Isle, Antibes, or Juan-les-Pins, he now was systematically going to extract variation upon variation from the same motif, one that would have rung familiar to everyone who had been in the French countryside. What better way to reaffirm the value of Impressionism and his leadership of French avant-garde art?

Monet interrupted his work on this series in early 1889 with a trip to the Creuse Valley

155 Claude Monet,
*Valley of the Creuse.
(Sunlight Effect)*, 1889,
65.1 × 92.4, W.1219,
Courtesy of Museum of
Fine Arts, Boston,
Juliana Cheney Edwards
Collection.

156 Claude Monet,
*Valley of the Creuse.
(Afternoon Sun)*, 1889,
73 × 92, W.1223,
Private Collection.

about three hundred kilometers south of Paris in the Massif Central. He was only going to stay a week or two with the poet Maurice Rollinat, a friend of Gustave Geffroy who had invited Monet to accompany him on the trip. However, Monet was so impressed with the area that he went back to Giverny to retrieve his painting supplies and returned to the Creuse for a stay of more than three months.[64] Monet was deeply moved by what he called the "lugubrious" qualities of the place with its primal hills and haunting sense of desolation, characteristics he deftly captured in the nearly two dozen paintings that he completed by late May 1889. Critics were impressed with these canvases, fourteen of which Monet exhibited (together with over one hundred and thirty other works) in a major retrospective with Auguste Rodin in the summer of 1889.[65] Of those fourteen, seven concentrated on the same site—the confluence of the Grande and Petite Creuse rivers (Pls. 155, 156). With their consistent focus and nearly uniform size, their extraordinary effects of light and color and their range in terms of the times of day, as well as the fact that they were all done with forethought during a limited period of time, these confluence pictures could be considered Monet's first completed series. Nearly every critic who mentioned these "tragic landscapes" was struck by the ruggedness of the motifs—"the narrow valleys filled with shadows, the ravines cut by a torrent, blocks of rock in tormented forms."[66] Paul Foucher, the critic for *Gil Blas*, found them to possess "an incomparable majesty" while the Belgian writer, Octave Maus, asserted that "of Monet's entire oeuvre it is perhaps these [canvases] that reveal the most extraordinary mastery."[67]

For almost a year after this very successful exhibition, Monet surprisingly did not paint a single picture. It was the first of many often unexplained spates of inactivity that he was to experience over the next thirty years. In this case, he had a legitimate excuse—he was completely preoccupied with a project that he had initiated to donate Manet's *Olympia* to the

157 Anonymous, "The Beautiful Olympia at the Louvre," caricature from *La Vie Parisienne*, 22 February, 1889, Musée Marmottan, Paris.

136

State, an undertaking that came to fruition only after an immense amount of time and effort.[68] The problem was not only raising the money—20,000 francs—which required an intense letter-writing campaign, but also overcoming the government's resistance. Officials did not relish the idea of having to accept the one canvas, with its blatant nudity, harsh chiaroscuro, and crude application of paint, that so clearly represented the avant-garde's successful assault on the country's heralded artistic traditions. That Monet devoted twelve months of his life to this project, therefore, is significant. On one level, it speaks about his affection for Manet and his widow who needed the money and his rightful recognition of the painting's value and stature. It also suggests his generosity, while underscoring the financial position he enjoyed—few, if any, of his colleagues could have afforded to take that much time off. On another, it attests to his self-appointed role as the leader of advanced painting in France. Despite their economic circumstances, none of his colleagues seemed to want to take on the project. None, therefore, probably felt more satisfaction when, after months of maneuvering that revealed his considerable skills as a tactician and negotiator, Monet finally received word that the picture would be accepted *sans engagement* and would be hung in the Musée du Luxembourg before eventually moving to the Louvre. The victory prompted more invective from conservatives and a hilarious, double-page caricature in the popular weekly *La Vie Parisienne* which depicted the cat-carrying Olympia striding through the columns of the Cour Apollion into a harem of women clipped from famous paintings and sculpture in the museum (Pl. 157). Monet must have found this image particularly satisfying as he owned at least one example of it. He did not go to the official opening ceremonies, however, demonstrating his continued disdain for such functions, but he could not resist visiting the museum a little while later. Nor could he hold back from telling Berthe Morisot that the painting "never looked better."[69] Monet had vindicated Manet and secured him his rightful place in the annals of nineteenth-century French art. As Manet's heir, Monet also had gained a toehold in those hierarchies for himself. And when he returned to his own work, specifically to his *Wheatstack* pictures, he knew that his art too could become part of the nation's patrimony, and that, like Manet, he also could be recognized as one of France's great artists. Unlike Manet, however, he would gain his due primarily by painting subjects drawn from the French countryside, especially ones that resonated with meaning for his countrymen and women in the 1890s.

158 Claude Monet, *Oat Fields (Giverny)*, 1890, 73 × 92, W.1257, Private Collection.

# 6 Monet in the 1890s: the Series Paintings

When Monet took up his palette and brushes again in the spring of 1890, he concentrated primarily on subjects around his Giverny estate that suggested the bounties of the soil and the poetry of rural light. The largest number of pictures he produced were more than a dozen views of flowing fields of hay, oats, and poppies, such as Pl. 158, all of which are filled with the freshness of the day. Despite the lack of human figures, these pictures exude a sense of fullness. It is felt in the way the oats stretch as far as the eye can see while appearing to extend well beyond the confines of the canvas on either side. It also is apparent from the rich, impastoed surfaces which even contain bits of straw, proof that they were at least begun en plein air.

For all of their visual fecundity, however, these paintings were really transitional pictures. They returned Monet to the occupation he had abandoned for so long and affirmed a new-found interest in distinctly agrarian subjects. But as soon as the wheatstacks rose once again on the landscape, Monet put these field canvases aside, not finishing some until months later and others not until 1892. Over the course of the next five or six months—from late August or early September 1890 to some time in February 1891—he threw himself into the series he had halted for his trip to the Creuse and his tribute to Manet.

He became so obsessed with his wheatstack project that he not only delayed the delivery of several oats and poppy paintings that Durand-Ruel had purchased, but also deferred making drawings after other paintings that the dealer wanted to reproduce in an up-coming issue of his newly founded magazine, *L'Art dans les deux Mondes*. Monet's excuse was always the same. "I am in the thick of work. I have a huge number of things going and cannot be distracted for a minute, wanting above all to profit from these splendid winter effects."[1] When Monet had been away from home on painting campaigns in the 1880s, he often became preoccupied with work in this manner. But when he was painting around Giverny he never had been quite as intense, suggesting the importance he placed on these *Wheatstack* pictures. In addition to the effects he found so attractive and the weather conditions that winter which were unusually accommodating (it rarely went below 15°F), his enthusiasm for his work surely rested on the fact that he was developing something entirely new. For no other painter up until then had ever conceived of painting a large number of pictures that concentrated on the same subject and that would be differentiated only by formal factors—color, touch, and composition—as well as by different lighting and weather conditions. Printmakers, of course, always worked in multiples and many artists, even during Monet's own day, thought nothing of making duplicate versions of particular paintings (Monet copied his own portrait of Camille). Artists also considered certain paintings they did as constituting suites or groups. But those pictures were always more varied in terms of their sites and subjects than Monet's more limited *Wheatstacks*, or they were done with a preestablished sequence in mind—the months of the year, for example, or the seasons, something Monet scrupulously avoided.

While Monet conceived, executed, and eventually exhibited these *Wheatstack* paintings as a series, he did not go about his task in a mechanical fashion. He did not use the same size canvas for all thirty paintings, for example; they vary considerably. Nor did he place them all in exactly the same frames; he exhibited at least two of them in white frames. More importantly, he neither stood in exactly the same spot for all of the pictures nor rendered the passage of time with such accuracy that the canvases would act like a collective chronometer. Thus when all of them are lined up they do not transport the viewer from dawn to dusk or demonstrate the changes the stacks underwent from one specific moment to the next. Most significantly, perhaps, the series did not derive from a single experience that Monet had on a particular day, despite his later claims to a biographer that the idea for the series came to him merely by accident. "When I started, it was just like the others," he asserted. "I thought two canvases were enough—one for a "gray" day, one for a "sunny" day. At that time I was painting wheatstacks that had caught my eye; they formed a magnificent group, right near here. One day," he continued, "I noticed that the light had changed. I said to my stepdaughter, 'Would you go back to the house, please, and bring me another canvas?' She brought it to me, but very soon the light had again changed. 'One more!' and, 'One more still!'" he cried. Poor Suzanne Hoschedé had very little time to rest between her commutes to the house because Monet said he "worked on each [canvas] only until I had achieved the effect I wanted; that's all. It's not very difficult to understand," he added coyly.[2]

Even a cursory glance at the paintings, however, reveals the duplicity of these statements, as their carefully constructed surfaces and striking color harmonies are clearly the result of many working sessions. The pictures also attest to the kind of decision-making process that was essential to their success. Monet pays special attention, for example, to the relationships of the stacks to each other and to the distant houses, barns, and poplars. He is also extremely sensitive to the positions of the stacks relative to the horizon and the meteorological activities above. Although he generally was faithful to what lay in front of him, he never felt bound merely to reproduce his chosen site. There were many stacks in the fields by his house where he painted these pictures (Pl. 159), but he always opted to include only one or two, thus

159 Anonymous, photograph of wheatstacks behind Monet's house at Giverny, 1905, from Louis Vauxcelles, "An afternoon with Claude Monet," *L'Art et les Artistes*, December 1905, 90.

keeping his scenes simple, something he accomplishes as well by dividing most of the canvases into three basic rectangular bands of field, hill, and sky, and by pulling the stacks into the foreground which makes them substantial actors on their respective stages. In order to achieve the most effective compositions, he even alters the size and positions of the stacks and occasionally changes the way their shadows fall upon the ground. He also tampers with effects that he initially set down in order to differentiate one canvas from another while preserving an internal unity for the group as a whole.[3] All of this editing and rearranging occurred not on the site but in the studio, thus undermining the claim he and his supporters professed that these pictures were done exclusively en plein air.

Although unreliable, Monet's insistence on the simplicity of his enterprise and its spontaneous origins parallels his admission to Gustave Geffroy that he was merely pursuing "instantaneousness" or the envelope of light that surrounded the stacks.[4] For all of these concerns focused attention on the distinctly Impressionist qualities of the series—that it was not programmatic, that Monet followed his instincts rather than his intellect, and that he ultimately was completely beholden to nature, all of which were exactly the opposite of the Neo-Impressionists' aesthetic as well as of mainstream academic art. This was a conscious part of Monet's strategy as these intricately related canvases were going to demonstrate the subtleties of Impressionism and its truthfulness to nature. They were also going to reveal its ability to evolve as a style. And by concentrating on a limited motif, Monet could show how difficult it was to paint an Impressionist picture, thereby silencing the critics who claimed the style was propagated by mindless individuals who manipulated their medium in a random and undisciplined manner.

One senses these concerns in the pictures themselves as the canvases breathe an air of extraordinary refinement. Nature becomes a source of wonder and fulfillment, a power at once elusive and omnipresent, chilling and restorative. Even more than previous paintings, particular moments in time seem to have been snatched—instantaneously—from the complex passage of hours, while lighting and weather conditions appear to have been rendered with greater accuracy than before. The paint itself seems to have been applied by someone who was deeply moved by the site while the colors appear to have been chosen for their emotive impact as much as for their allegiance to reality. The pictures, therefore, are imbued with grandeur and speak about issues that are larger than their apparent subjects—time and change, innocence and ageing, tradition and modernity.

Although essential to any contemporary landscape painter and evident in Monet's earlier pictures of the 1880s, these issues are expressed in the first canvases in the series, such as Pl. 160, with a unique combination of naivete and conviction. As the series progresses, they become even more insistent (Pl. 161), as the stacks themselves grow in size and majesty until they finally fill virtually half of the scene, as in Pl. 162. Monet might well have felt these urges more intensely following his campaign on Belle Isle and the paintings he completed in 1887 and 1888 that directly confronted his Neo-Impressionist challengers. But he also must have understood that such effects when heightened would serve to differentiate him from his contemporaries and make him appear free of all influence whether past or present. And by having such emotive effects dance across motifs that were so clearly linked to the French countryside, he also could affirm his affection for *la belle France* while demonstrating his ability to make new art out of old subject matter.

These tactics were not lost on his friends and supporters when Monet exhibited fifteen of his stacks at Durand-Ruel's in early May 1891. According to the outspoken novelist and cultural critic, Octave Mirbeau, for example, who became one of Monet's most vocal spokespersons from the later 1880s onwards, Monet's revolutionary work was "due to [his]

160   Claude Monet,
*Wheatstacks. (Full
Sunlight)*, 1890,
60 × 100, W.1267, Hill-
Stead, Museum,
Farmington.

161   Claude Monet,
*Wheatstacks. (Effects of
Snow, Morning)*, 1890–
91, 65 × 100, W.1276,
Private Collection.

moral isolation, self-focus, [and] immersion in nature." Mirbeau asserted Monet did not go
about his work in a haphazard fashion; he did it "according to a methodical, rational plan, of
inflexible rigor, in some ways mathematical." Mirbeau even went so far as to claim that
Monet's entire art was the product "of reflective thought, of comparison, analysis, [and] a
knowing will," a not-so-veiled claim to some of the science and forethought that critics felt
rested with his competitors, Seurat and the Neo-Impressionists.[5]

142

162  Claude Monet,
*Wheatstack. (Sunset)*,
1890–91, 73.3 × 92.7,
W.1289, Courtesy of
Museum of Fine Arts,
Boston, Juliana Cheney
Edwards Collection.

Gustave Geffroy had perhaps the most poetic response to the series, feeling that Monet had
"unmask[ed] changing portraits . . . of the landscape, the manifestations of joy and despair,
mystery and fate."[6] In the catalogue he wrote for the show, Geffroy focused specifically on
the stacks themselves, which he felt "look[ed] like gay little cottages set against a background
of green foliage and low hills. They stand erect beneath the bright sun in a limpid atmosphere
. . . . At the close of the warm days . . . the stacks glow like heaps of gems. Their sides split and
light up. Later still, under an orange and red sky, darkness envelops the wheatstacks which
have begun to glow like hearth fires."[7] Geffroy's empathy for the stacks is important as it
suggests their significance as a motif—something various other writers underscored as well.
No one perhaps was as moving or as surprising as Felix Fénéon, Seurat's primary supporter.
"In the evening sun especially, the wheatstacks are exalted," he wrote. "In summer, they are
given a halo of dark, red, flickering sparks; in winter, their phosphorescent shadows stream
over the soil and against the sky . . . they shimmer, enameled blue by a sudden frost."[8] While
"a fulcrum for light and shadow," as Geffroy put it, the stacks clearly touched common
chords, and rightfully so as their isolation, gestures to each other, reactions to the light, and
weighty, steadfast presence endowed them with deep feeling.

Having now lived in Giverny for almost a decade, Monet certainly knew the meanings
these stacks possessed for the farmers of the community. He suggests this in the ways in which
he pairs the stacks with the houses and barns in the distance, repeating their triangular shapes
as well as their thatched roofs. The pairings are as appropriate as they are poetic: the stacks
actually functioned as storage facilities, protecting the farmer's wheat until the spring when

163 Jean-François Millet, *The Angelus*, 1855–59, 55.5 × 66, Musée d'Orsay, Paris.

the grain could be more easily separated from the stalk and chaff. The stacks, therefore, were not only built by the occupants of those humble structures in imitation of the farmers' own houses, they literally were the farmers' livelihood as well as their hopes for the future. The stacks also represented the fruits of the farmers' labors and the fertility of their fields while standing as reassuring testimony to the continuities of agrarian traditions and the health of rural France. Little wonder, therefore, that one critic claimed the paintings "expressed the mysterious sounds of the universe [and] the impression of a generous and benevolent life," as this wholesome, fecund countryside, devoid of laboring peasants, ultimately represented the rural ideal, a place that could reaffirm widely shared ideas about the value of *la terre française* to the life and stature of the nation.[9]

The notion that France's greatest strength lay in the fields and forests of her rural acreage was as old as the country itself. But the idea had gained considerable appeal in the later nineteenth century as the country's cities and industries grew exponentially and the pace of life increased in kind. It was manifested in a variety of ways, although never so dramatically within the arts at least as in 1889 when one of France's most celebrated images of rural life— Millet's *Angelus* (Pl. 163)—was sold to an American collector, James Sutton of New York. The event caused a national outcry, with passionate protests in the press and heated debate in the Chamber of Deputies—all to no avail, as the picture left its native soil for the "land of the Yankees" as Monet referred to the United States.[10] But it did not stay abroad too long. The following year Sutton, recognizing a significant business opportunity, sold the painting to the head of the Magazin du Louvre who promised to leave it to the nation. When Sutton's courier arrived in France with the beloved picture, he was greeted by none other than President Carnot and his wife, the head of the Chamber of Deputies, and a section of the army band. Carillons in Paris churches rang out with joy and the country breathed a sigh of relief. The icon of rural France was now safely home for good.

Not surprisingly, when Monet began his *Wheatstacks,* landscape paintings—specifically, views of agrarian France—dominated the annual Salons and were some of the most popular subjects for decorative schemes in public buildings in Paris and its suburbs. They also comprised a third of all of the paintings in a huge exhibition organized for the world's fair in 1889 that traced French art since 1789. Monet's pictures, therefore, were perfectly timed, something Roger Marx noted in his review of the *Wheatstacks* when he stated that they "will be judged topical" for, like Barbizon art before him, these canvases for Marx "symbolize and sum up the labor, the sowing, and the harvesting, all of the harsh fight with the elements to fertilize the land, all the arduous and superb work of the earth."[11] With an implied reference to the temporary loss of the *Angelus*, Marx even regretted that "impatient America, who is always stealing our masterpieces, has already made off with more than one work in the series," as if these distinctly French paintings should remain in France because they proclaimed the national belief in *la belle France*.

By the early 1890s, the country needed that affirmation. It could take pride in its many advances, particularly in the light of its defeat in the Franco–Prussian war only twenty years earlier. But if it looked across its eastern border to its hated German neighbors or across the seas to England and America, it found that it had slipped behind those nations in virtually every area of production, including the arts. This had been made painfully apparent by the World's Fair of 1889. For the products these other countries had brought to Paris for that show were deemed vastly superior to those France herself exhibited, particularly in the realm of the decorative arts, formerly France's almost exclusive domain. This disaster caused the Minister of Culture to send envoys east and west to find out why these countries had been able to surpass his nation's once-exalted artisans, an inquiry that ultimately spurred the development of what became known as Art Nouveau.[12] Thus paintings like Monet's *Wheatstacks* with their evident novelty and skill as well as their emphasis on the beauty and prosperity of the countryside did much, no matter how naively, to allay nascent fears about the nation's state of affairs. Like all good art, they also clearly functioned in complex ways, "beyond their apparent subjects," as Désiré Louis, the critic for *L'Evénement*, wrote after seeing Monet's show. "His skies ... resonate with the mysterious sounds of the universe," Louis asserted. "He forces the spirit to think and to soar above these magisterial representations ... of reality. In front of [these] seductive painting[s], you have the impression of a full and benevolent life which makes you recall the intoxication one feels with the dawning of a new day."[13] Little wonder, therefore, that the critic for *Le XIXe Siècle* claimed that Monet was a "naive, sincere, moving, lyrical painter of nature and all things [who] will take his place among the greatest artists who painted the landscape of France."[14] It was a prediction that Monet soon would realize.

No sooner had he finished the *Wheatstacks* than Monet began his next series of paintings, this time of poplars along the Epte river just a few kilometers from his house (Pls. 164–67). He obviously was confident about his new mode of procedure; he started this series even before the *Wheatstacks* went on exhibition. But he also clearly wanted to challenge himself, as everything about these paintings—from their vertical formats and lyrical compositions to their more decorative palettes and broader handling—was the opposite of the *Wheatstacks*. It was one more way to demonstrate his versatility as well as the range of his Impressionist style and thus stay at the forefront of the Parisian avant-garde.[15]

His choice of subject again was significant in this regard as, like the *Wheatstacks*, poplars were distinctly associated with the French countryside. Svelte and elegant, the trees were traditionally planted along roads and entrances to châteaux as decorative additions. They also were used as windshields for tilled fields and as a form of fencing to divide rural property. They grew quickly—generally twenty-five to thirty feet in ten to fifteen years—making

them highly marketable. In fact, like the stacks, they often were grown as a crop, harvested at their peak for firewood or wood products such as matches, boxes, and building materials. The trees Monet chose to paint are a case in point as they had been planted by the town of Limetz on communal property about two kilometers south of Giverny. And on 18 June 1891, several months after Monet had begun his pictures, the town fathers voted to auction the trees off. When Monet learned of this, he immediately went to see the mayor to plead for a delay in the sale which was scheduled for 2 August. His words fell on deaf ears, however; the auction would proceed as scheduled. Monet then decided to go to the auction and some time before the bidding began met a wood merchant who was interested in purchasing the trees. "I asked him how high a price he expected to pay," Monet later told a biographer, "promising to make up the difference if the bid went over his amount, on the condition that he would buy the trees for me and leave them standing for a few more months." When the gavel came down, Monet and the lumberman were co-owners of the poplars.[16]

The story suggests how much Monet invested in his motifs, his financial commitment in this instance being the literal proof of the personal, aesthetic, and metaphorical significance that he found in his subjects. Although he would harmonize all of the *Poplars* in his studio after bringing them to a certain state of finish, just as he had with the *Wheatstacks*, the story also reveals how strongly Monet felt about working on the pictures en plein air. By choosing a subject that was so distinctly French and painting it, in this case twenty-four times, he also

was affirming the French roots of his art while appealing to strongly held beliefs about his nation and its character. For in addition to the poplar's familiarity and its practical applications, the tree had been selected after the French Revolution as the tree of liberty. Poplar-planting ceremonies occurred often throughout the century even down to Monet's own day (Pls. 168, 169).[17] Thus the tree resonated with meaning for patriotic citizens just as it spoke with eloquence and clarity about the charms of the French countryside—operating, therefore, like the wheatstacks, on many interrelated levels.

It is the beauty of the countryside, of course, which Monet emphasizes the most in these pictures, as many of the canvases are bathed in fresh, radiant light and are filled with bold colors that are applied with remarkable gusto. Unlike the staid and solid wheatstacks, the trees appear lithe and limber throughout the series. And instead of sitting immutably on the land like their conical counterparts, they move through their scenes in a seductive but stately fashion, often swaying to a kind of internal rhythm, their foliage rustled by an evident wind. For most of the canvases, Monet heightens these aspects of the series by assuming a low vantage-point, probably from the little *bateau atelier* that he had had built during his years at Argenteuil. He positioned his floating studio near where the river bent back on itself to form a reverse S-curve. This allowed him to stretch the trees and their reflections from the bottom of the canvas to the top and to counter that flexible grid with the slow sweep of the trees beyond as they curve right and then left before disappearing in the distance. The patterns the

166 (above left)
Claude Monet, *Poplars. (Summer)*, 1891, 93 × 73.5, W.1305, The National Museum of Western Art, Tokyo, Matsukata Collection.

167 (above right)
Claude Monet, *Poplars. (Evening Effect)*, 1891, 100 × 65, W.1292, Private Collection.

168 (above left)
Anonymous, *The Curé of Saint-Eustache Blessing the Tree of Liberty in the Marché des Innocents in Paris*, 26 March 1848, lithograph, from Roger Price (ed.), *1848 in France*, Ithaca, 1975, 65.

169 (above right)
Anonymous, *The Poplar as the Tree of Liberty*, ca. 1790s, Collection Flinck, Cabinet des estampes, Bibliothèque Nationale, Paris.

trees create, together with Monet's evident manipulation of paint and often striking color combinations, draw attention to the formal elements at his disposal. In Pl. 166, for example, the brushwork is so vigorous that description is almost overwhelmed by painterly bravura, just as the colors here or in Pl. 165 are so fanciful—down to the array of orange-yellows, blue-greens, and mauves in the trunks—that accuracy is clearly forsaken for pure chromatic flare reminiscent of Delacroix or eighteenth-century rococo predecessors. Even more than the *Wheatstacks*, therefore, these paintings create a tension between the artifice of the scene and Monet's desire to create the illusion of forms occupying space. By tipping the equation in favor of the former, however, and by allowing the most basic elements of art to carry visual weight, Monet clearly was encouraging his viewers to indulge in the aesthetic delights of the paintings, to immerse themselves, in the end, in the paintings' decorative powers.[18]

This was not new for Monet. His commission from Durand-Ruel in the mid-1880s entailed thirty-six decorative panels for the dealer's Paris apartment. He also had executed a number of pictures in the 1870s that he himself labeled and exhibited as *panneaux décoratifs*, including *The Luncheon* of 1873 (Pl. 96). His interest in the decorative was widely recognized, sometimes to his detriment. In the 1880s, for example, he was often criticized for indulging in this side of his craft, particularly by Degas who, according to Pissarro, went so far as to label Monet "a skillful but not a profound decorator" after seeing Monet's *Antibes* pictures of 1888.[19] Among their many achievements, the *Wheatstacks* undoubtedly had been a way to counter those charges, for while they gained in significance from being seen together, they also staunchly maintained their independence as individual canvases. The same is true for the *Poplars* although their relationships are often narrower and more intricate, as if Monet was testing the limits of his new procedure in order to extract even more startling variations.

That Monet stressed painting's decorative dimensions in these *Poplar* pictures more forcefully than before was hardly coincidental as the issue was of keen concern to many of his contemporaries. When Renoir went to Italy in the 1880s, for example, he was most attracted by Raphael's decorative paintings for the Vatican while Pissarro converted to Seurat's Neo-Impressionism not only for its more scientific orientation but also for the harmonious patterns and decorative surfaces it encouraged. In the later 1880s, younger artists, such as Paul Sérusier (1863–1927), Emile Bernard (1868–1941), and Paul Gauguin (1848–1903), had proclaimed their disdain for painting's age-old allegiance to description. They felt the craft now should explore more subjective phenomena by denying Renaissance perspective and traditional modeling. Thus one of their supporters, Archille Delaroche, could claim "the artist will interest us less by a vision tyrannically imposed . . . than by a power of suggestion that is capable of aiding the flight of the imagination or of serving as the decorator of our own dreams, opening a new door on the infinite and the mystery of things." In his opinion, Gauguin was the best of this new breed as "he seems to have understood the role of suggestive decoration. His procedure is notably characterized by a curtailing of particular features [and] by the synthesis of impressions. . . . If he represents jealousy for us it is by a blaze of pinks and violets in which all nature seems to participate . . . If mysterious waters gush from lips thirsty for the unknown, it will be in an arena of strange colors, in the ripples of some diabolical or divine beverage." Everything in his work hovered between "the indeterminate threshold of the conscious and the unconscious."[20] The ultimate extension of this anti-illusionism was expressed by Maurice Denis who declared in 1890 that "a picture—before being a battle horse, a nude woman, or some anecdote—is essentially a plane surface covered with colors assembled in a certain order."[21] This new orientation was championed by numerous other artists as well as writers, such as the distinguished critic Albert Aurier who asserted in 1891 that decorative art was the highest form of painting as it was "at once subjective, synthetic, symbolic, and ideistic."[22]

Monet did not intend to allow these challengers to Impressionism to co-opt the issue of decorative painting. Nor was he going to let them move the issue away from its inherent ties to nature, the most decorative of all phenomena in the world. In addition, he was not going to turn, like Gauguin and others, to "primitive," anti-naturalistic prototypes such as stained glass and non-Western sources, to accomplish his ends. Rather, he was going to root his work in forms that were easily recognizable and distinctly French, ones that strongly recalled the greatest achievement in decorative art the nation had ever known, namely the rococo. This again is not by coincidence. For the whiplash curves of the rococo, which derived from nature, and its evident artifice became the widely shared touchstone for decorative artists in France following the World's Fair of 1889. It also became the focus of the government's attention, as cultural officials initiated massive restoration projects in the 1890s of rococo buildings in and around Paris, including the Château de Chantilly and the long-neglected eighteenth-century rooms at the Bibliothèque Nationale. The government also devoted huge sums to establish a Department of Decorative Arts at the Louvre with a mandate to concentrate primarily on eighteenth-century artifacts.[23] Such measures reaffirmed France's traditions and collectively contributed to the nation's quest to reclaim the cultural supremacy she had so long enjoyed during the reigns of Louis XIV, XV, and XVI when the rococo became not only a national style but one that was imitated by virtually every other country in Europe (Pl. 170).

It was precisely this kind of stature that critics hoped French painting of the later nineteenth century would recover, after having languished from mid-century onwards in what was widely perceived as unfortunate mediocrity. In the early 1890s, many of these observers believed the breakthrough would occur if artists plumbed decorative painting of the past. Such study would lead artists back to the nation's patrimony and to some of her greatest painters, such as Le Brun, Watteau, and even Poussin, all of whom were considered to have

170  Jean-François Cuvilliés, the Yellow Room, the Amalienburg, Munich, 1734–39.

171 Andō Hiroshige, *Numazu, Yellow Dusk*, woodblock print from *Fifty-three Stations on the Tokaido*, Museum of Fine Arts, Boston.

been decorative artists. If their achievements could be united with the advances of the nineteenth century, France might rise once again as the international leader of the most heralded art form of painting.[24]

When Monet exhibited fifteen of the *Poplars* at Durand-Ruel's between 1 March and 10 March 1892, people saw them in this light, praising them for their novelty and their decorative splendor. Even to conservative critics, such as Raymond Bouyer, it appeared that Monet had been able to develop the ornamental aspect of painting to a greater degree in these pictures than ever before. Bouyer also felt that Monet had greatly contributed to the future of French landscape art, which he saw as tending toward the decorative and paintings "full of allurement and nobility."[25] Georges Lecomte, the liberal critic for *Art et Critique,* concurred, claiming that "decorative beauty ought to be the distinctive sign of our era" and that Monet should be seen as one of its leading practitioners. "Finally," he proclaimed, "the vigorous talent of Claude Monet . . . seems more and more to abstract the durable character of things from complex appearances, and by a more synthetic and premeditated rendering, to accentuate meaning and decorative beauty."[26] Lecomte was careful to distinguish Monet's achievement from the efforts of other painters engaged with the same problem by emphasizing Monet's attachment to nature. He insisted that the artist's desire to describe the world was "never sacrificed to decorative preoccupations," unlike people such as Maurice Denis who "cover canvases with flat tones that do not at all restore the luminous limpidities of the atmosphere, that do not at all give the envelope of things, the depth, the aerial perspective. . . . [Such artists] concern themselves with expressing faith by plastic means," he asserted, "and on behalf of religion they sacrifice the essential plastic qualities of [painting]."

The Japanese were widely seen by French observers as masters at extracting decorative patterns from nature, much as Monet achieved in his *Poplars*. Théodore Duret even went so far as to claim the series was inspired by Hiroshige's *Numazu, Yellow dusk*, from his *Fifty-three Stations on the Tokaido* (Pl. 171).[27] Although Duret's suggestion was too extreme, Japanese art was critical to this series, just as it had been important to Monet's thinking ever since the 1860s when nineteenth-century woodblock prints, which had begun to flood Paris at the time, started to make their impact felt in his work. His interest in these prints and those from the eighteenth century that soon followed eventually became a passion. He avidly collected them, particularly in the 1880s; by the 1890s, his house at Giverny was beginning to be filled with them. His keenness for things Japanese was also evident in his dining room which he painted two bold shades of yellow, imitating colors that Hiroshige's contemporary Katsushika Hokusai frequently used (Pl. 172). He even owned an everyday china service that was dark-blue imitation Japanese. Monet and his Impressionist colleagues were enamored with the accomplishments of their Eastern counterparts not only because they paralleled their own interest in contemporary subject matter and relied so obviously on the decorative elements of their medium, but also, and perhaps most importantly for Monet, because it was widely believed that Japanese artists derived their talent from their deep feeling for nature. Nature was their "constant guide," asserted Siegfried Bing, the great promulgator of things

150

Japanese in the 1890s, their "sole, revered teacher . . . and inexhaustible source of inspiration."[28] Geffroy even claimed that all Japanese artists, regardless of their ultimate speciality, began their careers as landscape painters because "life in the open air [in Japan] mingles man and nature together . . . and sets humanity against a background of earth, sky, and water."[29]

As these romantic comments imply, most people in France naively believed Japan was a kind of Eden and that Japanese artists were Rousseau-like innocents unaffected by the progressive changes that had so altered the West. According to most French commentators, therefore, Japanese artists were able to

172  Monet's dining room at Giverny.

move beyond verisimilitude to higher planes of sensation, which is why they were often perceived as being gifted decorative artists. It also is why someone like Roger Marx could assert in 1891 that Japanese art "is intuitive, spontaneous, full of unerring tact and innate delicacy," precisely what Monet was attempting to affirm in his *Poplar* paintings.[30]

But as is true with all of Monet's work, none of the *Poplars* actually looks like any Japanese prints. The surfaces of the paintings are more manipulated, their colors more varied, their effects more refined. Monet artfully evoked Eastern sensibilities while staunchly maintaining his native French roots, a combination that set him apart from his contemporaries who often copied Japanese forms or created "oriental" genre scenes based on information gleaned from Japanese art and romantic novels by Pierre Loti. The Frenchness of his pictures was brought home by the critic for *L'Ermitage* who pointed out that Monet would earn his rightful place in the annals of his country's art not only because he was so inventive and attuned to natural phenomena but also "because he understood the poplar, which summarizes all the grace, all the spirit, all the youth of our land."[31] His public seemed to concur; Monet had sold all fifteen *Poplars* by the end of the show.

Many of these sales were conducted before the show even opened, a marketing tactic Monet had devised with his *Wheatstack* exhibition. It automatically made the pictures rarer while giving them an immediate provenance, something Monet underscored by including the names of the owners in the catalogue for the show. The sales before the opening must have been a significant encouragement to this often-disgruntled artist. For in addition to providing him with substantial funds, they gave him the confidence to begin his next series before shipping any of the *Poplars* to Durand-Ruel. In fact, in February 1892, more than four months before the *Poplar* show opened, he was installed in the front rooms of a vacant apartment in Rouen with more than a dozen newly primed canvases that soon would be part of his great *Cathedral* series. The apartment looked out on to the place de la Cathédrale in the old medieval section of the town (Pl. 173). The square was lined on three sides with shops and houses and dominated on the fourth by the Cathedral itself (Pl. 174). It was from these quarters and from two others just down the street on the same side of the square that he painted what became his most challenging suite of pictures, twenty-eight views of the façade of the Cathedral and two of its old western tower.[32] These thirty pictures preoccupied him from early 1892 until May 1895 when he finally exhibited twenty of them at Durand-Ruel's, again to great acclaim. Monet had never spent so much time on any other paintings; nor had

he agonized quite so much. His letters to Alice during his stays in Rouen are filled with his cries of pain and woe. "Good God," he told Alice on 25 February barely two weeks into the project, "what work this Cathedral is! It's terrible."[33] "Things don't advance sensibly," he informed her about a month later, "primarily because each day I discover something that I hadn't seen the day before.... In the end, I am trying to do the impossible."[34] In mid-April 1892, he returned to Giverny "absolutely discouraged and unhappy with what I have done. I do not even want to unpack my canvases or see them for a long time," he complained to Durand-Ruel.[35]

His grousing was only part of the truth, however, as over the course of the next few weeks he willingly showed the pictures to various visitors—so often, it seems, that he felt obliged in early May to invite Durand-Ruel to come and see them for himself.[36] It is impossible to know what state the canvases were in, but it appears that he did not work on them again until the following February when he returned to Rouen for another three-month bout. During the almost ten-month interval, he painted very little, a lapse that was prompted both by what he described as "the deception" of his Rouen campaign and by family matters. Suzanne Hoschedé married the American painter Theodore Butler in July 1892; Monet himself married Alice just four days earlier as a way of legalizing their relationship and permitting him to walk Suzanne up the aisle as her lawful stepfather.[37] But when he returned to the ancient capital of Normandy in February 1893, he "got right back into my subject," as he told his new wife. "I am very happy that I made the decision to return, as it will be better [than last year]," although he admitted to her that "this confounded Cathedral is tough to do."[38] Monet voiced this complaint with increasing intensity as the weeks elapsed. "I am furious at myself," he told Alice at the end of the month. "I am doing nothing of value; I don't know how many sessions I have spent on these paintings, and do what I may, they don't advance.... It's depressing."[39] By the end of March, he admitted to Geffroy what the critic had heard often before: "Alas, I can only repeat this: the further I go, the more difficulty I have rendering what I feel; ... anyone who claims to have finished a picture is terribly conceited."[40]

As March gave way to April, Monet had to admit that conceit was one of his own problems. "I can certainly account for my state [of mind]. I am a proud person with a devilish self-esteem," he told Alice. "I want to do better and want these Cathedrals to be very good. [But] I can't."[41] One of the problems was the weather which proved to be enormously fickle, forcing him to abandon canvases for considerable periods of time until the same effects returned. Another problem was the fact that he had limited himself even more than in the *Wheatstacks* or *Poplars* to a permanent, man-made motif that he observed only from indoors in a major urban environment. Little wonder that he occasionally felt he was out of his element or that he had "not made any headway." It was a staggering undertaking that often required him to work on as many as a dozen canvases a day. One day in March 1893, he put his brush to a record fourteen.[42] Just keeping them all in order would have been a challenge.

Once again, however, the thirty in the series were not intended to be seen as charting the passage of light across the church's façade with such specificity that one could determine exactly what time of day each represented. Like the *Wheatstacks*, they were not to act like a collective chronometer. Monet emphasized this by painting many examples that have no evident time-frame and by giving titles to only a few of the thirty that indicate a moment during the day. Even there, however, the moments are generalized—morning effect, for example, or sunset. And Monet did not hang them sequentially, despite the fact that critics described them as moving from dawn to dusk.[43]

If this kind of tracking was not his intention, what was he attempting to achieve with these pictures? He told a journalist that the idea for the series originated in the late 1870s when he was painting the church at Vernon. "I discovered the curious silhouette of a church, and I undertook to paint it. It was the beginning of summer ... fresh foggy mornings were followed by sudden outbursts of sunshine whose hot rays could only slowly dissolve the mists surrounding every crevice of the edifice and covering the golden stones with an ideally vaporous envelope. This observation was the point of departure of my *Cathedral* series. I told myself it would be interesting to study the same subject at different times of day and to discover the effects of the light which changed the appearance and coloration of the building, from hour to hour, in such a subtle manner."[44] As with the story about the origins of the *Wheatstacks*, this statement cannot simply be accepted at face value. It, too, came long after the fact. In addition, it was the church at Vétheuil not Vernon that he had painted in the mist, a project that had occurred nearly fifteen years before he began the *Cathedrals*, making for an extremely long gestation period. The statement also fits the pictures too snugly while making them appear to be part of an underlying continuity in his work. Moreover, it separates the pictures from their immediate predecessors and Monet's aspirations of the moment. And it minimizes the importance of Monet's choice of motifs.

Few motifs could be more French than a Gothic cathedral. Born on the Ile de France in the twelfth century, the style first spread across the nation and then conquered the continent, penetrating remote villages and lasting for more than four hundred years. Its staying power was formidable—it had been enthusiastically revived in France in the nineteenth century, primarily through the efforts of people such as Viollet le Duc, Victor Hugo, and the Inspector-General of French Monuments, Ludovic Vitet (who had changed his name from Louis to its more medieval version). Viollet claimed the Gothic was "fashioned from our materials and in our climate, to suit our character," while Louis Courajod, the curator of medieval art at the Louvre in the 1890s, insisted in 1894 that people should shun a current vogue for the ancient world and turn to the era of the great cathedrals. "Let us loosen the stranglehold that pagan Rome has on us for a second time," he pleaded, "so that the nineteenth century will not end without our finding ourselves again completely, openly, and absolutely French."[45] Thus, even more than the wheatstacks and poplars, Rouen Cathedral could be read as uniquely nationalistic, just as it could be understood on multiple levels. It had

been built between the twelfth and the sixteenth centuries, so it encapsulated the entire medieval era while bearing witness to the changes the Gothic style experienced.[46] Its eclecticism was sometimes criticized by architectural purists but for Monet the different styles undoubtedly were physical testimony to the passage of time as well as to the ingenuity of the medieval architects and stonemasons. It was the largest and most impressive of the many churches in Rouen and one of the oldest Gothic structures in the province. It also was one of the most original, particularly in its detailing. Sitting in the old, medieval section of the city, it was one of the few major cathedrals in France that encouraged visitors to conjure up what the middle ages might have been like, something many artists who rendered it prior to Monet attempted to suggest. Rouen Cathedral had attracted dozens of French painters and printmakers as well as some of the greatest figures in English art, including Turner and Richard Parkes Bonington (1801–28), long before Monet decided to paint it. Thus, when he focused his attention upon it, he was placing himself in a long and distinguished tradition.

Equally important for Monet, perhaps, was the fact that the Gothic was widely understood as an organic style, grounded in nature and uniquely artful. Victor Hugo even claimed cathedrals were unique products of democracy.[47] The Gothic had its spiritual dimension, of course, something religious groups of the 1890s and artists such as Maurice Denis and Alexandre Séon tended to emphasize.[48] But, as a strident agnostic, Monet downplayed that

aspect of his subject; in fact, he did not even enter the Cathedral until he was well into his project and then only to attend a 300-person choral recital to which he had been given a free ticket.[49] Instead of evoking the mysticism of religion or what Pissarro called the plague of "superstitious beliefs" which were becoming increasingly popular in the 1890s, Monet emphasizes the wonders of nature, whose light and atmosphere literally invade the stone façade and transform it into a specter of extraordinary splendor.[50] Whether it be through the blues and pinks of early morning (Pl. 175), the heated oranges and whites of midday (Pl. 176), or the mauves, browns, and lavenders of a typically Norman overcast day (Pl. 178), it is nature and Monet's ability to translate it into paint that triumph here, not the dogmas that had been the Cathedral's initial *raison d'être*.

Monet's sensitivity to the natural effects he observed are just one factor that make these pictures so remarkable; the way he manipulates his medium contributes to their majesty as well. For the surfaces of these canvases are literally encrusted with paint that Monet built up layer upon layer like the masonry of the façade itself. In fact, they are so scumbled that they almost appear to contain small particles of stone in mock imitation of their motif. That is not the case, however, although it is extremely difficult to determine exactly how the pictures were painted. It is as if they were the product of someone endowed with atavistic powers, not merely a person laying paint with a brush on a flat surface. Little wonder that even Monet

177　Claude Monet, *Rouen Cathedral. Façade. (Morning Effect)*, 1892–94, 100 × 65, W.1355, Private Collection.

178 (above right) Claude Monet, *Rouen Cathedral. Façade. (Grey Weather)*, 1892–94, 100 × 65, W.1321, Musée d'Orsay, Paris.

could decry what he was doing, claiming near the end of almost six months of work on the series that his pictures were only "encrustation[s] of colors, and that's all." "That is not painting," he moaned, and by most traditional criteria, he was correct.[51]

Monet put the group aside in early 1895 to visit Jacques Hoschedé who had married a Norwegian widow and had moved to Christiania (present-day Oslo) where he plied his trade as a shipbuilder.[52] The trip seems to have been prompted primarily by Jacques's lack of communication with his mother and family and by Alice's desire to know if he was ever returning to Giverny. As his recently legalized stepfather, Monet may have shared Alice's concern. However, he also knew enough about the landscape of the north through friends such as Fritz Thaulow to be interested in seeing it at first hand. The trip from Giverny took three days. "It's a difficult voyage when you are no longer 20 years old," he joked to Alice.[53] When he arrived, he was disappointed. The fjords were frozen and everything was covered with snow. After two weeks, however, his opinion improved; he expressed his admiration for a 100-meter frozen waterfall, majestic mountains, and huge frozen lakes. Unfortunately, he found nothing he wanted to paint, which made him think seriously about going home. "I may suddenly take the path back to France," he informed Alice, "having no taste for a country that I cannot paint. In addition, I am too old to be going off to foreign lands."[54]

A few days later, Jacques took him to Sandviken about three-quarters of an hour outside of Christiania where he finally settled down to work, moved by a number of sites in the area. The most important of these was Mount Kolsaas, which rose like Cézanne's Mont Sainte-Victoire from the flattened plains on the outskirts of the town through a ring of conifer trees to an impressive though gradually assumed height (Pl. 179). When working on these pictures, Monet complained that the country "was very difficult to understand" and that he "needed to live there for a year to do anything good," but this mountain clearly touched significant chords in him as he painted it no fewer than thirteen times.[55] In addition to recalling Cézanne's favorite motif, the mountain made Monet think specifically of Japan. "I

156

am also doing a mountain that one can see from anywhere here and that makes me think of Fuji-Yama," he reported to Blanche Hoschedé on 1 March.[56] Never having been to the East, Monet clearly was associating the two mountains through his knowledge of Japanese prints. He owned several prints from Hokusai's thirty-six views of Mount Fuji (Pl. 180), which undoubtedly were his reference points. But Monet extended the analogy to the town as a whole, telling Blanche it "looks like a Japanese village." This association, too, may have been prompted by *ukiyo-e* images but it also may have arisen from the way the Norwegians lived close to nature, just as Monet believed their Japanese counterparts did. He therefore felt like a hero when he

180 Katsushika Hokusai, *Mount Fuji Seen from the Umezawa Manor in the Province of Sagami*, from *Thirty-six Views of Mount Fuji*, 1829–33, British Museum, London.

worked outside in the cold longer than any of his Scandinavian hosts. It was further proof that he was able to better the competition, even if it was hundreds of miles from France.[57]

When Monet returned to Giverny in the first week of April, he reported to Durand-Ruel that "I am not too unhappy with what I have done," an assessment that must have pleased the dealer since he had been waiting for over eighteen months to finalize plans for Monet's next exhibition.[58] That show occurred the following month when Monet finally put nearly fifty paintings before the public, including twenty of his *Cathedrals* and seven of his *Kolsaas* pictures. The former attracted the most attention, with some critics expressing real reservations about them. Ary Renan, for example, writing in the weekly *La Chronique des Arts et de la Curiosité*, thought Monet's handling of paint was "strangely troubling" while André Michel in the centrist *Journal des Débats* thought that these pictures were "the final exacerbated expression of sensation" and that Monet had taken painting to a point where it "had nothing left to say."[59] But they were in the minority, for the overwhelming number of people who saw the *Cathedrals* during the month they were exhibited agreed that they were a triumph. "I am carried away by their extraordinary deftness," Pissarro told his son. "Cézanne . . . is in complete agreement . . . this is the work of a well-balanced but impulsive artist who pursues the intangible nuances of effects that are realized by no other painter."[60] Viewers were struck with how vital the building became in Monet's hands. It seemed to become an animated object, growing ever more alive with the increased intensity of the light (an effect Monet enhanced by emphasizing the building's irregularities far more than its symmetries). Many people also saw poetic elements in the pictures, prompted particularly by Monet's handling of light. Others made analogies to musical harmonies.[61]

One of the most contentious issues concerned Monet's choice of subject. Critics saw it either as insulting and inappropriate, or as forceful and liberating according to their political bias. Camille Mauclair, for example, who by 1895 had become the cultural spokesperson for the Symbolist review *Mercure de France*, found it offensive. Although Mauclair called Monet "the most prodigious virtuoso that French painting has seen since Manet" and "the premier painter of his era," he felt that "musical, Provençal colors laid on to this medieval structure with such insolence is the disturbing sign of a genius without a sense of the order of things. . . . that Gothic art, the cerebral art *par excellence*, is being used as a motif by this superbly pagan [artist] is a bit repugnant."[62] Mauclair was a conservative Catholic, so it might be only natural that he felt a cathedral should be treated with greater respect, an opinion that also derived from his sense that subjects of national importance should be accorded a certain dignity. More open-minded Symbolist writers, however, such as Henry Eon, saw the issue differently. Eon artfully co-opted the pictures and their creator, feeling that Monet had painted "a phantom cathedral ... mysterious and mute ... and that the almost fantastic impression [he] has been able to draw from the Cathedral of Rouen adds a new and truly curious note of mysticism to his glory."[63] Monet undoubtedly was pleased to receive the support of Symbolist critics like Eon, who found much to enjoy in what he described as uncharacteristically "spiritual" paintings; the more praise the better, even if the accolades were based on skewed notions about the pictures. Given his unyielding agnosticism, however, it is much more likely that Monet would have found the reactions of people such as his new-found friend and soulmate, Georges Clemenceau, to be closer to the mark. Similarly skeptical about religious matters, particularly in the realm of the arts, Clemenceau felt that Monet's triumph rested precisely in his ability "to see the stone vibrate and to give [the Cathedral] to us ... bathed in luminous waves that collide in splashing sparks," which for Clemenceau was more truthful than any mysteries of the Church.[64]

By affirming the value of tangible experience over the inherited dogma of religion, Monet was expressing the progressive beliefs of his day, a fact the historian and cultural critic Léon Bazalgette affirmed several years later when he compared Monet's *Cathedrals* to J. Karl Huysmans' book entitled *The Cathedral* which appeared in 1898. For Huysmans, a Gothic cathedral was a religious symbol fraught with mystical powers. According to Bazalgette, such notions were backward and *retardataire*. In contrast, Monet's *Cathedrals* were "healthy, frank, vital, realist, alive. With him, it is no longer a question of dogma or of resurrection. . . . he considered the edifice only as a fragment of nature, according to reality, not to religion. Occult symbols cannot trouble him. Nor can Christian symbolism. . . . From his canvases, life spills out, stripped of . . . every kind of artifice or lie. It is there in front of us trembling and naked. If there really is a modern art," Bazalgette concluded, "an art linked to today's thought, the painter of the *Cathedrals*, from every point of view, is one of its representatives."[65] It is not surprising, therefore, that in his front-page review of the show, Clemenceau urged the President of France, Félix Faure, to "go and look at the work of one of your countrymen on whose account France will be celebrated throughout the world long after your name will have fallen into oblivion. . . . Remembering that you represent France," Clemenceau continued, "perhaps you might consider endowing [her] with these twenty paintings that together represent a moment for art, a moment for mankind, a revolution without a gunshot."[66] Unfortunately, Faure did not heed Clemenceau's call and the *Cathedrals* were soon scattered throughout the world, leaving Durand-Ruel's gallery and Monet's studio for the staggering sum of 12–15,000 francs apiece, more than five times what Monet had received for the *Wheatstacks*, *Poplars*, or any previous painting.[67]

Monet's financial success—he earned over 200,000 francs in 1895—afforded him the luxury of another long period of relative inactivity; he painted only a few pictures over the next ten months. It also permitted him another extended absence from the Paris art scene. His pictures continued to be bought and sold on the secondary market, but he did not return to the capital with a sizable collection of new paintings until June 1898 when he showed forty-two canvases at Georges Petit's, including twelve views of early morning light on the Seine (Pls. 185–88), and twenty-four paintings of the Normandy coast as seen from Pourville, Varengeville, and Dieppe (Pls. 181–84). The delay initially was due to difficulties Monet faced at home. During the summer of 1895, Alice, Suzanne, and Blanche Hoschedé all became ill, which taxed his time and patience. He also became embroiled in local affairs that summer and fall, after learning that the town of Giverny was intent on selling a piece of communally owned land to a chemical concern that planned to build a factory on the site. Monet felt the sale would spoil "the charm and beauty of the place" and wrote letter after letter to the mayor, the municipal council, the local prefect, and the prefect's assistant, protesting against the proposed action.[68] He even enlisted Mirbeau's help, convincing him to use his connections to influence the Minister of the Interior, Georges Leygues, to write a letter to the Giverny prefect supporting Monet's position. When it looked like his efforts might fail, Monet offered the town fathers 5,000 francs if they did not sell the land for fifteen years— a gesture the council spurned, which only made Monet angrier. But he quickly increased his offer to 5,500 francs which, after considerable haggling, was ultimately accepted.

The delay in the exhibition was also due to nature's lack of cooperation. When Monet finally left Giverny for the Normandy coast in February 1896, "to gain strength from the sea air," as he told the dealer Joyant, he was greeted by difficult weather conditions.[69] One day it was light-filled, the next overcast, causing him to begin one canvas after another and to become increasingly frustrated. Weather also was a factor with the *Mornings on the Seine,* as it rained for forty-one days in September and October of 1896, forcing him to abandon any hopes he may have harbored about finishing that new series in the fall.[70]

When the show finally opened, however, it was a sensation, just like the *Cathedrals.* In part, this was because it had been nearly three years since his previous exhibition, which made critics and colleagues eager to see what the master of Giverny had been up to. But it also was because Monet did not disappoint them. As a reminder of his previous achievement, Monet showed seven of his *Cathedral* pictures. But the heart of the exhibition consisted of the *Mornings on the Seine* and the Normandy coast paintings (Pls. 181–88). The latter were part of a group of almost fifty paintings he executed of these different Norman sites, while the twelve *Mornings on the Seine* were exactly half of the twenty-four examples of that campaign. The two groups are radically different in palette, touch, and effects. The former are open and expansive, windswept and volatile; the latter are contained and self-reflective, hushed and delicate. Many of the coastal views are filled with high-keyed color, often applied with vigorous brushwork; the *Mornings on the Seine* are much more uniform in hue, tending toward pale blues and light greens or sun-soaked yellows and purple whites, all of which are set down in a manner that minimizes brushwork and maximizes the translucent qualities of the paint as well as the flatness of the canvas.

The two groups, therefore, were perfectly paired. The coastal views attested to Monet's willingness to endure the challenging climate of the Channel in order to paint its moist fog and iridescence (Pls. 181, 182), its flickering light and mantle of gray (Pls. 183, 184). The *Mornings on the Seine,* in contrast, are testimony to his powers of control and his attention to the slightest nuances of nature. Unlike any previous series, these pictures were actually painted in a chronological fashion so that one canvas is intended to follow its predecessor, thus leading the viewer through the progressive moments of dawn's early light. As such, they reveal Monet's ability to track and capture quite specific effects more literally than ever before, just as they demonstrate his desire to bend painting's means to honor nature's intricacies in even more poetic ways. Thus, if the coastal views affirm the vitality of the northern tradition of landscape painting as handed down by the seventeenth-century Dutch, the views of the Seine assert the continuing potency of the pastoral and idyllic as practiced by Claude Lorrain and his Italianate followers as well as by Claude's great nineteenth-century counterpart, Camille Corot. Even the formats of the two groups of pictures confirm the complementary aspects of these radically different kinds of landscape traditions. The coastal views are generally horizontal canvases in which elements are arranged asymmetrically,

181 (following page top) Claude Monet, *Cliffs at Pourville. (Morning),* 1896–97, 64.8 × 99.1, W.1426, Private Collection.

182 (following page bottom) Claude Monet, *Val-Saint-Nicolas, near Dieppe. (Reflections on the Sea).* 1896–97, 65 × 92, W.1469, Private Collection.

185   Claude Monet,
*Morning on the Seine,*
*near Giverny. (Mist),*
1896–97, 89.9 × 92.7,
W.1475, The Art
Institute of Chicago,
Chicago, Mr. and Mrs.
Martin A. Ryerson
Collection.

186   Claude Monet,
*Morning on the Seine,*
*near Giverny. (Mist),*
1896–97, 92.7 × 88.9,
W. 1476, Kreeger
Museum, Washington.

183 (previous page
top)   Claude Monet,
*Gorge of the Petit Ailly.*
*(Varengeville),* 1896–97,
65.4 × 92.1, W.1452,
Fogg Art Museum,
Harvard University,
Cambridge, Gift of Ella
Milbank Foshay.

184 (previous page
bottom)   Claude
Monet, *Customs House*
*at Varengeville,* 1896–97,
61.6 × 90.8, W.1456,
Private Collection.

187 Claude Monet,
*Morning on the Seine,
near Giverny*, 1896–97,
81.3 × 92.1, W.1479,
Hiroshima Museum of
Art, Hiroshima.

188 Claude Monet,
*Morning on the Seine,
near Giverny*, 1896–97,
81 × 92.1, W.1480,
Private Collection.

189 Camille Corot, *Memories of Mortefontaine*, 1864, 65 × 89, Musée d'Orsay, Paris.

whereas most of the *Mornings on the Seine* are nearly perfect squares that are then divided in half horizontally so that water and sky are virtually equal, a pairing that emphasizes the mirror qualities of the scenes as a whole.

Monet's vantage points in both groups are a final point of contrast. To paint the *Mornings on the Seine*, he used his floating *bateau atelier* which he moored on the backwaters of the Seine. Although theoretically more vulnerable to change and movement by being on the river, Monet actually produced pictures that are some of the most limpid of his entire career. In the coastal views, the opposite occurs. He always stood on solid ground, which should have lent a measure of stability to his scenes. But that is not the case, except for the Pourville pictures, as he either assumes precarious positions that make the views appear risky, if not slightly dangerous, or he paints the land rising and falling unpredictably as if it were pulled by powerful, unseen forces. By building these contradictions into his pictures and then pairing these two groups with their evident contrasts, Monet once again could demonstrate his facility as a painter and proclaim his ability to rejuvenate time-honored landscape practices.

Even before the exhibition opened, a writer for *La Revue illustré*, Maurice Guillemot, predicted the show would be historic. Visiting Giverny in 1897 to interview Monet, Guillemot had the privilege of seeing "the master" working on the *Mornings on the Seine*. He declared they were "a marvel of contagious emotion [and] intense poetry," the product not of mindless spontaneity but of "prolonged, patient labor . . . anxiety . . . conscientious study, [and] feverish obsession." They were paintings, he asserted, that "will doubtlessly excite the wild prices currently reserved for Corot, Rousseau, and Daubigny" and "will be labelled masterpieces by posterity."[71]

Visitors to the exhibition agreed—almost unanimously—as the response to the show was more enthusiastic than for any previous gathering of Monet's work. Viewers were struck by Monet's seemingly unique combination of breadth and subtlety, vigor and detail. They also consistently marveled at his ability to wed novelty and tradition, particularly in the *Mornings on the Seine* which reminded people over and over again of the work of his recent predecessor, Corot.[72] The ties to tradition and specifically to the master of Ville d'Avray were evident to reviewers in the vaporous quality of many of the *Mornings on the Seine*, in the reverie that the soft, ill-defined forms generated, and in the bucolic world that the group as a whole suggested. The associations were certainly appropriate as the *Mornings* strongly recall well-known paintings by Corot, such as *Memories of Mortefontaine* of 1864 (Pl. 189).

Monet must have appreciated the association as he had long admired Corot, calling him later in life "the greatest landscape painter" of all time.[73] He was not alone in his enthusiasm for the artist, as Corot had been the subject of a huge retrospective in Paris that had run concurrently with Monet's *Cathedral* show and had been greeted with almost unrestrained pleasure. Consisting of more than 140 paintings, it was precisely what the public wanted to see—poetic views of the French countryside that reminded people of bygone days. These evocative paintings were widely perceived as the product of a humble but gifted man who, despite the time he spent in Italy, was able to preserve his national identity. His mastery, according to Roger Marx, was the logical product of his "temperament, ancestry, and race."[74] By evoking Corot more directly in the *Mornings on the Seine* than ever before, Monet was not just paying homage to one of his primary mentors and admitting to his status as a descendant of the master. He also was placing himself in the same position that Corot had assumed in

Supplément au Journal LE GAULOIS du 16 Juin 1898

# Le Gaulois

## A LA GALERIE GEORGES PETIT

## EXPOSITION CLAUDE MONET

*L'Exposition des Œuvres nouvelles de Claude Monet, ouverte en ce moment à la Galerie Georges Petit, est un événement trop important pour que Le Gaulois y demeure indifférent. Nous avons pensé que nos lecteurs seraient heureux d'en conserver un souvenir, et nous nous sommes fait un plaisir d'encadrer le portrait du célèbre artiste, et la reproduction de quelques œuvres de lui, de l'appréciation de son magnifique talent par les écrivains les plus autorisés de la critique contemporaine.*

Dans son numéro du 7 juin 1898, Le Journal publiait cet éloquent article de M. Gustave Geffroy :

### CLAUDE MONET

Claude Monet, qui n'avait pas fait d'exposition de ses œuvres depuis l'année où apparurent dans la lumière ses merveilleuses Cathédrales, réunit aujourd'hui, Galerie Petit, en une salle ouverte à tous, ses travaux de trois années. Il donne son point de départ, par une série de sept vues de la Cathédrale de Rouen : la grande forme dressée sur le sol, se perdant, s'évaporant dans le brouillard bleuâtre du matin, — le détail des sculptures, des anfractuosités, des creux et des reliefs, se précisant aux heures du jour, — le portail creusé comme une grotte marine, la pierre usée par le temps, dorée et verdie par le soleil, les mousses et les lichens, — la haute façade envahie d'ombre à sa base, le faîte éclairé par le soleil couchant, illuminé de la mourante lueur rose.

C'est le prodigieux poème de l'espace fixé aux aspects de la vieille église, une rencontre et une pénétration de la force naturelle et de l'œuvre humaine. L'artiste, toujours en travail et en recherche, accomplit là une

étape décisive, formula d'une manière neuve la loi d'unité qui régit les manifestations de la vie. Sa conception des choses, forte et subtile, se trouva davantage certifiée par une telle réalisation. Désormais, quelle que soit l'heure représentée sur la toile, un accord suprême se fera entre toutes les parties du sujet : l'eau, le ciel, les nuées, les feuillages, réunis par l'atmosphère, formeront un tout d'une irréprochable homogénéité, une image grandiose et charmante de l'harmonie naturelle.

Il est ainsi dans les effets de neige étudiés en Norvège, malgré le dépaysation visible, la surprise de se trouver devant une nature très différente de la nôtre, aux contours plus nets, aperçus distinctement à travers une atmosphère glacée et transparente. Le Mont Kolsaas, le fjord près Christiania, les bords du fjord, ont une parenté avec les justes découpures des estampes japonaises, relèvent du calcul mathématique par lequel l'étendue se trouve représentée en quelques lignes bien inscrites. Notre surprise est la même que celle-là éprouvée par Monet devant ces représentations d'un pays du Septentrion que l'on rêverait presque invisible, enfoui dans la brume opaque, sous une ouate atmosphérique, et que l'on découvre éclairé par une lumière nette, avec un accord pur et froid du blanc de la neige et du bleu de l'eau.

Revenu chez lui, en son village paisible, en sa maison fleurie, parmi les champs familiers, aux bords du fleuve et de la rivière, Monet erre parmi les prairies, sous l'ombre légère des peupliers, il monte et descend le courant en bateau, côtoie les îles, cherche avec une lenteur et un soin infinis l'aspect de nature propice par son arrangement, sa forme, son horizon, au jeu de la lumière, des ombres, des colorations. Car c'est une des nombreuses fantaisies nées au hasard de l'étiquette d'« impressionnisme », que de croire au non-choix des sujets par ces artistes réfléchis et volontaires. Le choix fut au contraire toujours leur vive et importante

relation to his own predecessors. "That Corot came from [Claude] Lorrain and reflects him is evident," Pissarro explained to his son after seeing the retrospective in 1895, "but it also is clear to what degree he transformed what he took, [and] in this lies all his genius." According to Pissarro, Corot was able to respect as well as transform Claude because Corot was French. "It is only here [in France]," Pissarro asserted, "that artists are faithful to the tradition of the masters, without robbing them."[75] By updating Claude, Corot was revealing his Frenchness and assuming the older artist's position as the pre-eminent landscape painter. It was precisely this strategy that Monet was practicing. For by doing the same to Corot, Monet was claiming that position for himself and asserting his ties to the time-honored French tradition.

The enthusiastic response to the show was ample proof of his success. Special supplements even appeared in liberal and conservative newspapers several weeks after the show opened that were devoted exclusively to Monet and the reception of his work over the previous ten years (Pl. 190). They featured a new photograph of the dashingly dressed artist taken by Nadar and a collection of favorable articles on previous shows that had appeared in other Parisian publications. The editor of the conservative *Le Moniteur des Arts* who followed the lead of his liberal counterpart at *Le Gaulois* even went so far as to admit that he had never been one of Monet's supporters but that this exhibition had made him a convert.[76]

190    Front page of *Le Gaulois* (supplement), 16 June 1898.

Such broad-based support suggests the opportune nature of these new paintings. Being closer to Corot and the French tradition, they were more restrained than Monet's *Cathedral* pictures and more palatable than his earlier work which, like that of his Impressionist colleagues, had just caused a kind of national crisis. In 1894 Gustave Caillebotte had died and had left his substantial collection of paintings by various Impressionists to the State. Many legislators, museum officials, and mainstream artists did not want the government to accept the donation, feeling that it was "an offense to the dignity of the [French] school." The conservative artist Jean-Léon Gérôme even claimed that accepting the bequest was tantamount to "the end of the nation."[77]

It took nearly two years to resolve the matter, which was exacerbated by the terms of the donation as much as by conservative factions. The government had to accept the gift *en bloc*, keep the paintings in Paris, exhibit all of the pictures at all times, and hang them all together. The Musée du Luxembourg was the only museum in the capital that could house such a gift, since it was the only one that accepted work by living artists. However, it was already overcrowded. Worse still, it operated on an unwritten policy of owning only three or four works by any one artist.[78] The Caillebotte bequest contained four Manets, five Cézannes, seven Degas, eight Renoirs, nine Sisleys, sixteen Monets, and eighteen Pissarros which meant the Impressionists would dominate the museum.

In late February 1896, the government announced it had reached a compromise with Caillebotte's executors and that it would accept two paintings by Manet, two by Cézanne, six by Renoir, six by Sisley, seven by Pissarro, seven by Degas, and eight by Monet. The works were delivered in November and hung in a new addition to the Luxembourg that was inaugurated in early 1897. But no sooner had the doors opened than the conservatives renewed their condemnations, this time with even greater truculence. The issue even made it to the floor of the Senate, where M. Hervé de Saisy attempted to convince his colleagues that the new acquisitions were "unhealthy" and "decadent"—the "antithesis of French art"—and that they would "pollute" the masterpieces in the Luxembourg's collection.[79]

Unlike Guillemot who made direct reference to the bequest, most people who reviewed Monet's show in 1898 went out of their way to convince their readers that the artist who had painted the *Mornings on the Seine* and the views of the Normandy coast was not the same one who had painted the earlier works in the Caillebotte collection, that they now were dealing with an artist whose intelligence and forethought measured up to higher standards. Georges Lecomte even felt Monet was now on the same level as Claude. "If one wants to relate his work to the past," he asserted, "it is to Claude Lorrain that he must be compared." In Lecomte's eyes, Monet was "the epic poet of nature . . . full of enthusiasm, indulgence, and serenity, extracting from nature all of its joy. Such a painter," he concluded, "passionate in his solitude about all of the hopes and fears of his time . . . is one of the crowning jewels of our epoch."[80] Reviewing Monet's work in a group show that Durand-Ruel mounted in 1899, Raymond Bouyer stated what Lecomte had implied—that "Monet's work above all expresses France, at once subtle and ungainly, refined and rough, nuanced and flashy." In Bouyer's opinion, Monet was "our greatest national painter; he knows the beautiful elements of our countryside whether harmonious or contradictory . . . the contours of the cliffs effaced by fog, the water running under the fresh foliage, the wheatstacks erected on the naked plains; he has expressed everything that forms the soul of our race." Although he felt some readers would not believe him, Bouyer proclaimed "an article of faith: for me [Monet] is the most significant painter of the century; yes, of the century."[81]

Given such extraordinary recognition and wide-ranging support, it is surprising to find that over the next twenty-eight years—from 1898 to his death in 1926—Monet painted over five hundred pictures, only a dozen of which depict a recognizable French site. There are approximately one hundred views of London painted between 1899 and 1904 and three dozen views of Venice from a trip Monet took there in 1906. The remaining three hundred and fifty concentrate on his water and flower gardens. It is difficult to know why the nationally recognized painter of *la France* and Corot's heir apparent abandoned French subjects for his own backyard.

There perhaps is no single explanation for this unique and peculiar development. It might have had something to do with Monet's advancing age; turning 60 in 1900, he might have wanted to stay closer to home and paint subjects that had always been dear to his heart. It may have been the result of the success he had achieved during the decade of the 1890s as his series paintings had netted him hundreds of thousands of francs, enough to live on comfortably for the rest of his days. It may have been his keen desire to make something special out of his Giverny acreage, an inclination he had begun acting upon early in the decade after purchasing the estate in 1890; it certainly had become a greater preoccupation as the years passed. However, it is difficult to believe that he could have made such a radical change without being prompted by some equally radical force.

Such a force struck France in 1898 when Emile Zola published his infamous article entitled "*J'accuse*" on the front page of Georges Clemenceau's liberal newspaper, *L'Aurore*. The article denounced the military and the French government, accusing them of a gross miscarriage of justice with regard to Alfred Dreyfus, a Jewish captain in the French army, who had been falsely accused and convicted of selling military secrets to the Germans in 1894. In early 1895, Dreyfus had been condemned to permanent exile on Devil's Island just off the coast of French Guiana in South America.[82] He perhaps would have been tragically forgotten—sparing France what became searing pain—if new evidence had not come to light suggesting that he was innocent, and that the real perpetrator was Count Charles Ferdinand Walsin Esterhazy, an infantry commandant attached to the French general staff who had been passing evidence to the general staff of the German army. In January 1898, Esterhazy was tried and acquitted, prompting Zola's article and ultimately a national catastrophe as friends and family members fought vociferously over the question of Dreyfus's innocence or guilt, making it an easy target for contemporary caricaturists (Pl. 191). The ferocity of the affair, which cannot be underestimated, was due to the fact that it turned on issues central to France—loyalty, patriotism, respect for the army, and distaste for foreigners. For liberal-minded citizens, Dreyfus was merely a victim of a completely corrupt system that would stop at nothing to protect its own malignant and venal concerns. For conservatives, the army could do no wrong: everyone knew Jews could not be trusted, especially when it came to sacred issues, such as national security. In their eyes, therefore, Dreyfus was not just a traitor, he was Judas incarnate who "for thirty shekels wanted to make all the women of France widows, cause small children to weep tears of blood, and turn his fellow soldiers over to enemy bullets."[83] Thus, when a subscription was mounted to aid the widow of another military figure, Lieutenant-Colonel Hubert Joseph Henry, who had been implicated in the affair and who had committed suicide, donations poured in from around the country, often accompanied by short but brutally anti-semitic notes. A parish priest from Poitiers who contributed one franc said he would be pleased "to sing a requiem for the last of the kikes." A resident of Baccarat wanted to see "all the kikes and kikettes and their kiddy-kikes placed in glass furnaces." Another self-declared "patriot" sent in twenty-five centimes to help "rent a deportation car."[84]

These harrowing comments, a bitter foretaste of Nazi Germany and Vichy France, make it clear that Dreyfus was considered by some to be "but a representative of the forces of evil

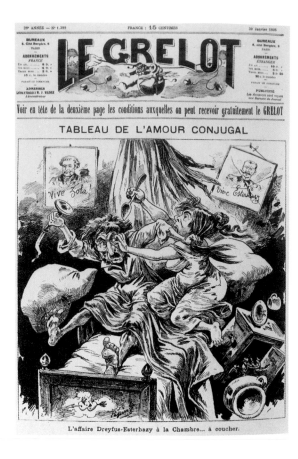

TABLEAU DE L'AMOUR CONJUGAL

L'affaire Dreyfus-Esterhazy à la Chambre... à coucher.

LA DEGRADATION

Composition de LIONEL ROYER. — Gravure de MÉAULLE.

191 (right)
Anonymous, *Picture of Conjugal Love*, from *Le Grélot*, 30 January 1898.

192 (far right)
Lionel Royer, *La Dégradation*, from *Le Journal illustré*, 6 January 1895.

destroying France" and that the problem went far beyond the verdict that was rendered and the consequent fate of the victimized captain. For what was at stake was nothing less than the very foundations on which France stood—her institutions, hierarchies, values, and traditions—as often expressed in popular illustrations (Pl. 192).[85] "Poor France," lamented Pissarro in February 1898. "Who could ever have imagined this nation, after so many revolutions, enslaved by the clergy like Spain. . . . She is sick. Will she ever recover?"[86]

As the bile rose to the surface, Monet acted with uncharacteristic forthrightness. After Zola wrote two initial articles in December 1897 defending Dreyfus on the basis of the information that was going to be presented in Esterhazy's trial, Monet wrote his old friend a heartfelt letter. "Bravo and bravo again for the two beautiful articles. . . . You alone have said what must be said and you have done it so well. I am happy to extend to you all of my compliments."[87] The day after "*J'accuse*" appeared, Monet wrote Zola another poignant letter. "Bravo once again," he exclaimed, "and all of my heartfelt sentiments for your valor and your courage."[88] Unlike Degas or Renoir, who became staunch anti-Dreyfusards, Monet even signed his name to the so-called Manifesto of the Intellectuals that *L'Aurore* published on 18 January 1898, supporting the paper's demands for the truth. And when Zola was brought to trial on libel charges later that year, Monet wrote to him to say he was unable to attend the proceedings only because of ill health. "Sick and surrounded by others who are ill, I could not come to your trial and shake your hand, as had been my desire. That has not stopped me from following all of the reports with passion. I want to tell you how much I admire your courageous and heroic conduct. You are admirable. It is possible that when calm is restored, all sensible and honest people will pay you homage. Courage, my dear Zola. With all my heart."[89]

Zola predictably was found guilty in July and was sentenced to a year in prison and a 3,000-franc fine, penalties he avoided by fleeing the country for England, where he lived in exile for almost a year. What else could one do in the face of the establishment's heinous conduct? Pissarro hoped that "it will end happily," a sentiment every sensitive individual shared. But unlike the older artist who told his son in November 1898 that "despite all these anxieties, I must work at my window as if nothing has happened," Monet could not continue doing what he had been doing.[90] The affair had altered his vision of his country just as it had for everyone else, whether they stuck to their course or not. Over the next fourteen months, Monet hardly picked up a paintbrush. And then in September 1899, he followed Zola's example and left his scandal-ridden homeland for a six-week stay in England.

Unconcerned about expenses, Monet settled into a sixth-floor suite in the fashionable Savoy Hotel, accompanied by Alice and Germaine Hoschedé. The room afforded him spectacular views of the Thames and south London. He returned to the same hotel for three months the following year and for the same period of time in 1901. The result of this extended effort (which did not end until he showed thirty-seven *London* pictures in 1904) was the largest series of paintings he had ever produced—nearly a hundred canvases that depict Charing Cross Bridge, Waterloo Bridge, and the Houses of Parliament (Pls. 193–99).[91] These pictures are filled with brilliantly diffused light and thick, rich atmosphere, the latter primarily the result of the smoke from the bituminous coal that Londoners burned at the time that mixed with the moist conditions of the region. The first two series are energized by the throbbing pulse of the city. Trains hurtle across the streaking Charing Cross Bridge puffing out trails of smoke, factory chimneys pierce the skyline behind the bustling traffic on the Waterloo Bridge, and boats ply the agitated waters of the murky Thames below both structures. These pictures are paeans to these various forces of modernity as much as poems about the extraordinary color and light that could transform this industrial area, in Monet's eyes at least, into a world of consummate beauty.

Similar effects, sometimes even more dramatically rendered, abound in the views of the Houses of Parliament where the often obscured orb of the sun pushes out from behind the almost impenetrable cloak of clouds and the haunting silhouette of the Gothic-revival buildings to shoot its rays of orange, yellow, and red across the darkened sky and river. Undefined except by outline, the Houses of Parliament in these pictures appear like specters, their towers rising to various heights as if replicating some ancient hierarchy or medieval form of competition. As in his *Cathedral* paintings, the buildings also seem to celebrate the magical, transformative powers of light. They stretch upwards to greet it and then stand like solemn sentinels as it spreads across the sky. Occasionally, Monet makes these associations more theatrical, as in Pl. 198 where the quivering towers seem to have set off an explosion of electrical energy, creating a dazzling display of light in the heavens (Pl. 197). The fiery bolts then descend to wrap the altered buildings in a kind of ritualistic veil that even extends into the waters below. Although taken to an extreme in this instance, what all of the *Houses of Parliament* paintings suggest are the mesmerizing irregularities of these Gothic-revival structures, as well as their style's long-standing ties to nature, just as Monet had expressed in his *Cathedral* pictures.

The extent to which Monet emphasized these factors is apparent when these *London* canvases are compared with a view of the Thames that he had completed in 1871 during his self-imposed exile in England during the Franco–Prussian War and Commune insurrection (Pl. 58). For its particular moment, the latter picture was remarkable for its atmospheric effects and handling of paint. Thirty years later, however, when set against the *Londons*, it appears almost naive or prosaic given its greater reliance on description and its abundance of

detail. The *Londons* by contrast have become immensely more complicated in their color combinations, brushwork, and spatial illusions, just as they have greatly increased in drama and reverie. This sea change is largely due to the three decades that divide the paintings and Monet's evident desire by the 1890s to evoke the magical powers of nature like a sorcerer or a priest. But the fact he decided to play this role in the heart of the English capital and not in France is significant and makes sense on a number of levels.

Besides being disillusioned with his homeland after the Dreyfus Affair, Monet seems to have been keen on expanding his market to include Great Britain. His work had never sold very well there, primarily because it had always carried a higher price than most avant-garde English art.[92] He therefore may have seen this London campaign as a way to appeal directly to English collectors, a suggestion that is underscored by his efforts in 1905 to stage an exhibition of these pictures in London after they were shown in Paris.[93] He would not have been interested in this enterprise if he did not admire the English. Holland may have been the only other country he held in equal or higher esteem. In addition to going to England several times prior to beginning his new *London* series, he had sent his sons, Jean and Michel, to live there and learn the language. Monet could hardly speak a word of English, but that did not cause him to complain about the difficulties of communicating or getting around. On the contrary, he enjoyed the time he spent in the company of his English acquaintances and went to enough fancy dinner parties during his stays in London (something he avoided in France) to suggest his fascination with the English upper crust. He even played tourist, visiting the Tower of London at least once and watching Queen Victoria's funeral procession which he claimed was "a unique spectacle."[94] His appreciation for the English extended to his own life at Giverny, which was similar to that of an English country gentleman, down to the English breakfast he had every morning complete with marmalade, ham, and tea, and to the suits of English wool that he had made to order, such as the one he wore for the *Le Gaulois* supplement.[95] Having housed a host of French refugees during difficult times in the nineteenth century, England had demonstrated a liberal bent that appealed to Monet. As Pissarro told his son in February 1898, "Now I see that you are right to stay in England, where you can expect a little more justice and common sense. Here, I fear the end has come."[96]

But most important, perhaps, England had produced some of the greatest landscape painters in the history of the genre, including the giants of the nineteenth century, Constable and Turner. It also had nurtured such an appreciation of nature that plein-air sketching was a national pastime, among women as well as men. Having triumphed in his bout with Corot

and paid vicarious homage to Corot's counterparts across the Channel, Monet must have felt that he had to meet the latter head on. If he were going to be a truly great landscape artist, it was a necessary challenge to face.

Although Monet must have had his friend James Whistler in mind when working on his *Londons*, knowing the American expatriate's *Nocturnes* quite well, he ultimately was doing battle with Turner. No one had gained greater stature for atmospheric scenes than the painter who once claimed to have strapped himself to a mast to experience a raging storm at sea. Turner also had done a great deal of work in France, including numerous prints of Rouen and its Cathedral to which Monet's series was often compared. So well known and admired was he in France that some people, such as Edmond de Goncourt, felt he put everyone else to shame, Monet included. "In the name of God," de Goncourt exclaimed in 1890 when looking at a painting of an ethereal blue lake by Turner, "if that doesn't make you despise Monet's originality and people of his ilk"—an evaluation Monet was out to contest in 1899.[97] Finally, even more than his English countrymen, Turner had settled his scores with earlier landscape painters with astonishing audacity, particularly when it came to one of France's greatest artists, Claude Lorrain. For not only did Turner copy paintings by Claude, he also insisted in his bequest to the National Gallery in London that his copies hang next to the originals by the French master, a wish the museum granted and still honors today.

Monet had long been interested in Turner and had the opportunity to see a great deal of his work in London during his visits there over the years. In a typical competitive barb he declared late in life that the Englishman was not a sophisticated colorist, but he spoke highly of him in the 1890s, referring to Turner's famous *Rain, Steam, and Speed—The Great Western Railway* of 1844 as well as to many of his watercolor studies from nature, making these some of the few works by any artist that Monet ever specifically cited.[98] Monet's interest was as natural as it was enduring. Few landscape painters had been as inventive or as passionate and few had captured nature's elusive ways with as much power and poetry. Few also were as individualistic or as moody, and few loved the sea more. Turner, therefore, was Monet's soulmate and guide as well as a special challenge.

That Monet had such difficulties finishing his *London* pictures, therefore, perhaps stands to reason. Although he completed twelve views of the Charing Cross and Waterloo bridges in 1899 and 1900, he did not finish the remaining eighty canvases in the three series until 1904. That is primarily because he was attempting to put an enormous chapter of the history of art behind him. With his views of the bridges over the Thames, he also was grappling with a

195 (above left)
Claude Monet, *Waterloo Bridge*, 1900, 64.5 × 91.25, Santa Barbara Museum of Art, Bequest of Katherine Dexter McCormick in memory of her husband, Stanley McCormick.

196 (above right)
Claude Monet, *Waterloo Bridge*. (*Grey Weather*), 1899–1901, 65 × 100, W.1561, Ordrupgaardsamlingen, Copenhagen.,

Claude Monet 1902

subject he had long abandoned. But if Turner had taken up the motif occasionally during his prodigious career, so too could Monet return to it at least for this engagement with the English master and his achievement. Monet's decision in 1901 to finish the series in his studio at Giverny and not in London, however, was a declaration of what he had probably felt all along but had been unwilling to admit—that modernity was not to be the focus of his attention, just as it ultimately had not been for Turner.

When he unveiled twenty-six bridge pictures and ten views of the Houses of Parliament at Durand-Ruel's in May 1904, all of the difficulties he had experienced must have seemed worthwhile as he received the accolades he had set out to earn. Georges Lecomte believed that Monet had never "attained such a vaporous subtlety, such power of abstraction and synthesis."[99] The stunned critic for the conservative *L'Action* was forced to agree: "In his desire to paint the most complex effects of light," he observed, "Monet seems to have attained the extreme limits of art. . . . He wanted to explore the inexplorable, to express the inexpressible, to build, as the popular expression has it, on the fogs of the Thames! And worse still, he succeeded."[100] Gustave Kahn understood precisely what Monet had been building on: "If it is true that Turner liked to compare certain of his works to certain of Claude Lorrain's, then one might place certain Monets beside certain Turners. One would thereby compare two branches, two moments of Impressionism, or rather . . . integrate two moments in a history of visual sensitivity."[101]

Monet was so pleased with the results that he went to England to try to find a space to show his *London* canvases "as an artist . . . for my personal satisfaction," as he told Durand-Ruel. This show never materialized but Monet was not disappointed. "Far from it," he wrote to his dealer, primarily because Durand-Ruel staged a major exhibition of Impressionist works in the English capital a year later in 1905 that was enthusiastically received. Monet had been handsomely represented in the show. In his mind, therefore, the desired end had been achieved. "I am delighted with the success [of your show]," he cooed to his dealer. "It is an excellent thing to have dealt London such a decisive blow," an aggressive expression of satisfaction that attests to how much Monet invested in this reckoning.[102] With victory declared and the art historical ledger rewritten, Monet returned to the project he had begun in the later 1890s and that would preoccupy him for the rest of his life—the development of his water and flower gardens and their transformation into art.

200    Anonymous, photograph of Giverny, ca. 1930, Copyright *Country Life*, Picture Library.

# 7  Monet and his Giverny Gardens: 1900–1926

When Monet moved to Giverny in April 1883, the town was similar to most of the farming communities that lay along the Seine between Paris and Rouen (Pl. 200). It had a modest church, a communal school, an unassuming town hall, a few *débits de boisson* (taverns), two mills, a blacksmith's shop, and a collection of low-slung houses built from local materials according to typical regional designs. Quiet and picturesque, it laid no claims to historical significance, boasted no major monuments, and counted no more than 279 residents, a number that had gradually declined during the century following the trend of most rural towns. The pink stucco house that Monet rented was one of the largest structures in the village. It sat on a sizable though curiously circumscribed plot of land. The back of the house was bordered by the rue de l'Amiscourt which wound into the village. Stretching out in front of the house were nearly two and a half acres that the former occupants had converted into a Norman kitchen garden with rows of vegetables and potatoes that were interspersed with fruit trees and berry bushes. Just beyond the stone wall that defined this space lay the chemin du Roy, a national road which ran along the southern edge of the property and led from Gasny, six kilometers to the east, to Vernon four and a half kilometers to the west. Though unpaved, it was the principle east–west axis for people who lived on that side of the Seine, which included everyone in Giverny. Parallel to the road adjacent to the property was an even more curious border   railroad tracks. The tracks had been laid in 1870 to link Vernon and Gisors—the latter about thirty-five kilometers to the east, right next to Eragny, home to Camille Pissarro and his family between 1884 and Pissarro's death in 1903. The Giverny station was a few hundred meters from Monet's house. When Monet leased the property, the train steamed by his garden four times a day. Though Monet had moved to the country, he clearly had not completely escaped the world he thought he had left behind.[1]

When the property came up for sale in November 1890, however, Monet quickly met the asking price of 22,000 francs, telling Durand-Ruel he was "certain of never finding a better situation or more beautiful countryside."[2] The first thing he did when he took ownership was to tear up the kitchen garden, visual beauty quickly replacing productivity. The fruit trees and berry bushes were uprooted, the vegetables plowed under, and the whole site redesigned. Sandy paths were imposed like a geometric grid on the plot and dozens of beds were raised on either side of the garden's main alley which was lined with trellises to support climbing roses. The fertilized beds were sown with a spectrum of flowers that were coordinated to bloom from early spring to late fall. Monet spent a great deal of time and money on this project, subscribing to horticultural magazines and encyclopedias, ordering his seeds from around the world, and consulting with friends, such as Mirbeau and Caillebotte, who shared his enthusiasm for gardening. He even received the advice of a

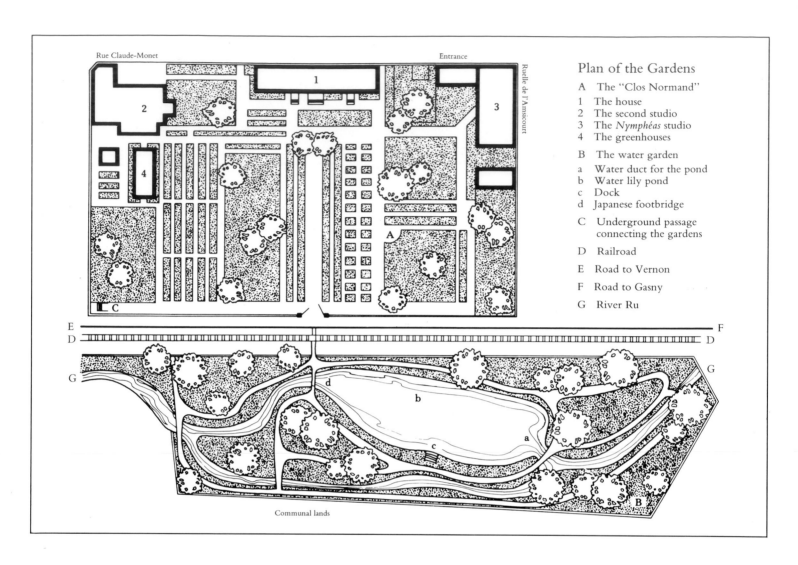

Plan of the Gardens

A   The "Clos Normand"
1   The house
2   The second studio
3   The *Nymphéas* studio
4   The greenhouses

B   The water garden
a   Water duct for the pond
b   Water lily pond
c   Dock
d   Japanese footbridge

C   Underground passage
    connecting the gardens

D   Railroad

E   Road to Vernon

F   Road to Gasny

G   River Ru

201   Map of Giverny and Monet's property.

Japanese gardener who came to Giverny in 1891, apparently at Monet's request. One critic said that "he reads more catalogues and horticultural price lists than articles on aesthetics."[3]

In early 1893, Monet was able to acquire additional land by purchasing a meadow that lay beyond the railroad tracks and was bordered on the far side by a small stream called the Ru, a tributary of the Epte, which ran parallel to his original property. The parcel covered close to an acre and contained a small pond that had once been used as a watering hole for farm animals. At the same time, he was able to negotiate the lease of an adjacent plot that went from the other bank of the Ru out to communally owned fields (Pl. 201). These were significant acquisitions. For although his property now was cut in half by the chemin du Roy and the railroad, he had the opportunity to expand his gardens, which is precisely what he did. On 17 March 1893, he wrote the Department Prefect a brief but revealing letter spelling out his intentions. The then 53-year-old artist requested permission "to install a *prise d'eau* [water trough] in the Epte by means of a small trench" in order to allow "for a small, intermittent diversion [of water]" that Monet claimed would not alter the level or flow of the river. "It merely would provide enough water," he told the Prefect, "to refresh the pond that I am going to dig on the land I own, for the purpose of cultivating aquatic plants." He also asked the Prefect for permission to build two small, light, wooden footbridges over the Ru "in order to pass from my land to the land I rent on the other bank and vice versa."[4]

These relatively modest requests initiated what would become one of Monet's most

176

grandiose works of art, namely his now famous water lily garden. Although local residents could never have foreseen the changes these proposals would ultimately bring to their town, they moved quickly to stop them. This odd Parisian was going to drain too much water from the river, they claimed, which he then would contaminate with his exotic cultures which they held to be suspicious since they were not local species. When he learned of these complaints, Monet became furious. "The hell with the natives of Giverny and the engineers," he raged to his wife. "I don't need to hire any of them nor order any lattice. Throw all of the aquatic plants in the river; they'll grow there." After two hearings on the matter over the next two months, another letter from Monet to the Prefect in which he defended his plans again, and at least two other letters to an attorney in Les Andelys and to the former publisher of an influential Rouen newspaper, the Prefect granted Monet his requests in July and issued the appropriate permits.[5]

These events attest to Monet's tenacity in the face of opposition and his ability to operate effectively as a political being. They also reveal how sharp-tempered he was and how differently he saw himself in relation to his neighbors. But, most important, they demonstrate his steadfast commitment to his vision, one that would preoccupy him for the remaining thirty-three years of his life and result in a spectacular legacy. For not only did Monet create a site that would become one of the most visited in France, he also completed over two hundred and fifty paintings that depict various aspects of this garden paradise.

Monet's keen interest in constructing his water lily pond was only the most ambitious manifestation of a long-standing passion for gardening. More than two decades earlier, he had devoted considerable time and resources to his gardens, even when they were only part

202 (below left) Claude Monet, *Camille Monet in the Garden at Argenteuil*, 1876, 81.7 × 60, W.410, From the Collection of Walter H. and Leonore Annenberg.

203 (below right) Claude Monet, *Monet's Garden at Vétheuil*, 1880, 150 × 120, W.685, National Gallery of Art, Washington, Ailsa Mellon Bruce Collection.

of the rented properties in Argenteuil (Pl. 202). When funds were short during that decade, he still made sure his gardens flourished. And when he left for Vétheuil, he was careful to choose a house that came with acreage that he could fill with flowers and potted plants (Pl. 203). Naturally, his art reflected his horticultural fervor. Of the more than eight hundred paintings he completed during the first half of his career before moving to Giverny, over one hundred are views of sun-dappled gardens or flower-rich still lifes. Little wonder, therefore, that he told a journalist that "I perhaps owe it to flowers for having become a painter."[6]

It was his estate at Giverny, however, that provided Monet with the ultimate in gardening opportunities. After receiving the Prefect's approval in July to divert the waters from the Epte he hired his construction crew and began work. The whole project was completed a few months later in the fall of 1893. Covering approximately 1,000 square meters, the water pond was soon ringed by an artful arrangement of flowers, trees, and bushes, crossed by a Japanese-style wooden bridge, and filled with water lilies. Monet eventually enlarged the pond several times (in 1901 and again in 1910), expanded its plantings, added a trellis to the Japanese bridge, and removed the concrete that he had originally poured for a floor in part of the pond.

In many ways, the water and flower gardens were perfectly paired. The flower garden, for example, was more traditional and more Western. It harked back to designs for formal, country-house gardens that had been devised in the eighteenth century and followed with some frequency thereafter, most notably at the Manoir d'Ango in Varengeville that Monet could well have known. The water lily garden was more Eastern, with its more natural layout, reflective waters, and Japanese bridge. It also contained many Eastern plantings—bamboo and ginkgo trees, for instance, as well as Japanese fruit trees. Silent and meditative, mysterious and foreign, it visually and emotionally was quite different from the bolder, more profuse flower garden across the tracks. With their emphasis on aesthetics and the evident expense of their creation, both gardens stood in marked contrast to the simpler plots of Monet's neighbors as well as to the acreage that friends such as Pissarro lovingly tended to produce food for his family at the very same time.

204 (below left)
Etienne Clémentel, photograph of Monet's water garden at Giverny, ca. 1917.

205 (below right)
Claude Monet, *Water Lilies. Water Landscape*, 1904, 90 × 92, W.1665, Private Collection.

It would be wrong to think of Monet's two gardens as polar opposites of each other, however, as the water garden (Pls. 204, 205) also contained plenty of Western trees and bushes and had been designed with as much rigor as the seemingly more geometric flower garden. Conversely, there were Eastern plantings in the flower garden, while its strict geometry was intentionally disguised by nasturtiums and wild geraniums that softened the edges of the beds, and aubretia and pink saxifrage that spilled out on to the intersecting paths (Pls. 206, 207). In the end, the two gardens were really complementary ways to appreciate the beauties of nature, thus affording Monet a wide range of visual incidents to paint. "Everything I have earned has gone into these gardens," he once told an interviewer. "I do not deny that I am proud of [them]."[7]

Given his devotion to these gardens, it is curious that Monet did not paint either of them seriously until late in the decade. He might have wanted to wait until his plantings matured. A photograph of the Japanese bridge taken around 1895 shows the pond to be rather sparse (Pl. 208). He also had not painted garden scenes for quite some time and was obviously preoccupied with his series paintings of the decade.

While working on these series pictures, Monet did not completely ignore his horticultural creations. There are at least two paintings of the Japanese bridge from 1895 and nearly eight of water lilies from 1897–98.[8] But in number and quality, these canvases do not compare with the *Wheatstacks*, *Poplars*, and *Cathedrals*, or any of the other series paintings of the decade. Wanting to attain national stature, it is likely that Monet waited to paint his gardens until he had realized his goals. For although gardening was a national pastime and landscape architecture a long standing art form, views of his own backyard could not engender the same kind of reaction as the evidently nationalistic subjects he chose for his primary efforts of the 1890s, no matter how beautiful his horticultural handiwork may have been.

It also is no coincidence that Monet turned to his water garden only after his rise to prominence and after the heinous Dreyfus Affair had broken. For it was only when that

206 (above left) Anonymous, photograph of Monet's flower garden at Giverny, ca. 1917, Archives, Musée Marmottan, Paris.

207 (above right) Claude Monet, *Path through the Garden at Giverny*, 1902, 81 × 92, W.1652, Private Collection.

208  [Lilla Cabot Perry?], photograph of the water lily pond and the Japanese bridge, ca. 1895, Perry Archives, Archives of American Art, Smithsonian Institution, Washington.

scandal spread its sordidness across the nation that Monet gave up his life-long project of immortalizing his native land and sought meaning elsewhere. He found it most often and most profoundly in a world of his own making.

By focusing almost exclusively on his gardens for the last two decades of his life, Monet was not emptying his art of significance. Just the opposite. Like Cézanne who spent the last twenty years of his life painting Mont Saint-Victoire outside his native Aix-en-Provence over and over again, Monet asserts the primacy of an individual vision and everyone's ability to find meaning in the fundamental relation of the human to the natural. Whether plumbing his floral fantasia or his water lily garden in these endlessly engaging pictures, Monet insists that individuals can begin to understand more fully the complexities of nature as the most awesome force in the world, to appreciate its beauty, and to respect its power. By his dogged devotion to this single, clearly defined task, Monet also suggests that certain human characteristics, such as order and discipline, steadfastness and confidence, are as essential to life as they are to art and that when they are applied to the study of nature they can yield enormous results, instilling in the novice viewer as well as the professional artist a complementary sense of humility and awe, knowledge and innocence. Cézanne admitted this many times although never perhaps as movingly as when he finally, at 70, told his son Paul, "as a painter I am becoming more lucid in front of nature." But he immediately countered that claim by confessing that "with me the realization of my sensations is always painful. I cannot attain the intensity that is unfolded before my senses. I have not the richness of coloring that animates nature."[9] Like Monet, he too was locked into an endless struggle, one that he similarly laid bare in his work. In doing so, both artists not only confirmed the principles of their own existence but also encouraged others to participate in the same exploratory process. For they insisted that once people come to know themselves better, they could recognize their place in the larger whole and, ultimately, act more responsibly in a world that appeared at the end of the 1890s to have abandoned that obligation.

These ideas are evident in the first extended group of paintings that Monet produced of his gardens which consists of eighteen views of his water lily pond and Japanese bridge that he began in 1899 and finished the following year (Pls. 209, 210). As with his late garden pictures at Argenteuil of 1875 and '76, Monet focuses on a very limited site, reducing his field of vision to compress the space in the scenes. He also closes the pictures off to any outside intrusion, allowing nothing to disturb the privacy of the moment or the exquisite solitude he manages to extract. Thus, lily pads float serenely out from under his watery vantage point, moving in seemingly arbitrarily arranged clusters into the shallow background where they meet the elliptical edge of the pond at a point halfway up the canvas. There, dense growth rises to merge with equally thick foliage, the myriad greens, yellows, blues, and lavenders blocking off the view while showering the shimmering surface of the pond with multicolored reflections.

What anchors the picture is the bridge. Truncated so that it almost seems to be levitating above the water, the blue-and-green structure stretches across the pond, linking the two unseen banks while acting as a mediator between the water and the foliage. Though viewed from an angle which causes it to appear asymmetrical, the bridge nonetheless provides a critical spatial demarcator for the scene while lending the view an important element of specificity; remove it, and the painting becomes nondescript if not overly picturesque. Forcefully imposed upon the site, the bridge's curving rectangles and vertical posts, continuous handrail and broadly painted truss (imitated by the darkened area in the foreground) all announce the presence of the human and designate the pond as a place for contemplation. Its strict geometry also suggests the existence of a rational relationship between the elements in the scene, alerting the viewer to the fact that everything has been carefully planned to allow nature to express herself on her own terms—thus the density of the foliage in the background, the plethora of water lilies, the sense of seclusion, and the timelessness of the moment.

What is most important, however, is the almost endless array of relationships that Monet has presented for the viewer to discover—the interaction between the various clusters of water lilies, for example, or between the water lilies with their horizontal distribution and the reflections around them which are predominantly vertical. Equally engaging are the reflections of the foliage in relation to the water's evident depths or the way the posts on the bridge spread apart as they move across the scene, a progression that is subtly coordinated with the cascade of willow strands on the left and the more bulbous configuration of leaves on the right. Even the undergrowth along the edge of the pond plays a role as it rises up to greet the bridge on either side, often twisting to imitate its arched form. It is these kinds of relationships that abound in the picture just as they do in the world, just as they do in Cézanne's works of which Monet owned at least a dozen. And it is these kinds of relationships that make experience meaningful: they sharpen one's senses and clarify one's own relationship to the physical surroundings. It is these kinds of relationships, finally, that Monet suggests should be recognized and contemplated, because they have the power to create harmony out of contrast and to extract beauty from the mundane.

These more meditative, semi-philosophical dimensions to Monet's work owe a great deal to what is most evident about these *Japanese Bridge* pictures, namely their Eastern orientation. In addition to the bridge itself which declares the series' obvious debt to Japanese phenomenon, the pictures strongly recall numerous prototypes in earlier Japanese art, such as Hiroshige's *The Tenjin Shrine at Kameido* (Pl. 211). More importantly, they appeal directly to the viewer's aesthetic sensibility in a way that is typically Oriental. Instead of Western worldliness, they stress contemplation and retreat. In place of traditional, occidental materialism, they offer innocence and simplicity.

That Monet would have chosen to concentrate so exclusively on these non-Western

209 Claude Monet, *The Water Lily Pond* [*Japanese Bridge*], 1899, 90 × 90, W.1506, The Art Museum, Princeton University, From the Collection of William Church Osborn, Class of 1883, Trustee of Princeton University (1914–1951), President of the Metropolitan Museum of Art (1941–1947); gift of his family.

210   Claude Monet, *The Water Lily Pond* [*Japanese Bridge*], 1899, 93 × 90, W.1507, Private Collection.

notions after trumpeting so many recognizable French sites and Western ideas is significant and begs explanation, especially as the Japanese bridge would appear in only three other paintings between 1900 and 1918. It might have been that he felt France could gain essential guidance at this critical juncture in her history by looking seriously at the East, specifically at Japan. After all, it was the Japanese who had so amply demonstrated the value of a deep engagement with nature, which had led most French observers to feel that the Japanese operated on a higher level of awareness. By Monet's own admission, it had made them "a profoundly artistic people. I once read something that struck me," he confided to a journalist who had come to see his gardens in 1904. "A [Japanese] bricklayer was building a wall and he placed a rose in front of him so that from time to time he could look at it and inhale its scent as he worked. As his wall progressed, he would move the rose so that it was always there before him. Don't you find that charming?" he asked his guest.[10] That was the kind of relationship to nature that Monet held dear.

Associations with the East also would have made viewers realize that Monet had been able to appropriate aspects of this foreign culture and adapt them to his own use. His *Japanese Bridge* pictures, for example, pulsate with life far more than any Japanese print, just as the forms in his scenes are more tangible and believable than the flatter ones in most *ukiyo-e* images. Monet's color schemes are also more distinctly European with their classical balance of blues and yellows, reds and greens. Even the particular way he applies the paint—in discrete, almost labored, touches reminiscent of the Impressionism of twenty years earlier—is unusually reserved for this moment in his career. With such a foreign subject, he clearly did not want to pursue the novel surfaces he had achieved in his previous series paintings, opting instead to reinstate his familiar, French Impressionist style. Monet's formal tactics were understandable, for what he was attempting to suggest in these *Japanese Bridge* paintings is the existence of a hybrid environment, a place where East becomes West through the powers of French culture and where nature becomes art through the tenacity of an Impressionist's vision.

He suggested this even more boldly when he got further into the series and abandoned some of his earlier restraint. In the six canvases of the same subject that date from 1900, for example, such as Pls. 212, 213, he shifts the bridge to a much more asymmetrical position, allows his paint to move more fluidly over the surface, and heightens his palette with various shades of red, yellow, and orange which often make his scenes much hotter, if not almost garish.

The paintings' ties to the East were not lost on reviewers when Monet showed twelve of the *Japanese Bridge* pictures at Durand-Ruel's in November and December of 1900. Some critics noted the existence of Japanese prints in which similar bridges appeared. One of them complained that Monet did not vary his view as much as his Oriental predecessors. Another felt that these new pictures were cause for concern. "I only fear," wrote Alphonse de Calonne in *Le Soleil*, "that these artistic divergences will make us lose the delicate and often very just sense that earned us so good and high a reputation in the past," a reminder that national status was a pre-eminent issue.[11] Others preferred Monet's earlier work, particularly his *Wheatstacks, Poplars*, and *Cathedrals*.[12]

However, there were those who strongly disagreed, such as Julien Leclercq, the critic for *La Chronique des Arts*. Having defended Monet and his Impressionist colleagues in previous years, calling their movement in 1899 "a glorious chapter to add to our history of French art," Leclercq believed that Monet surpassed the Japanese with his new series.[13] By maintaining a consistent vantage point in these pictures, he asserted, Monet was able to achieve a much broader range of lighting effects, and thus had endowed his naturalism with a freshness and vitality not evident in Oriental prints. As a group, Monet's series also engendered a sense of the ideal and the eighteenth century, a fact Leclercq felt would be better appreciated in the future. "We will understand one day better than we do now ... what limpidity of the soul, what incantation of the beautiful things of nature [these paintings represent], and how much the creator of these powerful and beautiful marvels belongs to the race of those lucid, welcoming, brilliant, sensible, and penetrating men who were the ever-gracious and intelligent painters of the eighteenth century." Like others who had come to associate Monet's work with French values, Leclercq defended this new series on the grounds that it embodied "the genius of an impassioned and measured people," going so far as to assert that "to discredit it is to discredit France."

Although unthinkable ten years earlier, Monet had reaped similar praise from critics who had reviewed the Fine Arts section of the Universal Exposition of 1900, which had closed three weeks prior to the opening of the *Japanese Bridge* show. Monet had been handsomely represented by fourteen paintings in that State-sponsored exhibition which covered French art of the previous hundred years. Roger Marx perhaps was the most euphoric. "Never were pictorial faculties put to the service of such a refined and sensitive eye.... Outside of Turner and Corot, modern landscape cannot count a master of more noble ability."[14] Even the arch-conservative Robert de La Sizeranne had to admit that Monet and his Impressionist colleagues had left their mark on artists far and wide. "If you walk through the rooms of the Décennale [a separate exhibition of art from 1889 to 1900 in which Monet was not represented] you will see traces [of Impressionism] not only among the quasi-Impressionists, such as M. Besnard, but also in the work of the most restrained people, such as Henri Martin." He even found their influence "in the lingering Romantics ... in France, ... the Alps, ... Hungary, even in the paintings coming from Oslo and Stockholm."[15] The critic for *La Liberté* found this influence commendable. "In the work of numerous artists, the effects of light are studied and expressed with more intelligence and truth than before; this represents progress in the discipline for which it is necessary to be grateful to the Impressionists."[16]

That Monet's *Japanese Bridge* pictures did not enjoy the same broad-based support stands to reason; they were not like his previous paintings and certainly not like the many earlier canvases he had selected for the Universal Exposition which by 1900 were more than thirty years old. Perhaps anticipating this, Monet included in his *Japanese Bridge* show twelve examples of his work since 1889, beginning with two *Creuse Valley* paintings and ending with three *Mornings on the Seine*. He clearly wanted to suggest that the *Japanese Bridge* pictures arose from the same steadfast commitment to nature that had produced these great series paintings. The liberal critic for *La Revue blanche*, Charles Saunier, gave Monet the highest praise for those earlier canvases of the 1890s. "Transport these *Mornings on the Seine*,

*Wheatstacks*, and *Cathedrals* around the world," Saunier wrote, "and no matter where these paintings will be, the spectator, whoever he is, will admire and envy a country where the hand of man . . . built such monuments in the middle of such beautiful sites. Glory thus to the artist," he concluded, "who with the aid of a few lines and some dashes of color can so grandly synthesize the land where he lives."[17] Monet was undoubtedly warmed by this review; it confirmed that national status had finally been accorded him.

Tellingly, Saunier did not include the *Japanese Bridge* pictures as part the group that was going to bring Monet—and France—such international acclaim. This was not an oversight as Saunier admired these new paintings, but not as much as he prized Monet's earlier series. For unlike the *Wheatstacks* and *Cathedrals*, which Saunier sensitively read as "speaking to us about the labor of man [and] his collaboration with the workings of nature," the *Japanese*

*Bridge* pictures were "deserted. . . . [the human] is totally absent." In addition, the vaporous atmosphere that Monet was able to capture, was "distilled," in his opinion, "from a suffocating heat [that] creates strange rainbow-like effects and allows this corner of nature to move from rose to mauve and from these tones to others." The experience was dissatisfying to Saunier. "In front of these pictures, one senses the secret design of a cinematographer who noted the color not the action—the color, I say, but not the nuance." By having these Eastern-orientated pictures constitute more than half the show, however, Monet clearly wanted to demonstrate that he was going to take his involvement with nature one step

213  Claude Monet, *The Water Lily Pond [Japanese Bridge]*, 1900, 89 × 100, W.1632, Private Collection.

further; that he now was going to concentrate on an even more limited motif than what he had chosen for those heralded earlier pictures, something Saunier sensed when he expressed his preference as well for the three *Mornings on the Seine* that Monet had included. Saunier liked these better than the *Japanese Bridge* pictures because "the site is so beautiful; nature appears so grandiose with the large, massive trees which hang over the river," which for him conjured up religious sentiments. "Man is not visible here as well, one might say. That's true, but the personality of the painter is." By limiting his site in the *Japanese Bridge* pictures and removing himself further than he had in his previous series, Monet was trying to transform the garden pictures into something more expansive and universal. The Symbolist poet, Emile Verhaeren, recognized this when he saw the exhibition. In his opinion, Monet "evoked the whole of nature" in these new paintings. "One senses the subterranean life at the bottom of the pool," he wrote, "the thick growth of roots; the intertwining of the stems, of which the flowers, massed on the surface, are only the continuation." For Verhaeran, Monet was like a great poet, who comes alive in [nature]. . . . In hours when work is fruitful," he concluded, "the union is complete. Individual life and universal life fuse. The poet becomes the universe which he translates."[18]

Monet aspired to achieve that union not only for himself but also for his times, as he firmly believed in the importance of nature to contemporary art and society, just like Cézanne or their mutual friend, Pissarro. When Pissarro's son turned to the Italian primitives, for example, to counter the commercialization of art in England in 1900, Pissarro reprimanded him harshly: "Commercialism can vulgarize these [arts] as easily as any other style, hence it's useless. Wouldn't it be better to immerse yourself in nature? I don't hold the view that we have been fooling ourselves and ought rightly to worship the steam engine with the great majority. No, a thousand times no! We are here to show the way! According to you, salvation lies with the primitives, the Italians. According to me, this is incorrect. Salvation lies in nature, now more than ever."[19]

Although Monet returned to his London series after completing these *Japanese Bridge* pictures, he aligned himself with Pissarro's sentiments by painting more than thirty views of his water and flower gardens between 1901 and 1904. More importantly, when his *Japanese Bridge* exhibition closed, he purchased more land—almost another acre—and expanded his water lily pond considerably. He also greatly increased the plantings in the garden, adding Japanese apple and cherry trees as well as rhododendron and bamboo. In addition, he constructed a trellis over the Japanese bridge to support wisteria which he introduced into the garden for the first time. And he mingled African water lilies with the French species he had concentrated upon previously.

This was a massive and costly undertaking that left no doubt about Monet's interests and orientation. He did not do the physical work himself, of course. In addition to hiring a construction crew, he relied upon a team of gardeners that he had formed in the 1890s. By 1901, when this expansion project began, the team numbered no fewer than six. He was able to support his staff and pay for the expansion in cash, as his considerable earnings of the 1890s continued through the turn of the century. In 1899, he sold enough paintings to make 227,400 francs. In 1901, he earned 127,000 francs; the following year, 105,000 francs. On top of these fabulous sums, he was netting about 40,000 francs a year from investments, making him a very rich man indeed.[20]

His wealth allowed him to enjoy many luxuries. In addition to supporting his extended family without worry and indulging his passion for gardening, Monet was able to order his twill suits from the fancy English outfitters Old England on the boulevard des Capucines, his ruffled cambric shirts from the best shirtmakers in Paris, and his boots from the same

bootmaker who outfitted the army regiment in Vernon (Pl. 214). He loved *foie gras,* especially that made in Alsace. When he had a craving for truffles, he bought those from the Périgord. He was not as particular about his wines, but he did not consume local vintages except Norman cider.[21] Monet's enthusiasm for food and drink contributed to his girth, which expanded from 1899 onwards, but it also made guests look forward to their visits to Giverny as they knew they would be treated to delicious fare. Monet's fortunes also permitted him to purchase not one but two automobiles, both Panhard-Levassors—the first in 1901, the second in 1904 (Pl. 215). When the first slowed down in 1913, Monet traded it in for a large limousine. He also bought cars for his son Michel, and his stepson Jean-Pierre Hoschedé. Monet loved riding around the countryside in his automobiles at high speeds. He always left the driving to someone else—generally his chauffeur, who also doubled as a studio assistant, a wine steward, and a mechanic. His money permitted him to travel, at least when he was not working. In 1904 he and Alice went to Spain, and in 1908 to Italy. In 1913, he took a two-week trip to Switzerland. Between 1890 and 1915, he also used the proceeds from the sale of his paintings to build a greenhouse and a second studio on his property, as well as a darkroom for his budding interest in photography. He also purchased a house in Giverny for his son Jean, built apartments for his stepchildren, and eventually constructed a huge third studio for himself in which he painted his last *Water Lilies.*

Despite these privileges and the earnings that continued to pour in, Monet never softened in his resolve to make something of his gardens. Even while he was finishing his paintings of the bridges in London and the Houses of Parliament, he painted the gardens nearly three dozen times. Two thirds of these pictures depict the water lily pond. That number grew exponentially when the show of his London paintings closed in 1904. Reports even circulated that he had begun as many as one hundred and fifty canvases of his pond alone, a number that undoubtedly was inflated to appeal to the public's keen interest in his serial procedure and the widespread fame his gardens had already earned.[22] In actuality, there are only approximately eighty extant canvases that date from 1903 to 1908. In addition to the mystique that came to surround Monet and his property, the discrepancy might have been due to the fact that Monet often became dissatisfied with his work and destroyed many canvases. He claimed to

214 (above left) Anonymous, photograph of Monet beside his water lily pond, ca. 1904, Archives, Musée Marmottan, Paris.

215 (above right) Anonymous, photograph of Monet in his Panhard-Levassor, Collection, Jean-Marie Toulgouat.

have disposed of at least thirty, although this may well have been hyperbole. Word of this practice leaked out to the press, however, and became blown out of proportion. Stories ran in nearly two dozen English-language papers on both sides of the Atlantic claiming the great Impressionist had slashed over $100,000 worth of his art.[23] This too appears to have been part of the myths about Monet. It might even have been a sly public relations campaign to encourage already enthusiastic American collectors to acquire more of his pictures, since they seemed to be becoming rarer. In any case, Monet become frustrated with his progress which caused him to postpone an exhibition of these *Water Lilies* several times, beginning in 1907, despite pleas from Durand-Ruel. Initially, he claimed he did not have enough good pictures to show and that he needed to work on the others from nature. A few weeks later, he felt he could not tell the good ones from the bad.[24]

His problems were well founded, as no one had ever tried to make so much out of so little. In the *Japanese Bridge* pictures and the views of the flower garden, he at least had selected sites that had definable dimensions and enough physical objects to allow the viewer to read the pictures in a logical fashion. When he began these *Water Lily* canvases with paintings such as Pl. 216, he retained a semblance of these traditional schemas but he stretched them to almost implausible extremes. In this picture, for example, he looks out across his pond to the foliated shore in the distance. Instead of allowing the pond to recede gradually into space, however, he raises it so radically that its shimmering surface occupies nearly nine-tenths of the canvas, leaving only a small strip of cropped undergrowth at the top of the scene to suggest the bank beyond. Even with the number of lily pad clusters acting as spatial demarcators, it is difficult to gage exactly how far the pond extends before it reaches the bank. It also is hard to know how tall that undergrowth might be, or how large the clusters of water lilies are. The latter becomes particularly problematic when scanning the picture from foreground to background given the way the lily pads increasingly move toward a single horizontal plane that is seen not from above, as in the immediate foreground, but from the side, as in the distance. It is almost as if Monet painted the lower half of the picture from one vantage point and the upper half from another. That is not the case, of course, but the compressed space and radical foreshortening places special stress on accepted notions of near and far while suggesting a kind of curvature to the pond's surface that is analogous to that of the earth itself.

These effects are as compelling as they are unprecedented and mark these paintings as extraordinary achievements. If that were not enough, however, Monet complicates the matter further, particularly in pictures such as Pl. 217, by greatly reducing the number of water lily pads and the amount of reflected foliage compared to what he had included in the *Japanese Bridge* pictures. In doing so, he increases the areas that have to exist without the benefit of floating matter or mirrored images. This must have been a formidable challenge for him, as it meant that color and brushwork alone had to bear the weight of description when there was virtually nothing physical to describe. It also meant he had to devise new strategies to suggest the illusion of the pond's depths.

All of this would have been sufficient to separate these first *Water Lily* pictures from their earlier *Japanese Bridge* counterparts in ways that few other paintings in Monet's career had been divided from their immediate predecessors. But Monet adds yet one more distinguishing feature: he permits the sky to be reflected in the water in Pl. 216—something he had scrupulously avoided in the *Japanese Bridge* pictures. In only two of the eighteen paintings in that series does the sky even appear and there it is sequestered to the upper left and right corners of the canvas—appropriate locations, given Monet's vantage point by the pond's edge. In Pl. 216, Monet has it occupy the lower half of the canvas, thus literally turning the traditional earth–sky relationship upside down. What he is really doing is reversing one of the most fundamental tenets of landscape painting—that sky is up and land is down. Monet adds one more complication to this notion by having the sky emerge from behind the reflected foliage whose relatively continuous edge across the middle of the pond corresponds to an inverse horizon. Little wonder, therefore, that Monet felt he needed more time with these paintings. He had embarked on a truly uncharted course that called the very structure of landscape painting into question. Even the title—*Les Nymphéas, séries de paysages d'eau* [*Water Lilies, series of water landscapes*]—on which Monet insisted for the exhibition of these pictures over Durand-Ruel's proposed *Les reflets* [*The Reflections*] indicates the problem, as the term "landscape" was now going to be stretched to include views in which little or no land appeared.[25]

The eighty-odd paintings that comprised this group of watery images make it clear that Monet was not quite certain where this new course might lead him. In 1903 and 1904, he vacillated between paintings such as Pl. 216 and Pl. 217 in which the bank in the distance disappears allowing the clusters of floating flowers and the reflections of sky and foliage to take over the entire canvas. In these latter paintings, which are less numerous than those that are similar to Pl. 216, there are no boundaries or divisions in the scene and thus no indications of where the site begins or ends. There also is no sense of where Monet or the viewer may be in relation to anything else, except to the elements in the immediate foreground. Where paintings such as Pl. 216 had placed stress on ideas of near and far or up and down, paintings like this one emphasize notions of presence and absence, of things physical and elusive, knowable and illusionary. Each cluster of lily pads, therefore, becomes essential to the effect of the whole image just as the relationship of those clusters to the reflections around them determines the cogency of the scene.

Given the complexities of these two groups of pictures, it perhaps is not surprising that after painting more than a dozen of them, Monet stepped back for a moment in 1905 and did three paintings that returned him to more traditional terrain. All three are similar to Pl. 218. They are easily readable views across the pond to the Japanese bridge which stretches between dense areas of foliage beneath a small section of brilliantly lit sky. All are painted with remarkable energy and contain passages of brilliant color. The pond in each is also surprisingly varied with an extraordinary mixture of visual incidents. With the surrounding garden, it appears wonderfully lush and much larger than it had in the earlier *Japanese Bridge*

218  Claude Monet, *Water Lily Pond. The Bridge*, 1905, 90 × 100, W.1668, Private Collection.

pictures: this effect is not illusory—in 1905, Monet had undertaken yet another expansion of the pond, an investment that might have inspired him to paint these three pictures. Despite their beauty and uniqueness, however, the three constitute more of a respite from the labors the previous twelve had extracted. Those dozen had taken Monet the better part of two years to complete. The three also were amalgams in which Monet attempted to wed the *Japanese Bridge* pictures to the discoveries he had made in the first dozen *Water Lilies*. He must have recognized this, for although he included one of these paintings in his 1909 exhibition, he quickly returned to the challenges that he had set for himself in those initial views of the pond, and specifically to paintings that contained nothing but lily pads, water, and reflections.

If there were lingering questions in some observers' minds after the 1900 exhibition of the *Japanese Bridges* about Monet's commitment or ability to make serious art out of what some reviewers perceived as shallow or inappropriate subject matter, the next three and a half years proved critical. For between late 1905 and January 1909 when Monet finally agreed to show these *Water Lilies* at Durand-Ruel's, the 65-year-old artist worked feverishly to produce pictures that in his opinion "would not disappoint the public."[26] In terms of their numbers alone, the results were astonishing—sixty pictures or about one every three weeks, all of which concentrated exclusively on the pond without the aid of banks, bridges, or background foliage (Pls. 219–26). While similar in subject, they differ in format. The first twenty from 1905 and '06 are mostly horizontal canvases, generally about a meter long. Within this relatively standard shape, Monet devised variation after variation, altering the arrangement of the lilies, reducing or increasing the amount of reflected material, and exploring a wide array of lighting effects. In all of them, time is suspended, just as it had been in the *Japanese Bridge* pictures. But here the paint is applied with such subtlety and breadth that the canvases seem to possess a kind of expansiveness that defies their relatively limited size and pushes well beyond the more restrained handling in the first *Bridge* pictures. In the watery

219   Claude Monet,
*Water Lilies*, 1905,
90 × 100, W.1673,
Private Collection.

220   Claude Monet,
*Water Lilies*, 1906,
81 × 92, W.1688,
National Museum of
Wales, Cardiff.

areas, for example, colors are laid one on top of the other to suggest the refractions of the light and the changing hues in the depths of the pond. The water lilies themselves are rendered with the most impasto to give them a sculptural presence, thereby affirming their position on top of the water. Wind sometimes seems to blow through the scenes suggested by passing clouds, while fleeting effects—quivering leaves, rippling water, and melding layers of light—are reflected in the pond's surface. Despite their immediacy and bravura, the twenty are surprisingly finished although most provide plenty of evidence of the pains Monet took to bring them to their state of completion.

The subsequent twenty from 1907 are much more experimental. Only three continue the horizontal format. The others are square, circular, or vertical, suggesting Monet was testing all of his options (Pls. 221–24). The vertical panels are the most venturesome. Instead of the lulling calm that the others possess, these vertical scenes are sliced down the middle by a meandering trail of sky, on either side of which are rivulets of reflected foliage and truncated clusters of flowers. The sky initially appears as a narrow but brilliantly colored intrusion that energizes the upper half of the picture at the same time as it divides it. As it descends generally on an angle to the right, it meets what is often the largest group of lily pads. The cluster sits almost exactly where the descending trail of light turns back to the left which is where the foliage on either side spreads out to reveal more of the reflected sky. Most often, that occurs slightly above the middle of the scene. This is a critical juncture, as it is here that the pictures change dramatically. From this point to the bottom, the lily pads float alone or in groups on the lighter sections of the water, often seeming to occupy a different plane from their counterparts above. They also are generally quite sketchily rendered as if proximity at this moment in the early twentieth century demanded an emphasis on process and expression, not an allegiance to mimetic description. Allowed to spread across the lower half of the picture, the sky also appears less constrained, something which is echoed in the way the light dissipates as it descends, losing the intensity it possessed at the top of the canvas until it finally turns dark by the time it reaches the bottom edge.

Many of the most challenging pictures in this group, such as Pl. 224, appear to depict evening effects. This is suggested by the fading light in the scenes and by the way Monet muddies his palette. Seductive pinks and greens all of a sudden become moodier mauves and murkier olives, meditation and seriousness replacing charm and delight. This is particularly evident when these pictures are compared with the circular versions from the same years (Pl. 222). Everything about those roundels—from their color schemes to their delicate surfaces—speaks of easy-going visual pleasure. Even their circular format, a throw-back to the eighteenth century, contributes to this effect, as it literally takes the edge off the image while leading the viewer to believe that the scene extends out on either side, like the ocean observed through a porthole.

The ethereal quality that these circular paintings possess is even more boldly expressed in the group of about thirteen pictures from 1907–08 that close the series of sixty (Pls. 225, 226). They are generally rendered with extremely delicate palettes—soft purples and yellows, light greens and pale blues—that do not change significantly across the canvas. They are also filled with equally even light, which is often so enormously restrained that it seems as if it were filtered through a theater scrim. The pearliness that results from this handling could not be further from the rough contrasts of the 1907 evening views, just as their almost chalky surfaces could not be less like the denser layers of pigment that distinguish their earlier counterparts.

The series as a whole, therefore, was remarkable not only for its size but also for its range and diversity, something critics noted when Monet put forty-eight of the canvases before the

223 (above left)
Claude Monet, *Water Lilies*, 1907, 100 × 73, W.1715, The Bridgestone Museum of Art, Ishibashi Foundation, Tokyo.

224 (above right)
Claude Monet, *Water Lilies*, 1907, 92 × 73, W.1706, Kawamura Memorial Museum of Art.

225   Claude Monet,
*Water Lilies*, 1908,
90 × 92, W.1721,
Private Collection.

public in May 1909. This was more than Monet had ever exhibited of any single series, which added to the novelty of the show. The show itself was hailed as an event; it had been greatly anticipated given the number of times it had been delayed and the fact people had not seen recent work since Monet's *Londons* of five years earlier. Visitors were not disappointed. They were astonished by Monet's versatility and prodigious output, as well as by the breadth and grandeur of the series. "One has never seen anything like it," declared the Paris correspondent for the *Burlington Magazine*. "These studies of water lilies and still water in every possible effect of light and at every hour of the day are beautiful to a degree which one can hardly express without seeming to exaggerate.... There is no other living artist," he claimed, "who could have given us these marvelous effects of light and shadow, this glorious feast of color."[27] Everyone was struck by the extraordinary harmony that the series exuded even though they recognized the differences between the various groups of pictures. Some, like Geffroy, found the decorative unity of the series to function like a spiritual balm and to possess a kind of universalism that transcended the specifics of the garden site. "Under the pretext of simplicity, there is everything that the eye can perceive and understand; there is the infinity of forms and nuances, [and] the complex life of things."[28] Others saw analogies to music and poetry. Roger Marx, one of Monet's long-time defenders, was moved by the way Monet mixed analysis and imagination to produce works which unabashedly declared their aesthetic essentials. One critic went so far as to say that the series ranked on the level of Michelangelo's Sistine Chapel and Beethoven's last quartets. In an imaginary interview with Monet, Marx quoted the artist as being more modest. "I have no other desire," Monet said, "than to merge myself more intimately with nature."[29]

Several writers bemoaned the inevitable dispersal of the canvases but they reminded their readers that Monet had an ultimate dream of decorating "a circular room of modest, well-calculated dimensions" which they hoped a millionaire might realize. "Around it, to half human height, there would . . . extend a painting of water and flowers passing though every possible modulation," wrote Arsène Alexandre. "Nothing else. No furniture. Nothing but a table in the center of the room which would be a dining-room encircled by these mysteriously seductive reflections."[30]

226 Claude Monet, *Water Lilies*, 1908, 92 × 90, W.1733, Worcester Art Museum, Worcester, Massachusetts.

227 Claude Monet, *Water Lilies*, 1897–98, 66 × 104.1, W.1501, Los Angeles County Museum of Art, Bequest of Mrs. Fred Hathaway Bixby.

This was a dream that Monet had expressed more than ten years earlier when a journalist, Maurice Guillemot, visited Giverny in 1897. "Imagine a circular room in which the walls above the baseboard," he told Guillemot, "would be covered with [paintings of] water, dotted with these plants to the very horizon, walls of a transparency by turns toned green and mauve, the still waters calm and silence reflecting the opened blossoms. The tones are vague, lovingly nuanced, as delicate as a dream."[31] Guillemot claimed Monet had already begun studies for this project, "large panels, which he showed me afterward in his studio." The only works that have survived that Guillemot might have seen are eight canvases, among them Pl. 227, which date from 1897 and 1898. If these were in fact related to this dream, it is easy to see why Monet took so long to realize it, for these pictures are greatly reduced in palette, brushwork, and ambition compared with the *Water Lilies* of 1903–09 as well as the larger such pictures that would follow. The water lily pads in these canvases sit flaccidly on an unmodulated section of the pond. The pond itself is almost opaque while its spatial dimensions have been severely limited, just like the number and variety of lily pads. The paintings also are modest in size, generally measuring about 70 × 100 centimeters, thus making them humble beginnings indeed for what ultimately would become Monet's most grandiose project.

It would be some time before Monet got to that project, however, as he could hardly think about work after his *Water Lily* exhibition closed in early June 1909. At 69½, he did not have the same energy he once enjoyed and was understandably exhausted from the six years he had spent on this painstaking series. He also was under no economic pressure to return to his labors right away. He sold nineteen paintings to Durand-Ruel and his rivals the Bernheim-Jeune brothers during the course of the year for a total of 272,000 francs, an extraordinary amount of money which only added to his already substantial bank account. So he did not work. He had promised Georges Bernheim-Jeune that he would complete a suite of paintings that he had begun when he and Alice Hoschedé had visited Venice for slightly more than two months in late 1908. But he reneged on that commitment, leaving the nearly forty canvases that comprised the series leaning up against the walls of his studio in various states of finish for almost two years.

In addition to his fatigue and advancing age, Monet was not able to bring himself to work on these Venetian views because they were removed from his more novel investigations of his water lily garden. They also were dissociated from the sites they depicted, as Monet had

228 Gobelins Tapestry Factory, water lily tapestry, 1910–13, 95 × 100, Mobilier National, Paris.

merely roughed in the canvases during his stay in Italy. Finishing them in his Giverny studio, therefore, really was work, as he had to rely on memory and invention, as opposed to the immediacy of *plein-air* experience. Not surprisingly, therefore, he saw them as "souvenirs" and insisted that after they were all gathered at Berheim-Jeune's for the exhibition in late May 1912 he would choose several for himself to remind him of his trip.[32] Not surprisingly as well, given the special circumstances surrounding their completion, the pictures vary a great deal in their handling and degree of finish, although individually most exude a striking mixture of airiness and nostalgia, grandeur and simplicity, as if Monet, while reliving a brief chapter of his own life, were paying homage to that ancient city of light and water and to the painters it had attracted over the centuries.

Finalizing the pictures between 1910 and 1912 became more of a problem because of three specific events. The first occurred in early 1910 when the Seine and the Epte surged over their banks and flooded both his gardens off and on for nearly two months. The waters were so high and turbulent that waves occasionally broke by the entrance to his house. Monet thought his life's passion had been ruined. "[He] does not speak, but moans," Alice confided in her daughter, Germaine; his "despair, like the Epte, will not abate."[33] The waters finally receded, however, and by summer the gardens were more radiant than ever before, due to the rich layers of sludge that the rivers had generously deposited across the property.

The second event was less distressing, although it preoccupied him from time to time during the period and undoubtedly planted ideas in his head that did the same. It involved a commission for a tapestry that would be based on one of his recent *Water Lily* paintings (Pl. 228).[34] The idea was the brainchild of Gustave Geffroy whom Clemenceau appointed in 1908 to head the Manufacture Nationale des Gobelins, the oldest and most prestigious tapestry maker in France. Initiating the commission had been Geffroy's first act as director, although it was not until the summer or fall of 1910 that it actually was awarded and not until

229  Claude Monet,
*The Grand Canal,
Venice*, 1908, 73 × 92,
W.1739, Private
Collection.

1913 that the tapestry was completed. During the three-year period when the Gobelin weavers were doing the work, the order grew from one tapestry to three. Because this was his first cooperative venture with the government and was going to result in a work of art that represented him, Monet became quite involved in the process, even down to consultations about colors and materials.

The third event was much more serious and ultimately more tragic. Alice Hoschedé fell ill as the waters rose in front of the house in early 1910. She was eventually diagnosed as having myeloid leukemia and was confined to bed. As her health declined, Monet became more and more distraught. "For a month, she has had to suffer four crises," he informed Geffroy in late December, "several very violent.... It's devastating as it diminishes the benefits of the radiotherapy treatment."[35] By 1 May 1911, her condition had drastically deteriorated; by the 7th, Monet thought it was "only a matter of hours."[36] Mercifully, her end came soon, early on the morning of 19 May. Monet was at her side. After more than thirty years together, the pain of her loss was excruciating for the master of Giverny; he grieved for months, unable to do anything else. "I am totally worn out," he told Bernheim-Jeune in August of that year. "Time passes and I cannot make anything out of my sad existence. I don't have the taste for anything and don't even have the courage to write."[37] When he attempted to find solace in his studio at the end of the year, he proclaimed he was "going to give up painting forever. All that I can do these days is completely ruin several Venice pictures which I will have to destroy," he told Blanche Hoschedé. "Sad results. I should have left them just as they were, as souvenirs of such happy days spent with my dear Alice."[38]

But just as the waters of the Seine and Epte eventually returned to their beds, so too did Monet gradually regain his strength. By the early spring of 1912, he was able to finish twenty-nine of his Venice pictures which, almost predictably by now, were enthusiastically received when they were exhibited at Berheim-Jeune's in May and June of that year (Pl. 229). The widespread praise was not much consolation to Monet, however, who told Paul Signac that even though "the insidious critics of the first hour [of my career] have left me alone,

I remain equally indifferent to the praises of imbeciles, snobs, and traffickers."[39] This uncharacteristically frank response was perhaps due to his sense that the pictures were not really on a par with his *Water Lilies*, something he admitted to Gustave Geffroy before the show opened. "I would like to be as satisfied with them as you appear to be. There are some that are not bad but . . . I fear that your friendship blinds you."[40] He also must have suspected that some of the praise the show received was prompted more by sentimentality than by honest reactions to the paintings; a few reviewers stated as much.[41] But most of all, he undoubtedly could not help but see the group as tragically linked to his deceased Alice, for whose loss no amount of praise could ever compensate.

The health of his oldest son, Jean, added to his concerns. Monet had sent Jean to England around 1890 to become a chemist. He had returned to France a few years later and had gone to work for his uncle, Léon Monet, who ran a chemical plant in Maromme-les-Rouen. In 1897, he married his stepsister Blanche Hoschedé, and had taken her from Giverny to live with him in Rouen. Disagreements with his uncle, however, ended his employment there and some time around 1912 he and Blanche left Rouen for Beaumont-le-Roger just up the Epte from Giverny, where Jean started a trout farm. Soon after, he began to experience serious health problems and was diagnosed as having syphilis, a disease he may have contracted while in the army in the late 1880s.[42] Just as the Venice show was ending, Jean's condition began to deteriorate; barely a week after it closed, he suffered a mental attack that was so intense Monet thought his son was actually going to lose his mind, something he eventually did two years later.[43]

If that were not enough, Monet had a frightening experience himself shortly after Jean's attack. While working in his studio that summer, he all of a sudden realized he could not see out of his right eye. Visiting several specialists, he learned he had a cataract and that his left eye "was also slightly affected."[44] Some of the doctors recommended an operation. Monet resisted, telling Geffroy he did not believe them when "they tell me the operation is not serious, that after it I will see as before. I am very disturbed and anxious," as he rightfully should have been.[45] Nothing was more precious to him than his sight. He therefore desperately tried to avoid surgery and in approximately twelve months felt his eyes were getting better. It is impossible to know whether that was the case or even how serious the problem actually was. But his condition did appear to stabilize; Monet did not mention it much until after the war when it worsened considerably, leaving him no alternative but to undergo the operation in 1923.

While terrifying, this problem actually increased his desire to paint, at least according to his letters. "Very happily," he told Durand-Ruel in August 1912, "[the doctor] did not forbid my continuing to paint, and if the weather finally wants to improve, I will once again bravely take up working, which more than ever is what I need."[46] Although the weather cooperated, Monet did not fulfill that desire with his typical aplomb. Over the course of the next twenty months, he produced only half a dozen pictures, a dearth that seems to have been the result of his despondency as much as his eye problems. In addition to his own health, he was worried about his family, particularly Jean, whose condition had become so critical that Monet bought him a house in Giverny in early 1913 so that he could be nearby on a permanent basis. Less than a year later, however, Jean became so incapacitated that he moved in with his father just after Monet himself had been bedridden for a month with a terrible cold. "What torture it is for me to witness this decline," he cried to his friend Charlotte Lysès, especially when it was happening "there, in front of me, that's what's hard."[47] A week later, Jean was dead, at the age of 46. "Our consolation is to think that he is no longer suffering," Monet told Durand-Ruel, "for he was a true martyr."[48] On top of all this, Monet's younger son Michel became ill the following month and had to undergo an operation which added to Monet's worries and forced him to spend over a week in Paris during the patient's convalescence.

By late April, however, something changed. "I'm feeling marvelous," he informed Geffroy on the 30th of the month, "and I'm obsessed with the desire to paint."[49] Just what caused this snap is difficult to say. Given his resilience and his uneasiness at being around the sick and the dying, he undoubtedly wanted to put all the health problems of the previous year and a half behind him and get back to work. But it is certainly no coincidence that his desire to return to his business as a painter was re-ignited exactly at the same time that his country was preparing for what appeared to be yet another conflict with the Germans. According to one leading historian, "most influential people in France, as elsewhere, accepted another European war as ultimately inevitable"; it was only a question of when and where it would occur.[50] Monet admitted to a friend that "for a long time" he too had thought about the possibility of armed conflict but he had not been able to bring himself to believe it actually would happen.[51] However, when Archduke Ferdinand of Austria, heir to the Hapsburg Empire, was murdered with his wife by fanatical Serbs on 28 June 1914 precipitating Austria's declaration of war on Serbia a month later, he obviously was proven wrong. Barely a week after that, on 2 and 3 August, seventy-eight German divisions began marching into Luxembourg and Belgium. By the 20th they had captured Brussels and by 1 September they were threatening Paris.

> "What will happen to all of us?" the cubist painter Juan Gris asked his dealer, Daniel-Henry Kahnweiler, in the middle of August of that fateful year. "All those who had sketched out our way through life must now change everything temporarily and get along as best we can. For my dear friend, I can see that in the nightmare through which we are passing, previous engagements are no longer valid and each of us must make his own way. How?" he asked. "I dont know."[52]

It was during those fateful months when the military machines on either side of the Rhine began their frightening build-ups causing tensions to rise in direct proportion to the hostile rhetoric in the press, that Monet returned to his beloved garden to try to make his way and realize the Grand Decorations he had dreamed about for so long. Like Henri Matisse, who volunteered for the army when the war broke out but was turned down because of his age, Monet at 74 felt the weight of the moment and responded accordingly. He turned to his work, just like his younger contemporary who described the plight of the artist during these difficult times. "I work enormously all day long, and with ardor," the Fauve-turned-classicist told his friend Charles Camoin. "I know there is only that, good and sure. I can't engage in politics as, alas, almost everyone does, so to compensate I have to make strong and sensitive paintings. Ours," he continued, "is a career of forced labor, without the certainties that allow one to sleep tranquilly. Every day I have to have worked all day long to accept the irresponsibility which puts the conscience to rest."[53] Unlike Matisse, however, who visited Monet several times during the war but who concentrated primarily on sober scenes in his Quai Saint-Michel apartment, the elder Impressionist was determined to celebrate nature's power to revivify the spirit. In so doing, he would provide his countrymen and women with wholesome reassurances about life and beauty that could counter what he described later in 1914 as the prevailing aura of "anguish and apprehension."[54]

Taking his cues from the more than one hundred paintings of his aquatic paradise that he had completed over the previous decade and a half, as well as from innumerable prototypes that would have appealed to him—from multi-paneled Japanese and Chinese scrolls to decorative projects by contemporaries such as Bonnard, Vuillard, Caillebotte, and

230   Claude Monet, *Water Lilies*, 1914–17, 150 × 200, W.1791, Musée Marmottan, Paris.

Whistler—Monet began some of the most ambitious canvases of his career, a series of views of his water lily pond that were characterized by an unprecedented breadth in terms of their size, touch, and vision (Pls. 230, 231). Nearly all of these pictures (which swelled to more than sixty in three years) were twice as big as his earlier *Water Lilies*. They also were more daring in their color schemes and compositions. And they were much looser in handling. Indeed, the majority are so open and free that they embody all the freshness of a work in progress or a new kind of grand-scale sketch, especially in comparison to the more modest and more finished water landscapes of 1900–09. That Monet considered these to be special essays is underscored by the fact that he did not exhibit or sell any of them until the 1920s when he parted with just one to the great Japanese collector, Kojiro Matsukata (Pl. 231). This canvas also was the only one in the group that Monet signed and dated, suggesting that he sold it to Matsukata as a gesture of friendship not out of a desire to put it in circulation.

Although all sixty concentrate on the water garden, they do not share enough compositional similarities to suggest Monet had conceived any of them as pairs or triptychs, which also supports the idea that they were working canvases of a new and different sort. Their formats imply this as well, as some are vertical, some horizontal, some almost square.

231 Claude Monet, *Water Lilies*, 1914–17, 200.5 × 201, W.1800, The National Museum of Western Art, Tokyo, Matsukata Collection.

Obviously, he had not set out to achieve the kind of continuity that would soon become critical to his notions about his decorative ensemble. At once exploratory and definitive, hesitant and assured, these paintings thus constitute a unique group of canvases in Monet's oeuvre. They were a sustained and evidently private enterprise in which Monet tested out his ideas for his decorative program on a scale he had never attempted for these watery motifs.

So engaged did he become with these canvases between May and June 1914 that he declined an invitation to attend the opening of new rooms at the Louvre that had been refurbished to receive the bequest of the Parisian collector, Count Isaac de Camondo, despite the fact that the donation included fourteen of his own paintings.[55] This event had historic dimensions: it marked the first time the museum had ever agreed to acquire and hang works by a living artist. Monet's excuse was the same to all of those who inquired about his absence—"work above all."[56] Monet also refused requests to visit friends and even cut back on his letter-writing. "I have thrown myself back into work," he told Durand-Ruel in late June, "and when I do that, I do it seriously, so much so that I am getting up at four a.m. and am grinding away all day long." Although exhausted in the evening, he said he could think

204

of nothing but his work. "I am as well as possible," he reported, "my sight is good, finally. Thanks to work, the great consolation, all goes well."[57]

His obsession with work, which he repeated in five of the nine letters he managed to write during these weeks, suggests how much he invested in this new project. In early July, he made this clear when he begged Geffroy to come to Giverny to see the results of his labors. At $74\frac{1}{2}$, he knew he was on to something significant, "the beginnings of a great work," he told Geffroy.[58] When war was declared less than a month later, he immediately became more sober. The inevitable had occurred. "We have been in a state of confusion for a month," he confessed to Geffroy on 1 September. "We don't know what we're doing." Isolated and fearful, he reached out to his old friend. "What I do know," he told him, "is that in the present state of things and in my isolation, a letter from a good friend like you is a comfort which helps me to endure their agonies."[59] The war clearly struck home and not just metaphorically. Less than ten days after it had been declared, Monet had to send his stepson, Jean-Pierre Hoschedé, off to the front, charging him to "be courageous and prudent and to rest assured that our hearts are with you. Think of us," he asked him. "Those who remain are also to be pitied."[60] Three weeks later, he learned that Clemenceau's son had been wounded and shortly after that his stepdaughter, Germaine, declared she and her children were leaving Giverny. "Many of my family have left," he told Geffroy, "without our knowing where they are. . . . Germaine, who was here with her children, left yesterday; a mad panic has come over our whole area."[61] A month later, he found out that Renoir's son had been shot, one of the tens of thousands that had become a statistic—either killed or wounded—in the first two months of the conflict. This was not a fact that Monet just read in the press. He witnessed it all around him. "The wounded are everywhere," he informed Durand-Ruel's son in October 1914, "even in the smallest villages."[62] In the face of this horror and attendant anxiety, Monet's resolve remained firm. "As for me, I'm here," he told Geffroy, "and if those savages must kill me, it will be in the midst of my canvases, in front of my life's work."[63]

Despite this almost blind determination so tinged with nationalism and a sense of fate that the war and old age had inevitably encouraged, Monet was not able to get back to work until the end of November. And even then the war weighed heavily upon him. Painting, he told Geffroy, "is still the best way not to think too much about the sad state of affairs although I am slightly embarrassed to think about little researches into form and color while so many people suffer and die for us."[64] He felt exactly the same way as the new year dawned. "I am not performing miracles," he told one of the Bernheim-Jeune brothers in February 1915. "I mix and use a great deal of color. It occupies me enough so that I don't have to think too much about this terrible, hideous war."[65] But like everyone else in France, Monet could not help but be haunted by all of those who "were suffering, fighting, and dying," as he described to Léon Wirth in March.[66] "A man not at the front feels rather good for nothing," the younger Matisse confessed soon after, a feeling he and Monet both fought to overcome.[67] Although it was against his principles during "ordinary times," Monet joined several war-related committees, one of which published a book in 1915 called *Les Allemands, déstructeurs des cathédrales et des trésors du passé* in which Monet's name appeared as a member of the group. He also went against his almost unbroken record of refusing to support patriotic causes when he donated money to an effort that Geffroy had mounted to aid "our poor soldiers." Equally remarkable, and even more generous, he participated in numerous exhibitions and sales for the benefit of war victims and various war-related relief initiatives, extending himself more than probably any other artist of his generation.[68] Most important, however, he did what he did best—he painted.

His commitment to his work and his doggedness served him well. By June 1915, his decorative program began to take shape as attested by a group of writers from the Académie Goncourt who came to Giverny for lunch on the 17th of that month. During the course of their visit, the writers were treated to a unique preview of the project when Monet gave them a tour of the second studio he had built on the property in 1899. As one visitor reported, they saw there "vast canvases of about 2 meters high by 3 to 5 meters long. He had already covered some, and he was having a studio built specifically for the series which he hoped to continue."[69] Although it is difficult to know exactly which canvases these were, they clearly were the outgrowth of the numerous rough sketches Monet had done since the previous May and constituted the first stages of what he clairvoyantly admitted to Mirbeau would be a five-year undertaking. It must have been difficult for the visitors to have seen these huge pictures given the spatial limitations of the studio, but even in their unfinished state the canvases left a lasting impression; one member of the group published four separate accounts of the experience over the next thirty years.[70]

As with the identity of these specific canvases, it is impossible to know whether Monet's plans for the new studio that one writer mentioned had been envisioned before he began the project, or whether it grew out of the practical considerations the over-sized canvases posed once Monet started to work on them in the modest space of the 1890s atelier. In either case, Monet does not appear to have submitted plans for the third studio until the late spring or early summer of 1915 as he did not receive the necessary permits from the local Prefect until 5 July of that year. When approval came, the structure rose at a remarkable pace, despite the shortages of manpower and materials during the war. By mid-August, the concrete foundations and floor had been poured and the building advanced far enough for Monet to regret its "ugly" external appearance. "I am ashamed to have made this myself," he admitted to his stepson, Jean-Pierre Hoschedé, "me who always cried out against those people who compromise Giverny's beauty."[71] He felt the whole project was something of a "folly" particularly "at my age"—just like the cost, which he admitted was "horribly expensive." The building ultimately ran to 35,600 francs, more than one and a half times what he originally had paid for his house and property combined. But he knew he was getting an unprecedented structure—23 meters long by 12 meters wide—whose iron truss system allowed the cavernous internal space to be free of any vertical supports. The trusses also permitted the roof to rise 15 meters at its peak and to be punctuated with huge skylights that washed the space with an abundance of natural light. It was, in short, a magnificent environment that Monet was thrilled to occupy in late October when it was sufficiently finished for him to move his canvases and materials in. Only then, he told Geffroy, did he finally have "the opportunity to judge what I have done."[72]

What Monet thought of his pictures when he first saw them in this new space or even how far they had progressed remains a mystery, as he was silent on both matters. But given his penchant for complaining, no word one way or the other suggests his satisfaction. A month later, however, he was "concerned and saddened" as the war had required another sacrifice—his younger son Michel was shipped off to the front at the end of November. To make matters worse, Monet had traveled to Versailles to wish him goodbye, only to find that he had left the day before. Having turned 75 only two weeks earlier, Monet confessed to Geffroy, "At my age, that's tough to take."[73] Work remained his only consolation over the next few months, although he often admitted his thoughts were elsewhere. All he could wish for, he announced to friends, was "the end to this terrible war and victory," a feeling that became particularly poignant when Michel was obliged to spend three frightening weeks in Verdun.[74] Not surprisingly, as the war dragged on making his wish all the more precious, the curmudgeon came out in the artist. He fell into nasty moods which he recognized were unfair

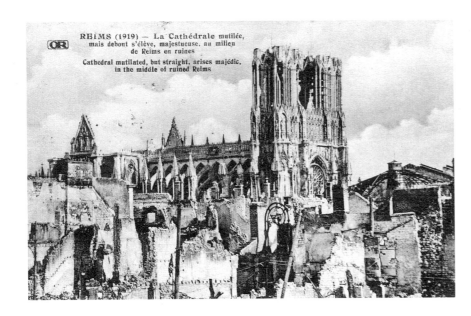

232 Anonymous,
photograph of Reims
Cathedral after the
bombing of 19
September 1914,
postcard. Courtesy of
Kenneth E. Silver.

to poor Blanche Hoschedé, his only companion in Giverny, just as he knew that such snits were unjust in the light of the suffering that the soldiers had to endure. When in these moods, he also tended to become discouraged about being able to realize his project which he feared was "beyond my powers and certainly beyond my age."[75] But he hung on and was thrilled when Clemenceau came to see him in early November 1916 and "left enthusiastic about what I have done," as he reported to Geffroy. He urged Geffroy to come as well since he had told Clemenceau "how happy I would be to have your advice about this formidable undertaking which is, to tell you the truth, a folly."[76] As 1916 gave way to another year of conflict, however, Monet's faith in the future and ability to realize his project began to slip. "Disgusted with what I am doing and seeing that I will not achieve my goal, I feel I am at the end of my rope and am no longer good for anything."[77]

To compound his concern, his good friend Octave Mirbeau died in February 1917. The critic's passing deeply affected the 76-year-old artist. In addition to losing a soulmate and supporter of almost thirty years, Monet felt it was one more member of the Impressionists' coterie gone and one more mark of the movement's passage into history, a fact that was underscored when Degas died in October of the same year at the age of 83. Of the original group, only Renoir was still alive and he would die two years later in 1919.

The heralded position that Impressionism and Monet in particular had achieved since its emergence in the 1860s was brought home to him soon after Mirbeau's funeral. On 30 April 1917 he had the pleasure of receiving two government officials at Giverny—Etienne Clémentel, the Minister of Commerce and Industry, and Albert Dalimier, the Under Secretary of State for Fine Arts. They had come to pay homage to the artist and to discuss the possibility of commissioning from him a painting of Reims Cathedral. Undoubtedly inspired by Monet's *Rouen Cathedral* series, one example of which the State had purchased in 1907, the commission was unique as the Cathedral in Reims had been bombed by the Germans (Pl. 232). Surprisingly perhaps, Monet found this opportunity "very interesting" and accepted it immediately. Although it took the government six months to process the official decree, Monet still was "flattered and honored" when the papers were delivered to him on 30 or 31 October.[78]

That Monet responded so quickly and so favorably to this opportunity demands some explanation, as initially it seems odd that the painter of nature's beauties would have wanted

233–36 [Paul or
Georges Durand-Ruel],
photographs of Monet's
*Grandes Decorations* in
the artist's Giverny
studio, 11 November
1917, Archives Durand-
Ruel, Paris.

to execute a picture that in theory would have borne witness to death and destruction. Selfishly, he might have seen it as an opportunity to curry favor with the government or as a way to lay the groundwork for whatever plans he may have been hatching regarding his "famous decorations," as he self-deprecatingly described his project. He also might have viewed it as a means to further his reputation as one of France's great national painters. But these explanations seem too cynical, even if the commission were going to bring him further recognition. They also are out of line with his genuine horror of the war. It seems instead that he saw it as an opportunity to apply his "little researches into color and light" to a subject that stated his position less equivocally than his equally impassioned but more metaphorical water lilies.

For reasons that remain unknown, however, Monet never seems to have begun the picture; he never even mentioned it after his official acceptance letter of 1 November 1917. Government personnel were equally silent on the subject. And no official documents exist that shed any light on its fate. But the fact that Monet was so receptive to the opportunity suggests how compatible it was with his orientation. It therefore also stands as a reminder of how much he invested in his huge decorative panels and the multiple ways in which those monumental canvases should be read. For they clearly were not just about light, color, and the splendor of his garden; they were bound up with larger issues, like all of Monet's work.

Monet soon made this apparent, but not before he permitted Durand-Ruel and his son to come to Giverny and photograph the panels on 11 November, an indication of his confidence in the paintings (Pls. 233–36). These photographs are remarkable documents. Not only are they among the first views of Monet's spacious new studio, they also provide the first glimpse of the progress he had made on his decorations after three years of work. They even suggest his methods while underscoring the ambitiousness of the project. What they show are at least twelve large panels of approximately 2 meters high by 4.25 meters long, most of which he clearly had conceived of as groups. Conveniently mounted on large, movable easels, one suite of four canvases depicts two cropped willow trees with their foliage cascading in front of water lily clusters (Pls. 233–36); another triptych to the right of the willow panels in Pl. 236 concentrates on agapanthus; and a lone canvas to the left of the willow panels in Pl. 233 seems to be a preliminary stage of what soon would be a suite of

three canvases depicting irises. It is clear that many of them are relatively advanced, that they were intended to occupy some kind of curving space, and that Monet had even gone so far as to consider what kind of frame, if any, he wanted for them (the latter is evident from the continuous wooden molding along the top edge of the panels). What also is interesting is the fact that very few, if any, of the sixty odd studies that Monet made over the previous three years seem to have served as specific models for these pictures, underscoring the amount of labor that went into the enterprise while validating Monet's worries about being able to complete it.[79] When the critic Thiébault-Sisson visited Monet in February 1918, the artist claimed he had already finished eight of the twelve canvases that were going to comprise his ensemble and that he could complete the other four in a year "as long as my eyes do not play any new tricks on me from now until then."[80] His estimate was as ambitious as the project itself, for although he worked on the pictures throughout the year, he would not finish them all for quite some time. In large part, the problem was of his own making as he decided to paint a whole group of new canvases at the same time, most of which were relatively large—up to 2 meters a side. Many of these are rough sketches like his first suite of studies; many of them extend the initiatives of their predecessors.

Perhaps the most remarkable works in this group of new canvases actually constituted an entirely independent series that Monet began in 1918 and largely completed that year. There are ten paintings in the series, all of which depict one of two weeping willows that stood at the northern end of the water lily pond (Pls. 241, 242). The ten vary slightly in size and composition but they are surprisingly uniform in their powerful impact. In each, the tree is located to the left of center. It twists and turns from the bottom of the canvas to the top, its branches stretching out to either side like the quivering arms of a frenzied dancer or shaman. The majority of the scene is filled with rivulets of multicolored foliage that fall like a shimmering deluge of flora from the sky. So thick is the foliage, however, that the sky is hardly visible, just as the area beyond the tree is almost entirely obscured. With surfaces troweled by his heavily loaded brush and colors bordering on the brazen, these are some of the most highly charged canvases Monet ever produced. They also are some of the most dialectical. Nothing seems quite rational in them and yet everything appears palpable and

237 Claude Monet, *Grandes Décorations. Morning*, four canvases, two 200 × 212.5, two 200 × 425, Musée de l'Orangerie, Paris.

keenly sensed. Light battles dark, description grapples with expression, space combats surface. The scenes brim with emotion but of similarly contrasting kinds. There are cries of pain and shouts of ecstasy, shivers of fear and clamors of celebration. Doubt pervades all the pictures but determination seems to prevail.

That Monet personally associated with these struggles is undeniable. He had staked that kind of claim thirty years earlier when painting an old oak tree in the valley of the Creuse (Pl. 243). Like a lone actor in a theater of natural splendor, the tree featured in more than half a dozen paintings from that campaign and became extremely important to Monet as a kind of personal symbol. Monet referred to it as "my tree" and even went so far as to tell Alice Hoschedé that he was "going to do a big sketch of my poor oak . . . through [which] you will realize the rages and difficulties I have had [here]."[81] Haunted by potential blindness and the horrors of the most devastating conflict the modern world had ever experienced, Monet's anger and distress had increased proportionately since that trip to the Creuse just as the formal elements at his disposal had been pushed to new extremes. But his association with his subjects had remained steadfast and meaningful.

238 Claude Monet, *Grandes Décorations. Morning with Willows*, three canvases, all 200 × 425, Musée de l'Orangerie, Paris.

That Monet saw these *Weeping Willows* as relevant to his war-torn country is also undeniable. Throughout those wretched years of killing, he never attempted to conceal his

outrage about the conflict or his sorrow at the toll it so excruciatingly exacted. When he began these *Weeping Willow* pictures, the Germans had mounted their most intense offensive against France; he and everyone braced themselves for the worst as the Germans broke through the British defenses in the Somme valley near Saint-Quentin in March and pressed on to capture Amiens only thirty-seven kilometers from Giverny. In May, they overran the French position along the Aisne and by the end of the month had occupied Château Thierry just ninety-six kilometers from Paris. "What an agonizing life we all are living," he cried to Durand-Ruel in June of that year. "I continue . . . to work, although at times, I long to give it all up. Sometimes, I have to ask myself what I would do if a new surprise attack by the enemy occurred." He answered his own question, however. "I think it then would be necessary to abandon everything like everyone else." This did not please him which is why he hoped that "all precautions are taken to withstand the enemy and that we arm ourselves with patience and courage. But even still," he admitted, "it would be hard for me to abandon everything to those dirty Krauts."[82] As he worked, the art world was taking measures to prevent such a catastrophe. The Rouen Museum, for example, less than an hour away, had removed its collections to safe storage that summer in anticipation of the German offensive, something Monet had learned at least by June. He also found out that museums and galleries in Paris

239 Claude Monet, *Grandes Décorations. The Setting Sun*, 200 × 600, Musée de l'Orangerie, Paris.

were in the process of doing the same. He was even asked by the Bernheim-Jeune brothers whether he wanted them to store work for him. He responded with the same mixture of anxiety and determination as he had expressed before. He thanked them for their gesture but said, "I do not want to believe that I would ever be obliged to leave Giverny; as I have written, I would much rather die here in the middle of what I have done."[83]

Like everyone else in France, however, Monet must have grown more fearful as the Germans appeared to be assuming control of the war that summer. For the first time in several years, Monet spoke unabashedly about mortality. "I do not have long to live," he told Georges Bernheim-Jeune, "and I must dedicate all of my time to painting, with the hope of arriving at something that is good, or that satisfies me, if that is possible."[84] He felt a measure of hope when the Allies mounted their counter-offensive in September and began pushing the Germans back along the Western Front while winning decisive battles in the Balkans and the Middle East. When Bulgaria surrendered to the Allies on the 30th of the month followed by the Ottoman Empire and Austria–Hungary at the end of October, the Germans were left isolated and reeling. The Allies pressed their case, pushing the enemy out of France and Belgium, forcing them to the peace table by early November. Monet was immensely relieved. He also was terribly proud of what his nation had endured and what the French army in particular had accomplished. To demonstrate his pleasure, he wrote Clemenceau a letter on 12 November 1918: "I am on the verge of finishing two decorative panels that I want to sign on the day of the Victory and am going to ask you to offer them to the State. . . . It's not much, but it is the only way I have of taking part in the victory. I would like these two panels to be placed in the Museum of Decorative Arts and would be happy that they were chosen by you."[85] He obviously would have to post-date them to have them coincide with the armistice, but his gesture was both moving and revealing. For not only does it attest to his nationalism; it also makes it clear that he saw his work as part of a larger whole, one that was deeply interwoven with the collective efforts of his country. Little wonder, therefore, that in addition to a *Water Lily*, Monet told Bernheim-Jeune that he was going to donate to the State one canvas from the *Weeping Willow* series. What more apt expression of the torment that had gripped the nation or the joy that she now could celebrate?[86]

As with the Reims commission, however, this donation did not materialize, at least not in the form Monet initially proposed; it grew into something much grander, undoubtedly because of Clemenceau. Ever since his front-page article on the *Cathedral* paintings in 1895, the "Tiger of France" had often expressed his profound admiration for Monet and his work, feeling that he alone exemplified the ideals of an artist and that his art rose above the rest because it was endowed with noble feelings and a heightened sense of purpose. It therefore spoke with a compelling mixture of poetry and urgency that could appeal to a wide range of people. And, most important, perhaps, it was original. In Clemenceau's mind, these attributes were truly admirable, and perfectly aligned with those that he held dear about the nation. Thus, instead of calling upon the President of France to purchase paintings by his celebrated friend, as he had done in 1895, Clemenceau now could do it for himself, since he had been named prime minister in November 1917. Gathering the necessary political support, appropriating the funds, and then seeing the project through to its completion would prove to be a challenge for both of these strong-minded men. But it appears that from the armistice onwards, the two had agreed that the donation would not be just two decorative panels but the monumental twelve that Monet had been working on since the beginning of the war.[87]

With the future of the project in Clemenceau's hands, Monet continued to work on these paintings off and on for the next two years although they were not his sole preoccupation. During that same period, he also began more than sixty other canvases, over a dozen of which were extremely large depictions of water lilies, such as Pl. 244. It is difficult to know whether he started these as sketches for parts of his decorative series (some of them remain extremely rough) or whether they were supposed to be independent paintings (he brought some to completion and sold at least four of them in 1919). More than likely it was a combination of the two, as Monet must have realized that Clemenceau could not deliver right away on whatever promises he had made to his friend, which allowed the artist time to paint some marketable pictures and to develop new ideas. Among the sixty canvases, for example, are a suite of eight views of *Wisteria* (Pls. 244, 245) that are unique in Monet's oeuvre. Never

240 Manuel, photograph of Monet and Clemenceau at Giverny, ca. 1923, Musée Clemenceau, Paris.

241 Claude Monet, *Weeping Willow*, 1918–19, 131.2 × 110.3, W.1869, Columbus Museum of Art, Ohio, Gift of Howard D. and Babette L. Sirak, the Donors to the Campaign for Enduring Excellence, and the Derby Fund.

before had he painted these flowering vines in such a lyrical yet forceful manner. Even their arabesque arrangement along the top part of the picture is completely new. So too is their scale; seven of the eight are larger than any of the *Water Lilies* that he was working on at the same time (the *Wisteria* measure 1.5 × 2 meters and 1 × 3 meters *versus* 1 × 2 meters for the *Water Lilies*). Monet appears to have conceived of these ethereal, yet highly energized, images not as independent canvases but as complements to the views of his pond and as part of his decorative ensemble. For, according to later accounts, he intended to hang them above the doors that led into the room that contained the decorative panels, thus bridging the only break in what he envisioned as a continuous sweep of water and light with a garland-like

242 (above) Claude Monet, *Weeping Willow*, 1918–19, 100 × 120, W.1875, Musée Marmottan, Paris.

243 Claude Monet, *Old Oak in Fresselines*, 1889, 81 × 92, W.1229, presumed destroyed during World War II. Document, Archives Durand-Ruel, Paris.

244 Claude Monet, *Water Lilies*, 1918–19, 100 × 200, W.1894, Private Collection.

frieze that recalled older decorative traditions.[88] None of these remarkable canvases ever made it into the final schema, however, primarily because of complications that arose about where the whole donation was going to be housed, a problem that proved to be extremely vexing and would ultimately take years to resolve.

The issue initially was exacerbated by Clemenceau's defeat in the Presidential election of January 1920. All of a sudden, the project lost its greatest supporter, and Monet his best political ally. The ageing statesman appears to have continued to fight for the donation, aided by Clémentel, who had moved from Minister of Industry and Commerce to Senator for Puy-de-Dôme. They also were assisted by several journalists who took up the cause, most notably Thiébault-Sisson who published several important articles on the donation based in part on confidential information that Monet had supplied him. Because of the pressure that these people applied, Monet must have received assurances from government officials some time in the late spring or early summer that they would continue to explore ways to realize the project, since Monet rather defiantly told Clémentel in July 1920 that "if the State wants me to work for it, it is imperative that it gives me the means."[89] This was not a demand for money but a request for the following winter's supply of coal which was being rationed after the war. Soon after, he was in deeper negotiations as that June the Ministry of Fine Arts had assumed control of the Hôtel Biron, Rodin's Paris house and studio, which the sculptor had left to the nation when he had died in 1916. The Ministry proposed to construct a new building on the grounds of Rodin's estate to house Monet's donation, an idea Monet must have found appealing given his long-standing friendship with the sculptor who occupied an equally heralded position in the annals of French art. They had even been born on the same day—14 November 1840—and had shared the limelight during their highly successful joint retrospective in 1889. In late summer or early fall, Monet began discussing ideas for the building with Louis Bonnier, one of the most sought-after architects of the time, who came up with a design by December 1920 that called for a single circular room, 18.5 meters in diameter, that would be enclosed in a modest rotunda set on the western edge of Rodin's garden with its back to the boulevard des Invalides (Pl. 246a).[90] Visitors would enter and leave the room through two narrow doors on either side of a vestibule (it was above these

245 Claude Monet, *Wisteria*, 1919–20, 100 × 200, W.1905, Musée d'art et de histoire Marcel-Dessal, Dreux.

doors that Monet had envisioned placing the *Wisteria* canvases). Once inside, they would literally be surrounded by the twelve panels which, as Arsène Alexandre described, would "dovetail to form a spectacle of uninterrupted water, reflected sky, and vegetation."[91]

Thiébault-Sisson broke the news of these plans on 14 October, long before they were finalized. He described the building and the arrangement of the panels in some detail. He also aptly noted that if a spectator stood in the middle of the room, "he will have the illusion of finding himself . . . on the island . . . in . . . the center of the water lily pond [itself]. . . . All that remains to be done," he claimed, "is to proceed with an exchange of signatures witnessed by a notary." Monet had confirmed that this was the case a few days prior to Thiébault-Sisson's story when the Bernheim-Jeune brothers and their friend, René Gimpel, had come to Giverny for lunch. What Monet's visitors also learned was that the cagey artist had extracted a rather serious compensation–cum–retribution; he had persuaded the State to agree to purchase his *Women in the Garden* (Pl. 42) for the staggering sum of 200,000 francs.[92] It must have been immensely satisfying for Monet to have turned the tables so decisively; this was a picture the jury had rejected for the Salon of 1867. In February 1921, the purchase became official and the painting left Monet's Giverny studio for the Musée du Luxembourg. Everything could not have looked more promising.

But then the problems began. First, Monet was offered the opportunity to be nominated to the Fine Arts section of the prestigious Institut de France, the highest award an artist could receive. In typical fashion, he declined. "I thank you gentlemen," he apparently told them, "but I have always been, I am, and always shall be independent," a rebuff that did not sit well with the members of this august and powerful organization.[93] Perhaps through their connections, certainly to Monet's dismay, the terms of the donation then became a topic of some debate among members of the Parliament. Acrimonious and divisive, the debate made it clear that funds were going to be difficult to find; many members balked at spending what the government's architect estimated would be 700–800,000 francs on a building that they asserted was going to contain half-finished works by an ageing artist. Others saw the expenditure as difficult to justify at a time when the economy was in crisis and the basic needs of the country remained to be met. In the summer of 1921, the Ministry of Fine Arts, then

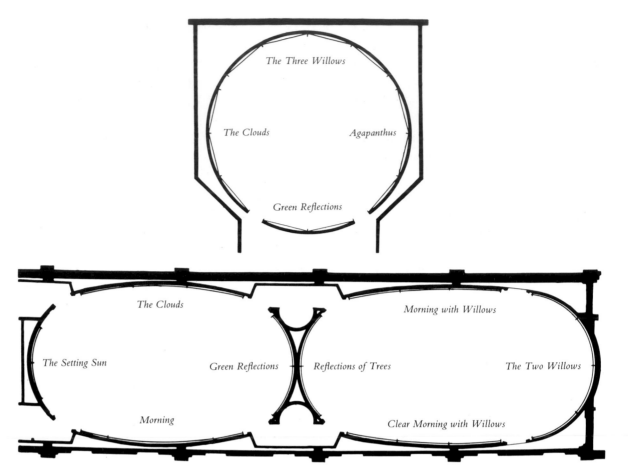

The Three Willows

The Clouds    Agapanthus

Green Reflections

The Clouds    Morning with Willows

The Setting Sun    Green Reflections    Reflections of Trees    The Two Willows

Morning    Clear Morning with Willows

246 a and b   Louis Bonnier, (a) plan for Monet museum on the grounds of Rodin's Hôtel Biron, twelve panels, 9 December 1920. (b) plan for reconfigured rooms in the Orangerie for Monet's expanded *Grandes Decorations*, 12 April 1922, with the final arrangement of twenty-two panels installed in 1927.

lead by Paul Léon, devised a compromise solution, using one of the existing buildings in Paris under its jurisdiction. More protracted negotiations ensued, primarily because Monet thought that the two proposed sites—the Jeu de Paume and the Orangerie of the Tuileries—were inadequate. He even threatened to withdraw his offer, despite having been paid for the *Women in the Garden*.

Under considerable pressure from Clemenceau, Monet finally acquiesced and in January 1922 he agreed to a completely revised proposal for the donation which now would be housed in the Orangerie. Because that building was long and narrow, it could not accommodate a circular room large enough to hold the original twelve panels in the manner Monet had envisioned. The revised plan, therefore, called for the space to be reconfigured into two elliptical rooms that would be interconnected and that would hold nineteen panels between them, nine in the first and ten in the second (Pl. 246b). This obviously was even more ambitious than Monet's first proposal and would require a great deal of additional work. Not only did Monet have to paint additional canvases, he also had to rethink completely the relationships between the original twelve panels and the way the new groupings would relate both to each other and to those in the adjoining room. Despite these challenges, Monet signed the Act of Donation on 12 April 1922.[94] After eight years of work on this project, the artist, now $81\frac{1}{2}$, in theory was finally going to realize the dream he had nurtured for almost a quarter of a century. It would not be soon in coming, however, nor would he ever see it in its final form. In fact, if Monet had known how difficult it would be to meet the obligations of his contract, he might not have agreed to it. Over the next four years, it haunted him like Marley's ghost. Part of the problem again was of his own making. Instead of getting started on the commission straight away, he turned to work on other pictures during the summer of 1922. On the one hand, he was following what had been his now long-standing practice of painting en plein air in the warmer months when his studio was too hot to work in and then taking the lessons he learned from those pictures into his atelier in the fall when the temperatures fell. He also undoubtedly was trying to finish a series of twenty-three views of his Japanese bridge that he had begun some time in 1918 as well as a group of ten pictures of the rose-covered pathway leading up to his house which he had started in 1920 (Pls. 248, 249). And thankfully he did, as these two groups of pictures constitute the most ferocious attack on traditional painting that Monet had ever mounted. Even more than most of the unfinished *Water Lily* studies or the emotive *Weeping Willows*, these canvases wreak havoc on all notions of propriety as paint streams across the surface virtually unchecked by any allegiance to vision, truth, or nature. Colors clash, cry, withdraw and assault; whole areas of the canvases seem given over to lyrical gropings or visual skirmishes. In many of the early pond pictures in this group, the bridge which in previous views held the image together now struggles to hold its own against the jungle of foliage and wisteria that threatens to consume it. In the views up the path, the house is obliterated, the trellises overrun with skeins of paint that are so densely woven that they defy definition. Strokes rise, fall, coagulate, twist, turn, and dance all at the same time, all the while luring the viewer down the striated path towards some threatening yet vulnerable darkness. In the last bridge pictures, everything explodes (Pl. 249). The foliage is ablaze in strident yellows, oranges, and red, the pond simmering in equally hot reflections. The bridge seems to tremble in the midst of this inferno as if fearing it is about to meld with destiny. How quiet those *Water Lilies* now appear; how controlled and classical! Even Fauvist extravagances which had rocked the French public almost twenty years earlier appear tame by comparison. That is because these pictures are the product of an old man crying at the light, knowing that his fate is upon him and that his nineteenth-century

247 Henri Manuel, photograph of Monet in his third studio in front of *Morning*, ca. 1924–25, Archives Durand-Ruel, Paris.

219

allegiance to nature, having been disparaged by younger contemporaries, is now drawing to a close.

While rooted in Monet's sense of history and the role he had played in the course of art historical events, his cries also arise from his battle with his vision. "I am working hard," he told Durand-Ruel that summer of 1922, "and I would like to paint everything before not being able to see anything any more."[95] That September, when visiting his ophthalmologist Dr. Coutela, he learned what he knew was true: he was legally blind in his right eye and had only ten per cent vision in his left. He insisted on treatments as opposed to an operation, which only postponed the inevitable. A few weeks later, he agreed to the procedure which was scheduled for the middle of November and would be performed in Dr. Coutela's Paris clinic on the boulevard Victor Hugo. But Monet caught a cold which postponed the surgery for two months. Finally, on 10 January, he underwent the first of what was a two-step operation to remove the cataract in his right eye; the second step occurred on the 31st of the month. Although Monet had been optimistic after the first part of the operation, he was shaken after the second and could not remain still in his bed as he was supposed to do. He apparently even tried to take off the bandages, claiming he would rather go blind than lie immobile (Pl. 250).[96] He made sufficient progress to be released from the clinic on 18

248 Claude Monet, *Japanese Bridge*, 1918–22, 89 × 116, W.1931, Minneapolis Museum of Art, Bequest of Putnam Dana McMillan.

February. Because of complications that developed from the second procedure, he had to undergo a third operation in July. Dr. Coutela later recalled that Monet was extremely depressed before then, fearful that he might become permanently blind. Blanche Hoschedé, however, claimed he was merely sad and concerned. Whichever was the case, the third procedure—which Dr. Coutela agreed to perform in Giverny—apparently went well. But Monet was disturbed by his condition several weeks after the operation. "All is deformed, everything is doubled, and it becomes impossible to see," he cried to Coutela.[97] Colors became distorted. "I still see what is green as yellow," he told Clemenceau a few days later, "and the rest as more or less blue. If I have to see nature as I see it now," he vowed, "I would prefer to be blind and to keep the memory of the beauties which I have always seen."[98]

In a few weeks, however, his condition improved, so much so that Dr Coutela proclaimed

249   Claude Monet, *Rose-covered Path in Monet's Giverny Garden*, 1920–22, 89 × 100, W.1936, Private Collection.

221

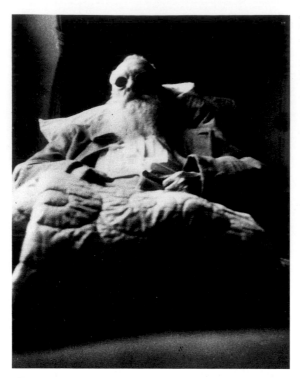

250  [Blance Hoschedé or Michel Monet?], photograph of Monet in bed wearing special glasses after his cataract operation, [February] 1922, Collection Jean-Marie Toulgouat.

his sight fully restored in his right eye for seeing things close up and reasonable for long distance if he wore special glasses that had been developed for cataract patients. His double vision was gone and color deformations were reduced to a minimum. Based on these results, the doctor recommended a fourth operation, this time on his left eye which he felt would restore his near sight and color balance, but Monet had had enough. He preferred to place his trust in various experimental glasses. They appeared to help. By October, colors essentially had returned and a few weeks later he was miraculously back at work.[99]

Having lost virtually a year on his Grand Decorations, he became set on "finish[ing] [them] by the date fixed," as he told Clémentel in November, which meant he had until April of the following year, the deadline stipulated in the 1922 contract.[100] Six months was hardly enough time to accomplish a task that had already occupied him for so many years. Not surprisingly, despite his good intentions and a lot of time in the studio, the April date came and went. Clemenceau interceded and negotiated an extension; he also provided constant encouragement. Monet needed as much of the latter as he could get. In addition to having to redesign the whole decorative program and then cover a woeful amount of canvas, Monet continued to have eye problems as colors tended to shift and occasionally disappear altogether. "I only see blue. I no longer see red . . . [or] yellow," he informed a new specialist, Dr. Mawas, a researcher with the Zeiss company who had come to Giverny probably in June 1924 through the intercession of Monet's artist friend, André Barbier. "I know these colors exist," Monet told Mawas, "because I know that on my palette there is red, yellow, a special green, a certain violet; I no longer see them as I once did, and yet I remember very well the colors which they gave me."[101] After trying several pairs of glasses from other manufacturers, none of which seemed to help, Monet received a pair from Dr. Mawas later that summer which he informed Barbier were "perfect."[102] But they apparently did not stay that way, as by October their advantages had declined, making Monet feel he had been completely abandoned by both of his doctors who, he claimed, no longer took an interest in his case.[103]

While irritating and often unjust, Monet's carping was at least understandable. How could he finish his project if he could not feel confident enough about his sight? Clemenceau saw the problem differently. He felt that Monet was merely stalling and that he had consciously let his vision deteriorate. When Monet told him that October that he was thinking about abandoning the project, Clemenceau exploded. "First you wanted to finish up some unfinished parts. It was not really necessary, but it was understandable. And then you got the absurd idea of improving others. . . . If you went back to the Cathedral of Rouen with your canvases, what would you not find to change? You created some new canvases, most of which were and still are masterpieces if you have not spoiled them. Then you wanted to make some super-masterpieces, and this with an instrument of sight that was imperfect because you yourself wanted it so. And then you get angry at the idea that you will never be able to satisfy

222

yourself. It is pure aberration. A true artist is never satisfied—you know that anyway. . . . at your request, a contract was passed between you and France, in which the State has met all of its obligations. . . . On your account the State is obliged to go to great expense, because of what you requested and even approved in person. You must therefore make an end of it, artistically and honorably, for there are no ifs in the commitments which you have made."[104]

Despite its tone, this rebuke from his old friend did not stop Monet from telling Paul Léon in late December 1924 or early January 1925 that he should not expect delivery of the decorations; Monet was backing out of the deal. Monet's decision is perplexing because that December he had obtained yet another new set of glasses from Dr. Mawas that had greatly improved his sight which in turn had lifted his spirits tremendously.[105] In any case, Léon must have contacted Clemenceau immediately after receiving Monet's letter. He naturally became enraged. "I don't care how old, how exhausted you are and whether you are an artist or not," he thundered at Monet on 7 January; "You have no right to break your word of honor, especially when it was given to France." Calling him a "spoiled child," Clemenceau told Monet in no uncertain terms that if he did not meet his obligations, he could be assured their friendship was finished.[106] This threat hit home, causing Monet to be inordinately depressed for months. At the end of March, he seemed to have given up even on himself, as he confided to Dr. Mawas: "I shall try to get accustomed to [the glasses] even though I am more certain than ever that a painter's vision can never be regained. When a singer has lost his voice, he retires; the painter, operated upon for a cataract, has to give up painting, and it is this which I did not know how to do. Excuse my candor."[107] Two months later, he was even worse. "I used the remedy you sent me," he told Barbier. "There was a very slight change in the blue vision but so what? I feel even more that it's the end for me in terms of painting. I'm beginning to think of nothing else (not without a great deal of sadness). It's the end."[108]

Though seemingly resigned to his fate, Monet grudgingly asked Dr. Mawas for yet another examination. He soon was thankful that he did. Almost exactly two months later, he experienced a radical change. "My sight is totally restored," he exclaimed joyously to Barbier, "I am working as never before, am satisfied with what I do and if the new glasses are even better, my only request will be to live to be a hundred."[109] It was in fact "a true resurrection," as he described it to Bernheim-Jeune three months later while still hard at work. Three days after his 85th birthday, he was just as buoyant, declaring to Barbier that he had every intention of delivering the decorations to the State in the spring.[110] He pressed on that winter and in February happily informed Clemenceau, with whom he had had a warm reconciliation, that the first set of panels only needed "for the paint to dry" before they could be sent to Paris. Clemenceau was thrilled, particularly because Monet had also admitted that he was "very pleased" with the results.[111] Soon thereafter, however, Monet's health began to fail. In early April he told Barbier, "I have not been doing very well for the past two months. . . . I'm feeling old and weak."[112] Unfortunately, his condition deteriorated even more that summer to such an extent that he could no longer hold a pen to write. But suddenly, like a phoenix rising from the ashes, he experienced a burst of energy in the fall and was able not only to scrawl Paul Léon a letter in early October but also to inform him that "I have regained my courage and despite my weakness am back at work," albeit, he admitted, "in very small doses." He even invited Léon and the architect for the reconfigured Orangerie to Giverny for a preview.[113] It was Monet at his best. It also was the last letter he wrote. Two months later, on 5 December 1926, in his bed overlooking his gardens, he died of pulmonary sclerosis. He had turned 86 three weeks earlier. At his side was the faithful Blanche Hoschedé,

251 and 252 Interior views of the Orangerie with the *Grandes Décorations*.

his younger son Michel, and his old friend Clemenceau. Appropriately, it was Clemenceau who closed his eyelids.

Three days later, he was laid to rest in the Giverny cemetery alongside Alice Hoschedé, her first husband Ernest, their two daughters, Suzanne and Marthe, and Monet's elder son Jean. Monet had insisted that the occasion be simple. Thus, only about fifty people attended the ceremony, which was strictly non-religious as Monet had requested. There were no eulogies

or flowers and nothing to mark the tomb but a single shaft of wheat, a reminder of his undying love for the land. Like his passing, the event was widely covered in the press. France had lost one of its great citizens.[114]

On 21 December Paul Léon came to Giverny to make arrangements for shipping the huge panels to Paris. Shortly after, the canvases arrived in the capital—twenty-two of them, not nineteen as the contract had called for. It was Monet asserting his disdain for such formalities to the end. During the first months of 1927, the paintings were taken off their stretchers and glued to the wall, their seams carefully concealed to ensure the desired effect of continuity. The official opening of the "Orangerie" took place on Tuesday 17 May 1926. It was presided over by Edouard Hérriot, Minister of Public Instruction and Fine Arts. On 20 May it opened to the public, with a special entrance fee that day of 20 francs—four times the prescribed 5 francs—in order to benefit widows from the war. Although that conflict had ended almost eight years earlier, it clearly continued to inform Monet's great project. Not many people attended the official ceremonies, and fewer still came to visit over the following weeks. But history can be as forgiving as it is fortuitous. Today that space is rightfully a kind of mecca, a place where people from all nations can be reminded of their essential ties to nature while being transported to realms of aesthetic reverie. As an artistic environment, it is a quintessential example of painting's powers; as the product of one man's unrelenting struggle, it is elegant testimony to the endurance of the human spirit. Like Monet's work as a whole, it could not be a more welcome haven or guide for us in the late twentieth century, or a more fitting legacy for those who follow. "I have only looked at what the universe has shown to bear witness to it through my paintbrush," Monet once told Clemenceau. "Put your hand in mine," he invited, "and let us help one another to see things better."[115]

253 (above left) Manuel, photograph of Monet's burial, 8 December 1926, Musée Clemenceau, Paris.

254 (above right) Anonymous, photograph of the inauguration (with Clemenceau) Monet's *Grandes Décorations* in the Orangerie, 1927, Musée Clemenceau, Paris.

# Notes

ABBREVIATIONS

AH       Alice Hoschedé
GBJ      Georges Bernheim-Jeune
GDR      Georges Durand-Ruel
GG       Gustave Geffroy
JBJ       Joseph Bernheim-Jeune
JPH      Jean-Pierre Hoschedé
PDR      Paul Durand-Ruel
W.I, II, III, IV, V      Daniel Wildenstein, *Claude Monet, biographie et catalogue raisonné*. Vol. I: 1840–1881; Vol. II: 1882–1886; Vol. III: 1887–1898; Vol. IV: 1899–1926; Vol. V: Supplément aux peintures, dessins, pastels, index.

Numbers preceded by an upper-case W. refer to paintings by Monet, as numbered by Wildenstein.

Numbers preceded by a lower-case w. refer to letters by Monet, as numbered by Wildenstein, and found at the end of each volume of his catalogue. A date enclosed in square brackets indicates the possible date of an undated letter.

The name of a city followed by a date refers to an exhibition and its accompanying catalogue.

1    MONET REVISITED

1    Monet's paintings, drawings, and letters have been meticulously catalogued and his life carefully documented by Daniel Wildenstein in his magisterial, five-volume biography and catalogue raisonné. Like all other Monet studies since Wildenstein's publication, the present book owes an immense debt to his work. This book is also informed by the rich harvest of recent Monet scholarship—as these notes and selected bibliography, I hope, justly attest.

2    Bomford et al., 1990, 168–69.

3    Zola, 1868.

4    Marx, 1891.

5    Charles Saunier, "Petite Gazette d'art: Claude Monet," *La Revue blanche*, vol. 21, no. 181 (15 December 1900), 624.

6    A. F., "Les Petits Salons: Claude Monet," *Gil Blas*, 12 May 1895.

7    GG, "Claude Monet," *Le Journal*, 7 June 1898, reprinted in *Le Gaulois (supplément)*, 16 June 1898.

2    BETWEEN THE CAPITAL AND THE COAST: MONET'S EARLY YEARS, 1840–60

1    Daniel Wildenstein has unearthed all pertinent documents regarding Monet's early life and presented them in W.I. They flesh out the "facts" of Monet's biography which the artist told François Thiébault-Sisson in 1900. See Thiébault-Sisson, 1900, cited and translated in Stuckey, 1985, 204–18. This lengthy interview became the basis of most subsequent retellings of Monet's life.

2    That the family had to take in boarders is suggested by Théophile Béguin-Billecocq in his unpublished journal quoted in W.I, 3.

3    On the school and some of its graduates see Abbé A. Anthiaume, *Le Collège du Havre*, 2 vols., Le Havre, 1905.

4    These tales are found in Monet's interview with Thiébault-Sisson, 1900, cited and translated in Stuckey, 1985, 204–05.

5    These sketchbooks are in the collection of the Musée Marmottan and are catalogued by Wildenstein in W.V, 59–122.

6    Jules Janin, *Itinéraire du chemin de fer de Paris au Havre*, Paris, Bibliothèque des chemins de fer, 1854, 101–02. Also see Frédéric de Coninck, *Le Havre, son passé, son avenir*, Havre, 1869; and Félix Laure, *Le Havre en 1878*, Havre, 1878.

7    The ties between Barbizon art and early Impressionism were recently reviewed in Champa et al., 1991, and Tinterow and Loyrette, 1994. On Barbizon art see Herbert, 1962 and 1982; Green, 1992; Grad and Riggs, 1982, and Adams, 1994.

8    On Monet's reputation as a caricaturist see Registre des délibérations du conseil municipal du Havre, séance du 18 May 1859, folios 157–162, quoted in W.I, 6. Also see W.IV, 133–51; Walter, 1976; and Edwards, 1943.

9    It was in his possession by the time he left for Paris in 1859 as he referred to it as "my Daubigny" when telling Boudin that Gautier had made an etching after it in early 1860. See w.4 to Boudin 21 April 1860. Unfortunately, the painting has never been identified. Charles Stuckey has astutely suggested that the painting may be the dark painting hanging on the wall in w.6. On paintings by Troyon and Millet hanging in the Le Havre art supply shop see w.2348 to

GG 8 May 1920.

10 "If I have become a painter," Monet confessed to Jean-Aubry, "I owe it all to Boudin." See G. Jean-Aubry, 1967, 27. Monet repeated this admission to Geffroy. See w.2348 to GG 8 May 1920. Also see Thiébault-Sisson, 1900. In this interview, Monet suggests he met Boudin in 1855 when he was 15. Wildenstein dates the meeting to 1858. See W.1, 5. House, 1979, 6, more correctly places it around 1856. Monet's letter w.2348 to GG 8 May 1920 supports House's suggestion as does a drawing Monet made of Boudin that dates to 1857. The drawing is presently in the Musée Boudin in Honfleur.

11 Boudin letter to Pierre-Firmin Martin 3 September 1868, as cited in Jean-Aubry, 1922, 72.

12 Stuckey, 1985, 205.

13 Stuckey, 1985, 205.

14 Stuckey, 1985, 206.

15 On these industrial images see Gabriel Weisberg, "François Bonhommé and early realist images of industrialization, 1830–1870," Arts Magazine, L (April 1980), 132–35; Gabriel P. Weisberg, The Realist Tradition: French Painting and Drawing, 1830–1900, Cleveland, The Cleveland Museum of Art, 1980; and Herbert, 1982.

16 w.1 to Boudin 19 May 1859.

17 w.2 to Boudin 3 June 1859.

18 w.3 to Boudin 20 February [1860].

19 w.4 to Boudin 21 April 1860.

20 w.1 to Boudin 19 May 1859.

21 On the Académie Suisse see W.1, 8; Henry Hérbert, "Physionomie d'un atelier libre à Paris," Revue illustré du Cercle des Beaux-Arts, Genève, 1 October 1879; E. R., "Les Arts. L'atelier Suisse," Paris Midi, 2 January 1925. On Monet's opinion of Couture as a "rageur" who had given up painting see w.3 to Boudin 20 February [1860].

22 w.3 to Boudin 20 February [1860].

23 w.1 to Boudin 19 May 1859.

24 w.3 to Boudin 20 February [1860].

3 MEETING THE COMPETITION: MONET IN THE 1860s

1 Thiébault-Sissons, 1900, cited and translated in Stuckey, 1985, 217, which also includes Monet's enthusiasm for Algeria. On the details of Monet's conscription see W.1, 12.

2 On workers' salaries in the Paris area see Louis Chevalier, La Formation de la population parisienne au XIXe siècle, Paris, Institute nationale d'études démographiques, 1949, 92–98. David H. Pickney, Napoleon III and the Rebuilding of Paris, Princeton, Princeton University Press, 1972, 160 notes that in 1860, "the usual wages for construction workers ran between 3 and 5 francs a day and the daily wage of a mason might go as high as 12 francs." In the Department of the Creuse in 1859, a prosperous year according to Pickney, "the daily wage for men in agriculture was 1.53 francs and in industry, where there were few jobs, 2.40 francs." In La Bête humaine of 1890, Emile Zola makes it clear that even near the end of the century many people were living on incomes of 2–3,000 francs a year. He speaks of a "young man, Henri Dauvergne, a guard who had lived there [in Paris] with his father a deputy stationmaster on the main line side, and his two sisters, Claire and Sophie, charming blondes of eighteen and twenty who, on six thousand francs from the two men, kept the house in a continual burst of gaiety" (translated by Leonard Tancock, Harmondsworth, Penguin, 1977, 20).

3 The standard biography of Gleyre is Charles Clément, Gleyre. Etude biographique et critique, Geneva, 1878. Two relatively recent exhibitions of his work were accompanied by thorough catalogues: Charles Gleyre ou les illusions perdues, Lausanne, Musée Cantonal des Beaux-Arts, 1974 and Charles Gleyre, New York Grey Art Gallery, 1980. On Gleyre's studio also see Boime, 1971.

4 On the exhibition in Rouen see W.1, 27; on the Le Havre commission see w.13 to Boudin [end of October–beginning of November 1864]; for appropriate Salon works see W.6, W.7, W.10, W.16, W.19 (which he completed in 1864 and submitted to the Salon of 1866), and W.21 which he may have exhibited at the Rouen show in 1864.

5 Paul Mantz, "Le Salon de 1865," Gazette des Beaux-Arts, 1st series, 19 (July 1865), 26.

6 Bazille letter to his mother [5 May 1865], W.1, pièce justificative #3. Pigalle, L'Autographe au Salon et dans les ateliers, no. 9 (24 June 1865), 76.

7 On this painting see in particular Isaacson, 1972; Herbert, 1988, 174–77; Champa, 1973, 4–9; and Adhémar, 1958. On Baudelaire and the demand for contemporaneity see Baudelaire, 1964; Clark, 1985; Crow, 1984; and Nochlin, 1971.

8 Wildenstein does not see Camille as the model for any of the women in the Luncheon and suggests that she may not have entered Monet's life until 1866 when she moved to Pigalle where she lived. See W.1, 30 especially n. 204. All other scholars disagree. Isaacson, 1972, 27 even asserts Camille posed for all of the women although it is evident from Monet's letter (w.19) to Bazille of 4 May that another woman was coming to Chailly—a certain "young Germaine," as Monet referred to her—who may have played a role in the enterprise. Camille's features seem to be those of the two central figures who are also distinguished by Camille's coiffure with its central part and lock of hair by the ear. On the influence of fashion plates see in addition to the references in note 7, Roskill, 1970. On photography see Poulain, 1937.

9 See Isaacson, 1972, 83 and 113, n. 94.

10 Willem Bürger [pseudonym of Théophile Thoré], "Salon de 1866," reprinted in Bürger, Salons (1861 à 1868), t. 2, Paris, J. Renoard, 1870, 285–86.

11 Emile Zola, "Le Salon de 1866: V. Les Réalistes du Salon," L'Evénement, 11 May 1866, reprinted in Zola, 1959. On Camille as Parisian queen, see Ernest d'Hervilly, "Les Poèmes du Salon," L'Artiste, LXXIX (15 June 1866), 207; Le Pavé de Chailly (W.19) was the accompanying landscape submission.

12 The caricature by Bertall appeared in Le Journal amusant on 12 May 1855; the other by Gill was published in La Lune on 13 May 1866. The dealer Cadart commissioned the replica, W.66.

13 On the sale of the Salon portrait of Camille see w.26 to Armand Gautier 22 May 1866. On the sale of other pictures during 1866 see w.26 to Amand Gautier 22 May 1866 in which he claims to have sold several paintings for a total of 800 francs. That sum would have covered the rent for his new studio in Pigalle for the entire year.

14 On this and the two other Paris pictures Monet painted at the same time see Isaacson, 1966.

15 On these and other pairs of pictures see Levine, 1975.

16 This interpretation owes a great deal to Herbert, 1988, 284–90.

17 Herbert, 1979, was the first to suggest a detailed social reading of this picture.

18 w.45 to Bazille [end of December 1868 or beginning of January 1869]. W.1 suggests this line refers to a lost canvas (W.107) but House, 1978, 681, rightfully argues that Monet was referring to the Garden at Sainte-Adresse.

19 On this enthusiasm see Chapter 6, pages 150–51 and Chapter 8, pages 181, 184–85. On Monet's collection of Japanese prints see Aitken and Delafond, 1983.

20 Elder, 1924, 64. For a review of this possibility see Joosten, 1986.

21 Deborah Johnson, "Confluence and Influence: Photography and the Japanese Print in 1850," in Champa et al., 1991, 78–98. Also see Johnson, 1984; Mabuchi, 1994; Flood, 1986; John Sandberg, "The Discovery of Japanese Prints in the nineteenth century before 1867," Gazette des Beaux-Arts (June 1968), 295–302; Geneviève Lacambre "Sources du Japonisme au XIXe siècle," in Paris, 1988, 22–32; and Gabriel P. Weisberg, "Félix Bracquemond and Japonisme Influence in Ceramic Decoration," The Art Bulletin 51 (December 1969), 277–80 and "Japonisme: Early Sources and the French Printmaker 1854–1882," in Japonism: Japanese influence on French art, 1854–1910, Cleveland, The Cleveland Museum of Art, 1975. Johnson in particular helps to debunk the often-told tale that Félix Bracquemond was the first to discover Japanese prints (in the form of Hokusai's Manga) in

his printer's shop who had found it in a shipment of ceramics from Japan. On this story see Cola Feller Ives, *The Great Wave: The Influence of Japanese Woodcuts on French Prints*, exhibition catalogue, New York, The Metropolitan Museum of Art, 1974, 7 and 12 and Siegfried Wichmann, *Japonisme. The Japanese Influence on Western Art in the 19th and 20th Centuries*, New York, Harmony Books, 9.

22 Pissarro letter to Lucien 3 February 1893, as cited and translated in Rewald, 1980, 207. Also see letter of 2 February 1893 in which Pissarro states "Damn it all, if this show [of Japanese prints at Durand-Ruel's] doesn't justify us!" Cited and translated in Rewald, 1980, 206.

23 Blunden and Blunden, 1976, 64–65 were among the first students of the period to make this assertion. Of all subsequent writers, House, 1986, 47–51 strikes the most appropriate balance. Some contemporaries of the Impressionists argued differently. The most insistent was Théodore Duret, a sensitive critic who supported the Impressionists early on and who amassed a large collection of Asian art from a trip around the world that he made in the early 1870s. In 1878 in the first study of Impressionism (*Les Peintres Impressionistes*), Duret claimed: "Only after seeing Japanese pictures, on which the most contrasting and intense colors are set side by side, did we finally understand that there were new techniques worth using for the reproduction of certain aspects of nature that have been neglected or considered impossible to render until this day.... Japanese art rendered particular aspects of nature with bold new techniques of coloration. It could not help but impress artists with open minds, and it strongly influenced the Impressionists." See Stuckey, 65–66. He repeated this claim in 1880 saying that Japanese prints and watercolors had introduced "a totally new system of coloration," one which he felt Europeans never would have been able to devise. See Duret, 1880, cited and translated in Stuckey, 1985, 71. Contemporaneous claims that "the catalyst for Impressionist landscape came from Japan" have greatly influenced Tinterow (Tinterow and Loyrette, 1994, 233–63).

24 On these sales see W.I, 158 and 164. Later in his life, Monet told a journalist that the Japanese "have taught us a different way of composing, that's for sure." See Trevis, 1920, as cited and translated in Stuckey, 1985, 340.

25 On finishing it in Honfleur see W.I, pièce justificative #13, letter from Dubourg to Boudin 2 February 1867. On Monet's claims about painting the picture entirely en plein air see GG, 1922, 36–37; de Trévise, 1927, 122–23; and Thiébault-Sisson 1926.

26 Zola, 1868.

27 For a sampling of laborers' wages see note 2. On Bazille's interest and ultimate purchase

of this painting see w.32 to Bazille [20 May 1867] and W.I, pièce justificative #15, letter from Bazille to Monet [2 January 1868].

28 Monet's ire can be seen increasing between w.33 to Bazille 25 June [1867] and w.39 to Bazille 1 January 1868.

29 See letter from Adolphe Monet to Bazille of 11 April 1867 cited in part in Gustave Poulain, *Bazille et ses amis*, Paris, La Renaissance du livre, 1932, 74–77 and in W.I, 37 and in whole in Mount, 1962, 133–34.

30 w.35 to Bazille 9 July 1867.

31 w.33 to Bazille 25 June 1867.

32 w.38 to Bazille 20 August [1867].

33 w.37 to Bazille 12 August [1867].

34 The early relationship between Monet and Alice Hoschedé remains cryptic despite frequent assertions that they had an affair in the 1870s and that Jean-Pierre Hoschedé was their illegitimate child. See for example W.I, 83 and n. 595. Alice's diaries, which I was able to consult thanks to the generosity of Jean-Marie Toulgouat and Claire Joyes, suggest a woman of deep religious convictions, which could be grounds to refute the charges of her impropriety. However, until further documents come to light, the issue will have to remain a mystery. For further information on the Hoschedés see W.I, 80–83; Alphant, 1993, 259–80; Distel, 1990, 94–107; and Hélène Adhémar, "Ernest Hoschedé," in Rewald and Weitzenhoffer, 1984, 52–71. Also see the Hoschedé bankruptcy records of 24 April 1877 in the Archives de Paris.

35 On Daubigny's intercession for Monet's port picture see W.I, pièce justificative #23 letter from Boudin to F. Martin 18 January 1869.

36 My thanks to Robert Herbert for sharing this previously unknown caricature of Monet's painting. It comes from a Le Havre source that remains obscure.

37 See w.43 to Bazille [end of October-beginning of November 1868] and W.I, pièce justificative #22 letter from F. Martin to Boudin 6 October 1868.

38 On his complaints see w.43. The portrait commission came from M. Louis-Joachim Gaudibert and resulted in the life-size depiction of his wife, Marguerite-Eugénie-Mathilde Gaudibert, W.121 and a now lost picture of him, W.122.

39 w.44 to Bazille [December 1868].

40 My thinking about this picture was particularly stimulated by Anne Wagner's brilliant article, "Why Monet Gave Up Figure Painting," *Art Bulletin*, vol. 74, no. 4, (December 1994), 613–29.

41 w.44 to Bazille [December 1868].

42 Wildenstein, for example, believes Camille posed for the woman leaning against the window but not necessarily for the seated figure. See W.I, 176.

43 See Seitz, 1960, 80 and Champa, 1972, 29–30.

44 Paris, Archives Nationales. F21 531. Note

pour Monsieur Tournois. Oppositions faites sur des ouvrages exposés. On the Le Havre sales see W.I, pièce justificative #23, letter from Boudin to F. Martin, 18 January 1869 and Boudin letter to Martin 25 April 1869, cited in Jean-Aubry, 1922, 74 and translated in Rewald, 1973, 214.

45 Paris, 1980, 56, n. 7. On Monet's solicitation see w.49 to Arsène Houssaye of 2 June 1869.

46 W.126 and W.133.

47 w.49 to Arsène Houssaye 2 June 1869. On the Sainte-Adresse painting in Latouche's see letter from Boudin to Martin 25 April 1869 in Jean-Aubry, 1922, 74.

48 w.53 to Bazille 25 September 1869.

49 On the site and Monet's paintings see Herbert, 1988, 210–19; Charles Harrison, "Impressionism, Modernism and Originality," in Frascina et al., 1993, 167–71; and Ronald Pinkvance, "La Grenouillère," in Rewald and Weitzenhoffer, 1984, 36–51.

50 Karl Bertrand [pseudonym for Arsène Houssaye], *L'Artiste* (1 June 1870), 319–20.

51 Discussions about an independent show, mounted by the artists themselves, appear to have occurred in the middle of the 1860s following the outrage of 1863 (which produced the Salon des refusés) and another refusés show in 1865. While a number of the Impressionists signed letters in the 1860s protesting the exclusivity of the annual Salon, the first tangible evidence of the Impressionists' efforts to mount a counter-exhibition is found in Bazille's letter to his parents of [May] 1867, as cited in Gaston Poulain, *Bazille et ses amis*, Paris, La Renaissance du livre, 1932, 208. This was followed by another attempt in 1869 reported again by Bazille (Poulain, 207–08) which unfortunately failed. On these efforts and their successful culmination in the so-called first Impressionist exhibition of 1874 see Chapter 4 and notes 28–36.

52 W.I, 45–46 which also includes a discussion of the wedding.

53 The richest discussion of Trouville and the Normandy coast is found in Herbert, 1994, and Herbert 1988, 293–99.

54 See, for example, W.158 and W.162, and Bomford et al., 1990, 126–31.

55 See, for example, Koppel S. Pinson, *Modern Germany. Its History and Civilization*, New York, Macmillan, 1966, 143–48. Also see Michael Howard, *The Franco–Prussian War*, New York, Macmillan, 1961.

56 On the Commune see Robert Baldick, *The Seige of Paris*, London, Batsford, 1964; and Alistair Horne, *The Fall of Paris. The Siege and the Commune, 1870–1871*, New York, St. Martin's Press, 1966. For the lasting effects of the war and Commune see the magisterial work by Claude Digeon, *La crise allemande de la pensée française, 1870–1914*, Paris, Presses Universitaires, 1959.

57 On Monet's stay in London see House, 1978 and 1980; *The Impressionists in London*, exhibition catalogue, London, Arts Council

of Great Britain, 1973; Rewald, 1973, 258–63; Alphant, 1992, 105–08; Spate, 62–68; and W.I, 52–55.

58 On the South Kensington show, see w.57 to the French Commission of the International Exhibition in London [nd]. The two figure paintings he showed were *Meditation. Camille Monet on the Couch* (W.163) and *Woman in a Green Dress* (W.66). The seascape remains obscure. On his relation with Durand-Ruel, see "Mémoires de Paul Durand-Ruel," in Venturi, 1939, vol. 2, 175–80.

59 w.55 to Pissarro 27 May 1871.

60 w.58 to Pissarro 2 June 1871. On Monet's time in Holland see Rijksmuseum, 1986; Alphant, 1992, 208–23; and W.I, 56–57.

61 w.59 and w.58 to Pissarro 17 and 2 June 1871.

62 w.58 to Pissarro 2 June 1871.

63 w.59 to Pissarro 17 June [1871]. Boudin expressed similar sentiments during his stay in Holland during the same period. "People make a great fuss about these towns in the Low Countries. I find them interesting, undoubtedly, but I'm not mad about them and the beautiful horizons of our France, not to speak of Brittany, mean just as much and even more to me." See letter to Martin 17 July 1871, cited in Jean-Aubry, 1922, 82.

64 For similar evidence of sobriety and restraint in France after the Commune, see Susanna Barrows, "After the Commune: Alcoholism, Temperance, and Literature in the Early Third Republic," in John M. Merriman, ed., *Consciousness and Class Experience in Nineteenth Century France*, New York, Holmes and Meier, 1979.

4 MONET AT ARGENTEUIL: 1871–1878

1 Letter from Boudin to F. Martin 2 January 1872 cited in Jean-Aubry, 1969, 82. On Monet's years in Argenteuil see Herbert, 1988, 219–46; Spate, 1992, 69–128; Alphant, 1993, 225–58, 281–96; and Tucker, 1982 upon which this chapter is largely based. The best modern history of Argenteuil is Edmund Réthoré, *Argenteuil et son passé*, 3 vols., Sannois, M. Theillet, 1968. Most nineteenth-century guidebooks and histories of the suburbs have ample sections on the town. See, for example, Emile de Labédollière, *Histoire des environs de nouveau Paris*, Paris, Gustave Barba, 1861, 147–48.

2 On Monet's house and lease see Walter, 1966; W.I, 71–72; and Tucker, 1982, 46–47.

3 Exact figures for French casualties during the war were never released but they were significantly more than German losses which totalled 28,208 men dead and 88,488 wounded. For these figures see Michael Howard, *The Franco-Prussian War*, New York, Macmillan, 1961, 453. E. J. Hobsbawm, *The Age of Capital 1848–1875*, London, Abacus, 1977, 97, claims "160,000

perished, mostly on the French side," but he provides no source for this estimate. Figures for the Commune are more secure. During the "Bloody Week," 17–20,000 insurgents were killed with the Versailles army sustaining 877 losses; 36–38,000 Communards were arrested, and 7,500 were sent to camps in New Caledonia. See Roger L. Williams, *The French Revolution of 1870–71*, London, Weidenfeld and Nicolson, 1969, 151. Also see Alistair Horne, *The Fall of Paris: The Seige and the Commune, 1870–71*, New York, St. Martin's Press, 1966; R. R. Palmer, *A History of the Modern World*, 4th edn., New York, Alfred Knopf, 1971; and Field Marshal Helmuth von Moltke, *The Franco-German War of 1870–71*, London, Greenhill Books, 1992.

4 Zola letter to Cézanne 4 July 1871 in Emile Zola, *Correspondance*, II, ed. H. B. Bakker, Montréal, Presses de l'Université de Montréal, 1978–91, 293–94.

5 Zola letter to Cézanne 4 July 1871 in *Correspondance*, II, ed. H. B. Bakker, Montréal, Presses de l'Université de Montréal, 1978–91, 293–94.

6 According to contemporary estimates, France could have raised almost ten times this amount or 43 billion francs. See Roger L. Williams, *The French Revolution of 1870–71*, London, Weidenfeld and Nicolson, 1969, 163.

7 Emile Galichon, "A nos lectures," *Gazette des Beaux-Arts* 4 (October 1871), 281–83 as cited and translated in Carl Baldwin, "The Salon of 1872," *Art News* 71 (May 1972), 20ff.

8 See for example the bridge at Chatou in *Le Monde Illustré*, XV (2 September 1871), 159, as illustrated in Tucker, 1982, 59.

9 On these earnings see note 38.

10 This is suggested by Etienne Moreau-Nélaton in *Manet raconté par lui-même*, Paris, H. Laurens, 1926, vol. 2, 22.

11 Jules Beaujanot, "Argenteuil 15 mars 1862," *Le Journal d'Argenteuil*, 16 March 1862, 1. For all of these changes see Tucker, 1982.

12 w.95 to Georges de Bellio 25 July 1876. On de Bellio as a collector see Robert Niculescu, "Georges de Bellio, l'ami des impressionnistes," *Revue roumaine d'histoire de l'art* vol. 1, no. 2 (1964), 209–78; and Distel, 1991, 109–23.

13 On the development of boating in France see Alphonse Karr et al., *Le Canotage en France*, Paris, Jules Taride, 1858. On Argenteuil's fame see articles on "Canotage," in *Le Sport* of 18 October 1855 and 25 October 1858.

14 On the importance of the rococo in the nineteenth century see Carol Duncan, *The Pursuit of Pleasure: the Rococo Revival in French Romantic Art*, New York, Garland Publications, 1976, and Silverman, 1989.

15 Renoir letter to PDR 27 September 1883, as cited in Venturi, vol. 1, 1939, 126 and translated in Herbert, 1988, 190.

16 A. Bonneville, "Moeurs de la banlieu de Paris," *Le Journal d'Argenteuil*, 23 March 1862, 1.

17 See Richard R. Brettell, *Pissarro and Pontoise: A Painter in the Landscape*, New Haven and London, Yale University Press, 1990, 64–71.

18 F. Lebeuf, "Ouverture de la nouvelle gare d'Argenteuil," *Le Journal d'Argenteuil*, 7 June 1863, 2.

19 Claude Collas, "Sur le nouveau chemin de fer d'Argenteuil," *Le Journal d'Argenteuil*, 28 June 1863, 2.

20 On this painting, so long associated with Impressionism, see Tucker, 1984.

21 On this project see Frédéric de Coninck, *Le Havre, son passé, son present, son avenir*, Havre, 1869, and Th. Negré, "Les travaux de l'avant-porte au Havre," *L'Illustration*, LXIII, 18 April 1874, 247.

22 In the fourth revised edition of *The History of Impressionism*, 1973, 339, n. 23, John Rewald asserted that another painting, W.262, was the work Monet submitted to this exhibition. Only one other scholar has agreed with him, Merete Bodelsen, 1968. On this issue, see Tucker, 1984, 470–71 and 476, n. 31–33, and W.I, 69 especially n. 493. On the First Impressionist Exhibition in addition to Rewald, 1973 and Tucker, 1984 and 1986, see Hélène Adhémar and Sylvie Gache, "L'Exposition de 1874 chez Nadar," *Centenaire de l'Impressionnisme*, Paris, 1974, 221–70; Ian Dunlop, "The First Impressionist Exhibition," *The Shock of the New*, New York, American Heritage Press, 1972, 54–87; W.I, 65–70; Lethève, 1959, 59–70; Isaacson, 1978, 2–4; Coe, 1976, 5–16; and Venturi, 1939, 255–6. The most recent reviews of the problems are Katsunori Fukaya, "The First Impressionist Exhibition" (in Japanese) in Tucker et al., 1994, 253–59, and Tokyo, 1994.

23 Georges Puissant, "Le Salon 1872," *Le Siècle*, 11 May 1872. Surprise and regret about the show not reflecting the moment were widely expressed. See, for example, A. Delzant, "Salon de 1872," *Courrier de France*, 21 May 1872, and Jules Clartie, "La Sculpture," *L'Artiste* (June 1872), 263–70.

24 Jules Castagnary, "Salon de 1872," *Le Siècle*, 11 May 1872.

25 On the Salon des refusés, see *Moniteur des Arts* (20 June 1873), and Tucker, 1986, 104. On "showing jealous Europe" see Claudius Stella, "Salon de 1872," *L'Opinion nationale*, 11 May 1872.

26 Paul Alexis, "Paris qui travaille, III, Aux peintres et sculpteurs, "*L'Avenir national*, 5 May 1873, cited and translated in Rewald, 1973, 309.

27 w.25 to Alexis 7 May 1873, published in *L'Avenir national*, 12 May 1873, cited and translated in Rewald, 1973, 309.

28 See Rewald, 1973, 310–12. The founding charter was published in "Société anonyme cooperative d'artistes-peintres, sculpteurs,

etc., à Paris," *La Chronique des Arts et de la Curiosité* (17 January 1874), 368. John Rewald found three other versions of the charter among Pissarro's papers and published them in the French version of *The History of Impressionism*, Paris, 1955, 358–64.

29 My thanks to Anne McCauley for this information which helps to solve a long-standing controversy regarding the location of the show. Rewald, 1973, 312–13 and then Coe, 1976, both decided that the show did not take place at 35 boulevard des Capucines but in rooms on the second floor of a contiguous building on the rue Daunou that they claimed Nadar occupied and then vacated. Their opinion was based in part on the windows in the building on the boulevard des Capucines which Coe claimed were not of the period, in part on the signs that Nadar had placed on the roof of the building facing the rue Daunou which appear in period photographs. However, the cadastral record shows that Nadar never had a studio on the rue Daunou; that he did occupy one on the boulevard des Capucines; that he renovated that one in 1869; and that he replaced the windows in that studio. The location of the advertisements is also logical. Photographers, particularly along the boulevard des Capucines which was over-populated by photographers, were renowned for putting advertisements wherever they could. Having one on the angle of the rue Daunou and the boulevard des Capucines made eminent sense as it would have been seen by people coming down the boulevard toward the Opéra, unlike the one on the face of the Capucines building visible in period photographs.

30 For a list of these see the Appendix in San Francisco, 1986, 460, and the list in Tokyo, 1994, 247–48. Attendance figures for the show come from the detailed records the group kept which Rewald found among Pissarro's papers and published in the French version of *The History of Impressionism*, 1955, 366–67. Unfortunately, no figures for shows at other private galleries of the time have been found. But even today, 3,500 people is far from a failure for an avant-garde exhibition in a communal gallery.

31 Emile Cardon, "Avant le Salon—L'Exposition des revoltés," *La Presse*, 29 April 1874.

32 Ernest Chesneau, "A côté du Salon. II, Le Plein Air, Exposition du Boulevard des Capucines," *Paris-Journal*, 7 May 1874; Philippe Burty, "Exposition de la Société anonyme des artistes," *La République Française*, 25 April 1874; Armand Silvestre, "Chronique des Beaux-Arts. Physiologie du Refusé. L'exposition des revoltés," *L'Opinion nationale*, 22 April 1874.

33 Louis Leroy, "L'exposition des Impressionnistes," *Le Charivari*, 25 April 2874. The four others were Silvestre and Chesneau, Marc de Montifaud, "Exposition du Boulevard des Capucines," *L'Artiste* (1 May 1874),

307–13, and Jules-Antoine Castagnary, "L'Exposition du Boulevard des Capucines—Les Impressionnistes," *Le Siècle*, 29 April 1874, 3. It is unfortunate that Leroy's satirical article has so long dominated ideas about the reception of the Impressionists' show. It was a serious spoof, but it was meant to be sarcastic and to poke as much fun at the conservative painters of the Academy as at the Impressionists.

34 The group was just as often referred to in the press as the "Intransigents" as the "Impressionists." The former was a term that described an anarchist wing of the Spanish Federal Party of 1872 that sparked a civil war in the country in 1873. Their radical political challenge was seen as parallel to the one the Impressionists posed to painting. On this term and its implications see Eisenmann, 1986. On the unique change for the third exhibition see Rewald, 1974, 390, and Georges Rivière, "Explications," *L'Impressionniste* (21 April 1877), 3, cited in Venturi, 1939, vol. 2, 322.

35 Prices the Impressionists were asking for their works appear in an annotated copy of the exhibition catalogue once owned by Claude Roger-Marx and now apparently lost. They are quoted in Adhémar et al., 1974, 224.

36 For positive reactions to the *Luncheon* see, for example, Léon de Lora [Louis de Fourcaud], "Petites nouvelles artistiques: Exposition libre des peintres," *Le Gaulois*, 18 April 1874, and Jules-Antoine Castagnary, "Exposition au boulevard des Capucines: Les impressionnistes," *Le Siècle*, 29 April 1874.

37 See Georges Lafenestre in the preface to the sales catalogue of the Desfosses Collection, 26 April 1895, as cited by Gustave Geffroy, 1924, I, 214.

38 Monet paid 1,400 francs a month for this new house which was a substantial increase over the 1,000 francs for his first place. On the new house see Walter, 1966; and W.I, 429. On the maid, the gardener, and the wines, see W.I, 87. Much of this was possible because Monet earned 12,100 francs in 1872, 24,800 francs in 1873, 10,554 francs in 1874, and 9,765 francs in 1875. (In 1876, he made 12,313 francs and in 1877, 15,197 francs.) These figures are recorded in Monet's hand in his account books, presently in the Musée Marmottan. They were first published by Wildenstein.

39 Gustave Flaubert, *Bouvard and Pécuchet* (1881), trans. A. J. Krailsheimer, Harmondsworth, Penguin, 1978.

40 Isaacson, 1982.

41 For a thorough discussion of this picture offering different conclusions see Colin B. Bailly et al., *Masterpieces of Impressionism and Post-Impressionism: The Annenberg Collection*, exhibition catalogue, Philadelphia, Philadelphia Museum of Art, 1990, 46–49.

42 Eugène Chapus, "La Vie à Paris: Le Carac-

tère de la société parisienne actuelle; les maisons de la campagne," *Le Sport*, 5 September 1860, 2–3.

43 Anthony Sutcliffe, *The Autumn of Central Paris, the Defeat of Town Planning 1850–1970*, London, Edward Arnold, 1970, 155 as cited in Herbert, 1988, 196.

44 On Monet's various studios see House, 1986, 147.

45 For Gautier's statement see Phoebe Poole, *Impressionism*, New York, Praeger, 1967, 161 which derives from an article he wrote in *Le Moniteur Universel*, 13 July 1868. The same enthusiasm for the subject was expressed by the critic Champfleury [Jules Husson], "Courbet in 1860," in *Le Réalisme*, ed. Geneviève Lacambre and Jean Lacambre, exhibition catalogue, Paris, Réunion des musées nationaux, 1973, 184.

46 Letter from Saint-Beuve to Charles Duveyrier 22 April 1862 quoted and translated in Albert Boime, "The Second Empire's Official Realism," in *The European Realist Tradition*, ed. Gabriel P. Weisberg, Bloomington, Indiana University Press, 1982, 90.

47 On Manet's ideas for the decoration see Antoine Proust, "Edouard Manet: Souvenirs," *La Revue blanche* (February–May 1897), 414–15, cited in Françoise Cachin et al., *Manet*, exhibition catalgoue, Paris, Réunion des musées nationaux, 1983, 515. For Couture's statement see Thomas Couture, *Méthode et entretiens d'atelier*, Paris, 1867, 254–55.

48 See, for example, Bertall [Charles-Albert d'Arnous], "Exposition des impressionnistes," *Paris-Journal*, 9 April 1877 in which he claimed "Manet's scepter is now held by Monet."

49 Jacques [pseudonym], "Menu propos: Salon impressionniste," *L'Homme Libre*, 11 April 1877, cited and translated in San Francisco, 1986, 227; Georges Rivière, "L'exposition des impressionnistes," *L'Impressionniste*, 6 April 1877, cited and translated in Stuckey, 1985, 61–62.

50 Léon de Lora [Louis de Fourcaud], "L'exposition des impressionnistes," *Le Gaulois*, 10 April 1877; Baron Grimm [Albert Millaud], "Lettres anecdotiques du Baron Grimm: Les impressionnistes," *Le Figaro*, 5 April 1877, cited and translated in San Francisco, 1986, 224 and 223.

51 Chevalier, 1877, 329–33.

52 On these changes and Monet's reaction to them see Tucker, 1982, 171–76.

53 See Tucker, 1982, 176–81. On Haussmann's sewer system see Pickney, 1972, 127–50.

5 MONET IN THE 1880S AND THE CHALLENGES TO IMPRESSIONISM

1 On Vétheuil see Annuaire de Commerce, Arrondissement de Mantes, Vétheuil, cited in W.I, 92. On Monet's time there see W.I,

92–120; Alphant, 299–321; and Spate, 132–48.

2  w.148 to de Bellio 20 December 1878.

3  See for example w.161 to de Bellio 17 August 1879. On Camille's condition see W.I, 97–99.

4  Clemenceau, 1928, 21–22.

5  See Chapter 3, n. 34.

6  w.173 to Théodore Duret 8 March 1880.

7  Letter from Pissarro to Caillebotte [27 January 1881], quoted in Janine Bailly-Herzberg, *Correspondance de Camille Pissarro*, vol. I, 1865–1885, Paris, Presses Universitaires de France, 146–47.

8  Tout Paris, "La Journée parisienne, Impressions d'un Impressionniste," *Le Gaulois*, 24 January 1880, cited and translated in Stuckey, 1985, 69–70. It appeared under the title "Les Impressionnistes" in *L'Artiste* (February 1880), 140–42.

9  w.172 to Pissarro 2 February 1880. The letter to de Bellio has been lost but the Doctor's response of 30 January 1880 indicates he had been approached about the matter. See W.I, 108, n. 806.

10  "Les Impressionnistes," *L'Artiste* (February 1880), 140–42. *Le Gaulois* ran a short notice indicating it had received a letter from Monet. See "Nouvelles diverses," *Le Gaulois*, 29 January 1880 and W.I, 108, n. 805.

11  Seiberling, 1981, 307, n. 53 in which she cites the following references: Nemo, "Exposition de Grenoble," *Moniteur des Arts* (13 August 1886), 272–73; Jean Limousin, "Exposition de Limoges: Partie moderne," *Moniteur des Arts* (27 August 1886), 283; Tabal, "Exposition de Nancy," *Moniteur des Arts* (29 November 1888), 110. According to Raymond Moulin, "Les Expositions des Beaux-Arts en Province, 1885–87," thèse, Faculté des lettres, Paris, 1967, 174–75, Monet also exhibited in Le Havre and Rouen in the 1880s. The former occurred in 1880 when three paintings were included in a show organized by the Société des amis des arts of Le Havre; see W.I, 115. On Monet's maneuvers in the marketplace see House, 1986, 10–11.

12  On Monet's work on the Normandy coast see Herbert, 1994.

13  w.1558 to AH [18] January 1897.

14  w.241 and w.242 to AH 14 and 15 February 1882.

15  w.263bis to AH 4 April 1882.

16  w.314 to AH 3 February 1883.

17  w.315 to AH 4 February 1883.

18  w.330 to AH 16 February 1883.

19  w.460 to [?] 25 March 1884.

20  w.451 to AH 21 March 1884.

21  w.460 to [?] 25 March 1884.

22  w.730 to AH 30 October 1886.

23  On being buried in a buoy, see House, 1986, 26.

24  Geffroy reiterates this point. See GG, 1924, I, 114–15.

25  w.310 to AH 31 January [1883]. For the richest discussion of these Étretat campaigns see Herbert, 1994, 61–89, 97–127. For the history of Étretat see R. Lindon, *Étretat, son histoire, ses légendes*, Paris, Editions de Minuit, 1949.

26  w.631 to AH [27 November 1885].

27  w.312 to AH 1 February 1883.

28  Gustave Flaubert, *Sentimental Education* (1869), trans. Robert Baldick, Harmondsworth, Penguin, 1976, 360.

29  w.236 to AH 8 February 1882. Zola may have encouraged Monet to move to Poissy as Monet asked him about the town. See w.218 to Zola 24 May 1881. Monet was settled there in December (w. 227 to PDR 17 December 1881) and by February had left to paint along the Normandy coast.

30  On Giverny and Monet's time there see Chapter 8.

31  w.388 to PDR [12] January 1884.

32  w.391 to PDR 23 January 1884.

33  w.394 to AH 26 January 1883.

34  w.404 to AH 3 February 1884.

35  w.404 to AH 3 February 1884 and w.403 to Théodore Duret 2 February 1884.

36  On the sales to PDR see w.532 to Pissarro 17 November 1884 and w.499 3 June 1884, w.501 7 June 1884, w.502 10 June 1884, w.503 14 June 1884 all to PDR. Also see W.II, 30–31, especially n. 348. Monet earned 34,541 francs in 1883, 31,241 in 1882, and 20,400 in 1881. See W.II, 9 and 21 and W.I, 119.

37  For detailed analyses of these eight exhibitions see San Francisco, 1986.

38  Caillebotte letter to Pissarro 24 January 1881, cited and translated in Roy McMullen, *Degas: his life, times, and work*, Boston, Houghton Mifflin, 1984, 330.

39  Renoir letter to PDR 26 February 1882, cited in Venturi, 1939, vol. I, 122. Gauguin's comments are in a letter to Pissarro 14 December 1881, cited and translated in Rewald, 1973, 462.

40  Stuckey, 1985, 92.

41  On Renoir's trip to Italy see Barbara Erlich White, "Renoir's Trip to Italy," *Art Bulletin* 51 (December 1960), 222–51. On his enthusiasm for Raphael see Barbara Erlich White, *Renoir, his life, art, and letters*, New York, Harry N. Abrams, 1984, 114–15.

42  Emile Zola "Nouvelles artistiques et littéraires" (trans. from the Russian), *La Revue politique et littéraire* (26 July 1879) in Zola, 1970, 320.

43  The most thorough study of this novel is Robert Neiss, *Zola, Cézanne, and Manet. A study of L'Oeuvre*, Ann Arbor, The University of Michigan Press, 1968.

44  w.664 to Zola 5 April 1886 as cited and translated in Rewald, 1973, 534. Also see W.II, 48–50.

45  Pissarro letter to Lucien [March 1886], cited and translated in Rewald, 1980, 73. Pissarro confirmed the intensity of this challenge the following year when he wrote his son on 15 May 1887 telling him, "Seurat, Signac, Fénéon, all our young friends, like only my works and Madame Morisot's a little; naturally they are motivated by our common struggle. But Seurat, who is colder, more logical, and more moderate, does not hesitate for a moment to declare that we have the right position, and that the impressionists are even more retarded than before." See Rewald, 1980, 110. Also see Pissarro letter to Lucien of 20 September 1887, cited and translated in Rewald, 1980, 120.

46  The most complete collection of contemporary reactions to Seurat's work of 1886 is in Henri Dorra and John Rewald, *Seurat, l'œuvre peint; biographie et catalogue critique*, Paris, Les Beaux-arts, 1959, 292–93; also see "Appendix," San Francisco, 1984, 495–96. On Seurat and the *Grande Jatte* see Robert L. Herbert et al., *Georges Seurat, 1859–1891*, exhibition catalogue New York, The Metropolitan Museum of Art, 1991, 170–219; Martha Ward, in San Francisco, 1984, 421–42; Clark, 1985, 259–68; Richard Thompson, *Seurat*, Oxford, Oxford University Press, 1985, 97–126; John House, "Meaning in Seurat's Figure Paintings," *Art History*, vol. 3, no. 3 (September 1980), 345–56; and the special issue of *The Art Institute of Chicago Museum Studies*, vol. 14, no. 2, "The Grande Jatte at 100," Chicago, The Art Institute of Chicago, 1989.

47  Taboureux, 1880, cited and translated in Stuckey, 1985, 92.

48  On Monet's campaign on Belle-Isle see Delouche, 1980 and 1992; W.II, 50–58; Alphant, 1993, 399–422, and Spate, 1993, 177–80.

49  w.686 to AH [14 September 1886].

50  w.688 to AH 18 September 1886.

51  w.694 to PDR 25 September 1886.

52  w.705 to AH [5 October 1886].

53  Joris-Karl Huysmans, "L'Exposition Internationale de la rue de Sèze," *La Revue Indépendante de Littérature et d'Art*, NS (3 June 1887), 345–55 cited in Levine, 1976, 84–85.

54  De Lostalot, "Exposition Internationale de peinture et de sculpture (Galerie Georges Petit)," *Gazette des Beaux-Arts*, 2nd ser., vol. 35 (June 1887), 522–27.

55  See Huysmans in particular.

56  GG, "Salon de 1887—Hors du Salon: Claude Monet," *La Justice*, 25 May and 2 June 1887.

57  w.712 to AH 14 October 1886.

58  On this campaign see W.III, 3–9; Alphant, 1993, 423–40; Spate, 1992, 191.

59  w.808 to AH 17 January 1888.

60  GG, "Dix tableaux de Claude Monet," *La Justice*, 17 June 1888; reprinted in GG, 1894, vol. 3, 77–81.

61  Pissarro letter to Lucien 8 July 1888, cited and translated in Rewald, 1970, 126.

62  Felix Fénéon, "Dix Marines d'Antibes de M. Claude Monet," *La Revue Indépendante de Littérature et d'Arts*, NS (8 July 1888), 154. On Degas's opinion see Pissarro letter to Lucien 19 July 1888, cited and translated in Rewald, 1970, 127.

63  Reported by Pissarro to Lucien 8 July 1888, cited and translated in Rewald, 1970, 127.

64  On this trip see W.III, 14–17; Alphant, 1993, 441–64; Spate, 1992, 198–200; and Tucker, 1989, 38–55.

65  This was Monet's largest and most important exhibition to date and was widely covered in the press, generally quite favorably. For critics' reactions see Levine, 1976, 95–116 and Tucker, 1989, 53–55 and 290. On the exhibition as a whole see W.II, 21–23 and Dunn, 1979.

66  Octave Maus, "Claude Monet–Auguste Rodin," L'Art moderne, vol. 9 (7 July 1889), 209–11.

67  Octave Maus, "Claude Monet–Auguste Rodin," L'Art moderne, vol. 9 (7 July 1889), 209–11; Paul Foucher, "Libres chroniques," Gil Blas, 28 June 1889.

68  See W.II, 23–30; Alphant, 1992, 465–82; and Tucker, 1989, 56–61. The Olympia had been offered at Manet's death sale in 1883 but had not met its reserve of 20,000 francs. It therefore had been bought in by the family. See Françoise Cachin et al., Manet, exhibition catalogue, Paris, Réunion des musées nationaux, 1983, 183. Monet's efforts were apparently prompted by the rumor that an American was going to purchase the picture although he had expressed his interest in doing something for Manet prior to that alarm. See w.897 to Mallarmé 19 June 1888.

69  w.1081 to Berthe Morisot 26 November 1890.

6   MONET IN THE 1890S: THE SERIES PAINTINGS

1   w.1096 to PDR 21 January 1891. On previous delays regarding the drawings for PDR's publication see w.1083 and w.1085 to PDR 5 and 14 December 1890.

2   Trévise, 1927, 126, cited and translated in Stuckey, 1985, 337. Arsène Alexandre tells a similar tale in Claude Monet, 1921, as does GG, "Meules de Claude Monet," preface to catalogue of the Meules exhibition, reprinted in GG, 1892, vol. 1, 22–29, cited and translated in Stuckey, 1985, 262–65. There is a more complicated version of the story that Monet told to François Thiébault-Sissons although this account too is problematic. See page 153 and notes 43 and 44 as well as Stuckey, 1985, 346.

    Herbert, 1979, was the first to recognize deeper meaning in the Wheatstacks. For further discussion of the series and its reception see W.III, 34–41; Brettell, 1984. Levine, 1976, 117–41; and Tucker, 1989, 31–37, 65–105. For different opinions see Alphant, 483–96; House, 1985, 19–23, and 1986, 28–32, 193–204; Moffett, 1984, 140–59; Seiberling, 1976, 84–110; and Spate, 1992, 205–18.

3   For some of these changes see House, 1986, 190–91 and Tucker, 1988, 80–82.

4   Monet letter w.1076 to GG 7 October 1890.

5   Octave Mirbeau, "Claude Monet," L'Art dans les deux Mondes (7 March 1891), 183–85.

6   GG, "Exposition Claude Monet: Galerie Durand-Ruel," L'Art dans les deux Mondes (10 May 1891), 297–98. This is a reprint of his catalogue preface cited in notes 2 and 7.

7   GG, Exposition d'œuvres récentes de Claude Monet dans les galeries Durand-Ruel, Paris, Imprimeur de l'Art, 1891, cited and translated in Stuckey, 1985, 262–65.

8   Felix Fénéon, "Œuvres récentes de Claude Monet," Le Chat Noir, 16 May 1891, reprinted in Halperin, vol. 1, 191.

9   Désiré Louis, "Claude Monet," L'Evénement, 19 May 1891. For further critical reaction see Levine, 117–41 and Tucker, 1989, 100–01 and 290–91.

10  On this affair see Robert L. Herbert, Jean-François Millet, exhibition catalogue, Paris, Réunion des musées nationaux, 1975, 106, and Tucker, 1989, 102–03. On Monet's comment about America see w.578 to PDR 28 July 1885. Also see w.868 to PDR 11 April 1888 concerning his regrets about "seeing all of his paintings leaving for America."

11  Roger Marx, "Les Meules de M. Claude Monet," Le Voltaire, 7 May 1891, parts reprinted in Le Journal des Artistes, 10 May 1891, and in Le Gaulois (supplément), 16 June 1898.

12  On this cry of alarm see Debora Silverman, 1989; Henry Havard and Marius Vachon, Les Manufactures nationales: Les Gobelins, la Savonnerie, Sèvres, Beauvais, Paris, 1889; Jean-Marie Mayeur and Medlience Reberious, The Third Republic from its Origins to the Great War, 1871–1914, Cambridge, Cambridge University Press, 1984; Georges Hanotaux, Histoire de la France contemporaine (1871–1900), Combet, 1908, and Claude Digéon, La Crise allemande de la pensée française, 1870–1914, Paris, Presses Universitaires de France, 1959.

13  Désiré Louis, "Claude Monet," L'Evénement, 19 May 1891.

14  Marcel Fouquier, "L'Exposition Claude Monet: le triomphe d'un maître—la série des meules," Le XIXe Siècle, 7 May 1891.

15  On this series see W.III, 41–43; Alphant, 1993, 496–503; Levine, 1976, 141–76; Seiberling, 1981, 111–33; Spate, 1992, 218–24; Tucker, 1989, 106–41.

16  The story is told by Elder, 1924, 12; J.P. Hoschedé, 1960, 47; and Gimpel, 1963, 318–19. On the decision to cut down the trees see Limetz town council minutes, cited in W.III, 43, n. 1047.

17  See, for example, C. Couillant and H. Legran, L'Arbre dans nos campagnes, Paris, 1924, 19; and Mona Ozouf, La fête révolutionnaire, 1789–99, Paris, 1976.

18  The issue of "the decorative" in later

Because of this letter, "instantaneousness" dominated thinking about the Wheatstacks until Herbert, 1979. For its most articulate defense see House, 1986, 193–204.

nineteenth-century French painting has yet to be fully sorted out. The most intelligent discussions of the problem are Herbert, 1984; Levine, 1977; and Gloria Groom, Edouard Vuillard: Painter–Decorator: Painter and Projects, New Haven and London, Yale University Press, 1993.

19  Pissarro letter to Lucien 8 July 1888, cited and translated in Rewald, 1980, 127.

20  Archille Delaroche, "Concerning the painter Paul Gauguin, from an aesthetic point of view," cited in Paul Gauguin's Intimate Journals, trans. Van Wyck Brooks, New York, Liveright, 1949, 53–54.

21  Maurice Denis, "Definitions of Neotraditionalism," Art et Critique, 23 and 30 August 1890, cited and translated in Herschel Chipp, Theories of Modern Art, Berkeley, University of California Press, 1968, 94.

22  G.-Albert Aurier, "Le Symbolisme en peinture: Paul Gauguin," Mercure de France, II (1891), 159–64, cited and translated in Herschel Chipp, Theories of Modern Art, Berkeley, University of California Press, 1969, 89–93.

23  On these various initiatives see Silverman, 1989, 142–58.

24  See, for example, Alphonse Germain, "De Poussin et des bases de l'art figuratif," L'Ermitage, vol. 4 (February 1893), 101–06.

25  Raymond Bouyer, "Le Paysage dans l'art: V. Projet d'une exposition historique du paysage," L'Artiste, NS 6 (August 1893), 118, cited and perceptively analysed by Levine, 1976, 160–76.

26  Georges Lecomte, "Beaux-Arts: Peupliers de M. Claude Monet," Art et Critique (5 March 1892), 124–25, partially reprinted in Le Journal des Artistes, 20 March 1892.

27  Théodore Duret, Histoire des peintres impressionnistes, Paris, H. Floury, 1906, 144. This claim is dubious, however, as Monet did not own a copy of this print. In addition, there are many others that could be associated with this series. This kind of exaggeration was typical of Duret who placed too strong an emphasis on the influence of Japanese art on the Impressionists in general. See, for example, Chapter 3, n. 23.

28  Evett, 1982, 49.

29  GG, "Japanese Landscape Painters," Artistic Japan, vol. 6, no. 32 (1891), 409, as quoted in Evett, 1982, 44. This notion was the natural offshoot of the belief that Japanese art was a direct copy of nature. The Goncourts asserted this in the mid-1860s: "Everything [Japanese artists] do is taken from observation. They represent what they see," Paris and the Arts, 1851–1896: From the Goncourt Journal, ed. and trans. by George J. Becker and Edith Philips, Ithaca, Cornell University Press, 1971, 91. It therefore followed that Duret could tell his readers in 1878 that when he was in Japan he "discovered the exact sensation of a Japanese countryside [as] reproduced on a fan or in an album. I look at a Japanese album and I say: 'Yes, this is

exactly how Japan appeared to me.'" See Duret, 1878, as cited and translated in Stuckey, 65.

30 Roger Marx, "Sur le rôle et l'influence des arts de l'Extrême-Orient et du Japon," *Le Japon Artistique*, vol. 6, no. 36 (April 1891), 142, extracted in Paris, *Le Japonisme*, 1988, 137–38.

31 L'Angèle [pseudonym for Raymond Bouyer], 1899, 399.

32 On this new series see Herbert, 1984; Hamilton, 1960; Rouen, 1994; W.III, 44–46, 50–60, 65–68; Alphant, 1993, 505–28; Levine, 1976, 177–239; Pissarro, 1990; Seiberling, 1980, 134–87; Spate, 1992, 224–32; and Tucker, 1989, 142–87. The apartment he worked in first was owned by Jean Louvet and was located at 31 place de la Cathédrale. It was from this location that he painted the head-on views of the Cathedral in both 1892 and 1893. The second location was a women's fashion and drapers' store at 23 place de la Cathédrale owned by Fernand Lévy. Monet worked here between 25 February and 15 April 1892. The third location was Edouard Mauquit's *magasin de nouveautés* at 81 rue du Grand-Pont, just at the south-east corner of the square. Monet worked there between mid-Febraury and mid-April 1893.

33 w.1136 to AH [25 February 1892].

34 w.1151 to AH [9 April 1892].

35 w.1153 to PDR 13 April 1892.

36 w.1156 to PDR 11 May 1892.

37 On this dual marriage see W.III, 47. Initially, Monet had opposed the idea of Suzanne marrying Theodore Butler. Butler was not known to Alice or himself and had not properly presented himself to them. Monet was also upset that Butler was an American. Worse still, he was a painter. "Sacrebleu!" he exclaimed. "[T]o marry a painter, if he can't do anything else, it's stupid, certainly for someone like Suzanne." He became so enraged that he threatened to sell his Giverny estate and move his extended family elsewhere. When he realized that Suzanne really loved the man, however, he relented and condoned their union. See w.1141 and w.1139 to AH 9 April and 19 March 1892.

38 w.1179 to AH 22 February 1892. On getting back into his subject see w.1175 to AH 15 February 1892.

39 w.1184 to AH 7 March 1893.

40 w.1201 to GG 18 March 1893.

41 w.1209 to AH 7 April 1893.

42 w.1203 to AH 29 March 1893.

43 Based on two letters to Geffroy [w.2938 (1300b) and w.2939 (1300c) to GG 24 and 29 May 1895], Charles Stuckey has rightfully suggested that while Monet did not hang the *Cathedrals* sequentially at the outset he seems to have been quite willing to rearrange them in that way and to extend the show a few days in order to allow Clemenceau the opportunity to see them as Clemenceau had

romantically described them in his famous front-page review in *La Justice*. In w.2938, Monet says to Geffroy, "We can see about doing the arrangement Clemenceau dreamed about. It's really the least I can do to please him after the wonderful article he wrote." While reaffirming the fact Monet did not intend the paintings to be seen as a kind of chronometer, these letters also reveal how far Monet would go in response to the actions of people in important positions—whether those actions were positive or negative, the *Olympia* fight being an example of the latter. Monet may have been interested in seeing how the paintings looked in Durand-Ruel's space the way Clemenceau described them, although he undoubtedly had already tried that kind of sequencing in his own Giverny studio prior to the show and had found it unsatisfactory.

44 Thiébault-Sisson, 1920, as cited and translated in Stuckey, 1985, 346.

45 Louis Courajod, *Les Origines de l'Art Moderne*, Paris, E. Leroux, 1894, 34. The Viollet le Duc quotation comes from Georges Germann, *Gothic Revival in Europe and Britain: Sources, Influences, and Ideas*, London, Lund Humphries, 1972, 7. In addition to the innumerable Gothic monuments he restored, Viollet also wrote a ten-volume *Dictionnaire raisonné de l'architecture française du XIe au XVIe siècle*, Paris, B. Bance [etc.], 1858–68 which remained the century's primary source of technical information about the Gothic and the theoretical underpinnings of the era. A strident anti-cleric, Viollet grounded his opinion of the Gothic in strictly secular terms; see *Viollet le Duc*, exhibition catalgue, Paris, Réunion des musées nationaux, 1980.

46 The Tour d'Albane, for example, was completed in the twelfth century but was given a new crown in the fifteenth when the Tour de Beurre on the other side of the façade was built. The two side aisle portals date from the twelfth and thirteenth centuries, the center one from the sixteenth. The screen above the portals was built between the thirteenth and sixteenth centuries while the iron spire that towers over the church was completed in the 1870s. On the Cathedral see L. Petit, *Histoire de la Cathédrale de Rouen*, Rouen, 1858 and Louis de Foucaud, "Rouen: Les monuments religieux," in *La France Artistique et Monumentale*, vol. 2, Paris, Librairie illustrée 1892–93, 49–88.

47 On Hugo see Neil Levine, "The book and the building: Hugo's theory of architecture and Labrouste's Bibliothèque Ste.-Geneviève," in *The Beaux-Arts and nineteenth-century French architecture*, New York, Museum of Modern Art, 1982, 150 and *La Gloire de Victor Hugo*, exhibition catalogue, Paris, Réunion des musées nationaux, 1985. Pissarro was equally ardent about the Gothic with which he aligned his art. See letters to Lucien of 28 February, 6 March, and 8 April

1895, cited and translated in Rewald, 1980, 261–63.

48 See in particular Alphonse Germain, *Notre art de France*, Paris, Edmond Girard, 1894 and Alphonse Germain, "La Vrai Renaissance," *L'Ermitage*, vol. 5 (June 1894), 343.

49 w.1196 to AH 23 March 1895.

50 Hamilton, 1960 was the first to emphasize Monet's agnosticism while Herbert, 1984 was the first to recognize the ways in which nature replaces religion in these paintings. By grounding his work in secular terms, Monet was following ideas expressed by liberal thinkers on the matter, such as Viollet le Duc who was a strident anti-cleric.

51 w.1206 to AH 4 April 1983.

52 On this trip and the paintings that resulted see W.III, 60–65; Alphant, 1993, 529–58; and Tucker, 1989, 168–74.

53 w.1263 to AH 31 January 1895.

54 w.1268 and w.1266 to AH 13 and 9 February 1895. Monet also missed his routine in Giverny and the relative anonymity he enjoyed there. In Norway, he was celebrated as a hero, which he did not like. He told Alice (w.1266) he "was used to living modestly *dans mon coin* and although very flattered [about a banquet in his honor], I did not like those kinds of things." In the end, however, he confessed to Alice, "I was touched by their testimony, which seemed so sincere." On these testimonial dinners see w.1297 and w.1287 to AH 24 February and 23 March 1895. Monet's status was further underscored by numerous articles on him in the Norwegian press and by a visit paid to him by the Prince of Norway just before the artist's departure. See w.1287 and w.1290 to AH 23 and 30 March 1895.

55 w.1274 to GG 26 February 1895.

56 w.1276 to Blanche Hoschedé 1 March 1895.

57 See w.1290 to AH 30 March 1895.

58 w.1291 to PDR 7 April 1895.

59 André Michel, "Les Salons de 1895. IV. De quelques manières de peinture. Huile et détrempe," *Journal des Débats*, 17 May 1895. Ary Renan, "Petites Expositions: 50 Tableaux de M. Claude Monet," *La Chronique des Arts et de la Curiosité* (18 May 1895), 186.

60 Pissarro letter to Lucien 26 May 1895, cited and translated in Rewald, 1980, 269.

61 Ary Renan, "Petites Expositions: 50 Tableaux de M. Claude Monet," *La Chronique des Arts et de la Curiosité* (18 May 1895), 186; Louis Lumet, "Sensations d'art: Claude Monet," *L'Enclos*, I (1895), 44–45; and Theodore Robinson letter to J. Alden Weir, May 1892, cited in Dorothy Weir Young, *The Life and Letters of J. Alden Weir*, ed. Lawrence W. Chisolm, New Haven, Yale University Press, 1960, 190; also quoted in Seiberling, 1981, 146–47.

62 Camille Mauclair, "Choses d'art," *Mercure de France*, NS 14 (June 1895), 44–45.

63 Henry Eon, "Les Cathédrales de Claude Monet," *La Plume*, no. 147 (1 June 1895), 259.

64 Clemenceau, 1895.

65 Bazalgette, 1898.

66 Clemenceau, 1895.

67 Monet's prices were based on how much time he had spent on these pictures, on the toll that they had exacted, and on his sense of what the market would bear. While working on the series in 1892, for example, he had learned that one of his early views of Rouen (presumably of the 1870s) had sold at auction for 9,500 francs. At the Duret sale in March 1894, his *View of the Seine at Vétheuil* of 1879 (W.528) brought 7,900 francs and his *Turkeys* of 1876 (W.416) reached 12,000 francs. The price for the *Cathedrals* made Durand-Ruel balk but Monet was able to sell almost half-a-dozen of them prior to the show (four to the Comte Camondo and one to a Rouen collector, François Depeaux). On these dealings see Tucker, 1989, 165–68.

68 w.1300, w.1301, w.1303, w.1305, w.1313, w.1314 to various government officials written between May and August 1895. On this affair see W.III, 69 and n. 1314.

69 w.1322 to M. Joyant 8 February 1896.

70 On these two series see W.III, 73, 78–79, 83–86; Levine, 228–39; Seiberling, 1981, 188–92; Spate, 1992, 233–35; and Tucker, 1989, 189–235. Two eye-witness accounts are also useful. They are Guillemot, 1898 and Perry, 1927.

71 Guillemot, 1898.

72 See, for example [Arsène Alexandre], "Expositions individuelles: I. Paysages de Claude Monet," *L'Estampe*, 29 May 1898, reprinted in *Le Figaro*, 3 June 1898, and in *Le Gaulois (supplément)*, 16 June 1898.

73 Gimpel, 1963, entry for 11 October 1920, quoted in Stuckey, 1985, 309. So enthused was Monet with Corot as a landscape painter that he bought one of his paintings from the Doria Sale in 1899 and would have purchased a second if it had not exceeded his limit of 7,000 francs. Monet was able to separate Corot's talent from his personality, however, as in the same conversation he also condemned the older artist for not having helped the Impressionists with Salon juries, calling him a "swine". See Stuckey, 1985, 306. Like Monet, Pissarro held Corot in high esteem as an artist. See letters to Lucien 26 July 1893, 19 April 1895, and 19 August 1898, cited and translated in Rewald, 1980, 211–12, 266–67, and 328–39.

74 Roger Marx, "Claude Lorrain," *Le Votaire*, 7 June 1892, 1. On Corot's retrospective see Georges Lecomte, "Corot," *La Nouvelle Revue*, 94 (May–June 1895), 616–23; Louis de Foucaud, "Camille Corot," *Le Gaulois*, 24 May 1895; and L. Roger-Milès, *Album classique des chefs-d'œuvre de Corot*, Paris, Braun Clément, 1895.

75 Pissarro letter to Lucien 23 March 1898, cited and translated in Rewald, 1980, 323.

76 Maurice Mery, "Petit Salons: Œuvres nouvelles de Claude Monet," *Le Moniteur des Arts* (10 June 1898), 574–75.

77 On Gérôme's remarks see *Le Journal des Artistes*, 8 April 1894, quoted in Jeanne Laurent, *Arts et pouvoirs en France de 1793 à 1981*, St.-Etienne, 1982, 89–90 and in Varnedoe, 1987, 198 and 209, n. 1. On the Caillebotte bequest see Vaisse, 1983; Berhaut, 1983; and Vaisse and Berhaut, 1983

78 On the Luxembourg's collection and policies see Geneviève Lacambre, "Introduction," *Le Musée du Luxembourg en 1874*, exhibition catalogue, Paris, Musée du Luxembourg, 1974 and Varnedoe, 1987, 197–204.

79 Berhaut and Vaisse, 1983, Appendix XXVI. Members of the Institut de France and the Académie des Beaux-Arts called the bequest "an offense to the dignity of our school" and claimed that if it were accepted it would create "a strange confusion [in the public's mind] between what is worthy of being admired and what deserves strong disapproval." See Berhaut and Vaisse, 1983, Appendix XXIII and XXIV. Renoir was responsible for negotiating with the government since he was Caillebotte's executor. Monet was his voice of conscience, however, constantly urging him to accept nothing less than what the will stipulated, particularly with regard to keeping the paintings in Paris. See Monet letter to Renoir of 22 April 1894 in Berhaut and Vaisse, 1983, Appendix X, cited in Varnedoe, 1987, 207, n. 16.

80 Georges Lecomte, "La Vie artistique: Claude Monet," *Droits de l'homme*, 10 June 1898.

81 L'Angèle, "Lettre d'Angèle. Chronique du mois: L'Impressionnisme: Corot–Monet, etc.," *L'Ermitage*, vol. 10 (May 1899), 390–400.

82 On the Dreyfus Affair see Jean-Denis Bredin, *The Affair: The Case of Alfred Dreyfus*, New York, George Braziller, 1986; Norman L., Kleeblatt, ed., *The Dreyfus Affair: Art, Truth, and Justice*, Berkeley, University of California Press, 1988; Patrice Boussel, *L'Affair Dreyfus et la presse*, Paris, A. Colin, 1960; and John Grand-Carteret, *L'Affair Dreyfus et l'image*, Paris, E. Flammarion, [1897].

83 "Le Traître," *Le Rire*, 5 January 1898.

84 Jean-Denis Bredin, *The Affair: The Case of Alfred Dreyfus*, New York, George Braziller, 1986, 350–53.

85 Jean-Denis Bredin, *The Affair: The Case of Alfred Dreyfus*, New York, George Braziller, 1986, 290, 309.

86 Pissarro letters to Lucien of 19 November and 10 February 1898, cited and translated in Rewald, 1980, 332 and 321–22.

87 w.1397 to Zola 3 December 1897.

88 w.1399 to Zola 14 January 1897.

89 w. 1402 to Zola 24 February 1898. Monet also expressed his disgust with the situation and his support of Zola to Geffroy. See w.1401 and w.1403 of 15 and 25 February 1898 and another letter of 14 February 1898 in the Stanford University Art Museum.

90 Pissarro letters to Lucien 19 November 1898, cited and translated in Rewald, 1980, 332.

91 On these campaigns see Seiberling, 1988; W.IV, 10–16, 23–25; Alphant, 1993, 591–618; Levine, 197, 270–96; Spate, 1992, 239–50; and Tucker, 1989, 242–53.

92 Flint, 1984.

93 w.1748 and w.1751 to PDR 5 and 8 December 1904.

94 w.1592 to AH 2 February 1901; on the Tower of London visit see w.1533 to AH 19 March 1900. On his high opinion of the English see w.421 and w.466 to AH 17 February and 29 March 1884. On his dinners in London see w.1528 to AH 11 March 1900.

95 On his English suits and eating habits see Joyes, 1975, 23 and 31.

96 Pissarro letter to Lucien 10 February 1899, cited and translated in Rewald, 1980, 321–22.

97 Edmond and Jules de Goncourt, *Journal*, vol. 16, Monaco, 1956, 207.

98 Theodore Butler, diary, September 1892, quoted in John Gage, *Turner, Rain, Steam, and Speed*, New York, George Braziller, 1972, 75, and Seiberling, 1988, 42.

99 Georges Lecomte, "Un Homme," *Petit République Socialiste*, 11 May 1904.

100 Le Masque Rouge, "Notes d'Art: L'Exposition Claude Monet," *L'Action*, 12 May 1904, cited and translated in Seiberling, 1988, 96.

101 Gustave Kahn, "L'Exposition Claude Monet," *Gazette des Beaux-Arts*, ser. 3, 32 (July 1904), 82–88. Others noted the relationship to Turner; see, for example, "Claude Monet Exhibition," *The Daily Telegraph* 24 May 1904 which even invokes *Rain, Steam, and Speed*.

102 w. 1768 to PDR 8 March 1905. On his own show in London see w.1748 and w.1751 to PDR 5 and 8 December 1904.

7 MONET AND HIS GIVERNY GARDENS: 1900–1926

1 The best sources on Giverny and Monet's time there are Joyes, 1975; Gordon, 1973; Hoschedé, 1960; Varnedoe, 1978; Wildenstein, "Monet's Giverny," in Moffett et al., 1978; and Paris, Centre Culturel du Marais, 1983. Specific studies of Monet's *Water Lily* paintings include House, 1983; Hooge, 1987; Gordon and Stuckey, 1979; and Stuckey, 1979. On Giverny's appeal to foreigners see David Sellin, "Giverny 1887–1900," and "Giverny 1900–1910," in *Americans in Brittany and Normandy 1860–1910*, exhibition catalogue, Phoenix, Phoenix Art Museum, 1982, and William Gerdts, *Monet's Giverny: an impressionist colony*, New York, Abbeville Press, 1993.

2 w.1079 to PDR 21 January 1890. On the purchase of the property see W.III, 37.

3 Guillemot, 1898. On the Japanese gardener

coming to Giverny see w.111bis to Paul Helleu 9 June 1891. Among the horticultural publications he purchased were the magazine *La Revue horticule* (which he subscribed to from 1893 to 1925), the five-volume *Dictionnaire d'horticulture*, the twenty-three-volume *Flore des jardins de l'Europe*, and the twenty-six-volume *Flore des serres et des jardins de l'Europe* published in Ghent in 1845 and still considered one of the best reference works at the end of the century.

4   w.1191 to Prefect of Eure 17 March 1893.

5   w.1193 to AH 20 March 1893. On the objections of the Giverny residents see w.1219 to Prefect of the Eure 17 July 1893. On his solicitations of the attorney see w.2889 (1212a) to M. A. Louvray 20 April 1893 and of the Rouen journalist see w.1195 to AH [21 March 1893].

6   Thiébault-Sisson, July 1927. For plant identification see Joyes, 1975, 33, 37–38 and Georges Truffaut, "The garden of a Great Painter," *Jardinage*, November 1924, translated in Stuckey, 1975, 313–17.

7   Joyes, 1975, 37.

8   W.1392, 1419, and 1419bis, of 1895 and W.1501–1508, of 1898.

9   Cézanne letter to his sons, Paul, 8 September 1906, as quoted and translated in John Rewald, *Cézanne: a biography*, The Netherlands, Harry N. Abrams, B.V., 1990, 258–59.

10  Maurice Kahn, "Le Jardin de Claude Monet," *Le Temps*, 7 June 1904, quoted in Charles Stuckey, 1985, 244. On the reaction to things Japanese see Evett, 1982; Paris, *Le Japonisme*, 1988; Johnson, 1986; and Tucker, 1989, 124–32.

11  Alphonse de Calonne, "Beaux-Arts: M. Claude Monet," *Le Soleil*, 26 November 1900.

12  See for example G. D., "Tribune Artistique: Petits Salons," *Le Voltaire*, 4 December 1900.

13  Julien Leclercq, "Le Bassin aux Nymphéas de Claude Monet," *La Chronique des Arts et de la Curiosité* (1 December 1900), 363–64; Julien Leclercq, "Petites Expositions: Galerie Durand-Ruel," *La Chronique des Arts et de la Curiosité*, 15 (15 April 1899), 130–31.

14  Roger Marx, "Un Siècle d'art [1900]," in *Maîtres d'hier et d'aujourd'hui*, Paris, Calmann-Lévy, 1914, 100.

15  Robert de La Sizeranne, "L'Art à l'Exposition de 1900. II. Le Bilan de l'Impressionnisme," *Revue des Deux-Mondes*, vol. 70 (1 June 1900), 628–51.

16  A. Pallier, "XXX," *La Liberté*, 8 June 1898 Armand Silvestre declared that the Impressionists had affected "their worst enemies" at the Salon des Champs-Elysées who were finally "condescending not to disdain all of their methods." See Armand Silvestre, "Notes d'art. Plein air," *La Petite Gironde*, 3 February 1899. The following year, Louis

de Fourcaud asserted that if Monet and Manet, "the two masters of Impressionism," were written out of the history of French art, "aestheticians would no longer understand anything about the transformations of French color at the close of the nineteenth century." See Louis de Fourcaud, "L'Exposition Universelle: La Peinture; I. L'Ecole française," *La Revue de l'art ancien et moderne* (10 September 1900), 145–58.

17  Charles Saunier, "Petit Gazette d'art: Claude Monet," *La Revue blanche*, vol. 22, no. 181 (15 December 1900), 624.

18  Emile Verhaeren, "L'Art moderne," *Mercure de France*, February 1901, 544–45.

19  Pissarro letter to Lucien of 26 April 1900, cited and translated in Rewald, 1980, 340–41.

20  On Monet's earnings see his carnets at the Musée Marmottan and W.IV, 10, 25, 34, 77, 90.

21  On these personal habits see Joyes, 1975, 31 and 23, and Paris, Centre Culturel du Marais, 1982, especially 229 and 279–80.

22  On the fame of Monet's garden see for example Arsène Alexandre, "Les jardins de Claude Monet," *Le Figaro*, 9 August 1901; C.I.B., "Monet and Giverny," *The New York Tribune*, 8 September 1901; Alice Kuhn, "Claude Monet Giverny," *Femme d'Aujourd'hui*, 10 August 1904; Maurice Kahn, "Au jour le jour. Le jardin de Claude Monet," *Le Temps*, 7 June 1904; and Arsène Alexandre, "Un Jardinier," *Le Populaire* [Nantes], 11 June 1904. The first to include photographs of the gardens was Louis Vauxcelles, "Un Après-midi chez Claude Monet," *L'Art et les Artistes*, 2 (November 1905), 86. On the rumors that he began 150 canvases see Spate, 1992, 254.

23  All of these newspaper reports are in the Durand-Ruel Archives and are listed in W.IV, 56 n. 517. One from the *Washington Post* of 16 May 1908 and one from *The Standard* of 20 May 1908 (which corrects the others by saying they are slightly exaggerated) are quoted in Stuckey, 1985, 250–51. On Monet's claims to have destroyed thirty canvases see w.1832 to PDR 27 April 1907.

24  See w.1831 and 1832 to PDR 8 and 27 April 1907.

25  On the title of the 1909 show see w.1875 to DR 28 January 1909. On the inversion of earth and sky see Butor, 1963. Critics drew attention to the fact no sky appeared in the 1900 pictures. See, for example, Louis Aubry, "Notes d'art; L'impressionnisme.—Exposition d'œuvres nouvelles de Claude Monet," *Le Soir*, 3 December 1900. Its inclusion in the paintings of 1909 was noted by critics such as Edouard Sarradin in the *Journal des Débats*, 12 May 1909 while others spoke about the perfect balance Monet had struck between water and sky; "Les Nymphéas" *Critique Indépendant*, 15

June 1909.

26  w.1832 to PDR 27 April 1907. The overwhelming majority of the twenty-five reviews the 1900 show provoked were positive but there were a few that were negative or that expressed reservations. The strongest of the negatives is Alphonse de Calonne, "Beaux-Art. M. Claude Monet," *Le Soleil*, 26 November 1900. Even Arsène Alexandre was concerned; see *Le Figaro*, 23 November 1900.

27  Robert E. Dell, "Art in France," *Burlington Magazine*, 15 (June 1909), 193.

28  GG, 1893, vol. 2, 142.

29  Roger Marx, "Les 'Nymphéas' de Claude Monet," *Gazette des Beaux-Arts*, ser. 4, I (1909), 524–29, which also includes analogies to music and poetry, quoted and analyzed in Levine, 1976, 303–14; on comparison to Michelangelo and Beethoven see Henry Ghéon, "Les 'Paysages d'eau' de Claude Monet," *La Nouvelle Revue Française*, 1 (1 July 1909), 534–35. Also see Edmond Epardaud, "Les Nymphéas de Claude Monet," *Journal de Maine et Loir*, 31 May 1909.

30  Arsène Alexandre, "Un Paysagiste d'aujourd'hui et un portraitiste de jadis," *Comœdia*, 8 May 1909; and Roger Marx, "Les 'Nymphéas' de Claude Monet," *Gazette des Beaux-Arts*, ser. 4, I (1909), 529.

31  Guillemot, 1898.

32  w.2001b to GBJ or JBJ 1 April 1912. On the series as souveniers see the same letter as well as w.2019 to GG 6 July 1912.

33  Alice Hoschedé letters to Germaine Salcrou of 28 January and 2 February 1910, quoted in Paris, Centre Culturel du Marais, 1983, 275, and translated in Spate, 1992, 265.

34  On this commission see W.v, 178–9 and the following letters all to GG: w.1944 11 November 1910; w.1947 and w.1949 3 and 27 December 1910; w.1950 12 January 1911; w.1959 11 April 1911; and w.1987 25 November 1911.

35  w.1949 to GG 27 December 1910.

36  w. 1962 to GG 7 May 1911.

37  w.1976a to GBJ or JBJ 28 August 1911.

38  w.1989 to Blanche Hoschedé 4 December 1911.

39  w.2014 to Paul Signac 5 June 1912. On the critical reception of the Venice pictures see Levine, 1976, 336–73, and W.IV, 75, ns. 688 and 689.

40  w.2009 to GG 6 May 1912 and w.2019 to GG 6 July 1912.

41  On critics who implied praise out of deference to the master see, for example, George Besson, "Exposition Claude Monet," *La Phalange*, 20 June 1912, 552–53.

42  Jean's biography remains cryptic, like that of the rest of Monet's children and stepchildren. We know at least that his health problems surfaced in late August 1890 while in the army as he was hospitalized in

Le Havre where he was visited by his father. See w.1074 to Berthe Morisot 22 September 1890.

43   w.2019 to GG 6 July 1912.

44   w.2023 to GG 26 July 1912. On Monet's ocular problems see W.IV, 77, n. 711; Ravin, 1985, 394–99; J. Haut Roger and Amalric, "L'operation de la cataracte de Claude Monet, correspondance du peintre et G. Clemenceau au Docteur Coutela," *Histoire de la Science Medicale*, vol. 18, no. 2 (1984), 109–27; P. G. Moreau, "La cataracte de Claude Monet," *L'Ophtalmologie des origines à nos jours*, vol. 3 (1981), 141; and Dittière, 1973, 126–32.

45   w.2023 to GG 26 July 1912; w.2024 to PDR 1 August 1912; and w.2024I to GBJ or JBJ 5 August 1912.

46   w.2024 to PDR 1 August 1912.

47   w.2097 to Charlotte Lysès 5 February 1914. On purchasing a house for Jean see w.2062 to PDR 10 April 1913.

48   w.2101 to PDR 16 February 1914.

49   w.2116 to GG 30 April 1914.

50   George F. Kennan, *The Fateful Alliance, France, Russia, and the Coming of the First World War*, New York, Pantheon Books, 1984, 30.

51   w.2148 to Joyant 25 February 1915.

52   Gris letter to Daniel-Henry Kahnweiler, 16 August 1914, in *Letters of Juan Gris, collected by D.H. Kahnweiler*, trans. and ed. Douglas Cooper, London, Print. Priv., 1956, 8–9, cited in Kenneth E. Silver, *Esprit de Corps: the Art of the Parisian Avant-Garde and the first World War*, Princeton, Princeton University Press, 1989, 4.

53   Matisse letter to Charles Camoin, 10 April 1918, in Danièle Giraudy, "Correspondance Henri Matisse–Charles Camoin," *Revue de l'Art*, no. 12 (1971), 21, cited and translated in Kenneth E. Silver, *Esprit de Corps: the Art of the Parisian Avant-Garde and the First World War*, Princeton, Princeton University Press, 1989, 34.

54   w.2132 to JDR 6 November 1914; Monet even claimed later that he began the Grand Decorations on 1 August 1914, a suggestion that is clearly untrue but which indicates the way the war in hindsight came to inform these pictures; see Thiébault-Sisson, "Un nouveau musée parisien: Les Nymphéas de Cl. Monet à l'Orangerie des Tuileries," *La Revue de l'Art* (June 1927), 48; also see Marthe de Fels, 1929, 205–07.

55   w.2119 to Felix Fénéon [c. 1 June 1914].

56   w.2121 to Felix Fénéon 17 June 1914.

57   w.2123 to PDR 29 June 1914.

58   w.2124 to GG 6 July 1914.

59   w.2128 to GG 1 September 1914.

60   w.2126 to JPH 10 August 1914.

61   w.2128 to GG 1 September 1914 which also includes the reference to Clemenceau's son.

62   w.2129 to Joseph Durand-Ruel 9 October 1914, which also includes the reference to Renoir's son.

63   w.2128 to GG 1 September 1914.

64   w.2135 to GG 1 December 1914.

65   w.2145 to GBJ or JBJ 10 February 1915.

66   w.3031 (2148b) to Léon Wirth 1 March 1915. He expressed the same sentiments throughout the year. See, for example, w.3032 (2155a) to Theo van Rysselberge 23 August 1915.

67   Matisse letter of 1 June 1916, cited and translated in Alfred Barr, *Matisse. His art and his public*, New York, Museum of Modern Art, 1951, 182.

68   On the benefit exhibitions and sales see W.IV, 86 ns.798–800; w.2169 to GBJ or JBJ 20 January 1916, w.2171 to Madame Clémental 19 February 1916, w.2174 to GBJ or JBJ 10 March 1916, w.2176 to Madame Clémental 2 April 1916, and w.2220 to GDR 26 March 1917; on the financial donation see w.2130 to GG 20 October 1914; on committees see w.2143 to unknown recipient 16 January 1915, and w.3030 (2148a) to F. Déconchy of 1 March 1915.

69   Lucien Descaves, "Chez Claude Monet," *Paris–Magazine*, 25 August 1920.

70   See, for example, Lucien Descaves, "L'Academie Goncourt chez Cl. Monet," *L'Œuvre*, 11 December 1926, 1, and *Souvenirs d'un ours*, Paris, 1946, 246–47.

71   w.2155 to JPH 19 August 1915.

72   w.2160 to GG 24 October 1915; also see w.2162 to GBJ or JBJ 30 October 1915 in which he announces he is finally installed; on the cost of the studio see W. IV, 84; on his complaints about the ugliness of the building see w.2155 to JPH 19 August 1915.

73   w.2164 to GG 30 November 1915.

74   On Michel in Verdun see w.2193 to GG 11 September 1916. On the end of the war see w.2168 to GDR 17 January 1916 and w.2173 to Thérèse Janin 2 March 1916; on Monet's thoughts being elsewhere see w.2172 to GBJ or JBJ 29 February 1916.

75   On fears about the project see w.2186 to André Barbier 14 June 1916; on his nasty moods see w.2178 to Charlotte Lysès 19 April 1916 and w.2205a to GBJ or JBJ 12 December 1916.

76   w.2200 to GG 13 November 1916.

77   w.2210 to GG 25 January 1917. He had slipped in and out of these phases in 1916 as well, as he admitted to Clemenceau; see w.2192 11 September 1916.

78   See w.2230 to GG 1 May 1917; on this commission and the purchase of Monet's *Rouen Cathedral* see Hoog, 1981 and W.IV, 54.

79   This would change over the next few years as Monet added or substituted various canvases, several of which are extremely close to specific sketches. The two *Willow* panels, for example, became three *Willows* with the third panel being based on W.1848–51; W.1820 served as a veritable cartoon for part of one of the *Agapanthe* panels while other works in the group, such as W.1811, are extremely close to another section of that suite. This change in working habits might have been precipitated by constraints of time and health. Stuckey and Gordon, 1979, were the first to try to sort out these changes.

80   Thiébault-Sisson, 1927, 49.

81   w.974 to AH 6 May 1889.

82   w.2275 to JDR 15 June 1918.

83   w.2277 to GBJ 21 June 1918.

84   w.2278 to GBJ 3 August 1918; for another such bald statement see w. 2281 to GG 10 September 1918.

85   w.2287 to GC 12 November 1918. Monet was not the only artist to celebrate the victory. Matisse painted a still life that he titled "Flowers, 14 July" to commemorate the celebration of the end of the war that occurred on Bastille Day following the signing of the Treaty of Versailles on 28 June 1919. See Kenneth E. Silver, *Esprit de Corps: The Art of the Parisian Avant-Garde and the First World War*, Princeton, Princeton University Press, 1989, 226.

86   w.2290 to GBJ or JBJ 24 November 1918.

87   Thiébault-Sisson "Un Don de M. Claude Monet à l'Etat," *Le Temps* 14 October 1914; Marcel Pays, "Un Grand Maître de l'impressionnisme—Une visite à M. Claude Monet dans son ermitage à Giverny," *Excelsior*, 26 January 1921; and Geffroy, "Claude Monet," *L'Art et les artistes*, 1920, 80–1.

88   See Thiébault-Sisson, 1920.

89   w.2362 to Clémentel 12 July 1920.

90   W.IV, 431–2, pièce justificative #297 Louis Bonnier to Monet 5 October 1920.

91   Arsène Alexandre, "L'Epopée des Nymphéas," *Le Figaro*, 21 October 1920, 1.

92   Gimpel, 1963, 177, cited in Stuckey, 110; Thiébault-Sisson, 1920, 2.

93   Monet may have embellished his response slightly as it was based on a recollection he made more than four years after the fact. See René Delange, "Claude Monet," *L'Illustration*, vol. 85 (15 January 1927). Whatever he said certainly prompted a negative reaction among Institute members. See "M. Claude Monet et l'Institut," *Le Bulletin de l'art ancien et moderne*, no. 658 (10 January 1921), 2. Monet did not hesitate to fire back, discussing his refusal openly with a journalist later that month. See Marcel Pays, "Une visite à Claude Monet dans son ermitage à Giverny," *Excelsior*, 26 January 1921.

94   The contract called for the delivery of nineteen *Water Lily* panels to be placed in two contiguous rooms in the Orangerie of the Tuileries to be called the Musée Claude Monet. The first room was to hold eight 4.25-meter-long panels—three entitled *The Clouds*; three more, *Morning*, and two others *Green Reflections*—together with

one 6-meter panel entitled *Setting Sun*. For the second room, there were to be four 4.25-meter panels representing *The Three Willows*, four 6-meter panels entitled *Morning*, and two final panels of 4.25 meters called *Tree Reflections*. Monet had the right to make any modifications to the program up until the time of delivery, which was to occur as soon as the State completed the construction of the galleries. The State guaranteed the galleries would be ready no later than two years from the date of the agreement. That meant Monet had to deliver the paintings by 12 April 1924. No other paintings or sculpture could ever be placed in the rooms, the arrangement of the panels could never be altered after they were on the walls, and the paintings could never be varnished. See Hoog, 1987, 113–15. For the negotiations that led to this contract and the changes entailed to the original proposal see Gordon and Stuckey, 1979.

95 w.22503 to JDR 7 July 1922.

96 W.IV, 109.

97 w.★2662 and w.★2659 to Dr Coutela 14 September and 26 August 1923.

98 w.2529 to Clemenceau 30 August 1923.

99 See w.2663, w.2664, w.2665 to Dr Coutela 13 and 23 October and 10 November 1923.

100 w.2541 to Clémentel 7 November 1923.

101 Recollections of Dr Jacques Mawas, [7] June 1924, cited in W.IV, 120.

102 w.2572 to André Barbier 5 August 1924.

103 w.2577 to André Barbier 5 October 1924 and w.★2677 to Dr Coutela 6 October 1924.

104 Clemenceau letter to Monet, 8 October 1924, cited in Hoog, 1987, 110.

105 w.2583 to Dr Mawas 8 December 1924, w.2584 and w.2585 to André Barbier 9 and 27 December 1924.

106 Clemenceau letter to Monet, 7 January 1925, cited and translated in Stuckey, 120, and in Hoog, 1987, 110–111 although with slight changes in translation.

107 w.2596 to Dr Mawas 25 March 1925.

108 w.2600 to André Barbier 22 May 1925.

109 w.2609 to André Barbier 17 July 1925.

110 w.2615 to André Barbier 17 November 1925. On his recovery as a resurrection see w.2612 to GBJ 6 October 1925.

111 Clemenceau letter to Monet, 8 February 1926, cited in Hoog, 1987, 112.

112 w.2621 to André Barbier 5 April 1926.

113 w.2630 to Paul Léon 4 October 1926. On no longer being able to hold a pen see w.2626 to E. Chartres 21 June 1926 which was dictated to Blanche Hoschedé-Monet.

114 See for example Gillet, "Claude Monet," *Le Gaulois*, 6 December 1926; Jean Botrot, "Claude Monet est mort," *Le Journal*, 6 December 1926; Roger Dardenne, "Un Grand Peintre. Claude Monet," *Le Figaro*, 6 December 1926.

115 Clemenceau, 1928, 101–02. For the mixed reviews about the Grand Decorations at the Orangerie see, for example, Marcel Sauvage, "Les 'Nymphéas' de Claude Monet au Musée de l'Orangerie," *Comoedia*, 17 May 1927; Francois Thiébault-Sisson, "Art et Curiosité. A l'Orangerie des Tuileries. Les 'Nymphéas' de Claude Monet," *Le Temps* 18 May 1927; Pierre Guillais, "A l'Orangerie. M. Hérriot dans les salles des 'Nymphéas' de Claude Monet," *Le Soir*, 18 May 1927; Louis Paillard, "Un musée Claude Monet est installé aux Tuileries," *Le Petit Journal*, 17 May 1927; and L'Imagier, "Claude Monet au Musée de l'Orangerie," *L'Œuvre*, 17 May 1927.

# Selected Bibliography

Adams, Steven. *The Barbizon School and the Origins of Impressionism*. London, Phaidon, 1994.

Adhémar, Hélène. "Modifications apportées par Monet à son 'Déjeuner sur l'herbe' de 1865 à 1866," *Bulletin du Laboratoire du Musée du Louvre* (June 1958), 36–49.

——, et al. *Centenaire de l'impressionnisme*. Exhibition catalogue, Paris, Réunion des musées nationaux, 1974.

——, et al. *Hommage à Monet*. Exhibition catalogue, Paris, Réunion des musées nationaux, 1980.

Aiken, Geneviève and Marianne Delafond. *La Collection d'estampes japonaises de Claude Monet à Giverny*. Paris, La Bibliothèque des Arts, 1983.

Alexandre, Arsène. *Claude Monet*. Paris, Bernheim-Jeune, 1921.

Alphant, Marianne. *Claude Monet, une vie dans le paysage*. Paris, Hazan, 1993.

Amsterdam, Rijksmuseum Vincent Van Gogh. *Monet in Holland*. Exhibition catalogue, Zwolle, Waander, 1987.

Bailly-Herzberg, Janine (ed.). *Correspondance de Camille Pissarro*. Vol. 1 1865–1885, Paris, Presse Universitaires de France, 1980; Vol. 2 1886–1890, and Vol. 3 1891–1894, Paris, Editions du Valhermeil, 1986 and 1988.

Baudelaire, Charles. *The Painter of Modern Life and Other Essays*. Trans. and ed. Jonathan Mayne. London, Phaidon, 1964.

Bazalgette, Léon. "Les deux cathédrales, Claude Monet et J.-K. Huysmans," in *L'Esprit nouveau dans la vie artistique, sociale et religieuse*. Paris, Société d'éditions litteraires, 1898.

Berger, Klaus. "Monet's Crisis," *Register of the Museum of Art*, University of Kansas, 2, Nos. 9–10 (May 1963), 17–21.

Berhaut, Marie. "Le Legs Caillebotte, Verités et contre-verités," *Bulletin de la Société de l'Histoire de l'Art français* (1983), 209–23.

Bernier, R. R. "The Subject and Painting: Monet's 'Language of the Sketch,'" *Art History*, Vol. 12, No. 3 (September 1989), 298–321.

—— and Pierre Vaisse. "Le Legs Caillebotte; Annexe: documents," *Bulletin de la Société de l'Histoire de l'Art français* (1983), 223–49.

Blunden, Maria and Godfrey. *Impressionists and Impressionism*. Geneva, Skira, 1970.

Bodelsen, Merete. "Early Impressionist Sales 1874–94 in the light of some unpublished 'procès-verbaux,'" *Burlington Magazine* 110 (June 1968), 330–49.

Boime, Albert. "The Salon des Refusés and the Evolution of Modern Art." *Art Quarterly*, Vol. 32, No. 4 (Winter 1969), 411–26.

——. *The Academy and French Painting in the Nineteenth Century*, London, Phaidon, 1971.

Bomford, David, et al. *Impressionism (Art in the Making)*. Exhibition catalogue. London, National Gallery, 1990.

Boston, Museum of Fine Arts. *Monet Unveiled, A New Look at Boston's Paintings*. Exhibition catalogue, Boston, Museum of Fine Arts, 1977.

Bouyer, Raymond. *Le Paysage dans l'art*. Paris, L'Artiste, Revue de Paris, 1894.

Brettell, Richard R. "Monet's Haystacks Reconsidered," *The Art Institute of Chicago Museum Studies*, Vol. 11, No. 1 (Fall 1984), 4–21.

———, et al. *A Day in the Country: Impressionism and the French Landscape*. Exhibition catalogue, Los Angeles, Los Angeles Museum of Art, 1984.

Bricon, Emile. "L'Art impressionniste au musée du Luxembourg," *La Nouvelle Revue*, 114 (15 September 1898), 288–304.

Butor, Michel. "Claude Monet ou le monde renversé," *L'Art de France*, Vol. 1 (1963), 277–81, trans. and reprinted in *Art News Annual*, 1968.

Byvanck, W. G. C. *Un Hollandais à Paris en 1891: Sensations de litterature et d'art*. Paris, Perrin, 1892.

Callen, Anthea. *Techniques of the Impressionists*. Secausus, Chartwell Books, Inc., 1982.

Champa, Kermit. *Studies in Early Impressionism*. New Haven, Yale University Press, 1973.

———. *"Masterpiece" Studies: Manet, Zola, van Gogh, and Monet*. University Park, Pennsylvania University Press, 1994.

———, et al. *The Rise of Landscape Painting in France. Corot to Monet*. Exhibition catalogue, Manchester, The Currier Gallery of Art, 1991.

Chevalier, Frédéric. "Les Impressionnistes," *L'Artiste*, 1 May 1877, 329–33.

Chicago, The Art Institute of. *Paintings by Monet*. Exhibition catalogue, Chicago, The Art Institute of Chicago, 1975.

Chisaburo, Yamado, (ed.) *Japonsime in Art: An International Symposium*. Tokyo, Committee for the year 2001, 1980.

Clark, T. J. *The Painting of Modern Life: Paris in the Art of Manet and his Followers*. New York, Knopf, 1985.

Clemenceau, Georges. "Révolution de cathédrales,'' *La Justice*, 20 May 1895, 1.

———. *Claude Monet. Les Nymphéas*. Paris, Librairie Plon, 1928; reprinted as *Claude Monet: Cinquante ans d'amité*. Paris, Palatine, 1965.

Crow, Thomas. "Modernism and Mass Culture in the Visual Arts," *Modernism and Modernity*. Halifax, The Press of the Nova Scotia College of Art and Design, 1983, 215–64.

Daulte, François, "Claude Monet et ses sympathies avec l'art japonaise," *Connaissance des arts,* 256 (June 1973), 122–29.

Delouche, Denise. "Monet et Belle-Ile en 1886," *Bulletin des Amis du Musée de Rennes*, No. 4 (1980), 27–55.

———. *Monet à Belle-Ile*. Saint-Herblain, Le Chasse-Marée/ArMen, 1992.

Dewhurst, Wynford. "Claude Monet – Impressionist: An Appreciation," *The Pall Mall Magazine*, 6 (1900), 209–24.

———. *Impressionist Painting. Its Genesis and Development*. London, George Newnes, 1904.

Distell, Anne. *Impressionism: The First Collectors*. Trans. Barbara Perroud-Benson. New York, Harry N. Abrams, 1990.

Dittière, Monique. "Comment Monet retrouvera la vue après l'operation de la cataracte," *Sandorama*, Vol. 32 (January–February 1973), 26–32.

Dunn, Roger Terry. *The Monet–Rodin Exhibition at the Gallery Georges Petit in 1889*. New York, Garland Publishing, 1980.

Duret, Théodore. *Les peintres impressionnistes: Claude Monet, Sisley, C. Pissarro, Renoir, Berthe Morisot*. Paris, H. Heyman et J. Perois, 1878; reprinted as *Critique d'avant-garde*. Paris, Charpentier, 1885.

———. *Le Peintre Claude Monet*. Paris, G. Charpentier, 1880.

Durosell, Jean-Baptiste, et al. *Georges Clemenceau à son ami Claude Monet. Correspondence*. Paris, Réunion des Musées Nationaux, 1993.

Eisenman, Stephen F. "The Intransigent Artists or How the Impressionists got Their Name," in San Francisco, 1986, 50–59.

Elder, Marc [Marc Tendron]. *A Giverny, chez Claude Monet*. Paris, Bernheim-Jeune, 1924.

Elderfield, John. "Monet's series," *Art International* Vol. 18, No. 9 (15 November 1974), 28–29, 45–46.

Evett, Elisa. *The Critical Reception of Japanese Art in Europe in the Late Nineteenth Century*. Ann Arbor, UMI Research Press, 1982.

Fels, Marthe de. *La vie de Claude Monet*. Paris, Editions Gallimard, 1929.

Fitzgerald, Desmond. "Claude Monet: Master of Impressionism," *Brush and Pencil*, 15 (March 1905), 181–95.

Flint, Kate (ed.). *Impressionists in England: The Critical Reception*. London, Routledge and Kegan Paul, 1984.

Flood, Phyllis. "Documentary Evidence for the Availability of Japanese Imagery in Europe in Nineteenth-Century Public Collection," *Art Bulletin*, Vol. 68, No. 1 (March 1986), 105–41.

Frascina, Francis, et al. *Modernity and Modernism: French painting in the nineteenth century*. New Haven and London, Yale University Press, 1993.

Fuller, William H. *Claude Monet*. New York, Gilliss Bros., 1891.

———. *Claude Monet and His Paintings*. New York, J. J. Littler, 1899.

Garb, Tamar. "L'Art Féminin: The Formation of a Critical Category in Late Nineteenth-Century France", *Art History*, Vol. 12, No. 1 (March 1989), 39–65.

Geffroy, Gustave. "L'Impressionnisme," *Revue encyclopédique*, 15 December 1893.

———. "Histoire de l'impressionnisme," in *La Vie artistique*, Vol. III, Paris, E. Dentu, 1894.

———. *La Vie artistique*. 8 vols. Paris, E. Dentu (1–4) and H. Floury (5–8), 1892–1903.

———. *Claude Monet: sa vie, son temps, son œuvre*. 2 vols. Paris, G. Cres, 1924.

Gimpel, René. "At Giverny with Claude Monet," *Art in America,* Vol. 15, No. 4 (June 1927), 168–74.

———. *Diary of an Art Dealer*. Trans. Joseph Rosenberg. New York, Farrar, Strauss, and Giroux, 1963.

Goldwater, Robert. "Symbolic Form: Symbolic Content," in 'The Reaction against Impressionism in the 1880s, Its Nature and Causes,' *Problems of the 19th and 20th Centuries*, Acts of the 20th International Congress of the History of Art, IV. Princeton, Princeton University Press, 1963, 111–21.

Robert Gordon. "The lily pond at Giverny: the changing inspiration of Monet," *The Connoisseur*, Vol. 184, No. 741 (November 1973), 154–65.

———, and Andrew Forge. *Monet*. New York, Harry N. Abrams, 1983.

———, and Claire Jones. "Claude Monet in Giverny," *Du*, (December 1973), 872–93, 952.

———, and Charles F. Stuckey. "Blossoms and Blunders. Monet and the State," *Art in America*, Vol. 67, No. 1 (January-February 1979), 102–17.

———, and Charles F. Stuckey, "Dealing in temperaments: economic transformation of the artistic field in France during the second half of the nineteenth century," *Art History*, Vol. 10, No. 1 (March 1987), 59–78.

Grad, Bonnie L. and Timothy Riggs. *Visions of City and Country, Prints and Photographs of 19th Century France*. Exhibition catalogue, Worcester, Worcester Art Museum, 1982.

Green, Nicholas. *The Spectacle of Nature: Landscape and Bourgeois Culture in Nineteenth-century France*. Manchester, Manchester University Press, 1990.

Greenberg, Clement. "The Latin Monet," *Art News Annual* (1957), 132–48, 194–96.

Gsell, Paul. "La Tradition artistique française. I, L'Impressionisme". *La Revue bleue*, Vol. 49, No. 13 (26 March 1892), 403–06.

Guillemot, Maurice. "Claude Monet," *Revue illustré*, 13 (15 March 1898).

Halperin, Joan U. (ed.). *Felix Fénéon: Œuvres plus que complètes*. 2 vols., Geneva, Librarie Droz, 1970.

Hamerton, Philip Gilbert. "The Present State of the Fine Arts in France. IV. Impressionism," *The Portfolio* (1891), 67–74.

Hamilton, George Heard. *Claude Monet's Paintings of Rouen Cathedral*. Charleton Lecture, 1959. London, Oxford University Press, 1960.

Herbert, Eugenia W. *The Artist and Social Reform: France and Belgium 1885–1895*. New Haven, Yale University Press, 1961.

Herbert, Robert L. *Barbizon Revisited*. Exhibition catalogue, Museum of Fine Arts, Boston, 1962.

———. "Method and Meaning in Monet," *Art in America*, Vol. 67, No. 5 (September 1979), 90–108.

———. "Industry and the Changing Landscape from Daubigny to Monet," in J. M. Merrimann (ed.), *French Cities in the Nineteenth Century*. London, Yale University Press, 1982.

———. "The Decorative and the Natural in Monet's Cathedrals," in Rewald and Weitzenhoffer, 1984, 160–79.

———. "Impressionism, Originality, and Laissez-Faire," *Radical History Review*, 38 (Spring 1987), 7–15.

———. *Impressionism. Art, Leisure, and Parisian Society*. New Haven and London, Yale University Press, 1988.

———. *Monet on the Normandy Coast. Tourism and Painting, 1867–1886*. New Haven and London, Yale University Press, 1994.

Hoog, Michel. "'La Cathédrale de Reims' de Claude Monet, ou le tableau impossible," *La Revue du Louvre et des Musées de France*, Vol. 31, No. 1 (1981), 22–24.

———. *Les Nymphéas de Claude Monet au Musée de l'Orangerie*. Paris, Editions de la Réunion des musées nationaux, 1984.

Hoschedé, Jean-Pierre. *Claude Monet, ce mal connu*. 2 vols., Geneva, Pierre Cailler, 1960.

House, John. "New Light on Monet and Pissarro in London in 1870–71," *Burlington Magazine*, Vol. 120, No. 907 (October 1978), 636–42.

———. "The New Monet Catalogue," *Burlington Magazine*, Vol. 120, No. 907 (October 1978), 678–82.

———. "The Impressionist Vision of London," in Ira Bruce Nadel and F. S. Schwarzbach (eds.), *Victorian Artists and the City*. New York, Pergamon Press, 1980.

———, "Monet: le jardin d'eau et la 2e série des Nymphéas (1903–9)", in Paris, 1983, 150–71.

———. "Monet in 1890," in Rewald and Weitzenhoffer, 1984, 124–39.

———. "The Origins of Monet's Series Paintings," in *Claude Monet. Painter of Light*. Exhibition catalogue, Auckland, Auckland City Art Gallery, 1985.

———. *Monet, Nature into Art*. New Haven and London, Yale University Press, 1986.

———. "Time's Cycles", *Art in America*, Vol. 80, No. 10 (October 1992), 126–35.

Huth, H. "Impressionism comes to America," *Gazette des Beaux-Arts*, ser. 6, Vol. 29 (April 1946), 225–52.

Isaacson, Joel. "Monet's Views of the Thames," *Bulletin of the Art Association of Indianapolis*, 52 (1965), 44–51.

———. "Monet's views of Paris," *Allen Memorial Art Museum Bulletin* (Oberlin), 24 (Fall 1966), 5–22.

———. *Monet: Le Déjeuner sur l'herbe*. New York, Viking Press, 1972.

———. *Claude Monet. Observation and Reflection*. Oxford, Phaidon, 1978.

———. "'La Débâcle' by Claude Monet," *University of Michigan Museum of Art Bulletin*, Vol. 1 (1978) 1–15.

———. *The Crisis of Impressionism: 1878–1882*. Exhibition catalogue, Ann Arbor, The University of Michigan Museum of Art, 1979.

———. "Impressionism and Journalistic Illustration," *Arts Magazine* 56 (June 1982), 95–115.

———. "Constable, Duranty, Mallarmé, Impressionism, Plein Air, and Forgetting," *Art Bulletin*, Vol. 76, No. 3 (September 1994), 427–50.

Jean-Aubry, G. *Eugène Boudin, d'après les documents inédits: L'Homme et l'œuvre*. Paris, Bernheim-Jeune, 1922. Trans. Caroline Tisdall. Greenwich, New York Graphic Society, 1969.

Jensen, Robert. *Marketing Modernism in Fin-de-Siècle Europe*. Princeton, Princeton University Press, 1994.

Johnson, Deborah Jean. *The Impact of East Asian Art Within the Early Impressionist Circle, 1856–1868*. Ann Arbor, UMI Research Press, 1986.

Jooster, Joop M. "'Claude Monet's Discovery'. Japanese Prints Given Away in Holland As Wrapping Paper?", in *Amsterdam*, 1986, 72–82.

Joyes, Claire, et al. *Monet at Giverny*. London, Mathews, Miller and Dunbar, 1975.

———. *Monet's Table*. New York, Simon and Schuster, 1989.

Koechlin, Raymond, "Claude Monet," *Art et Décoration*, 51 (February 1927), 5–47.

Lecomte, Georges. "L'Art contemporain," *La Revue indépendente de Litterature et d'Art*, Vol. 23, No. 66 (April 1892), 30–48.

———. *L'Art impressionniste d'après la collection privée de M. Durand-Ruel*. Paris, Chamerot et Renouard, 1892.

Lehmann, A. G. *The Symbolist Aesthetic in France, 1885–1895*. Oxford, Basil Blackwell, 1968.

Lethève, Jacques. *Impressionnistes et symbolistes devant la presse*. Paris, Armand Colin, 1959.

Levin, Miriam R. *Republican Art and Ideology in Late Nineteenth Century France*. Ann Arbor, UMI Research Press, 1986.

Levine, Steven Z. "Monet's 'Cabane du Douanier,'" *Fogg Art Museum Annual Report (1971–1972)*. Cambridge, Harvard University, 32–44.

————. "Monet's Pairs," *Arts Magazine*, 49 (June 1975), 72–5.

————. *Monet and his Critics*. New York, Garland Publishing, 1976.

————. "Monet, Lumière and Cinematic Time," *The Journal of Aesthetics and Art Criticism*, Vol. 36, No. 4 (Summer 1978), 441–47.

————. "Decor/Decorative/Decoration in Claude Monet's Art," *Arts Magazine*, 51 (February 1977), 136–39.

————. "The 'Instant' of Criticism and Monet's Critical Instant," *Arts Magazine*, 55 (March 1981), 114–21.

————. "Monet, Fantasy, and Freud," *Psychoanalytic Perspectives on Art*, ed. Mary Mathews Gedo. Hillsdale, N. J., The Analytic Press, 1985, 1, 29–55.

————. "Seascapes of the Sublime: Vernet, Monet and the Oceanic Feeling," *New Literary History*, Vol. 16, No. 2 (Winter 1985), 377–400.

————. "Monet's Series: Repetition, Obsession," *October*, No. 37 (Summer 1986), 65–75.

Loevgren, Sven. *The Genesis of Modernism*. Bloomington, University of Indiana Press, 1971.

London, Arts Council of Great Britain. *Claude Monet*. Exhibition catalogue, London, Tate Gallery, 1957.

————. *The Impressionists in London*. Exhibition catalogue, London, Arts Council of Great Britain, 1973.

London, Royal Academy of Arts. *Post-Impressionism: Cross Currents in European Painting*. Exhibition catalogue, New York, Harper and Row, 1979.

Mabuchí, Akiko. "Claude Monet's Japonisme: Nature and Decoration," in Tucker et al., 1994, 232–38.

Mallarmé, Stéphane. "The Impressionists and Edouard Manet," *Art Monthly Review*, Vol. 1, No. 9 (30 September 1876), 117–22, reprinted in San Francisco, 1986, 26–35.

Marlais, Michael. *Conservative Echoes in Fin-de-Siècle Parisian Art Criticism*, University Park, The Pennsylvania State University Press, 1992.

Marx, Roger. "Les meules de M. Claude Monet, "*Le Voltaire*, 7 May 1891.

————, "Les 'Nymphéas' de M. Claude Monet" *Gazette des Beaux Arts*, ser. 4,1, (1909), 523–31.

Mauclair, Camille [Camille Faust]. *Claude Monet*, Paris, F. Rieder, 1924.

Maupassant, Guy de. "La Vie d'un paysagiste," *Gil Blas*, 28 September 1886.

Mirbeau, Octave. *Des Artistes*. 2 vols. Paris, Flammarion, 1922.

Moffett, Charles S. "Monet's Haystacks," in Rewald and Weitzenhoffer, 1984, 140–59.

————, et al. *Monet's Years at Giverny: Beyond Impressionism*. Exhibition catalogue, New York, Metropolitan Museum of Art, 1978.

Monneret, Sophie. *L'Impressionnisme et son époque*. 4 vols. Paris, Denoël, 1978–81.

Nochlin. Linda. *Realism*. Harmondsworth, Penguin Books, 1971.

———— (ed.). *Impressionism and Post-Impressionism. Sources and Documents*. Englewood Cliffs, Prentice Hall, 1966.

Paradise, JoAnne Culler. *Gustave Geffroy and the Criticism of Painting*. New York, Garland Publishing, 1985.

————. "Three Letters from Claude Monet to Gustave Geffroy," *Bulletin of the Stanford Museum* Vols. 12–13 (November 1985).

————. *Women, Art, and Power and Other Essays*. New York, Harper & Row, 1989.

————. *The Politics of Vision. Essays on Nineteenth-Century Art and Society*. New York, Harper & Row, 1989.

Paris, Centre Culturel du Marais. *Claude Monet au temps de Giverny*. Exhibition catalogue, Paris, 1983.

Paris, Grand Palais. *Le Japonisme*. Exhibition catalogue, Paris, Editions de la Réunion des musées nationaux, 1988.

Patin, Sylvie. "Les séries dans l'œuvre de Monet," *Conférences du Musée d'Orsay, Quarante-huit/Quatorze*, No. 4, Paris, Editions de la Réunion des musées nationaux, 1992, 51–60.

Perry, Lilla Cabot. "Reminiscences of Claude Monet from 1889 to 1909," *The American Magazine of Art*, Vol. XVIII, No. 3 (March 1927), 119–25.

Piquet, Philippe. *Monet et Venise*. Paris, Editions Herscher, 1987.

Pissaro, Joachim. *Monet's Cathedral. Rouen 1892–94*, London, Pavilion, 1990.

Pollock, Griselda. "Modernity and the Spaces of Femininity," in *Vision and Difference: Femininity, Feminism and the Histories of Art*, London, Routledge and Keegan Paul, 1988.

Poulain, Gaston. "L'origine des *Femmes au Jardin* de Claude Monet," *L'Amour de l'Art*, March 1937.

Ravin, James G. "Monet's Cataracts," *The Journal of the American Medical Association*, 19 July 1985, 394–99.

Rewald, John. *The History of Impressionism*. 4th revised edition, New York, The Museum of Modern Art, 1973.

———. *Post-Impressionism. From Van Gogh to Gauguin*. 3rd revised edition, New York, The Museum of Modern Art, 1978.

——— (ed.). *Camille Pissarro. Letters to his son Lucien*. 4th edition, London, Routledge and Kegan Paul, 1980.

——— and Frances Weitzenhoffer (eds.). *Aspects of Monet: A Symposium on the Artist's Life and Times*. New York, Harry N. Abrams, 1984.

Rifkin, Adrian. "Cultural Movement and the Paris Commune," *Art History*, Vol. 2 No. 2 (June 1979), 201–20.

Robinson, M. S. "Zola and Monet: The Poetry of the Railways," *Journal of Modern Literature*, Vol. 10, No. 1 (1983), 55–70.

Robinson, Theodore. "Claude Monet," *The Century Magazine*, XLIV (September 1892), 696–701.

———. Diary, 1892–1896. Frick Art Reference Library, New York.

Roger-Marx, Claude. "Le Commerce des tableaux sous l'impressionnisme et à la fin du XIXè siècle," *Médecine de France*, 95 (1958), 17–32.

Roos, Jane Mayo. "Within the 'zone of silence': Monet and Manet in 1878," *Art History*, Vol. 11, No. 3 (September 1988), 374–407.

Roskill, Mark. "Early Impressionism and the Fashion Print," *Burlington Magazine*, CXII, No. 807 (June 1970), 391–95.

———. *Van Gogh, Gauguin and the Impressionist Circle*. Greenwich, New York Graphic Society, 1970.

Rouen, *'Les Cathédrales' de Monet*. Exhibition catalogue, Rouen, Musée des Beaux-Arts, 1994.

Royer, J., J. Haut and P. Amalric. "L'opération de la cataracte de Claude Monet, correspondance inédit du peintre et de G. Clemenceau au Docteur Coutela," *Histoire des Sciences Médicales*, Vol. 18, No. 2 (1984), 109–27.

Sabbrin, Celen. *Science and Philosophy in Art*. Philadelphia, William F. Feld, 1886.

San Francisco, The Fine Arts Museums of San Francisco. *The New Painting. Impressionism 1874–86*. Exhibition catalogue, Geneva, Richard Burton SA, 1986.

Seiberling, Grace.

———. "The Evolution of an Impressionist," in *Chicago*, 1975, 19–40.

———. *Monet's Series*. New York, Garland Publishing, 1978.

———. "Monet's 'Les Roches à Pourville, marré base,'" *Porticus: The Journal of the Memorial Art Gallery of the University of Rochester*, 3 (1980), 40–48.

———. *Monet in London*. Exhibition catalogue, Atlanta, High Museum, 1989.

Seitz, William C. *Claude Monet*. New York, Harry N. Abrams, 1960.

———. *Claude Monet. Seasons and Moments*. Exhibition catalogue, New York, Museum of Modern Art, 1960.

Shattuck, Roger. "Approaching the Abyss: Monet's Era," *Artforum*, Vol. 20, No. 7 (March 1982), 35–42.

Shiff, Richard. *Cézanne and the End of Impressionism*. Chicago, University of Chicago Press, 1984, 60–89.

———. "The End of Impressionism: A Study in Theories of Artistic Expressionism," *The Art Quarterly* (new series), Vol. I, No. 4 (Autumn 1978), 338–78, revised in San Francisco, 1984, 60–89.

Silverman, Debora L. *Art nouveau in fin-de-siècle France: politics, psychology, and style*. Berkeley, University of California Press, 1989.

Spate, Virginia, *Claude Monet. Life and Work*, New York, Rizzoli, 1992.

Stuckey, Charles F. "Blossoms and Blunders. Monet and the State. II," *Art in America*, Vol. 67, No. 5 (September 1979), 109–25.

———. "What's wrong with this picture?" *Art in America*, Vol. 69, No. 7 (September 1981), 96–107.

——— (ed.). *Monet: A Retrospective*. New York, Hugh Lauter Levin Associates, 1985.

———. *Monet Water Lilies*. New York, Hugh Lanter Levin Associates, 1988.

Suckale, Robert. *Claude Monet. Die Kathedrale von Rouen*. Munich, 1981.

Taboureux, Emile. "Claude Monet," *La Vie moderne*, 12 June 1880, 380–82.

Thiébault-Sisson, François. "Une histoire de l'impressionnisme," *Le Temps*, 17 April 1899.

———. "Claude Monet, les années des épreuves," *Le Temps*, 17 April 1900.

———. "Claude Monet," *Le Temps*, 6 April 1920.

———. "Un don de M. Claude Monet à l'Etat," *Le Temps*, 14 October 1920.

———. "Autour de Claude Monet, anecdotes et souvenirs," I and II, *Le Temps*, 29 December 1926 and 8 January 1927.

———. "Un nouveau musée parisien. Les Nymphéas de Claude Monet à l'Orangerie des Tuileries," *La Revue de l'art ancien et moderne*, 52 (July 1927), 41–52.

Tinterow, Gary, and Henri Loyrette. *Origins of Impressionism*. Exhibition catalogue, New York, The Metropolitan Museum of Art, 1994.

Trévise, Duc de. "Le Pèlerinage de Giverny," *La Revue de l'art ancien et moderne*, 51 (January–February 1927), 42–50 and 121–34.

Tucker, Paul Hayes. *Monet at Argenteuil*. New Haven and London, Yale University Press, 1982.

———. "The First Impressionist Exhibition in Context," in San Francisco, 1984, 92–117.

———. "The First Impressionist Exhibition and Monet's 'Impression: Sunrise': A Tale of Timing, Commerce, and Patriotism," *Art History*, Vol. 7, No. 4 (December 1984), 465–76

———. *Monet in the 90s: The Series Paintings*. Exhibition catalogue, Boston, Museum of Fine Arts, 1989 and New Haven and London, Yale University Press, 1990.

———. "Passion and Patriotism in Monet's Late Work," *Monet: Late Paintings of Giverny from the Musée Marmottan*. Exhibition catalogue, New Orleans and San Francisco, The New Orleans Museum of Art and The Fine Arts Museums of San Francisco, 1994.

———, et al. *Monet: A Retrospective*. Exhibition catalogue, Tokyo, The Bridgestone Museum, 1994.

———. Tokyo, National Museum of Western Art, *Paris in 1874: The Year of Impressionism*. Exhibition catalogue, Tokyo, National Museum of Western Art, 1994.

Vaisse, Pierre. "Le Legs Caillebotte d'après les documents," *Bulletin de la Société de l'Histoire de l'Art français*, (1983), 201–08.

Varnedoe, Kirk. "In Monet's Gardens," *The New York Times Magazine*, 2 April 1978, 30–41.

———. "Artifice or Condor: Impressionism and Photography Reconsidered," *Art in America*, Vol. 68, No. 1 (January 1980), 66–78.

———. *Gustave Caillebotte*. New Haven and London, Yale University Press, 1987.

Vauxcelles, Louis. "Un après-midi chez Claude Monet," *Le Monde illustré*, 7 December 1905.

Venturi, Lionello. *Les Archives de l'impressionnisme*. 2 vols. Paris, Durand-Ruel, 1939.

Villain, Jacques, et al. *Claude Monet – August Rodin. Centenaire de l'Exposition de 1889*. Exhibition catalogue, Paris, Musée Rodin, 1989.

Wagner, Anne. "Why Monet Gave Up Figure Painting," *Art Bulletin*, Vol. 74, No. 4 (December 1994), 613–29.

Walter, Rudolphe. "Emile Zola and Claude Monet," *Cahiers Naturalistes* XXVI (1964), 51–61.

———. "Les Maisons de Claude Monet à Argenteuil," *Gazette des Beaux-Arts*, LXVIII (December 1966), 333–42.

———. "Claude Monet as a Caricaturist: A Clandestine Apprenticeship," *Apollo*, Vol. 103, No. 172 (June 1976), 488–93.

———. "Saint-Lazare l'impressionniste," *L'Œil*, 292 (November 1979), 48–55.

Webster, James Carsten. "The Technique of Impressionism: a reappraisal," *College Art Journal*, 4 (November 1944), 2–33.

Weitzerhoffer, Francis; *The Havemeyers. Impressionism comes to America*, New York, Harry N. Abrams, 1986.

White, Harrison and Cynthia. *Canvases and Careers. Institutional Change in the French Painting World*. New York, John Wiley and Sons, 1965.

Wildenstein, Daniel. *Claude Monet, biographie et catalogue raisonné.* 5 vols. Lausanne, Bibliothèque des arts, 1974–1985.

———. "Monet's Giverny," in Moffett, et al., 1978, 15–40.

Wilson, Mark, et al. "Monet's 'Bathers at La Grenouillère,'" *National Gallery Technical Bulletin*, Vol. 5 (1981), 14–25.

Zola, Emile. "Mon Salon. IV. Les Actualistes," *L'Evénement illustré*, 24 May 1868.

———. *Salons*. Ed. F. W. Hemmings and Robert J. Niess, Geneva, E. Droz, 1959

———. *Mon Salon, Manet, Ecrits sur l'art*. Ed. Antoinette Ehrard, Paris, Flammarion, 1970.

# Index

## Photograph Credits

In most cases the illustrations have been made from photographs or transparencies provided by the owners or custodians of the works. Those for which further credit is due are:

Photo © RMN, Paris: vi, 17, 24, 25, 42, 51, 72, 89, 96, 97, 102, 115, 134, 163, 178, 189, 237, 238, 239, 251, 252; Photo N. D. Roger-Viollet, Paris: 3, 62, 81, 83, 119, 120, 123; Sotheby's, London: 8, 15; Photo © 1994, The Art Institute of Chicago: 9; Courtesy Bridgestone Museum of Art, Tokyo: 12, 68, 194, 197, 198, 224; © cliché du M. B. A. de Bordeaux: 13; Scala, Florence: 29, 85, 103; Courtesy Christie's, New York: 43, 80, 92, 125, 127, 136, 222; Sotheby's, New York: 54, 60, 113, 150, 167, 229; Photograph courtesy of the Lefevre Gallery: 58, 205; Acquavella Galleries, Inc: 61, 107, 146, 151, 153, 164, 219; Photo Peter Schächli, Zurich: 67; Courtesy Museum of Fine Arts, Boston: 74, 158, 182, 185, 188; Courtesy of Thomas Gibson Fine Art Ltd: 77; Photo Metropolitan Museum of Art, New York: 93, 98, 165, 202, 207, 210; Galerie Nichido, Tokyo: 109, 111, 225; Cliché photothèque des musées de la Ville de Paris, © by SPADEM, 1995: 117; Courtesy of the Miniature Gallery: 179, Christie's Images, London: 213; Dallas Museum of Art: 216.